T0190447

Arduino Software Internals

A Complete Guide to How Your Arduino Language and Hardware Work Together

Norman Dunbar

Apress®

Arduino Software Internals: A Complete Guide to How Your Arduino Language and Hardware Work Together

Norman Dunbar
Rawdon, West Yorkshire, UK

ISBN-13 (pbk): 978-1-4842-5789-0   ISBN-13 (electronic): 978-1-4842-5790-6
https://doi.org/10.1007/978-1-4842-5790-6

Managing Director, Apress Media LLC: Welmoed Spahr
Acquisitions Editor: Natalie Pao
Development Editor: James Markham
Coordinating Editor: Jessica Vakili

Distributed to the book trade worldwide by Springer Science+Business Media New York, 233 Spring Street, 6th Floor, New York, NY 10013. Phone 1-800-SPRINGER, fax (201) 348-4505, e-mail orders-ny@springer-sbm.com, or visit www.springeronline.com. Apress Media, LLC is a California LLC and the sole member (owner) is Springer Science + Business Media Finance Inc (SSBM Finance Inc). SSBM Finance Inc is a Delaware corporation.

For information on translations, please e-mail rights@apress.com, or visit http://www.apress.com/rights-permissions.

Apress titles may be purchased in bulk for academic, corporate, or promotional use. eBook versions and licenses are also available for most titles. For more information, reference our Print and eBook Bulk Sales web page at http://www.apress.com/bulk-sales.

Any source code or other supplementary material referenced by the author in this book is available to readers on GitHub via the book's product page, located at www.apress.com/978-1-4842-5789-0. For more detailed information, please visit http://www.apress.com/source-code.

Printed on acid-free paper

This book is dedicated to my wife, Alison, who sometimes allows me to have some time to myself, programming, attempting to build things (with or without "Internet of"), and writing notes, articles, and/or this book.

Another person, to whom I am grateful, is Alison's late maternal grandmother, Minnie Trees (yes, I did call her Bonsai!), who gifted me an Arduino Duemilanove starter kit and rekindled my long-lost (for over 35 years) interest in building things with electronics.

The book is also dedicated to the myriad of people and companies or organizations around the world who freely give their time and skills to produce open source software and hardware, for the benefit of others or just for fun.

If I may paraphrase the words of Isaac Newton, I too stand on the shoulders of giants, so here's to the giants, the little people, and all the medium-sized ones too, who may or may not become giants themselves. Let's hope the fun never stops.

Finally, my own motto is Don't think! Find out! *Hopefully this book will help you do exactly that.*

Table of Contents

About the Author

Norman Dunbar is an Oracle database administrator. Norman has had a long-running relationship with electronics since childhood and computers since the late 1970s, and the Arduino was a perfect marriage of the two interests. With a love of learning new things, examining and explaining the Arduino Language and the hardware became a bit of a hobby, and as piles of notes expanded, Norman has now decided to publish his work.

About the Technical Reviewer

Sai Yamanoor is an embedded systems engineer working for an industrial gases company in Buffalo, New York. His interests, deeply rooted in DIY and open source hardware, include developing gadgets that aid behavior modification. He has published two books with his brother, and in his spare time, he likes to contribute to build things that improve quality of life. You can find his project portfolio at `http://saiyamanoor.com`.

Preface

If I have seen further it is by standing on ye sholders of Giants.

—Sir Isaac Newton (1643–1727), Letter to Robert Hooke

There are many books which discuss the abilities of the Arduino *hardware* and how best the maker can use this to their benefit. I have many of them in my bookcase, and digital versions on my phone and tablet – in case I get bored with life and need something interesting to read. Many of these books explain what the hardware does; and some even dig deeper into the hardware to explain how, in fairly easy to understand terms, it does it.

There are no books which take a similar view of the Arduino *software*. There is now! This book takes you on a *journey* (why do we *always* have to be on a journey these days?) into the world of Arduino sketches and the various files involved in the compilation process. It will delve deep into the supplied software and look at the specific parts of the Arduino Language which deal with the underlying hardware, the ATmega328P (or ATmega328AU) microcontrollers – henceforth referred to as ATmega328P.

Once the Arduino Language has been explained, the book takes a short look at how you can strip away the Arduino *hand holding* and get down and dirty with the naked hardware. It's not easy, but equally it's not too difficult. Don't worry, this is still the C/C++ language, there's no assembly language required. Perhaps!

CHAPTER 1

Introduction

The Arduino is a great system for getting people into making with electronics and microcontrollers. I was reintroduced to a long-lost hobby when I was gifted an Arduino Duemilanove (aka 2009) by my wife's late grandmother, and since then, I've had lots of fun learning and *attempting* to build *things*. I've even built a number of Arduino *clones* based on just the AVR microcontroller and a few passive components – it's cheaper than fitting a new Arduino into a project!

Much has changed over the intervening years. LEDs used to cost about £10 each and came in one color, red. These days I can get a pack of 100 LEDs for about £2 in various different colors. Even better, my old faithful Antex 15W soldering iron still worked, even after 35 years.

The Arduino, and I'm concentrating on either the Uno version 3 or the Duemilanove here, as those are two of the ones I've actually purchased (or been given), is based on an Atmel ATmega328 microcontroller. On the Uno it's the Atmel ATmega328P-AU, while the Duemilanove uses the ATmega328P-PU.

Roughly, the only difference between the two is the UNO's AU version is a surface mount, while the PU version is a 28-pin through-hole device. They are/should be identical to program, although the AU version does have two additional analogue pins that are not present on the ATmega328P-PU.

Occasionally though, I may mention in passing the Mega 2560 R3 – as I have a cheap Chinese clone of one of these – which is based on the Atmel ATmega2560 microcontroller.

© Norman Dunbar 2020
N. Dunbar, *Arduino Software Internals*, https://doi.org/10.1007/978-1-4842-5790-6_1

Some older Arduino boards had the ATmega168 microcontroller, which also was a 28-pin through-hole version, but it only had 16 Kb of flash memory as opposed to the 32 Kb in the later 328 chips. The EEPROM and RAM size is also half that of the ATmega328P devices.

The Arduino was designed for ease of use, and to this end, the software and the "Arduino Language" hides an awful lot from the maker and developer. Hopefully, by the time you have finished reading this book, you will understand more about what it does and why and, when necessary, how you can bypass the Arduino Language (it's just C or C++ after all) and use the bare metal AVR-specific C or C++ code instead. Doing this can lead to more space for your code, faster execution, and lower power requirements – some projects can be run for months on a couple of batteries.

1.1. Arduino Installation Paths

The version of the Arduino software used in this book is 1.8.5.

I used an installation on Windows 7 and another on Linux while writing this book although Linux is my operating system of choice. Both versions were installed by downloading the zip file version, as opposed to the appropriate installer, and extracting it. The locations I used are as follows:

- On Linux – `/home/norman/arduino-1.8.5`

- On Windows 7 – `c:\users\norman\arduino-1.8.5`

Within this book, there are references to various files provided by the Arduino software. Because of the way I've installed my software and the fact that the installer versions of the download may install to a different location, all paths used in this book will be relative to the preceding locations.

Paths used will be as follows:

- $ARDBASE is the preceding given location where I've extracted the zip file – /home/norman/arduino-1.8.5. This is where you will find the file arduino.exe on Windows or arduino on Linux which is the Arduino IDE.

- $ARDINST is the location of the main Arduino files for AVR microcontrollers. This is $ARDBASE/hardware/ arduino/avr and is where the various cores, bootloaders, and so on can be found, beneath this directory. On my Linux system, this is the path /home/ norman/arduino- 1.8.5/hardware/arduino/avr.

- $ARDINC is the location of many of the *.h header files and most of the *.c and *.cpp files that comprise the Arduino Language for AVR microcontrollers. This is $ARDINST/cores/arduino. The expanded path is / home/norman/arduino-1.8.5/hardware/arduino/avr/ cores/arduino on my Linux system.

- $AVRINC is where the header files for the version of the AVR Library provided by the Arduino IDE are located. The Arduino Language (eventually) compiles down to calling functions within the AVR Library (henceforth referred to as AVRLib), and the header files are to be found in location $ARDBASE/hardware/tools/avr/ avr/include. The fully expanded path here is /home/ norman/arduino-1.8.5/hardware/tools/avr/avr/ include.

So, if you see $ARDINC/Arduino.h mentioned, you will know that this means the file

- /home/norman/arduino-1.8.5/hardware/arduino/ avr/cores/arduino/Arduino.h on Linux

- c:\users\norman\arduino-1.8.5\hardware\arduino\ avr\cores\arduino\Arduino.h on Windows

You can see why I'm using abbreviations now, can't you?

In addition, most of the file paths I refer to will be in Linux format with the "/" as a path separator, unless I'm specifically referring to a Windows file, in which case the file's path will use the "\" Windows path separator character.

If you wish to examine the files that I am discussing in the book on your system, see Appendix A for a couple of useful tips on how to avoid always having to type the full paths.

1.2. Coding Style

Code listings in the book will be displayed as follows:

```
#define ledPin LED_BUILTIN
#define relayPin 2
#define sensorPin 3

...

void loop()                                    ①
{
    // Flash heartbeat LED.
    digitalWrite(ledPin, HIGH);
    delay(100);
    digitalWrite(ledPin LOW);          ②

    ...

}
```

① This is a *callout* and attempts to bring your attention to something in the code which will be described beneath the code listing in question.

② This is another callout – there can be more than one.

In the book's main text, where you see words formatted like USCR0A or PORTB, then these are examples of Arduino pin names, AVR microcontroller registers, bits within those registers, and/or flags within the ATmega328P itself, as well as references to something listed in the data sheet for the device. Where code listings are being explained, then variables from the code will be shown in this style too.

Arduino pin numbers will be named Dn or An as appropriate. This is slightly different from the normal usage of the digital pins, which normally just get a number. I prefer to be a little more formal and give the digital pins their full title. <grin>

Tips are exactly that. They give you a clue or information about something that may not be too well known in the Arduino world, but which might be incredibly useful (or, maybe, just slightly useful!).

This is a note. It brings your attention to something that may require a little more information. It could be useful to pay attention to these notes. Maybe!

Cautions are there to highlight potential problems with something in the software, or just something that the data sheet needs you to take extra care over. There may be a possibility of damage to your Arduino if you don't pay particular attention. Occasionally, the data sheet warns against doing something – so it's best not to do what it says not to do!

1.3. The Arduino Language

I should perhaps point out that there isn't *really* such a thing as the Arduino Language. I may refer to it frequently within the pages of this book, but technically, it doesn't exist. What it is is simply an abstraction of the C/C++ language, written in such a way as to make life easier for people learning to make *stuff* with their Arduino. Which of the following is easier to understand?

```
digitalWrite(13, HIGH);
```

or

```
PORTB |= (1 << PORTB5);
```

The first is definitely easier to understand; however, the latter is by far the quicker of the two as it just does what it says – it sets pin 5, on PORTB of the ATmega328P, to HIGH. The name, digitalWrite(), appears to be a different language, but it isn't; it's that abstraction away from plain AVR C/C++ which makes life easier for us all.

1.4. Coming Up

In Chapter 2, I explain how a sketch gets massaged into a proper C++ program and how the libraries used in the sketch are incorporated into it. Following the brief overview of how compiling a sketch operates, I then document the Arduino's main() function, the various header files that it includes, and the initialization carried out by the init() function. These initializations are part of every sketch that you compile, so it helps if you know what the Arduino system is doing, in the background, for you.

In Chapter 3, I explain about the features and facilities of the Arduino Language. This will include all the commands such as pinMode(), digitalWrite(), and so on. I talk through all the functions that relate to the Arduino, with particular emphasis on the code that applies to the standard Arduino boards, those based on the ATmega328P family of AVR microcontrollers.

Chapter 4 looks into a number of the C++ classes (or objects) which are supplied with, and used by, the Arduino Language. The classes of main interest here are the `HardwareSerial` class which provides us with the `serial` interface and its commands like `Serial.begin()` or `Serial.println()`. However, the `HardwareSerial` class is not fully self-contained, so the other, lesser known, supporting classes are also explained in this chapter.

Chapter 5 takes a brief look at how to cast off the bonds of the Arduino Language and delves into the brazen world of AVR C++ itself, where you bypass the likes of `pinMode()` calls and talk to the AVR microcontroller in something akin to its own language. In here you will learn how you can set the `pinMode()` for up to eight pins with a single instruction or how to `digitalWrite()` those same eight pins, again with one instruction, and other efficient methods of communication with your board.

Chapter 6 demonstrates a couple of alternatives to the Arduino IDE. Some people don't get on with it. I myself have a sort of love-hate relationship with it as I find the editor a little clumsy and slow for my liking.

In this chapter, I will show you how you can write code for Arduino boards in both the Arduino Language and plain AVR C/C++ code using the "PlatformIO" system and, also, give you a sneak preview of the forthcoming "Arduino Command-Line Interface (CLI)."

The Arduino Command-Line Interface is to be the basis for a forthcoming release of the Arduino IDE, but you can also use it in make files, the command-line environment, and so on. It does not require you to install Java as the current IDE does.

Chapter 7 is where I delve deeper into some features of the ATmega328P which, while not strictly software, are fundamental to configuring the ATmega328P how *you* might like it and not as the Arduino designers, however talented they may be, have decided. In this chapter, I'll be looking at the ATmega's fuses, power reduction modes, sleep modes, and similar features which determine how the ATmega328P works, but not necessarily what it does.

Chapters 8 and 9 are where I delve deeper into some features of the ATmega328P which, while not strictly software, are either important in understanding the Arduino Language or just useful to know about. Hardware features such as the Analogue Comparator, timer/counters, Analogue to Digital Converter (ADC), and Universal Synchronous/ Asynchronous Receiver/Transmitter (USART) are covered in some detail.

Finally, in the appendices, there are a number of topics that may be of interest, or are kept together in one place for reference. In here you will find all the helpful reference material you might need such as pinout diagrams and potentially useful (or unusual) code to upload to your Arduino.

There's even an index!

Without any further ado, let's dive in to what happens when you want to compile a sketch in the Arduino IDE.

CHAPTER 2

Arduino Compilation

This chapter is all about what happens when you compile an Arduino sketch and how the various header files are used. Hopefully, by the time you have read (and understood) this chapter of the book, you'll have a much better idea of what happens during the compilation of an Arduino sketch. However, before we dive into the gory details of a sketch's compilation, we need to understand a bit about some of the text files that live in and around the $ARDINST directory.

These files are used to set up the IDE's menu options and to define the AVR microcontroller and Arduino board to be used. Additionally, the IDE needs to know how to compile and upload sketches, and with lots of different boards nowadays, not just those with AVR microcontrollers, these numerous text files help the IDE configure the build tools and so on, for the specific board chosen from the Boards menu in the IDE.

Once we have discussed the various text files, we can *then* get down and dirty in the compilation process and also take a look at the hidden C++ files that the Arduino environment keeps well away from us.

2.1. Preferences.txt

The file preferences.txt holds all the preferences for the Arduino IDE and under recent versions of the IDE is no longer found within the location of the various IDE files, but in a separate area so that future upgrades to the IDE do not overwrite any changes that you make to the file. This explains

© Norman Dunbar 2020
N. Dunbar, *Arduino Software Internals*, https://doi.org/10.1007/978-1-4842-5790-6_2

why, when you configure the IDE on one version, an upgrade will pick up your preferences without you having to reapply them all every time you upgrade.

You should find the file in one of the following locations, however, as the file is created when you first run the IDE. If you have not yet done so, there will not be a preferences.txt file to be found. The initial set of defaults is defined in the file $ARDINST/lib/preferences.txt so those are the ones that will get written to the preferences.txt file, in the appropriate location, on first execution of the IDE. You may also delete the preferences.txt file if your edits have rendered it unusable, and it will be recreated by the IDE next time you open it.

You *could* edit $ARDINST/lib/preferences.txt to set your own preferred default settings, but as the file will be overwritten by IDE updates, it's probably not a good option to consider.

The one thing about looking in $ARDINST/lib/preferences.txt is the fact that everything is commented nicely to advise you as to what the options are used for. The file which the IDE actually uses is not commented at all. If you need to know what you are about to change, look at the $ARDINST/lib/preferences.txt file but change the one that is in the correct location for your system. The file used by the IDE is found in a number of places, depending on your operating system of choice:

- On Linux – Look in /home/<YOUR_NAME>/.arduino15.

- On Windows 7 – Look in C:\Users\<YOUR_NAME>\ AppData\Local\Arduino15. I believe that on older versions of Windows, the file can be found in c:\ Documents and Settings\<YOUR_NAME>\Application Data\Arduino or even C:\Program Files (x86)\ Arduino\lib which I believe is where 32-bit applications get installed on 64-bit machines.

- On MacOS – I believe you can look in /Users/<YOUR_
  NAME>/Library/Arduino, but I don't have access to a
  Mac to check, sorry.

The easiest way to determine the location of the preferences.txt file
is to open the IDE and select File ➤ Preferences; and on the "Settings"
tab, at the bottom, you will see the full path to the preferences.txt file
documented. Take heed of the warning to only *edit the file when the IDE is
closed* – the IDE writes to the file when you shut it down and will overwrite
any changes you made if the IDE was open when you changed the file.

The preferences.txt file contains all the configuration changes
that you made using the IDE. The changes you make here will be saved
between IDE upgrades. There are some additional preference changes that
you need to make by editing the preferences file directly as the IDE doesn't
"surface" those options. A couple of examples follow.

⚠ If you have your preferences nicely set up, beware if you
subsequently install and use the new Arduino command-line utility
arduino-cli (see Chapter 6, Section 6.2, "*Arduino Command
Line,*" for details). It uses the same location for all its files and will
pick up whatever preferences you have configured for the IDE.

💡 If, by some chance, you make a mistake editing the file and
things stop working (properly), you can reset everything to defaults by
simply deleting the preferences.txt file while the IDE is closed
and running the IDE again.

2.1.1. Using an ICSP for All Uploads

Are you using an ICSP (In-Circuit System Programmer) to do all your uploads? Do you get fed up having to configure it in every sketch you write and try to upload? Wouldn't it be nice to tell the IDE that you are always using an ICSP? Try this:

- Close the IDE if it is open.

- Edit the `preferences.txt` file in your favorite text editor. (No, do not use Microsoft Word!)

- Search for "upload.using". It should currently look like this:

  `upload.using=bootloader`

- Change it to use the name of the device you are using. The device name you change it to must match one of the device names in the file `$ARDINST/programmers.txt`. In my case, I use a USB Tiny clone, from eBay, and I set my option to the following:

  `upload.using=USBtinyISP`

- Save the file.

With this done, all sketches will now default to using the ICSP rather than the bootloader. This means that I no longer have to worry about remembering to change the programmer in the IDE, and, as a bonus, I will always overwrite the bootloader area and regain the use of that part of the Flash RAM for my own use. My Uno board will have an extra 512 bytes (1.5625% of the total) of flash for my programs, while my Duemilanove will regain an extra 2 Kb or 6.35% from the bootloader space.

Uploading with any ICSP device does still require you to press the Shift key when you click the upload button or to select Sketch ➤ Upload Using Programmer, even with this preference set.

I can still set the IDE to use a bootloader though. I just have to remember to select it from the Tools menu when I wish to create a sketch for a system that I cannot, or don't want to, use the ICSP for uploads.

What's an ICSP? Normally beginners would use a USB cable between the computer and the Arduino to upload programs. However, look at your Arduino and see if you can see a set of six pins in two rows of three. My Duemilanove has them beneath the reset switch. Those pins are where an ICSP can be plugged in to program the Arduino. Using one of these frees up the space taken by the bootloader program and gives you a bit more program space.

Unfortunately, it does prevent the Arduino from talking back to your computer using the Serial Monitor facility – Tools ➤ Serial Monitor. You will need an ICSP if you have to replace the ATmega328P on your board, and it comes with the default fuse settings. You will need to purchase one with an Uno bootloader already programmed in or use an ICSP to program your own.

My ICSP is from an eBay seller "finetech007" which no longer exists. There are lots of them if you search for "usbtiny isp" – here's one example [www.ebay.co.uk/itm/USBTiny-USBtinyISP-AVR-ISP-programmer-for-Arduino-bootloader-Meag2560-uno-r3-CF/191780957944?epid=1138358692&hash=item2ca7092ef8:g:4-UAAOSwhvpd-fY7], identical to mine. (Sorry about the length of that URL!)

2.1.2. Change the Action of Home and End Keys

> **ⓘ** I'm reliably informed that this applies to Apple Mac users. It
> certainly has no effect on Windows 7 or Linux.

In the editor, when you press the Home key, the caret jumps to the very
start of the sketch. When you press the End key, it jumps to the very end of
the sketch. Apparently, this gets quite annoying when you expect the caret
to be positioned at the start or end of the line you are editing. This sort of
thing definitely needs changing!

There isn't an option in File ➤ Preferences which enables this action
to be changed so that the cursor goes to the start or end of the current line
and not to the start or end of the current sketch. The preferences.txt file
must be edited directly:

- Close the IDE, if it is open.

- Edit the preferences.txt file.

- Look for the following setting:

    editor.keys.home_and_end_beginning_end_of_doc = true

- Change it to the following and save the file:

    editor.keys.home_and_end_beginning_end_of_doc = false

When you next open the IDE and load a sketch, the Home and End
keys should now do your bidding.

i Issue 3715 on the GitHub issues page for the IDE has some interesting details about this preference. It only exists from version 1.6.6 onwards. Prior to that, it was called `editor.keys.home_and_end_travel_far`.

In the first incarnations of version 1.6.6, the setting was coded backward. Setting it to `false` meant that the Home and End keys sent the cursor to the start or end of the document. You had to set it to `true` to get it to go to the beginning or end of the current line.

Since August 28, 2015, that was fixed; and it now works as it should. You can find all the details at `https://github.com/arduino/Arduino/issues/3715`.

2.1.3. Setting Tab Stops

Now, you would think that an editor, for writing code, would at least allow you the ability to adjust the width of the tab stops and whether or not they are to be converted into spaces. Not so the Arduino IDE!

All is not lost, as we do have that ability, but it involves editing the `preferences.txt` file again:

- Close the IDE if you currently have it open.

- Edit the `preferences.txt` file.

- Look for the following two lines:

```
editor.tabs.expand=true
editor.tabs.size=2
```

- Change the second line as per the following:

```
editor.tabs.expand=true
editor.tabs.size=4
```

- Save the file.

This causes tabs to indent four characters from the default of two characters. I don't know about you, but I find two-character indents quite unreadable when looking at the structure of a sketch. I use four for just about everything I do. The preceding first line, which was not changed, determines if the IDE will convert tab characters into spaces. When set to true, the IDE will convert tabs to spaces, while false will leave the tab characters as they are, unchanged.

This makes editing in the IDE a little more comfortable, in my opinion.

2.2. Globally Defined Paths

Before the various text files are read, the Arduino IDE defines some properties defining various paths and others for itself. These properties are *global* and can be used within any of the other configuration files, including your own. These globally defined properties are listed in Table 2-1.

Table 2-1. *Globally defined properties*

Property Name	Description
{runtime.hardware.path}	The absolute path of the `hardware` directory which is the folder containing the current `platform.txt` file.
{runtime.ide.path}	The absolute path of the directory where the `arduino` (or `arduino.exe`) application, the Arduino IDE, is found.
{runtime.ide.version}	The version number of the Arduino IDE as a valid number. Each component of the version number will be converted to use two digits. Then all the dots are stripped out, and finally, any leading zeros are removed leaving the final value. For example, the Arduino IDE version 1.8.5 will become "01.08.05" which becomes "010805" before finally being assigned as `runtime.ide.version=10805`. IDE versions prior to version 1.6.0 used a single digit for the IDE version number. For example, version 1.5.6 was 156 as opposed to 10506.
{ide_version}	Compatibility alias for `runtime.ide.version`.
{runtime.os}	The operating system that the IDE is currently executing on. The values are "linux", "windows", and "macosx".

These global settings may be used in `platform.txt`, `boards.txt`, or, perhaps, but not very likely, `programmers.txt`. You may also use these paths in your amendments to the configuration files or in the various "local" versions that you create.

💡 Various configuration files can have a local version; `boards.txt`, for example, may have `boards.local.txt`. This local version allows you to make changes to the system configuration and not have to reconfigure every time the Arduino IDE is updated. Unfortunately, not all of the configuration files have a local version – `programmers.txt` is one that I have come across that doesn't. See `https://github.com/arduino/Arduino/issues/8556` for details, if you are interested.

2.3. Boards.txt

The `$ARDINST/boards.txt` file defines the various menu options for different types of microcontroller devices. These options either will appear on the Boards menu in the Arduino IDE or will be used when a specific board is selected from that menu. The file is read, and the various options are decoded and used by the IDE at startup. New boards can be added quite simply, if desired, by editing this file. Let's look inside at the entry for the Arduino Uno.

2.3.1. Arduino Uno Example

The following is the complete listing of all entries for the Arduino Uno, in the IDE version 1.8.5 - other releases, both older and potentially newer, may be different:

```
uno.name=Arduino/Genuino Uno                    ①

uno.vid.0=0x2341                                ②
uno.pid.0=0x0043
uno.vid.1=0x2341
```

```
uno.pid.1=0x0001
uno.vid.2=0x2A03
uno.pid.2=0x0043
uno.vid.3=0x2341
uno.pid.3=0x0243

uno.upload.tool=avrdude                              ③
uno.upload.protocol=arduino
uno.upload.maximum_size=32256
uno.upload.maximum_data_size=2048
uno.upload.speed=115200

uno.bootloader.tool=avrdude                          ④
uno.bootloader.low_fuses=0xFF
uno.bootloader.high_fuses=0xDE
uno.bootloader.extended_fuses=0xFD
uno.bootloader.unlock_bits=0x3F
uno.bootloader.lock_bits=0x0F
uno.bootloader.file=optiboot/optiboot_atmega328.hex

uno.build.mcu=atmega328p                             ⑤
uno.build.f_cpu=16000000L
uno.build.board=AVR_UNO
uno.build.core=arduino
uno.build.variant=standard
```

① Board name.

② This section defines identification settings used to determine the board's identity when it is plugged into the USB port on your computer.

③ These settings define parameters used for uploading compiled code to the board.

④   Bootloader settings are listed in this section.

⑤   Various build options are specified here.

The Arduino Wiki at `https://github.com/arduino/Arduino/wiki/ Arduino-IDE-1.5-3rd-party-Hardware-specification` mentions, at least for IDE version 1.5.3 which appears to be the most recently documented, that

> *This file contains definitions and meta-data for the boards supported. Every board must be referred through its short name, the board ID. The settings for a board are defined through a set of properties with keys having the board ID as prefix.*

What it doesn't mention is how the system is supposed to know that "uno", for example, refers to the Arduino/Genuino Uno device.

From the preceding listing, it is pretty obvious that the Uno's short name must be "uno" as that is the prefix in use for every entry in this section of the file.

2.3.1.1. Board Identifier

The `name` parameter here identifies the board and defines what will be displayed in the Boards menu in the IDE:

```
uno.name=Arduino/Genuino Uno
```

2.3.1.2. Identification Settings

This section's settings help to identify a genuine Arduino Uno. When you plug a device into a USB port, the device is queried to obtain a vendor and product identifier. This helps the system load the correct drivers (mainly Windows) or, on the very first time, to prompt you to load the appropriate drivers for the device. For the Uno, the following four pairs of vendors and product identifiers are known to be genuine:

```
uno.vid.0=0x2341
uno.pid.0=0x0043
uno.vid.1=0x2341
uno.pid.1=0x0001
uno.vid.2=0x2A03
uno.pid.2=0x0043
uno.vid.3=0x2341
uno.pid.3=0x0243
```

In the settings:

- Vid is the vendor identifier.

- Pid is the product identifier for the specific vendor.

From the preceding text, we can clearly see two vendors – "0x2431" and "0x2A03" – and the appropriate product identifiers to suit each vendor. Bear in mind that it isn't necessarily the actual manufacturer of the Arduino board that is being identified; it is most likely to be the chip that converts the data on the USB port into the correct format for the microcontroller. Some Uno boards have another AVR microcontroller taking care of the communications, while others have an FTDI chip – both will register as different pids.

ℹ Genuine boards, such as my own Duemilanove, which use an FTDI chip for communications, will not necessarily be recognized as the correct board. This is due to the FTDI chip which uses a generic pid and vid and is used by numerous different boards. However, this is nothing to worry about.

2.3.1.3. Upload Settings

When you click the upload button in the IDE, the settings defined in this section of the boards.txt file are used to set various parameters as desired, to enable proper communication with the currently chosen board:

```
uno.upload.tool=avrdude
uno.upload.protocol=arduino
uno.upload.maximum_size=32256
uno.upload.maximum_data_size=2048
uno.upload.speed=115200
```

To specify the tool to be used to carry out the upload, the upload.tool parameter is used. In this example, the tool in use is the program named avrdude. This tool is installed at the same time as the Arduino IDE.

The communications protocol to be used when uploading is defined in the upload.protocol parameter, while the maximum Flash and Static RAM (SRAM) sizes for the particular AVR microcontroller in use are defined in upload.maximum_size and upload.maximum_data_size parameters, respectively.

ℹ The maximum size of an ATmega328P's Flash RAM is 32,768 bytes, so why does upload.maximum_size only allow 32,256 bytes? It's because the remaining 512 bytes are used for the bootloader. The Optiboot bootloader is 512 bytes in size, so that amount of Flash RAM needs to be reserved from the maximum available.

Actually, the Optiboot bootloader is only 500 bytes in size. You can see this when you look at the start and end addresses in the compilation listing file, `$ARDINST/bootloaders/opitiboot/optiboot_atmega328.lst`, which are $7E00_{hex}$ and $7FF3_{hex}$, respectively. Subtracting gives $1F3_{hex}$ which is $499_{decimal}$, but we need to add one because we started counting from zero.

Communications will be carried out at the baud rate specified in upload.speed. For this Uno example, that will be at 115,200 baud.

2.3.1.4. Bootloader Settings

This section of the boards.txt file defines various parameters to be used when you choose Burn bootloader from the IDE menu.

It should be obvious (shouldn't it?) that burning a bootloader will require an In-Circuit System Programmer (ISCP) device as the AVR microcontroller you are burning a bootloader into doesn't yet have a bootloader to allow uploading via the normal USB connection to the board!

You should be very careful to ensure that you have selected the correct board when burning a bootloader – on a good day, it will simply fail to work. On a bad day, it will set the fuses to something that might cause you some grief trying to unravel and get reprogrammed. On a *really* bad day, it could convert your prized Arduino board into something resembling a brick.

Okay, it's probably not *that* bad, but you might end up with a need to purchase a new ATmega328P, and hopefully, it will be one that comes complete with an Uno bootloader burned in. Otherwise, you'll have to do the bootloader burning exercise all over again.

Yes, I admit it. I *did* brick an Arduino board, so that's how I know. It was a Digispark board with an ATtiny85 microcontroller, but I bricked it anyway! Investigation showed that I set the fuse to disable the RESET pin so that it could be used as a normal I/O pin. No amount of programming with a high-voltage programmer would rescue it, so there must have been some other settings that I broke as well.

I still have the device, somewhere, and one day, I will find out what I did wrong and, hopefully, fix it. Perhaps.

Continuing to look at the standard settings for an Arduino Uno, we can see the following settings:

```
uno.bootloader.tool=avrdude
uno.bootloader.low_fuses=0xFF
uno.bootloader.high_fuses=0xDE
uno.bootloader.extended_fuses=0xFD
uno.bootloader.unlock_bits=0x3F
uno.bootloader.lock_bits=0x0F
uno.bootloader.file=optiboot/optiboot_atmega328.hex
```

To specify the tool to be used to carry out the upload, the bootloader.tool parameter is defined. In the case of the Uno we are looking at here, the tool in use is the program named avrdude – the same as in the preceding text for uploading compiled sketches.

As described in Chapter 7, Section 7.1, *"ATmega328P Fuses,"* the AVR microcontroller has a number of fuses that can be utilized to set various configurations of the AVR microcontroller itself. The bootloader.low_fuses, bootloader.high_fuses, and bootloader.extended_fuses parameters define the required hardware settings for the microcontroller on the board.

Finally in this section, the `bootloader.file` parameter defines which of the many bootloaders supplied with the IDE is to be used for this board. The Uno uses the file `optiboot/optiboot_atmega328.hex` which is to be found in the `$ARDINST/bootloader/` directory.

You can, if you wish, change the bootloader by either editing the `boards.txt` file to change the appropriate parameter or duplicating an existing section and changing the bootloader. The latter option is preferred. It's worth bearing in mind that any updates to the IDE will most likely overwrite your changes to `boards.txt`, so how do we avoid this problem?

2.3.1.4.1. Boards.local.txt

Since release 1.6.6 of the Arduino IDE, a new file has been introduced, `boards.local.txt`, in which you can define various parameters that you wish to use instead of those in the `boards.txt` file. To continue the preceding example of changing the bootloader, you could create the file, if it doesn't exist, and add the following to it:

```
uno.bootloader.file=my_new_bootloader/my_new_bootloader_
atmega328.hex
```

This assumes that you won't need any additional Flash RAM space for the bootloader over and above that required by the current bootloader. If you do, then add the following as well:

```
uno.upload.maximum_size=<what ever is required>
```

2.3.1.5. Build Settings

```
uno.build.mcu=atmega328p
uno.build.f_cpu=16000000L
uno.build.board=AVR_UNO
uno.build.core=arduino
uno.build.variant=standard
```

The `build.mcu` setting defines the name of the microcontroller for this particular board. For the Uno, only an ATmega328P is defined. For other boards, the Nano, for example, there are two different microcontrollers available, the ATmega168 and the ATmega328P. Within each of those two boards, there are two different configurations, and the `boards.txt` has entries for each variant with global settings for all Nanos as well as the specific settings for the different microcontroller boards and the variants thereof.

The parameter `build.f_cpu` defines the system clock (CLK_{cpu}) for the board. The Uno has a 16 MHz crystal installed, so that's the speed that is defined in this example. This setting is used in your sketches, although you won't actually see it, as the `F_CPU` variable is used, for example, if calculating the desired baud rate when using the Serial interface.

The `build.board` property is used to set a compile-time variable `ARDUINO_{build.board}` to allow the use of conditional code between `#ifdefs` in sketches and/or header files. The Arduino IDE automatically generates a `build.board` value if not defined. In this example, the variable defined at compile time will be `ARDUINO_AVR_UNO`.

To determine which file path is to be used when the compiler is looking for various files, `main.cpp,` for example, the `build.core` setting is used. The parameter is used to build a path to the files in `$ARDINST/cores/<uno.build.core>/`, which, for the Uno in this example, will be `$ARDINST/cores/arduino/`.

The variant of the board is then defined using the `build.variant` setting. This is used to build a path to the files that live in `$ARDINST/variants/<uno.build.variant>/` and is where you will find the file named `pins_arduino.h` which defines any variations over the standard settings that apply to this particular board. For this example of an Uno, the path defined will be `$ARDINST/variants/standard/`.

ℹ The IDE defines a number of global settings for the various paths to the cores and variants. These are available in other configuration files, but they don't have the board's prefix, so uno.build.core would correspond to the IDE's global setting of build.core. If the board doesn't specify a setting, the global one will be used; however, where a board does have an appropriate setting, that will override the global one created by the IDE, when the appropriate board is selected from the Boards menu in the IDE.

You can see some of these global settings in the file platform.txt.

2.3.1.6. Configuring an ICSP

If you always want to use an ICSP (In-Circuit System Programmer) to program a particular board, you can add the following line to the $ARDINST/boards.txt or $ARDINST/boards.local.txt file, probably as part of the build settings as detailed earlier, for example:

```
uno.upload.using=USBtinyISP
```

The name you use here is one of the ones that are to be found in the $ARDINST/programmers.txt file which is itself described later in this chapter, in Section 2.5, *"Programmers.txt."*

You should make this change while the IDE is closed. When you next open the IDE, any time you select the Uno device as your board, it will automatically select the USB Tiny ISP device, in this case, to perform the uploads, rather than the bootloader.

If you wish to make this change as the default for *all* boards, then you should edit the preferences.txt file, as documented in Section 2.1, *"Preferences.txt,"* earlier in this chapter.

2.4. Platform.txt

The `$ARDINST/platform.txt` file defines platform-specific features and command-line tools, where libraries live and what they are called, and so on. It contains the various recipes used by the IDE in order to compile, build, upload, and/or program various devices and boards according to their different needs.

What is a platform? Well, in the case of the ATmega328P, or other AVR microcontrollers, the platform defines all the tools, compilers, linkers, command lines to be used and so on, for Atmel AVR microcontrollers. Other non-AVR microcontroller boards will have their own platform to define the specific tools and others for that particular microcontroller. Arduino boards with, for example, an ARM chip on them will use a different platform from those with the AVR microcontrollers.

Using this method allows for a fairly simple manner in updating the system to cope with new boards.

The Arduino system requires that this file define the following meta-data:

```
name=<platform name>
version=<platform version>
```

The name will be shown in the Tools ➤ Boards menu of the Arduino IDE, in grayed-out text, above the list of boards that conform to this particular platform. According to the documentation on the Arduino web site at `https://github.com/arduino/Arduino/wiki/Arduino-IDE-1.5-3rd-party-Hardware-specification`, the `version` is currently unused and is reserved for future use.

For the Arduino IDE version 1.8.5, we see this at the top of the file:

```
name=Arduino AVR Boards
version=1.6.22
```

Obviously, the version number of the platform can, and does, differ from the version of the IDE. Don't be confused if you see something different.

2.4.1. Build Recipes

The platform.txt file, as mentioned earlier, contains a large amount of meta-data that configures the IDE to be able to compile sketches and upload them, among other things, for the Arduino boards running with AVR microcontrollers. It does this using *recipes*. Having different recipes for all the different platforms allows the IDE to be used for a myriad of different devices.

When you select a build in the IDE, a small number of settings are created automatically for you. These are as follows:

- build.path – The path to the temporary folder to store various files created by the build process.

- build.project_name – The project (sketch) name.

- build.arch – The microcontroller architecture, which in our case is "avr" but, depending on the board, may be "sam", "arm" and so on. The IDE gets this from the paths to $ARDINST.

  On my system, $ARDINST is defined as $ARDBASE/hardware/arduino/avr – and the path portions define the hardware folder location, $ARDBASE/hardware; then the vendor name, arduino; and finally the architecture, avr for boards with the ATmega328P. For Arduino SAM boards, the path would be $ARDBASE/hardware/arduino/sam instead. The final part of the path gives the build.arch name.

A number of additional settings are defined within the $ARDINST\
boards.txt file based on the particular board chosen on the Tools ➤
Boards menu – see Section 2.3, *"Boards.txt,"* for those details – and the IDE
global variables can be used within this file too. You can find more details
on those variables in Section 2.2, *"Globally Defined Paths."*

The compilation process can read source files written in plain C – these
are the .c source files, C++ (.cpp), or even assembly language (.S). It
has to know how to convert these files into object files (.o) which can be
gathered together by the linker to create an executable file. The way this
happens is by using the recipes within the platform.txt file.

The recipes are variables in the format

```
recipe.<source_format>.o.pattern
```

And the "source_format" is simply the file extension for the files in
question. This gives us the following variables:

- recipe.c.o.pattern – To convert C files to object files

- recipe.cpp.o.pattern – To convert C++ files to
  object files

- recipe.S.o.pattern – To convert assembly language
  files to object files

You will notice, I hope, that the source format in each is case sensitive.
Assembly language files must have an upper case .S extension.

Taking one of them as an example, this is what I found in my
platform.txt file for the Arduino IDE version 1.8.5:

```
## Compile c files
recipe.c.o.pattern="{compiler.path}{compiler.c.cmd}"
{compiler.c.flags}
-mmcu={build.mcu} -DF_CPU={build.f_cpu} -DARDUINO={runtime.ide.
version}
```

```
-DARDUINO_{build.board} -DARDUINO_ARCH_{build.arch}
{compiler.c.extra_flags}
{build.extra_flags} {includes} "{source_file}" -o "{object_file}"
```

If we break the preceding recipe down into its constituent parts, we see the following variables and command-line options:

- "{compiler.path}{compiler.c.cmd}" defines where the compiler tool can be found – {compiler.path} – and what it is called, {compiler.c.cmd}. The use of double quotes allows for spaces and other non-alphanumeric characters in the path or command name.

  In the IDE, I see that {compiler.path} is defined as {runtime.tools.avr-gcc.path}/bin/; and as you can see, these recipes can refer to other variables defined in this file or elsewhere. The {compiler.c.cmd} is defined as avr-gcc, and this is not actually the compiler, but a front end to all phases of the compilation process and which can be used to control the whole process.

- {compiler.c.flags} defines a list of flags and options to be passed to the {compiler.c.cmd} utility to define how the build should progress, what outputs are required and so on. There are numerous options in IDE 1.8.5; but one in particular, -c, tells the compiler front end to stop compiling after the object file has been created and not to run the link phase.

- -mmcu={build.mcu} defines another compiler option. It tells the C compiler which microcontroller is in use on the board. It comes from $ARDINST/boards.txt and, for the Uno, is defined as uno.build.mcu=atmega328p. The name part, uno, is stripped off first.

- `-DF_CPU={build.f_cpu}` is very useful when writing code for multiple boards. The speed of the AVR microcontroller clock is defined in the compilation process, as opposed to being hardcoded in the actual source files, for example, `#define F_CPU 16000000L`. This would require editing before running on a board with a different clock speed.

  The variable is defined in `$ARDINST/boards.txt` and, for the Uno, is `uno.build.f_cpu=16000000L`. The name part, "uno.", is stripped off first.

- `-DARDUINO={runtime.ide.version}` defines a numeric value for the Arduino IDE version in use. It is created automatically by the IDE and is described in Section 2.2, "*Globally Defined Paths*." For IDE version 1.8.5, for example, it becomes 10805.

- `-DARDUINO_{build.board}` references the `uno.build.board=AVR_UNO` variable from the `$ARDINST/boards.txt` – the example shown is, once more, for the Uno. This can be used in conditional code to determine the board in use and, from that, whether certain features are available or otherwise. In this example, it would define a variable named `ARDUINO_AVR_UNO`.

- `-DARDUINO_ARCH_{build.arch}`, as described earlier, defines the architecture we are building for. For the purposes of this book, this will be "avr" giving `ARDUINO_ARCH_avr`.

- `{compiler.c.extra_flags}` are some additional flags that you or I can define in `$ARDINST/platform.local.txt` to be added to the command line for this recipe. By default, these are blank.

- {build.extra_flags} are some additional flags that you or I can define in $ARDINST/boards.local.txt to be added to the command line for this recipe. By default, these are blank.

- {includes} is the list of paths that the compiler will use to search for files #included in the various source files. The format is -I/include/path and so on. You can have more than one path. The documentation online has this to say:

  Note that older IDE versions used the recipe.preproc. includes *recipe to determine includes, which is undocumented here. Since Arduino IDE 1.6.7 (arduino-builder 1.2.0) this was changed and* recipe.preproc. includes *is no longer used.*

  This is not really very helpful, as includes remains undocumented, and even the "no longer used" recipe recipe.preproc.includes actually has {includes} as part of its definition.

- "{source_file}" is the path to the single source file being compiled. The double quotes allow for spaces and other non-alphanumeric characters in the file name.

- -o "{object_file}" is the path to the single object file which will be created by the compilation phase. The double quotes allow for spaces and other non-alphanumeric characters in the file name.

2.4.2. Pre- and Post-build Hooks

Pre- and post-build hooks were introduced in Arduino version 1.6.5 and are found in the $ARDINST/platform.txt file. In version 1.8.5, the following hooks are available for your use:

- recipe.hooks.sketch.prebuild.NUMBER.pattern – Called before sketch compilation

- recipe.hooks.sketch.postbuild.NUMBER.pattern – Called after sketch compilation

- recipe.hooks.libraries.prebuild.NUMBER. pattern – Called before libraries compilation

- recipe.hooks.libraries.postbuild.NUMBER. pattern – Called after libraries compilation

- recipe.hooks.core.prebuild.NUMBER.pattern – Called before core compilation

- recipe.hooks.core.postbuild.NUMBER.pattern – Called after core compilation

- recipe.hooks.linking.prelink.NUMBER.pattern – Called before linking

- recipe.hooks.linking.postlink.NUMBER.pattern – Called after linking

- recipe.hooks.objcopy.preobjcopy.NUMBER. pattern – Called before objcopy recipe execution

- recipe.hooks.objcopy.postobjcopy.NUMBER. pattern – Called after objcopy recipe execution

- `recipe.hooks.savehex.presavehex.NUMBER.`
  `pattern` – Called before savehex recipe execution

- `recipe.hooks.savehex.postsavehex.NUMBER.`
  `pattern` – Called after savehex recipe execution

These are identified by the `recipe.hooks` part. The next part determines which stage in the compilation the hook will be called. `Prexxxxx` and `postxxxxx` indicate that the pattern will be called before the appropriate stage or afterward.

In order that multiple hooks can be called at any stage, the `NUMBER` part is a sequence number which should be 1, 2, 3, 4, and so on – there's one number for each hook to execute at a given stage in proceedings. The end of the recipe is always the word `pattern`.

ℹ️ If you find that you require ten or more hooks, then your NUMBER parts should be 01, 02, ..., 10, 11, and so on.

Following the equals sign are the commands you want to execute. For example, in `$ARDINST/platform.local.txt`, you could add the following on Linux:

```
recipe.hooks.sketch.prebuild.1.pattern=echo Compiling sketch:
{build.source.path}
recipe.hooks.sketch.postbuild.1.pattern=echo Compiled
```

Or the following on Windows:

```
recipe.hooks.sketch.prebuild.1.pattern=cmd /C echo Compiling sketch:
{build.source.path}
recipe.hooks.sketch.postbuild.1.pattern=cmd /C echo Compiled"
```

I noticed that some, but not all, variables do not get expanded. Using "{source_file}", for example, doesn't expand, but {build.source.path} does. Also, the entire text after the equals sign becomes part of the message, not just the command's output. The preceding code, on Linux, displays the text "echo Compiling sketch: /full/path/to/my/sketch/here" rather than just "Compiling sketch:
    /full/path/to/my/sketch/here". A similar thing happens with Windows.

⚠ The command used *cannot be a built-in command* and *must* be found on your system's path ($PATH on Linux and MacOS, %path% on Windows.)

On Windows, the echo command is a built-in command. It cannot be found on %path% when the compilation is started, so the whole compilation fails because echo can't be found. This is because of the way that the Java command exec, from Runtime.getRuntime(), works.

So how did the preceding echo command work for Windows? I created an echo.bat file and put it on my Windows %PATH%.

Commands to be executed in the hooks must be found on the $PATH; if not, they will not be executed, and the recipe will fail.

2.5. Programmers.txt

The programmers.txt file is very much the least documented of the various text files used by the Arduino IDE. The Wiki pages describe the other files, but nothing at all, other than a brief mention of its name, for programmers.txt.

It is assumed, possibly incorrectly, that people creating and building new ICSP devices know what all the parameters mean and will supply a list of required entries, for their device, to be added to `programmers.txt`.

It is also likely that whenever anyone creates or updates a programming device, or settings, it would be submitted to the Arduino maintainers for inclusion in the next release of software.

⚠️ The `programmers.txt` file *will* be overwritten by each new IDE update, so if you have made any changes, you *really* should keep a record of them prior to upgrading.

`$ARDINST/programmers.txt` holds details about the various programming devices that the Arduino IDE can use to upload code to your Arduino board. Unlike `boards.txt` and `platform.txt`, the IDE doesn't seem to recognize a local variant, `programmers.local.txt`, even if one exists. Therefore, any changes that you make to your own installation will need to be made to the supplied `$ARDINST/programmers.txt` file, and this will be overwritten when the IDE is upgraded.

As this is a bit of a nuisance, I logged issue 8556 about it at `https://github.com/arduino/Arduino/issues/8556`. It could be that this is by design and not an actual problem. We shall see what transpires.

The file contains parameters that are relevant to the various programming devices that can be used, and depending on the settings, these may appear in the various menu options under the Tools menu in the IDE.

An example of an entry in the file is as follows:

```
usbtinyisp.name=USBtinyISP
usbtinyisp.protocol=usbtiny
usbtinyisp.program.tool=avrdude
usbtinyisp.program.extra_params=
```

This is for the "USB Tiny" ICSP (In-Circuit System Programmer) and shows the following:

- The device name, as it will appear in the Tools ➤ Programmer menu. In this case, it is "USBtinyISP." You can change this if you prefer to use a different name.

- The protocol to be used when executing the IDE option to "Upload using programmer."

- The tool that will be used when uploading. Here we can see that it is defined as using the avrdude utility.

- Any extra parameters that may be needed to do the upload. In this example, there are none. However, if any were needed, they would be required to be consistent with the syntax of the programming tool in use.

If, for example, the device required a serial port to be used for the upload, then you could add the following:

```
usbtinyisp.program.extra_params=-P{serial.port}
```

This would allow the command line passed to avrdude to be supplied with the -P option, to select a serial port, and it would be set to the value chosen in the IDE on the Tools ➤ Port menu option.

ℹ This is obviously just an example; the USB Tiny device doesn't need a serial port.

2.6. Compiling a Sketch

When you open a project in the Arduino IDE, you will notice that all files in the project directory with an `.ino`, `.h`, `.c`, or `.cpp` extension get placed on a tab of their own. These are assumed to be all the source files that make up your project. You can, if you wish, open other files within the IDE, but these will not automatically open in separate tabs when you subsequently reopen the project. They will have to be manually opened if editing or viewing is required.

You should also be aware that there is *not* a function called `main()` in any of the files open in the project. Anyone who has programmed in C or C++ will know that `main()` is the program's entry point. What's going on?

The Arduino IDE supplies its own `main()` function, so that you don't have to. In order to make life easier for budding microcontroller makers and developers, the Arduino system hides a lot of *stuff* from you. I'll be taking a look at the `main()` function soon.

When you compile a project in the Arduino IDE, a number of things take place, and these separate processes are described in the remainder of this chapter. Your sketch will be converted into a C++ file by the Arduino Preprocessor.

2.6.1. Arduino Sketch (*.ino) Preprocessing

An Arduino sketch is a very much simplified C++ source file which may be composed of many files with the extension `.ino` and, occasionally, some additional files with the extension `.cpp`. To convert the sketch into a valid C++ file, a number of actions are carried out:

- *Maybe* create a temporary compiler working folder in the system's main temporary folder or directory. This will be within `/tmp` on Linux and something along the lines of `c:\users\<your_name>\AppData\Local\Temp\arduino_build_<some_number>\` on Windows.

This happens only on the very first compilation of this particular sketch. For the rest of this discussion, I shall refer to this folder as $TMP.

- If your sketch is composed of a number of .ino files, those files are concatenated into a single .ino.cpp file, in the $TMP/sketch subfolder, starting with the main sketch file which is the .ino file with the same name as the sketch's folder name. The remainder of the .ino files are appended to the end of the main one, in alphabetical order. If your sketch was named Blink.ino, then the generated file would be named $TMP/sketch/Blink.ino.cpp.

- The line #include <Arduino.h> is added at the beginning of the .ino.cpp file, if not already present.

- All libraries used in the sketch are detected, and the include paths for those libraries are discovered. This is done by running a dummy compilation with the output being discarded (to the null device on Windows and /dev/null on Linux) and processing any relevant error messages.

- Prototypes for all functions in the .ino.cpp file are generated. If, as *occasionally* happens, a valid function prototype cannot be automatically generated, you will need to add one explicitly to the .ino file that defines the failing function.

- The .ino.cpp file is processed so that there are relevant compiler preprocessor #line and #file directives so that error reporting will be accurate and refer to the correct lines in the correct source files, as opposed to referencing the lines within the concatenated .ino.cpp file.

These actions are performed by the `arduino-preprocessor` tool which lives on GitHub at `https://github.com/arduino/arduino-preprocessor`.

2.6.2. Arduino Sketch (*`.ino`) Build

After preprocessing, the build is then completed by the `arduino-builder` tool, found at `https://github.com/arduino/arduino-builder`, which

- Compiles the `.ino.cpp` file, created by the preprocessing stage, into a module with a `.ino.cpp.o` extension. This module file is stored in the `$TMP/sketch` subfolder created by the Arduino Preprocessor tool described earlier.

- Compiles all other `.c` or `.cpp` files, including `main.cpp`, into separate modules in the `$TMP/sketch` subfolder.

ℹ️ If the sketch's configuration – the board and so on – has not changed since the previous compilation, then some of these modules may be reused rather than recompiled. This saves time on the second and subsequent compilations. This is only done if the source file(s) for the module to be reused has not been edited or changed of course.

- Any libraries used by the sketch will be compiled as separate modules too. Once again, these will be written as `.o` files in the `$TMP/libraries` subfolder.

- The Arduino core files are compiled as `.o` files into `$TMP/core`. These core files are the like of `wiring_analog.c`, `wiring_digital.c` and so on, as installed under the IDE.

- The individual core modules (*.o) are then built into a single static library, core.a, in the $TMP/ core subfolder – for example, on Windows, c:\ users\<your_name>\AppData\Local\Temp\arduino_ build_<some_number>\core\core.a.

- After all the modules have been created, the linker combines them all into a single elf format binary file. This file lives in the main temporary folder created earlier and will be named $TMP/<sketch_name>.ino. elf, $TMP/Blink.ino.elf, for example.

- The $TMP/<sketch_name>.ino.elf file is then used to create a file named $TMP/<sketch_name>.ino. eep which contains data to be written to the AVR microcontroller's EEPROM area.

- The $TMP/<sketch_name>.ino.elf file is also used to create a file named $TMP/<sketch_name>.ino. hex which contains the code used to flash the AVR microcontroller with your sketch. This code is in "Intel Hex" format.

This ends the compilation process. If the upload button is clicked in the IDE, rather than the compile (or verify) button, then the $TMP/<sketch_name>.ino.hex file is uploaded to the AVR microcontroller, using an *Arduino-specific* version of the avrdude tool which can be found on GitHub at https://github.com/arduino/avrdude-build-script.

There's a menu option, Sketch ➤ Export Compiled Binary, which will export the compiled hex files to the sketch's folder. This could be used for passing copies of your application for your friends to upload, without letting them see your source code. There are two files created:

- `Sketch_name.ino.standard.hex` – This is the hex file to upload your code and only your code.

- `Sketch_name.ino.with_bootloader.standard.hex` – This file, if uploaded, will write both the bootloader and your application code.

If you have a bootloader installed on your ATmega328P, then you can use it to upload the files using avrdude. Normally, when using an ICSP to program your device, the bootloader will be overwritten when the chip is wiped. However, if you use the ICSP to upload the preceding file with the bootloader, then you effectively burn a bootloader as well as your application's code into the Arduino board.

Either file can be uploaded using the bootloader – if it is still installed on your device – and after doing so, regardless of which of the two files you upload, the bootloader will still be present afterward.

All this "just works" and it makes life easy; however, what is the Arduino system hiding from you?

💡 You can see all of this happening, before your very eyes, if you edit the preferences in the IDE to show verbose compiling and/or upload messages.

The following chapters describe the various files that your sketch ends up including when the compilation process has completed.

2.7. The Arduino `main()` Function

As previously noted, the main() function is where all C or C++ applications start executing. As an Arduino developer though, you don't have to supply one as the system does it for you. The Arduino main() function in version 1.8.5 is found in the file $ARDINC/main.cpp beneath the Arduino installation directory and is shown in Listing 2-1.

Listing 2-1. The Arduino main() function

```
#include <Arduino.h>                                         ①

// Declared weak in Arduino.h to allow user redefinitions.
int atexit(void (* /*func*/ )()) { return 0; }

// Weak empty variant initialization function.
// May be redefined by variant files.
void initVariant() __attribute__((weak));
void initVariant() { }

void setupUSB() __attribute__((weak));
void setupUSB() { }

int main(void)
{
    init();                          ②

    initVariant();                   ③

#if defined(USBCON)                  ④
    USBDevice.attach();
#endif

    setup();                         ⑤

    for (;;) {                       ⑥
```

```
        loop();
        if (serialEventRun) serialEventRun(); ⑦
    }

    return 0;
}
```

① The first point to note is the inclusion of the file
Arduino.h (found in the folder $ARDINC), and
this is where numerous constants and other
definitions specific to the Arduino are declared. If
you look at this file, it makes *interesting* reading;
there are numerous tests to determine which
board is in use and which features of the AVR
microcontroller can be used. The Arduino.h
header file is described in Section 2.8, "*Header
File Arduino.h.*"

② Within the main() function itself, there is a call
to init() which is found in $ARDINC/wiring.c.
This initializes a whole raft of features for the
Arduino and carries out this based on the actual
microcontroller in use on the board. If you decide
to dive into this function, make sure that you are
armed with a copy of the data sheet for your specific
microcontroller; otherwise, nothing much will make
sense.

③ The next function call, initVariant(), carries out
any special initialization for boards that are possibly
not covered by the standard initialization. The
function defaults to doing nothing (you can see it at
the top of main.cpp); but as it is declared as weak, it
can be overridden, as required, in a sketch.

45

④ Some boards like the Leonardo use USB for serial communications and thus require USB setting up, so there is a test to see if this is required. If so, then the USBDevice.attach() function is called to do the needful.

⑤ The sketch's setup() function is called next. This is where the sketch's own initialization gets carried out.

⑥ After the call to setup(), an endless loop is entered where the sketch's loop() function is called once on every pass through the loop.

⑦ The function serialEventRun() is called each time through the loop as well. This in itself calls out to another (weak) function named serialEvent(), if it exists in the sketch, and this is used to collect up any data that has been received into the Serial input buffer but not yet read by the sketch.

There is an example of its use on the Arduino Tutorials web site at www.arduino.cc/en/Tutorial/SerialEvent.

This is how the sketch's ino file fits into the real world: the setup() function is called once, and the loop() gets called repeatedly until the Arduino runs out of power or is turned off.

Calling the loop() function many times in this manner will impart some overhead to each execution. There is the stack frame setup prior to the function call and the stack teardown at the end prior to the function returning. These housekeeping instructions take time to execute and *can* slow down your code. You can avoid this by defining your own loop with a for, while, or do block within the loop() function, so that loop() only ever gets called once and never has to return to main(). Listing 2-2 shows a brief example.

Listing 2-2. A "never returning" loop() function

```
void loop() {
    while (1) {
        // Do your loop code here.
    }
}
```

⚠ Bear in mind that if you do decide to create your own loop in the manner described earlier, you *might* cause problems with any serial communications that would have been processed by the call to serialEventRun() in the main() function.

Check the documentation on the Arduino Tutorials web site at www.arduino.cc/en/Tutorial/SerialEvent to be sure that you will not be causing yourself any worries.

2.8. Header File `Arduino.h`

As mentioned previously, when you compile a sketch in the Arduino IDE, there is a certain amount of *reorganization* taking place to convert your sketch into something resembling a proper C/C++ program. The file Arduino.h, which can be found in $ARDINC as can all the other Arduino-specific header files, is included at the top of the converted source code. It is in, or from, this file that much of the initialization of a sketch takes place.

The following list outlines the actions of the Arduino.h file:

- Various standard C/C++ header files are included. I will not be discussing those here.

- A number of AVR-specific header files are included from the AVRLib sources, in $AVRINC. These are as follows:

  - avr/pgmspace.h

  - avr/io.h

  - avr/interrupt.h

- A *strange* header file, binary.h, is included next.

- All the Arduino-specific function headers are defined, for example, pinMode(), digitalWrite() and so on, along with a number of useful constants such as HIGH, LOW, INPUT, OUTPUT amongst others.

- If the compilation is using the C++ compiler (avr-g++) as opposed to the C compiler (avr-gcc), then

  - WCharacter.h is included.

  - WString.h is included.

  - HardwareSerial.h is included.

  - USBAPI.h is included.

  - If the compiler discovers that the microcontroller in use has both hardware serial and CDC serial, then it cannot continue with the compilation, so an error is displayed and the compilation ends.

- Finally, the header file pins_arduino.h is included.

The relevant header files are described in the following sections, as are any other headers that they themselves include.

2.8.1. Header File `avr\pgmspace.h`

This header file is included from $AVRINC, to allow pins_arduino.h, as described in the following, to create lookup tables within the program space – in flash memory, as opposed to in the scarce Static RAM (SRAM) on the device. It defines a number of typedefs and functions to copy data between the program space, in flash, and the variable space in RAM. It doesn't make for very interesting reading I'm afraid.

2.8.2. Header File `avr\io.h`

This file, from $AVRINC, sets up all the AVR-specific *stuff* for the appropriate AVR microcontroller that is in use on the Arduino board. The settings you chose in the IDE for Tools ➤ Boards will determine the specific device file that will be included. In the majority of cases, and for our purposes here, this will be the ATmega328P, and so this file simply causes the AVR definitions for that microcontroller to be read in from the file avr/iom328p.h.

This file also includes sfr_defs.h to set up numerous macros for memory address simplification, some functions to handle looping until a bit is clear (or set) and so on. These are not discussed here.

Other files included by avr/io.h are as follows:

- `<avr/portpins.h>`
- `<avr/common.h>`
- `<avr/version.h>`

- `<avr/xmega.h>` (only if we are compiling for an XMega device, which we are not, so this header will not be discussed further)
- `<avr/fuse.h>`
- `<avr/lock.h>`

The AVRLib header files are to be found in $AVRINC, under your Arduino 1.8.5 installation, unless otherwise stated. These header files are not part of the Arduino IDE *per se*, but are supplied as part of the AVRLib, which the IDE uses.

2.8.2.1. Header File `avr/iom328p.h`

If you've ever looked at the data sheet for the ATmega328P, then you will notice that the various registers, and the bits thereof, have strange-sounding acronyms. This header file, from $AVRINC, is the one which creates all the constants so that you can refer to those acronyms in your code. In addition to these acronyms, various other constants are defined to manage RAM sizes, fuse bits, sleep modes, interrupt vectors and so on. This is another important header file, but it really doesn't make for good bedtime reading.

If your Arduino board uses a different AVR microcontroller device, then a different `iomxxx.h` file will be included, rather than this one, so the definitions will be suitable for the board and/or microcontroller in use.

The exact file which will be included is defined by the IDE's Tools ➤ Boards settings.

2.8.2.2. Header File `avr/portpins.h`

This header file, from $AVRINC, is a continuation of the device-specific `avr/iom328p.h` file and defines some additional constants which are common to all of the other devices. Some of the definitions in this file will not be relevant to all devices, but the code in this file does do some checks to see if a definition will be relevant, before defining it. It does this by checking for constants defined in the avr/iom328p.h header file and, if defined, sets up the additional constants.

ℹ️ Obviously, if the board in use is not based on the ATmega328P, then the reference to avr/iom328p.h in the preceding text would of course be to a different header file for the device actually in use on the board.

2.8.2.3. Header File ⟨avr/common.h⟩

According to the comments in this header, *This [sic] purpose of this header is to define registers that have not been previously defined in the individual device IO header files, and to define other symbols that are common across AVR device families.*

I think that about covers it!

The file can be found in $AVRINC.

2.8.2.4. Header File ⟨avr/version.h⟩

This is a header file specific to the AVRLib code and not to the AVR devices. It defines various constants to indicate which version of the AVRLib is in use. For example, for a version 2.0.0 AVRLib, we see the constants shown in Listing 2-3.

Listing 2-3. AVRLib constants

```
#define __AVR_LIBC_VERSION_STRING__  "2.0.0"
#define __AVR_LIBC_VERSION__          20000UL
#define __AVR_LIBC_DATE_STRING__     "20150208"
#define __AVR_LIBC_DATE_            20150208UL
#define __AVR_LIBC_MAJOR__           2
```

```
#define __AVR_LIBC_MINOR__          0
#define __AVR_LIBC_REVISION__       0
```

You could use these constants to check whether a specific version of the library is in use and, from that, determine if some function can be used or otherwise.

Once again, the file can be found in $AVRINC.

2.8.2.5. Header File `<avr/fuse.h>`

Fuses are programmable bits in 1, 2, or 3 bytes inside the AVR microcontroller. These are used to set various features of the hardware and are covered in some detail in Chapter 7, Section 7.1, "*ATmega328P Fuses*." The data sheet for the appropriate AVR device has full details, and warnings!

This header file, from $AVRINC, sets up a structure type (__fuse_t) that corresponds to the fuse bits for the appropriate board.

2.8.2.6. Header File `<avr/lock.h>`

This header file, from $AVRINC, sets up lock bit details for the specific AVR microcontroller in use. This will not be discussed further here, so see the data sheet for full details.

2.8.3. Header File `avr\interrupt.h`

Because the init() function, as described in the following, sets up Timer 0 with an interrupt routine to keep track of the number of milliseconds (millis) that have passed since a sketch started, this header file is required. In essence, and among many checks, it creates the ISR() macro which allows you to create interrupt handlers when using AVR-specific C/C++ code. The Arduino Language uses a slightly different system, attachInterrupt(), for example, for external interrupts. Arduino interrupts will be described in Chapter 3, Section 3.5, "*Interrupts.*"

This file is also part of the AVRLib and is found in $AVRINC.

2.8.4. Header File `binary.h`

This header file defines a constant for every numeric value from 0 through to 255, in the value's *binary* number format. The constants defined, using #define, are of the format

```
#define B0 0
#define B00 0
#define B000 0
#define B0000 0
#define B00000 0
#define B000000 0
#define B0000000 0
#define B00000000 0

#define B1 1
#define B01 1
#define B001 1
#define B0001 1
#define B00001 1
#define B000001 1
#define B0000001 1
#define B00000001 1
...
...
#define B11111110 254
#define B11111111 255
```

It looks strange, yes? The header is defining as many different *binary* style constants for every number between 0 and 255. Why does 0 get so many different constants while 255 only has one? This allows the programmer to specify zero in as many ways as there are leading zeros in the binary representation of the number zero. This applies to all the numbers, but once you reach 128, there are no more leading zeros, so those values only have a single constant defined.

As I said, a little strange, but it allows you to write code such as

```
DDRD = B11110000;
```

Set the D port on the AVR microcontroller to have the top 4 bits as OUTPUT and the bottom 4 as INPUT, equivalent to the following Arduino code:

```
pinMode(7, OUTPUT);     // Port D, pin 7.
pinMode(6, OUTPUT);     // Port D, pin 6.
pinMode(5, OUTPUT);     // Port D, pin 5.
pinMode(4, OUTPUT);     // Port D, pin 4.
pinMode(3, INPUT);      // Port D, pin 3.
pinMode(2, INPUT);      // Port D, pin 2.
pinMode(1, INPUT);      // Port D, pin 1.
pinMode(0, INPUT);      // Port D, pin 0.
```

Only *one* line of code? To do all that? Yes, one line of AVR code can correspond to numerous lines of Arduino code. This is another example of how the Arduino makes life easier for the beginner – which of the two preceding code sections is the easier to read and understand?

2.8.5. Header File **WCharacter.h**

This header file defines a number of inlined functions which can be used to determine if a character is numeric, alphanumeric, and so on. This is not specific to the Arduino software and will not be discussed further.

What are inlined functions?

Inlined functions get copied verbatim into the code where they are called. Normally, functions are set up in the executable once and called from many places. Inlining them improves runtime efficiency but at the expense of code size.

Have a look at the header file, and if you are short of space in your device, try not to use the functions defined here too often; or if you have to use them, do something similar to the code in Listing 2-4.

Listing 2-4. Avoiding inlined code to save space

```
// Define my own function to avoid too many copies of
// 'isAlphaNumeric()' which is always inlined.
// See 'WCharacter.h' for details.
boolean isAlphaNum(int c)
{
    return isAlphaNumeric(int c);
}
```

Then call the `isAlphaNum()` function frequently from your own code, rather than calling the `isAlphaNumeric()` function frequently.

2.8.6. Header File `WString.h`

The `WString.h` header file defines a C++ class named `String`. I have to admit to not seeing any Arduino code that uses this class, but maybe I haven't been reading enough code. As this isn't specifically Arduino code, even though the class has been written for Arduino, it will not be discussed further.

Okay, I lied. `String` *is* used by the `Serial` class, but deep down. `Serial` inherits from `Stream` which inherits from `Print`, and `Print` uses `String` internally.

⚠️ Using this class will seriously increase the size of your sketches and may result in *very difficult to diagnose* runtime errors if too much dynamic memory is allocated – which this class does internally.

2.8.7. Header File `HardwareSerial.h`

This is the header file that defines the `Serial` interface whereby your Arduino board can talk back to your main computer over the USB cable. There's a lot going on in this file, and it makes interesting reading to see how the Arduino library works.

If your device has less than 1024 bytes of RAM, then two buffers of 16 characters each are created. One is for serial receiving and the other is for serial transmission. The buffer sizes are increased to 64 characters if you have more than 1024 bytes of RAM available. The ATmega328P has 2048 bytes, so the larger-sized buffers are created.

The buffers are set up as what is known as *circular* buffers. They have a pointer to the first free character for insertion into the buffer and a pointer to the next character to be removed from the buffer. Hopefully, never the twain shall meet, but if they do happen to meet, the sketch will suspend for a while until some data has been removed from the buffer allowing the new data to be inserted.

Circular buffers are described in some detail at https:// en.wikipedia.org/wiki/Circular_buffer.

Also set up in this file are a couple of interrupt routines which are called automatically by the AVR microcontroller whenever there is an empty transmit or a full receive buffer for the built-in USART device. The Serial class will, in the case of a transmission, read the next character from the Arduino transmit buffer and write it into the hardware register as appropriate to have it transmitted out via the USART. A similar process takes place for the receive interrupt. The hardware buffers on the AVR microcontroller are a single byte in size.

In the case where the AVR device has more than one USART, the Mega 2560 series, for example, then these are also set up from other header files included by this one. These additional hardware serial devices are not discussed further as the default Arduino board using the ATmega328P only has a single USART and they are all similar.

2.8.8. Header File USBAPI.h

This is a header specifically for devices which have built-in *hardware* USB features – these being boards based around the ATmega32U4 microcontroller which is on board the Arduino Leonardo, Pro Micro, Micro, and a few other models. As the ATmega328P doesn't have hardware USB on board, this file will not be discussed any further.

2.8.9. Header File pins_arduino.h

The version of pins_arduino.h that is included is dependent on the Arduino board in use and, thus, the AVR microcontroller in use on that specific board. For the default board, the file is located in $ARDINST/

`variants/standard,` using an ATmega328P, while the Adafruit Gemma board has its `pins_arduino.h` in `$ARDINST/variants/gemma` and uses an ATtiny85 device. The included file sets up the pin assignments for the appropriate device.

The board is chosen by the developer using the IDE's Tools ➤ Boards menu option.

It is this header file that defines constants for the analogue pins, `A0` which has the value 14 through `A7` which is defined as 21, for example.

Also created within the program space on the AVR device are a number of small lookup tables that are used to

- Convert an AVR port name (Px) to the Data Direction Register for that port (DDRx). This is table `port_to_mode_PGM`.

- Convert an AVR port name (Px) to the output port register for that port (PORTx). This is table `port_to_output_PGM`.

- Convert an AVR port name (Px) to the input port register for that port (PINx). This is table `port_to_input_PGM`.

- Convert a digital pin number (0–13) to the AVR port (PORTB, PORTC, or PORTD). This is table `digital_pin_to_port_PGM`.

- Convert a digital pin number (0–13) to the specific pin number (or bit number) on the AVR port (PORTB, PORTC, or PORTD). This is table `digital_pin_to_bit_mask_PGM`. The entry stored in this table is a bitmask with only 1 bit set, the bit that corresponds to the pin number.

- Convert a digital pin number (0–13) to one of the timer outputs on the device (6 on the standard Arduino board). This is table `digital_pin_to_timer_PGM` and is used in the `analogueWrite()` function for pulse width modulation (PWM).

2.9. The `init()` Function

This function is located within the file $ARDINC/`wiring.c`.

At the start of *every* Arduino sketch, the `init()` function is responsible for

- Enabling the global interrupt flag

- Configuring Timer/counter 0 to provide PWM on pins D5 and D6 and initiating the `millis()` counter facility by setting up the Timer/counter 0 Overflow interrupt handler

- Configuring Timer/counter 1 to provide PWM on pins D9 and D10

- Configuring Timer/counter 2 to provide PWM on pins D3 and D11

- Initializing the Analogue to Digital Converter

- Disabling the USART from pins D0 and D1

2.9.1. Enabling the Global Interrupt Flag

The function `init()` begins by enabling interrupts globally as shown in Listing 2-5. Arduino boards require interrupts to be enabled so that the `millis()` function can begin counting, once the appropriate timer (Timer/counter 0) is configured and started.

ℹ️ In the following walk-through of the source code for the `init()` function, and as with many other code listings in this book, the code that is not relevant to the ATmega328P has been removed to reduce the amount of source code listed and to avoid confusing this author!

Listing 2-5. Setting interrupts on

```
void init()
{
    // this needs to be called before setup() or some
    // functions won't work there
    sei();                                    ①
```

    ① Turns on global interrupts. This is required to make functions such as `millis()` and `micros()` work.

The code continues to enable Timer/counter 0 next.

2.9.2. Enabling Timer/counter 0

Timer/counter 0 is used to count the milliseconds which have passed since the sketch began operating after power on, system reset, or uploading a sketch. It does this by setting up the following for Timer/counter 0:

- The prescaler for Timer/counter 0 is set to divide the system clock (16 MHz) by 64 so that every 64 ticks of the system clock, the timer/counter's own clock will tick once and increment the counter value by 1. As this is an 8-bit timer, it can only count from 0 to 255 and then roll over, or overflow, to 0 again and so on. The overflow will occur every 256 timer/counter clock ticks which equates to 64 * 256 system clock ticks.

- The interrupt on Timer/counter 0 overflow is set up and enabled. The interrupt will fire every time the timer/counter's value overflows from 255 to 0. The Timer/counter 0 Overflow interrupt will update the millis counter once every 256 *timer* clock ticks (256 *Timer/counter 0* clock ticks.) This is calculated as

```
1/ (CPU Frequency / prescaler) * Timer ticks until
overflow
= 1/(F_CPU / 64) * 256
= 1/(16000000 / 64) * 256
= 1/250000 * 256
= 4 microseconds * 256
= 1024 microseconds
= 1 millisecond plus 24 microseconds.
```

The interrupt takes account of those extra 24 microseconds and will adjust the millis() result to account for them whenever they accumulate enough to add an extra millisecond to the timer.

Timer/counter 0 is also used to provide 8-bit PWM (pulse width modulation for analogueWrite()) on pins D5 and D6.

The init() function code walk-through continues in Listing 2-6.

Listing 2-6. Timer/counter 0 configuration

```
// on the ATmega168, timer 0 is also used for fast
// hardware PWM (using phase-correct PWM would mean
// that timer 0 overflowed half as often resulting in
// different millis() behavior on the ATmega8 and
// ATmega168)
```

```
#if defined(TCCR0A) && defined(WGM01)
    sbi(TCCR0A, WGM01);                      ①
    sbi(TCCR0A, WGM00);
#endif

    // set timer 0 prescale factor to 64

    ...

#elif defined(TCCR0B) && defined(CS01) && defined(CS00)

    // this combination is for the standard
    // 168/328/1280/2560.
    sbi(TCCR0B, CS01);                       ②
    sbi(TCCR0B, CS00);

    ...

#else
    #error Timer 0 prescale factor 64 not set correctly
#endif

    // enable timer 0 overflow interrupt

    ...

#elif defined(TIMSK0) && defined(TOIE0)
    sbi(TIMSK0, TOIE0);                      ③
#else
    #error Timer 0 overflow interrupt not set correctly
#endif
```

① Setting these 2 bits in the TCCR0A register ensures that the PWM waveform generator is running in Fast Hardware PWM mode, instead of Phase Correct PWM mode, which would interfere with the timer for the millis() function.

② Setting these 2 bits in register TCCR0B sets the timer clock to be the system clock divided by 64.

That equates to 16 MHz for the system clock, divided down to 250 MHz, or one tick of the timer clock for every 64 ticks of the system clock.

③ Setting this bit in the TIMSK0 register enables the Timer 0 Overflow interrupt. Now every time the timer goes from 255 to 0, the interrupt routine will be called to accumulate counts for millis() and micros().

Listing 2-7 shows the source for the Timer 0 Overflow interrupt routine, which is separate from the code in the init() function. The remainder of the init() function walk-through follows later.

2.9.3. Timer/counter 0 Overflow Interrupt

The Timer 0 Overflow interrupt is used to update the millis() count. It does this every 1.024 milliseconds, and, as this is slightly over 1 millisecond, it accumulates these extra fractions; and when there are enough accumulated, the millis count gets incremented by an extra *leap* millisecond. This takes place roughly every 42 interrupt handler executions – it's actually every 41.666 (recurring) executions, but you cannot have a fraction of an execution!

The code to do all this is shown in Listing 2-7, taken from $ARDINC/ wiring.c.

Listing 2-7. Timer/counter 0 Overflow interrupt handler

```
#if defined(TIM0_OVF_vect)
ISR(TIM0_OVF_vect)
#else
ISR(TIMER0_OVF_vect)
#endif
{
    // copy these to local variables so they can be
    // stored in registers (volatile variables must be
    // read from memory on every access)

    unsigned long m = timer0_millis;        ①
    unsigned char f = timer0_fract;

    m += MILLIS_INC;                        ②
    f += FRACT_INC;
    if (f >= FRACT_MAX) {
        f -= FRACT_MAX;
        m += 1;
    }

    timer0_fract = f;                       ③
    timer0_millis = m;
    timer0_overflow_count++;                ④
}
```

① The current values of the variables timer0_millis and timer0_fract are copied locally from memory (Static RAM) so that they can be used in registers for faster processing.

② The current `timer0_millis` count, in `m`, is incremented by `MILLIS_INC`. The current accumulated fractions of a millisecond, `timer0_fract` used locally in variable `f`, are incremented by `FRACT_INC`. If `f` is then larger than `FRACT_MAX`, then an extra "leap" millisecond is accumulated and the counts adjusted accordingly.

③ The new values are copied back to the original two variables.

④ A counter, `timer0_overflow_count`, keeps track of the number of times the ISR has been fired. This counter is used in the `millis()` function, and that is itself used in the `delay()` function.

"What are `MILLIS_INC`, `FRACT_INC`, and `FRACT_MAX`?", I hear you ask. These are defined in `$ARDINC/wiring.c`, and an extract is shown in Listing 2-8.

Listing 2-8. Variables used in counting `millis`

```
// the whole number of milliseconds per timer0 overflow
#define MILLIS_INC (MICROSECONDS_PER_TIMER0_OVERFLOW / 1000)

// the fractional number of milliseconds per timer0 overflow.
// we shift right by three to fit these numbers into a byte.
// For the clock speeds we care about - 8 and 16 MHz - this
// doesn't lose precision.)

#define FRACT_INC
    ((MICROSECONDS_PER_TIMER0_OVERFLOW % 1000) >> 3)

#define FRACT_MAX (1000 >> 3)
```

The other helper definitions we need here are as follows. The first is also defined in $ARDINC/wiring.c:

```
// the prescaler is set so that timer0 ticks every 64
// clock cycles, and the overflow handler is called
// every 256 ticks.
#define MICROSECONDS_PER_TIMER0_OVERFLOW \
    (clockCyclesToMicroseconds(64 * 256))
```

From $ARDINC/Arduino.h, we have

```
#define clockCyclesToMicroseconds(a) \
    ( (a) / clockCyclesPerMicrosecond() )
```

and also

```
#define clockCyclesPerMicrosecond() ( F_CPU / 1000000L )
```

So, working backward, we see that the number of clockCyclesPerMicrosecond is 16e6/1e6 or 16. From that, we can then see that MICROSECONDS_PER_TIMER0_OVERFLOW is (64 * 256)/16, which gives us 1024.

This then allows MILLIS_INC to be calculated as 1024/1000 which is a solitary one, as this is integer division, not floating point. And, finally, FRACT_INC is 1024 – (1024/16) >> 3 or 24/8 which gives us 3.

FRACT_MAX is easy; it's effectively 1000/8 or 125.

So, every 256 Timer/counter 0 clock ticks, we increment the number of millis by 1 and add 3 to the fractions accumulator, and if that is more than 125, we add an extra 1 to millis and reduce the fractions accumulator by 125, thus holding on to any *spare* fractions. Eventually, these will add up and generate another millisecond.

If you are wondering why we add 3 and check for 125, then consider that there are 24 microseconds spare each time through the interrupt handler – that's 41.666 (recurring) to gain an extra millisecond. 125/3 is exactly the same value – 41.666 (recurring) – so it works out the same.

ℹ️ Is adding 3 and checking against 125 more efficient than adding 24 and checking against 1000? Yes, indeed, the former method fits a byte, while the latter requires a 16-bit value, and the ATmega328P is an 8-bit device without a 16-bit compare instruction.

2.9.4. Configuring Timer/counter 1 and Timer/counter 2

On the ATmega328P, Timer/counter 1 is a 16-bit timer; however, the Arduino system sets it up so that it appears as an 8-bit timer which makes it similar to Timer/counter 0 and Timer/counter 2.

Timer/counters 1 and 2 are used to provide PWM on four of the six pins that are PWM enabled on an ATmega328P.

Both timers have their prescaler set to divide the system clock by 64 and are set up in 8-bit Phase Correct PWM mode.

Timer/counter 1 provides PWM on pins D9 and D10, while Timer/counter 2 provides PWM on pins D3 and D11.

The init() function source code continues in Listing 2-9, where it configures Timer/counter 1.

Listing 2-9. Timer/counter 1 configuration

```
// timers 1 and 2 are used for phase-correct
// hardware PWM. this is better for motors as it
// ensures an even waveform
// note, however, that fast PWM mode can achieve a
// frequency of up 8 MHz (with a 16 MHz clock) at
// 50% duty cycle
#if defined(TCCR1B) && defined(CS11) && defined(CS10)
    TCCR1B = 0;                                    ①
```

```
    // set timer 1 prescale factor to 64
    sbi(TCCR1B, CS11);                            ②

#if F_CPU >= 8000000L
    sbi(TCCR1B, CS10);                            ③
#endif

    ...

#endif

    // put timer 1 in 8-bit phase correct PWM mode
#if defined(TCCR1A) && defined(WGM10)
    sbi(TCCR1A, WGM10);                           ④
#endif
```

① This shouldn't be necessary as init() is called at the start of a sketch, after a reset, or on power on, so the default for register TCCR1B is zero anyway. However, sometimes it's best to be explicit.

② Setting only the CS11 bit sets the timer's prescaler to divide by 8, which is fine for slow system clock speeds. This would give a standard Arduino board a 2 MHz timer clock speed – a tad excessive perhaps!

③ For faster clock speeds, setting CS10, plus the preceding CS11, finally sets the prescaler to divide by 64, giving the required 250 KHz timer clock speed.

④ The WGM10 bit, in the TCCR1A register, sets the PWM waveform generator to run in 8-bit Phase Correct PWM mode.

After configuring Timer/counter 1, the next part of the init() function sets up Timer/counter 2 as shown in Listing 2-10.

Listing 2-10. Timer/counter 2 configuration

```
    // set timer 2 prescale factor to 64
#if defined(TCCR2) && defined(CS22)

    ...

#elif defined(TCCR2B) && defined(CS22)
    sbi(TCCR2B, CS22); ①

//#else
    // Timer 2 not finished (may not be present on this CPU)
#endif

    // configure timer 2 for phase correct PWM (8-bit)
#if defined(TCCR2) && defined(WGM20)

    ...

#elif defined(TCCR2A) && defined(WGM20)
    sbi(TCCR2A, WGM20); ②

//#else
    // Timer 2 not finished (may not be present on this CPU)
#endif

    ...
```

① Setting bit CS22 in register TCCR2B sets the timer's prescaler to divide the system clock by 64. This results in a 250 KHz timer clock.

② Setting the WGM20 bit, in the TCCR2A register, sets the PWM waveform generator to run in 8-bit Phase Correct PWM mode.

The function continues, now that all three timers are configured, to set up the Analogue to Digital Converter (ADC) so that the Arduino analogRead() function will work.

2.9.5. Initializing the Analogue to Digital Converter

According to the data sheet for the ATmega328P, the ADC (Analogue to Digital Converter) runs best, and most accurately, when it is running at a speed between 50 and 200 KHz. The system clock on the microcontroller is running at 16 MHz, so is a *little* on the speedy side.

In order to get the ADC into a valid speed range, it has its prescaler set to divide the system clock by 128. This puts the speed at 125 KHz, which is within the desired range specified by the data sheet.

The ADC is then enabled, as shown in Listing 2-11, which is a continuation of the init() function.

Listing 2-11. ADC configuration

```
#if defined(ADCSRA)
    // set a2d prescaler so we are inside the
    // desired 50-200 KHz range.

    #if F_CPU >= 16000000 // 16 MHz / 128 = 125 KHz
        sbi(ADCSRA, ADPS2);          ①
        sbi(ADCSRA, ADPS1);
        sbi(ADCSRA, ADPS0);

        // Code removed - not relevant.

    #endif

    // enable a2d conversions
    sbi(ADCSRA, ADEN);               ②
#endif
```

① The system clock needs to be divided down to obtain an ADC clock speed in the range 50–200 KHz which, according to the data sheet, is the optimal clock range for the ADC. For the standard Arduino boards, this requires a divisor of 128 to get the 16 MHz system clock into this range. The resulting ADC clock speed is 125 KHz, which is well within the requirement.

② Setting the ADEN bit in the ADCSRA register ensures that the ADC is enabled. It will not start converting until it is told to do so by analogRead().

The preceding code implies that even if you don't want the ADC in your sketches, it is active and consuming additional power that might be better used keeping your batteries from running down!

If you are sure that you don't need or want analogRead() in your sketch, and you are running on batteries, then perhaps adding the following line to your setup() function could help:

```
#include <wiring_private.h>
...
cbi(ADCSRA, ADEN);
```

This disables the ADC. If you also add

```
sbi(PRR, PRADC);
```

then you will also stop power reaching the ADC clock, saving a few more microAmps, alternatively:

```
#include <avr/power.h>
...
void setup()
{
    ...
    power_adc_disable();
}
```

This uses the AVRLib facility to turn off the power to the ADC clock and, in my opinion, is a lot more readable, and understandable, than the preceding one.

2.9.6. Disabling the USART

The final task for the init() function is to disable the Universal Synchronous/Asynchronous Receiver/Transmitter or USART for short.

This is left attached to Arduino pins D0 and D1 by the bootloader, and the two pins used need to be disconnected so that they can be reused for digitalRead() and/or digitalWrite() in sketches. On the ATmega328P, these *digital pins* are the *physical pins* 2 and 3.

If the USART is required for the Serial Monitor tool, for example, then the two USART pins will be reconnected by a call to Serial.begin() in the sketch. Listing 2-12 shows the pins being disconnected from the USART.

Listing 2-12. USART configuration

```
    // the bootloader connects pins 0 and 1 to the
    // USART; disconnect them here so they can be used
    // as normal digital i/o; they will be reconnected
    // in Serial.begin()
#if defined(UCSRB)

    ...

#elif defined(UCSR0B)
    UCSR0B = 0;
#endif

}       // End of init().
```

This concludes the initialization that occurs at the start of every sketch and the walk-through of the init() function's source code.

CHAPTER 3

Arduino Language Reference

In this chapter, I look at the Arduino-specific features of the C/C++ language which relate to the AVR microcontroller and how it operates, as opposed to looking at the C/C++ language in general.

⚠️ This chapter, and the following one, are long chapters, my apologies for that. I would advise that you do not try to get through them both in one sitting. Take a break every so often and go and do something with your Arduino – to take your mind off it! Sorry!

The features of the Arduino that I will be covering in the next two chapters of the book are those that the Arduino Reference site (www.arduino.cc/reference/en/) refers to as

- Digital I/O – meaning pinMode(), digitalRead(), and digitalWrite(). These functions can be found in the file $ARDINC/wiring_digital.c.

- Analogue I/O – meaning analogReference(), analogRead(), and analogWrite(). These functions can be found in the file $ARDINC/wiring_analog.c.

© Norman Dunbar 2020
N. Dunbar, *Arduino Software Internals*, https://doi.org/10.1007/978-1-4842-5790-6_3

- Advanced I/O – meaning `tone()`, `noTone()`, `pulseIn()`, `pulseInLong()`, `shiftIn()`, and `shiftOut()`. These functions can be found in the file `$ARDINC/wiring_shift.c`.

- Time – meaning `delay()`, `delayMicroseconds()`, `micros()`, and `millis()`. These functions can be found in the file `$ARDINC/wiring.c`.

- Interrupt-related language features such as `interrupts()`, `noInterrupts()`, `attachInterrupt()`, and `detachInterrupt()` which can be found in the file `$ARDINC/WInterrupts.c`.

- Various bit manipulation functions as found in the header files `$ARDINC/Arduino.h` and `$ARDINC/wiring_private.h`.

I will not be discussing the general C/C++ language functions, only those related to the Arduino Language. For the general ones, you should arm yourself with a good book on the subject.

Where possible, each function mentioned in the preceding text will be listed here in full, then dissected, and explained. If there are any foibles to be aware of, those will be discussed too. However, as the Arduino software for AVR microcontrollers covers many different types of AVR microcontrollers, I shall restrict the discussion of the software to that pertaining to the ATmega328P, and I will not be covering other microcontrollers – unless absolutely necessary.

Finally in the next chapter, I discuss the various C++ *classes* declared by the Arduino software that are included in almost every sketch. These are the `Print`, `Printable`, `Stream`, `HardwareSerial`, and `String` classes – although I don't have much to say on the latter, apart from *avoid*!

Read on…

3.1. Digital Input/Output

This section takes a look at the functions which carry out digital input and output within the Arduino Language. These functions are pinMode() to set the pin's mode and direction; digitalRead() to read the voltage state, HIGH or LOW, on a pin; and digitalWrite() to set the pin's voltage, HIGH or LOW.

3.1.1. Function pinMode()

In Arduino sketches, you will often see code such as that shown in Listing 3-1.

Listing 3-1. Example pinMode() usage

```
#define switchPin 2;
#define sensorPin 3;

void setup()
{
    pinMode(LED_BUILTIN, OUTPUT);
    pinMode(switchPin, INPUT_PULLUP);
    pinMode(sensorPin, INPUT);

    ...
}
```

The pinMode() function sets the direction of a specific pin so that it can be used for input or output depending on what purpose the project is designed for. The three modes shown in the preceding example code are the only three that are available. These allow that particular pin to be used for

- Input, where the pin state is determined by the voltage applied to it. The pin's state would be read using digitalRead() and will result in a returned value of HIGH or LOW according to whatever voltage is currently being applied to the pin by external devices or components.

- Input with the internal pullup resistor enabled,
  where the pin is used again for input, but the default
  state is pulled to HIGH when nothing else attached
  to the pin is attempting to pull it LOW. Using pullup
  resistors in this way can be done internally, as with
  the pinMode(switchPin, INPUT_PULLUP) example
  in Listing 3-1, or externally where there would be a
  resistor of about 10 K connected to the pin and to 5 V or
  3.3 V depending on your Arduino board.

- Output, where the pin state is set to HIGH or LOW by a
  call to digitalWrite(). Output pins, when set to HIGH
  or LOW by a call to digitalWrite(), will see the supply
  voltage 5 V or 3.3 V on the pin if set to HIGH or 0 V if set
  to LOW.

A pin may be configured as an INPUT pin, but then written to, as
if it was an OUTPUT pin, with digitalWrite() to set it HIGH. This
will enable the internal pullup resistor which means that a
digitalRead() on the pin will now see a HIGH unless the pin is
being pulled to ground by some external influence.

This is exactly how the INTERNAL_PULLUP setting for pinMode()
works.

When reading or writing a digital pin, the pin can take one of two
different values. These are defined in $ARDINC/Arduino.h as HIGH and LOW,
but what does this mean in relation to the voltage applied to, or seen on,
the pin itself?

For Arduino boards running on a 5 V supply, a call to `digitalRead()` will return HIGH if the voltage on the appropriate pin is 3 V or higher. A LOW will be returned if the voltage on the pin is less than 1.5 V.

For Arduino boards running on a 3.3 V supply, a call to `digitalRead()` will return HIGH if the voltage on the appropriate pin is 2 V or higher. A LOW will be returned if the voltage on the pin is less than 1 V.

What about voltages in between? These are considered to be *floating* voltages, and the call to `digitalRead()` could return either a HIGH or a LOW depending on other circumstances and not necessarily the same result each time it is called for the same voltage. For this reason, it is best to avoid having input pins floating – so either use pullup resistors (internal or external) or, alternatively, pulldown resistors, which are external only.

Floating pins are a *really* bad thing to have. A pin that is not electrically connected to supply or ground is a problem waiting to happen. How does your code see the value on the pin? It could be seen as HIGH sometimes, or LOW, and the code thinks that it is a valid reading — it is not. The value seen on the pin may be affected by many things — temperature, stray capacitance on the board, induced currents from external sources, or even you walking past. *Never* leave a pin floating.

It may not be a major problem on a project designed to flash an LED from time to time, but for a high-powered laser cutter, for example, you really don't want the laser turning on because the Arduino board *thought* a button had been pressed!

The file `$ARDINC/Wiring_digital.c` is where the source code for the digital functions `pinMode()`, `digitalRead()`, and `digitalWrite()` can be found. Additionally, there is one other function in this file, but it can only be called from the three functions listed. This helper function is `turnOffPWM()`, which is not discussed further, is declared `static`, and is there simply to turn off any PWM on a pin that is about to be used for `digitalRead()` or `digitalWrite()` purposes.

The `pinMode()` function takes two input parameters, a pin number and a mode, and sets the requested pin to the mode given. The modes are as discussed in the preceding text, while the pin number is just a number corresponding to the actual pin required.

You may not be aware, but the eight analogue pins A0–A7 on your Arduino board can also be used for digital I/O. They are numbered from D14, for pin A0, to D21 for pin A7. So a call to `digitalWrite(14, HIGH)` will set pin A0 to HIGH. This is useful when you need more digital pins than apparently supplied on the Arduino board.

Hang on! What do I mean A7? Surely I mean A5?

Some Arduino boards have been built with the surface mount versions of the ATmega328 device. These surface mount devices have a couple of extra pins connected to the ADC input, these being A6 and A7. Many clone boards have added two extra connectors to allow the boards to use these two additional pins, while some have not.

If you have an Arduino Nano, for example, then look carefully at the pin labels and you will see A6 and A7. These extra pins are *not* present on the 28-pin through-hole ATmega328P devices.

Sometimes you might see code referencing an additional ADC input pin, pin A8, which is an internal connection for the temperature sensor built in to the AVR microcontroller itself. You can read this input and get an idea of how hot the AVR microcontroller is running. Sadly, the Arduino Language does not make this visible using `analogRead()`. See the sketch in Appendix A for details on how to use this internal feature.

Getting back to pinMode(), we need to be aware first of all that the Arduino pin numbering system is completely different from that used by Atmel (now Microchip) who manufactures the AVR devices. What we call D1 is known to Atmel/Microchip as PD1, and the built-in LED on pin D13 is attached to the ATmega328P's PB5 pin.

It helps if there's a pinout diagram for our specific AVR microcontroller. Look at Figure 3-1 which shows the pin functions and names for an ATmega328P.

ALT	Arduino	PCInt	AVR	Pin		Pin	AVR	PCInt	Arduino	ALT
RESET		PCINT14	PC6	1	U	28	PC5	PCINT13	D19/A5	SCL
RX	D0	PCINT16	PD0	2		27	PC4	PCINT12	D18/A4	SDA
TX	D1	PCINT17	PD1	3		26	PC3	PCINT11	D17/A3	
INT0	D2	PCINT18	PD2	4		25	PC2	PCINT10	D16/A2	
OC2B/INT1	D3/PWM	PCINT19	PD3	5		24	PC1	PCINT9	D15/A1	
XCK/T0	D4	PCINT20	PD4	6		23	PC0	PCINT8	D14/A0	
			VCC	7		22	GND			
			GND	8		21	AREF			
XTAL1/OSC1		PCINT6	PB6	9		20	AVCC			
XTAL2/OSC2		PCINT7	PB7	10		19	PB5	PCINT5	D13	SCK
OC0B/T1	D5/PWM	PCINT21	PD5	11		18	PB4	PCINT4	D12	MISO
OC0A/AIN0	D6/PWM	PCINT22	PD6	12		17	PB3	PCINT3	D11/PWM	OC2A/MOSI
AIN1	D7	PCINT23	PD7	13		16	PB2	PCINT2	D10/PWM	OC1B/SS
ICP1/CLKO	D8	PCINT0	PB0	14		15	PB1	PCINT1	D9/PWM	OC1A
ALT	Arduino	PCInt	AVR	Pin		Pin	AVR	PCInt	Arduino	ALT

Figure 3-1. *Pin names on the ATmega328P*

The Arduino pin numbers are easily enough recognized as they are listed by name, in the two columns labeled **Arduino**, and there you will see names like D0 or A5 and so on. The Arduino Language has given these names to the various pins that are accessible using that language. However, Atmel/Microchip named the pins differently, and the Atmel/Microchip pin names can be seen in the **AVR** columns. Here you see names like PB2 or PD4 and so on. These are the actual pins that are used for digital input and output, or analogue input.

On an AVR microcontroller, pins are arranged in banks of up to eight pins, which happily is the same number of bits in a byte. On the ATmega328P, there are three banks of pins – these are B, C, and D. In order to use pinMode() on an Arduino pin, you need three things:

- The bank's Data Direction Register or DDR
- The bank's Pin Input Register or PIN
- The bank's Pin Output Register or PORT

On the ATmega328P, we have

- DDRB, DDRC, and DDRD
- PORTB, PORTC, and PORTD
- PINB, PINC, and PIND

On the pinout image, when a pin is named PCn, where "n" is a number, then that particular pin belongs to bank C and uses DDRC, PORTC, and PINC.

The pinMode() function, among others, has to convert between the Arduino pin naming convention and the AVR's own names. If, for example, pin D2 is being set to OUTPUT, the pinMode() function needs to convert D2 to DDRD, PORTD, and PIND2 so that manipulating that pin in Arduino code manipulates the PD2 pin on the ATmega328P.

Getting from D2, which is nothing more than the value 2, to a PORT, PIN, and DDR is done with the help of a few small data tables, set up in $ARDINST/variants/standard/pins_arduino.h.

Listing 3-2 is the code which makes up the pinMode() function.

Listing 3-2. The pinMode() function

```
void pinMode(uint8_t pin, uint8_t mode)
{
    uint8_t bit = digitalPinToBitMask(pin);      ①
    uint8_t port = digitalPinToPort(pin);        ②
    volatile uint8_t *reg, *out;
```

```
if (port == NOT_A_PIN) return;                    ③

// JWS: can I let the optimizer do this?
reg = portModeRegister(port);                     ④
out = portOutputRegister(port);

if (mode == INPUT) {                              ⑤
    uint8_t oldSREG = SREG;
    cli();
    *reg &= ~bit;
    *out &= ~bit;
    SREG = oldSREG;

} else if (mode == INPUT_PULLUP) {                ⑥
    uint8_t oldSREG = SREG;
    cli();
    *reg &= ~bit;
    *out |= bit;
    SREG = oldSREG;

} else {                                          ⑦
    uint8_t oldSREG = SREG;
    cli();
    *reg |= bit;
    SREG = oldSREG;
}
}
```

①   If we continue the preceding example with
     D2, then this pin has the value 2. This call to
     digitalPinToBitMask() converts D2 into an 8-bit
     value in which only bit 2 is set. This is therefore the
     value 4 as bit 2 in a byte indicates whether there are
     any 4s present in the value. The bitmask returned
     will look like 0000 0100$_{binary}$ with only bit 2 set.

② D2's value, 2, is used again in a call to
digitalPinToPort() which returns a value known
as PD from the table digital_pin_to_port_PGM. PD
is defined in Arduino.h to be the value 4. We now
have the bitmask in bit and the port in reg. These
are still not AVR microcontroller register names yet;
they are still just numbers – both of them 4 in this
example.

③ The port is validated; and if it is NOT_A_PIN, which
has the value -1, we exit from the function.

④ The value for our port, 4, is then converted to a
Data Direction Register and a PORT register using
portModeRegister() and portOutputRegister().
These two functions read the tables port_to_mode_
PGM and port_to_output_PGM and return pointers to
the internal registers named DDRx and PORTx for the
appropriate pin. In this example, these will be DDRD
and PORTD. At this stage, pointers to the desired DDR
and PORT registers are available in reg and out and
can be manipulated to set a single pin to output
mode.

⑤ If the requested mode is INPUT, we have to clear
the appropriate bit in the DDR to configure an
input pin, and as pullup has not been requested,
the appropriate bit in the PORT register is also
cleared to turn off the input pullup resistor for the
pin. The current state of the status register is saved,
and interrupts are turned off for the duration of
the preceding changes. When the status register

is restored, interrupts are reset to how they were before being disabled.

⑥   If the requested mode is INPUT_PULLUP, we have to clear the appropriate bit in the DDR to configure an input pin as in the preceding text, and as pullup has been requested, the appropriate bit in the PORT register is set to turn on the input pullup resistor for the pin. As earlier, the current state of the status register is saved, and interrupts are turned off for the duration of the preceding changes. When the status register is restored, interrupts are reset to how they were before being disabled.

⑦   If the requested mode is OUTPUT, we have to set the appropriate bit in the DDR to configure an output pin. There is no pullup on output pins. As before, when these changes are being made, the current state of the status register is saved and interrupts are turned off. When the status register is restored, interrupts are reset to their previous setting.

In the AVR microcontroller, writing a one to the DDRx register sets the pin to output, while writing a zero sets the pin to input. Input is the default when the AVR microcontroller is reset or powered on.

💡 Even though the default mode for a pin is INPUT in Arduino code, it is always beneficial to ensure that you *explicitly* set the pin in your code. It isn't mandatory, but it can help make your code more readable and self-documenting.

As the example needs to set PORTD, bit 2, to output, then a one is required in the *third* bit of the bitmask – remember bits number from zero – and that is all. The code line *reg |= bit; does exactly that; it takes the bitmask 0000 0100$_{binary}$ and ORs it with whatever is currently in the register DDRD. This sets the pin to output, as required, and *does not change* the direction of any other pins on PORTD.

Had the mode requested been INPUT, then bit 2 in the DDRD register would need to be set to zero. The code *reg &= ~bit; does this by inverting the bitmask from 0000 0100$_{binary}$ to 1111 1011$_{binary}$ and then ANDing that with the current contents in the DDRD register. That would change only the third bit to a zero and would not affect any other pin. *out &= ~bit; then ensures that the pullup resistor is disabled for this pin.

If the mode is INPUT_PULLUP, then the *out |= bit; code makes sure that the pin is set to have its internal pullup resistor enabled by writing a 1$_{binary}$ to the PORTD register.

3.1.2. Function digitalRead()

Once a pin has been set for INPUT with pinMode(), then you can read the voltage on that pin with the digitalRead() function and change the behavior of your project according to the result obtained. The function will return either HIGH or LOW according to the voltage on the pin at the time of the function call.

Listing 3-3 shows the source code for the digitalRead() function.

Listing 3-3. The digitalRead() function

```
int digitalRead(uint8_t pin)
{
    uint8_t timer = digitalPinToTimer(pin);      ①
    uint8_t bit = digitalPinToBitMask(pin);      ②
    uint8_t port = digitalPinToPort(pin);        ③
```

```
if (port == NOT_A_PIN) return LOW;

// If the pin supports PWM output, we need to turn it off
// before getting a digital reading.
if (timer != NOT_ON_TIMER) turnOffPWM(timer);             ④

if (*portInputRegister(port) & bit) return HIGH;          ⑤
return LOW;                                                ⑥
}
```

①   This converts the pin's number to a timer/counter number. This will be 0, 1, or 2. Timer/counters are used on pins that we can use analogWrite() upon. This is required as any pin which can be used for analogWrite() may be set to a value which is not a HIGH and not a LOW – a floating value in other words – and we need to avoid floating values.

②   The pin's number is converted to an 8-bit value where the only bit set will correspond to this pin's position in the PINx register. Given the D2 example from earlier, this would be a bitmask of 0000 0100$_{binary}$ with only bit 2 set.

③   The pin is now also converted to the correct PINx register.

④   In order to read a digital value, LOW or HIGH, the pin should not be carrying out PWM. If the pin is one of the six that can be used with analogWrite(), then its ability to do so is temporarily disabled.

⑤   The correct PINx register is read and ANDed with the pin's bitmask. If the result of the AND operation leaves the pin's bit set in the PINx register, then HIGH is returned.

⑥   The pin must be at GND potential, so return a value of LOW.

> **ℹ** Timers, or, more correctly, timer/counters, are internal hardware features of the ATmega328P. These will be discussed in great detail in Chapter 8, along with many other useful features of the AVR microcontroller. What follows here is a brief discussion with only as much information as necessary to help understand the `digitalRead()` and `digitalWrite()` functions.

The timer/counters in the ATmega328P are named Timer/counter 0, Timer/counter 1, and Timer/counter 2. As described previously, Timer/counter 0 is used to ensure that the `millis()` count is incremented correctly (see Chapter 2, Section 2.9, "*The init() Function*," for details). All three timer/counters are used to provide PWM facilities (`analogWrite()`) on two pins each. If there is a call to `digitalWrite()` for pins D3, D5–D6, or D9–D11, then the PWM must be turned off. This is done by finding out if the pin in question is connected to a timer/counter and, if so, calling `turnOffPWM()` for the particular timer.

The timer/counter in question is converted from a pin number by accessing the table `digital_pin_to_timer_PGM` which is defined in `$ARDINST/variants/standard/pi s_arduino.h`.

As with `pinMode()`, the port and bitmask are worked out from the two tables set up in `$ARDINST/variants/standard/pins_arduino.h`, and the port name (e.g., PD) is converted to an actual PINx register and the current value of that register is read. To continue the D2 example, this would be `PIND`, and the bitmask would be $0000\ 0100_{binary}$; bit 2 is set.

The PINx registers are connected to the physical pins on the AVR microcontroller, and reading those registers returns an 8-bit value where any external pin connected to a high enough voltage will be set to 1 and the others will be set to 0, if they are seeing a low enough voltage. Floating pins, always a bad idea, will return a fairly random value in the bit, which cannot be relied upon.

As digitalRead() is only interested in one single pin's value, all the other bits are masked out by ANDing the returned value with the bitmask holding the correct pin. The function returns the result according to whether or not the bit in the PINx register was set to one or zero.

3.1.3. Function digitalWrite()

Once a pin has been set for OUTPUT with pinMode(), then you can set the voltage on that pin with the digitalWrite() function and change the behavior of your project by lighting up LEDs, activating relays and so on.

Listing 3-4 shows the source code for the digitalWrite() function.

Listing 3-4. The digitalWrite() function

```
void digitalWrite(uint8_t pin, uint8_t val)
{
    uint8_t timer = digitalPinToTimer(pin);        ①
    uint8_t bit = digitalPinToBitMask(pin);        ②
    uint8_t  port  =  digitalPinToPort(pin);       ③
    volatile uint8_t *out;

    if (port == NOT_A_PIN) return;                 ④

    // If the pin supports PWM output, we need to turn it
    // off before doing a digital write.
    if (timer != NOT_ON_TIMER) turnOffPWM(timer);  ⑤

    out = portOutputRegister(port);                ⑥

    uint8_t oldSREG = SREG;                         ⑦
    cli();
```

```
if (val == LOW) {                                    ⑧
    *out &=  ~bit;
} else {
    *out |= bit;
}

SREG = oldSREG;                                      ⑨
}
```

① The pin number is converted to a timer number, 0, 1, or 2. As with `digitalRead()`, this is required in case the pin is capable of being used with the `analogWrite()` function call.

② The pin number is also converted to an 8-bit value where the only bit set will correspond to this pin's position in the PORTx register.

③ The pin number is converted to a port number.

④ If the port number is discovered to be invalid, `digitalWrite()` will quietly exit without changing the requested pin and without error. Your sketch will be none the wiser!

⑤ If the requested pin supports PWM, then the pin has PWM turned off.

⑥ The port number returned is converted to an actual PORTx register address and stored in a pointer variable, out.

⑦ The current value of the status register is saved to preserve the current state of global interrupts. Interrupts are then disabled globally. This will affect the status register and stops `millis()` from being accumulated.

⑧   If the value to be written to the pin is LOW, then the
     appropriate bit in the PORTx register is cleared
     to zero; otherwise, it is set to one. This turns the
     physical pin on the AVR microcontroller LOW or HIGH
     as appropriate.

⑨   The status register is restored which restores the
     previous state of the global interrupts.

As previously mentioned, all three timer/counters available in the
ATmega328P are used to provide PWM facilities on two pins each. If
there is a call to digitalWrite() for pins D3, D5–D6, or D9–D11, then the
PWM on the requested pin must be turned off. This is done by finding out
if the pin in question is connected to a timer/counter and, if so, calling
turnOffPWM() for the particular timer/counter.

As with digitalRead(), the port and bitmask are worked out from
the two tables set up in $ARDINST/variants/standard/pins_arduino.h,
and the port name (e.g., PD) is converted to an actual PORTx register. To
continue the D2 example, this would be PORTD, and the bitmask would be
$0000\ 0100_{binary}$ in binary; bit 2 is set.

The PORTx registers are, like the PINx registers, connected to the
physical pins on the AVR microcontroller; and writing to those registers
will cause the voltage on the physical pin to change to supply or ground
potential, depending on whether the bit in the PORTx register is a one or a
zero.

As digitalWrite() is only interested in setting a single pin's value, all
the other bits are masked out by ANDing or ORing the bitmask holding the
correct pin with the current contents of the PORTD register. This affects only
the bit that is set in the bitmask, and none of the other pins change. AND is
used to clear the bit, while OR is used to set it.

3.2. Analogue Input/Output

This section takes a look at the functions which carry out analogue input and output within the Arduino Language. These functions are analogReference() to set the reference voltage for the analogue circuitry in the ATmega328P , analogRead() to read a voltage between 0 V and the reference voltage on a pin, and analogWrite() to set a pin's voltage to somewhere between 0 V and the reference voltage.

3.2.1. Function analogReference()

The AVR microcontroller, in this case, the ATmega328P, has the ability to read analogue voltages – those that are not just defined as HIGH or LOW – using the analogRead() function. In order to do this, the comparator built in to the device needs a reference voltage to compare the unknown voltage against. This can be supplied from a number of different sources, these being the following:

- The default, which is to use the supply voltage of 5 V or 3.3 V depending on the device. The ATmega328P on Arduino boards uses a 5 V supply.

- An internally generated 1.1 V reference voltage. This must be used if the internal temperature sensor is being used as the ADC input. See Appendix E for a small sketch showing how this can be done.

- An external reference voltage on the AREF pin. This must be between 0 V and 5 V, or damage to the AVR microcontroller will occur.

The data sheet for the ATmega328P warns that *If the user has a fixed voltage source connected to the* AREF *pin, the user may not use the other reference voltage options in the application, as they will be shorted to the external voltage. If no external voltage is applied to the* AREF *pin, the user may switch between* AVCC *and 1.1V as reference selection.*

The preceding warning *must* be noted. On my own Arduino boards, AREF isn't connected at all (according to the schematics), and the temperature measuring sketch mentioned earlier works fine. There is a location on one of the headers labeled "AREF" where the maker can supply a voltage to the AREF pin. I have never connected anything to that pin, so I'm safe.

There are many, many places on YouTube, on the Internet in general, and in some books where there are circuit diagrams, usually created in Fritzing, which show how you can remove all the extraneous *gubbins* from an Arduino board and create your own pseudo-Arduino on a breadboard. These *usually* show that there are three connections to the 5 V supply – VCC, AVCC, *and* AREF.

This connection of AREF to VCC is *completely wrong* as it prevents you from being able to select the internal 1.1 V reference for the ADC or the Analogue Comparator and will have the result, if you upload a program that does select the internal reference voltage, of potentially bricking your AVR microcontroller. Not a good idea.

My advice is to treat those circuits with disdain and never connect AREF to any supply voltage, unless you absolutely need to do so, as this will help your AVR microcontroller live long and prosper. (This, I think, is a phrase taken from some 1960s space exploration series on TV!)

The source code for the analogReference() function follows in Listing 3-5. This code can be found in the file $ARDINC/wiring_analog.c.

Listing 3-5. The analogReference() function

```
uint8_t analog_reference = DEFAULT;

void analogReference(uint8_t mode)
{
    // can't actually set the register here because
    // the default setting will connect AVCC and the
    // AREF pin, which would cause a short if there's
    // something connected to AREF.
    analog_reference = mode;
}
```

As you can see, it just changes the value in the analog_reference variable, which will be used later by analogRead(). The values that can be passed to this function, for the ATmega328P, are

- DEFAULT which has value 1.

- INTERNAL which has value 3.

- EXTERNAL which has value 0.

All of these are defined as constants in the $ARDINC/Arduino.h header file. You may be wondering about why those exact values have been used. The description of analogRead() will tell all!

3.2.2. Function `analogRead()`

The `analogRead()` function connects the pins A0–A5, or A0–A7 if your board has the surface mount version of the ATmega328 *and* the manufacturer chose to connect A6 and A7 to header pins, to the multiplexed inputs of the AVR microcontroller's Analogue to Digital Converter (ADC).

The ADC can read a voltage on those pins; and using a method called successive approximation, it can work out, with reasonable accuracy, what the voltage was. Wikipedia has a good explanation of how successive approximation works at https://en.wikipedia.org/wiki/Successive_approximation_ADC if you are interested further.

If you think back to the previous section on the `analogReference()` function, you may remember I asked why the constants defined for DEFAULT, INTERNAL, and EXTERNAL had the values 0, 3, or 1? The simple reason is because when they are shifted left by six places, they take up position in the REFS1 and REFS0 bits of the ADMUX register and are ready to go without any further processing being required. Sneaky! (And efficient.)

ℹ️ The register names may not be very meaningful to you at this stage; however, in Chapters 7, 8, and 9 where I look at the hardware features of the ATmega328P, which the code here depends upon, all will, hopefully, become clear. You may, if you wish, skip to Chapter 9 and read all about the ADC or just take my word for it until then!

Basically, there are two bits in the control registers for the ADC which tell it where to obtain the reference voltage it needs to convert from an analogue voltage to a digital value representing the voltage. Those two bits are named REFS1 and REFS0. By shifting the DEFAULT, EXTERNAL, or INTERNAL values into those bits, the correct reference voltage is selected.

Table 3-1 shows the different values allowed and how they relate to the analogue reference voltage used by the ADC.

Table 3-1. *AnalogReference values and sources*

Name	Value	Binary	REFS1	REFS0	Reference Used
DEFAULT	0	00	0	0	Default reference is the supply voltage, 5 V or 3.3 V depending on the device.
EXTERNAL	1	01	0	1	Default reference is the voltage supplied on the AVCC pin, 5 V or 3.3 V depending on the device.
INTERNAL	3	11	1	1	Default reference is the internally generated 1.1 V voltage.

ℹ️ The data sheet notes that the value 2 or 10_{binary} is reserved and should not be used.

It should be noted that the data sheet for the ATmega328P states that if INTERNAL or EXTERNAL references are being used, there should be a small capacitor between the AREF pin and ground. The Duemilanove and Uno boards use a 100 nF capacitor according to the schematics.

Listing 3-6 shows the source code for the analogRead() function.

Listing 3-6. The analogRead() function

```
int analogRead(uint8_t pin)
{
    uint8_t low, high;
    if (pin >= 14) pin -= 14;        ①
```

```
    // set the analog reference (high two bits of
    // ADMUX) and select the channel (low 4 bits).
    // this also sets ADLAR (left-adjust result)
    // to 0 (the default).

    ADMUX = (analog_reference << 6) | (pin & 0x07);     ②

    // without a delay, we seem to read from the        ③
    // wrong channel
    //delay(1);
#if defined(ADCSRA) && defined(ADCL)
    // start the conversion
    sbi(ADCSRA, ADSC);                                  ④

    // ADSC is cleared when the conversion finishes
    while (bit_is_set(ADCSRA, ADSC));                   ⑤

    // we have to read ADCL first; doing so locks both ADCL
    // and ADCH until ADCH is read. reading ADCL second
    // would cause the results of each conversion to be
    // discarded, as ADCL and ADCH would be locked when
    // it completed.

    low = ADCL;                      ⑥
    high = ADCH;
#else
    ...
#endif

    // combine the two bytes
    return (high << 8) | low;     ⑦
}
```

① Here, the pin number passed in is adjusted to ensure that it is between 0 and 7. In case anyone passed D14, or 14, for A0, which is perfectly valid, this adjustment ensures D14 becomes A0 which has the numeric value of zero.

② Whatever the user sets as the desired value for analog_reference is copied up into the appropriate bits of the ADMUX register, alongside the correct three bits for the desired analogue pin.

③ This comment is obviously incorrect in this version of the Arduino IDE, as the desired delay(1) is itself commented out!

④ Ask the ADC to initiate a conversion of the voltage on the requested pin to a digital value. ADSC is the "ADC Start Conversion" bit.

⑤ Hang around here, burning CPU cycles, while the ADC does its conversion. When it is complete and a result is available, bit ADSC in the ADCSRA register will be cleared. The result of the ADC's conversion will be available in the ADCL and ADCH registers.

⑥ As per the comment, and the data sheet, we *must* read the low value first and then the high value; otherwise, we would potentially get an incorrect reading. Reading ADCL locks the result until ADCH is read; it is then unlocked again. The ADC can be configured in other modes which make repeated readings – you would not want to have read the ADCL and get a different reading's value in ADCH!

⑦   The highest 2 bits of the value are in high, while the
      lower 8 bits are in low – here we combine these into
      a 16-bit value to return as the result.

ℹ The source code shown in the preceding text is not *exactly* as it
appears in $ARDINC/wiring_analog.c. I have stripped out a lot of
checks, function calls, and assignments which are not relevant to the
ATmega328P. Hopefully, this makes things a lot easier to understand.
It certainly saves space on the page!

3.2.3. Function analogWrite()

The code for the analogWrite() function is found in the file $ARDINC/
wiring_analog.c.

The analogWrite() function is used to write an 8-bit data value to one
of the six pins that support pulse width modulation (PWM) which allows the
voltage read on the pin to appear as a value between GND and VCC. Chapter 8
explains the various timer/counter features, including the various forms
of PWM that are available, how PWM works, and how a supposedly digital
device is able to make analogue voltages appear on its pins.

The analogWrite() function takes a value between 0 and 255 and uses
it to define the *duty cycle* (see Chapter 8, Section 8.1.7.1, "*Duty Cycle*") of
the PWM timer/counter connected to the appropriate pin. The higher this
value is, the longer the duty cycle of the PWM signal on the pin will be and,
therefore, the higher the apparent voltage on the pin will appear to be.

The analogWrite() function will *always* set the appropriate pin to
be in OUTPUT mode, and if the pin requested is not one that allows PWM,
then a digitalWrite() takes place on the pin, with values less than 128
indicating that the pin should be set to LOW and higher values setting the
pin to HIGH.

As you will see from Listing 3-7, all that the analogWrite() function does is decide which timer/counter and channel that the requested pin number should be connected to, connects it to that timer/counter and channel, and sets the duty cycle. Each timer/counter has two separate channels available for PWM output, and as there are three timer/counters on the ATmega328P, we have PWM on six pins.

The pins with PWM are D3, D5-D6, and D9-D11; and Table 3-2 shows which pin is controlled by which timer/counter and the timer/counter's channel. The timer/counters have two channels each, hence why there are only six PWM pins on an ATmega328P.

Table 3-2. *PWM pins, timers, and channels*

PWM Pin	Timer Used	Timer Channel
D3	Timer 2	Channel B
D5	Timer 0	Channel B
D6	Timer 0	Channel A
D9	Timer 1	Channel A
D10	Timer 1	Channel B
D11	Timer 2	Channel A

The various timer/counters are separate parts of the ATmega328P and operate separately from the brain of the microcontroller – the CPU. This allows the timer/counters to be set and left to get on with timing or counting while the CPU continues running the program.

ℹ️ The two channels of each timer/counter operate independently of each other. This allows pin D5 to have one value written by analogWrite() and pin D10 to have another, different value. This applies because of the PWM mode chosen by the designers of the Arduino Language and system and is explained in some detail in Chapter 8 which deals with the timer/counter hardware in the ATmega328P.

The source code for the analogWrite() function is shown in Listing 3-7 and, as usual, has had all nonrelevant sections removed.

Listing 3-7. The analogWrite() function

```
void analogWrite(uint8_t pin, int val)
{
    // We need to make sure the PWM output is enabled for
    // those pins that support it, as we turn it off when
    // digitally reading or writing with them. Also, make
    // sure the pin is in output mode for consistently with
    // Wiring, which doesn't require a pinMode call for the
    // analog output pins.

    pinMode(pin, OUTPUT);                                    ①
    if (val == 0)
    {
        digitalWrite(pin, LOW);
    }
    else if (val == 255)
    {
        digitalWrite(pin, HIGH);
    }
```

```
else
{
    switch(digitalPinToTimer(pin))                      ②
    {
            ...

            #if defined(TCCR0A) && defined(COM0A1)       ③
            case TIMER0A:
                // connect PWM  to pin on timer 0, channel A
                sbi(TCCR0A, COM0A1);
                OCR0A = val; // set PWM duty
                break;
            #endif

            #if defined(TCCR0A) && defined(COM0B1)        ④
            case TIMER0B:
                // connect PWM  to pin on timer 0, channel B
                sbi(TCCR0A, COM0B1);
                OCR0B = val; // set PWM duty
                break;
            #endif

            #if defined(TCCR1A) && defined(COM1A1)        ⑤
            case TIMER1A:
                // connect PWM  to pin on timer 1, channel A
                sbi(TCCR1A, COM1A1);
                OCR1A = val; // set PWM duty
                break;
            #endif

            #if defined(TCCR1A) && defined(COM1B1)        ⑥
            case TIMER1B:
                // connect PWM  to pin on timer 1, channel B
```

```
        sbi(TCCR1A, COM1B1);
        OCR1B = val; // set PWM duty
        break;
    #endif

    ...

    #if defined(TCCR2A) && defined(COM2A1)        ⑦
    case TIMER2A:
        // connect PWM  to pin on timer 2, channel A
        sbi(TCCR2A, COM2A1);
        OCR2A = val; // set PWM duty
        break;
    #endif

    #if defined(TCCR2A) && defined(COM2B1)        ⑧
    case TIMER2B:
        // connect PWM  to pin on timer 2, channel B
        sbi(TCCR2A, COM2B1);
        OCR2B = val; // set PWM duty
        break;
    #endif

    ...

    case NOT_ON_TIMER:                             ⑨
    default:
        if (val < 128) {
            digitalWrite(pin, LOW);
        } else {
            digitalWrite(pin, HIGH);
        }
    }
  }
}
```

① The pin is made an output pin, and as a quick test and return, if the value is either 0 or 255, the two limits for analogWrite(), then the pin is simply set to ground or supply voltage using digitalWrite(). This avoids a slight timing error when the timer/counter is in PWM mode and is set to one of its limits. The data sheet has details, if you wish to investigate further.

② The pin is converted to a timer/counter and channel by way of a call to digitalPinToTimer() which uses the table digital_pin_to_timer_PGM created in $ARDINST/variants/standard/pins_arduino.h to determine if the pin is a PWM pin or otherwise. This returns a value of NOT_ON_TIMER if the pin is purely digital, and that will be handled by the default case.

③ This is where pin D6 is configured. The pin is connected to the timer/counter, and the OCR0A register is loaded with the value passed to analogWrite() to enable the correct duty cycle for the timer/counter's PWM output. D6 is on Timer/counter 0, channel A.

④ Configuration of pin D5 is performed here and sets up D5 on Timer/counter 0, channel B.

⑤ This is where pin D9 is configured to use Timer/counter 1, channel A.

⑥ Pin D10 configuration happens here. Pin D10 uses Timer/counter 1, channel B.

⑦ Pin D11 is configured here and uses channel A on Timer/counter 2.

⑧ Pin D3 is configured here. D3 is configured to use channel B on Timer/counter 2.

⑨   In the event that the supplied pin number is not able to output PWM, this part of the code digitally sets the pin LOW or HIGH according to the requested PWM value passed to analogWrite().

The Arduino Reference web site at www.arduino.cc/reference/en/ language/functions/analog-io/analogwrite/ warns that

> *The PWM outputs generated on pins 5 and 6 will have higher-than-expected duty cycles. This is because of interactions with the* millis() *and* delay() *functions, which share the same internal timer used to generate those PWM outputs. This will be noticed mostly on low duty-cycle settings (e.g. 0–10) and may result in a value of 0 not fully turning off the output on pins 5 and 6.*

Looking at the code in Listing 3-7, a value of zero will ignore PWM altogether and simply use digitalWrite() to turn off the pin. I suspect the warning may refer to older types of Arduino boards. The ATmega328P data sheet also advises against PWM values of zero or *TOP* where TOP is the configured highest value for the timer/counter in use. I would say that the checks in Listing 3-7 which test for 0 or 255 are obviously there to get around the problem.

ℹ️ A pin can be HIGH or LOW. PWM turns a pin HIGH and LOW, and the sum of one HIGH plus one LOW is the period. This is related to the PWM frequency which is defined by the timer/counter's prescaler – Chapter 8, Section 8.1.7.2, "*PWM Frequencies*", has all the gory details.

Duty cycle is usually expressed as a percentage. It defines the time that the pin is HIGH as a percentage of the period. A duty cycle of 10% means that the pin is HIGH for 10% of its period and LOW for the remaining 90%. A 10% duty cycle would appear as a voltage very close to 10% of VCC on the PWM pin.

3.3. Advanced Input/Output

In this section, I take you through the advanced input/output functions which allow you to make sounds and measure logic levels on pins to determine how long a specific state was held for and an easy way to shift a byte value from a variable out onto a digital pin and vice versa.

3.3.1. Function `tone()`

The code for the `tone()` function is found in the file `$ARDINC/Tone.cpp`.

The `tone()` function generates a square wave of the specified frequency, with a 50% duty cycle, on any pin. A duration can be specified; otherwise, the wave continues until a call to `noTone()`. The pin can be connected to a piezo buzzer or another speaker to play tones.

If `tone()` has been called, then PWM on pins D3 and D11 will be affected. These analogue pins are maintained by Timer/counter 2, and it is Timer/counter 2 that the `tone()` function uses to generate a square wave.

If you have, for example, a pair of LEDs, fading in and out, on pins D3 and D11, then whenever the `tone()` function is called, and while sounding a tone, the LEDs will be off. Fading LEDs, on the other pins available for `analogWrite()`, will not be affected. Those are pins D5, D6, D9, and D10. Only pins D3 and D11 are affected by this problem.

Brett Hagman's GitHub site, `https://github.com/bhagman/Tone#ugly-details`, which is linked to the Arduino Reference web site, `www.arduino.cc/reference/en/language/functions/advanced-io/tone/`, has the following to say, as a warning:

⚠ Do not connect the pin directly to some sort of audio input. The voltage on the output pin will be 5 V or 3.3 V and is considerably higher than a standard line-level voltage (usually around 1 V peak to peak) and can damage sound card inputs and others. You could use a voltage divider to bring the voltage down, but you have been warned.

You *must* have a resistor in line with the speaker, or you *will* damage your microcontroller.

The resistor mentioned is shown on Brett's circuit diagram as having a value of 1 K. That should, if I can do the calculations properly, restrict the current to 5 milliAmps.

ⓘ Brett is the author of the Tone Library, a simplified version of which has been included with the Arduino IDE, since version 0018.

Listing 3-8 shows how the tone() function can be called in one of two ways.

Listing 3-8. Example tone() function calls

```
tone(pin, frequency)
```

```
// or
```

```
tone(pin, frequency, duration)
```

The duration, if it is omitted or zero, causes the tone to sound *forever* or until noTone() is called.

On the Arduino boards based around the ATmega328P, only one pin can be generating a tone at any time. If a tone is already playing on a pin, a call to tone() with a different pin number will have no effect unless noTone() was called first. If the call is made for the same pin as the one currently playing, the call will set the tone's frequency to that specified in the most recent call.

In order for tone() to function correctly, a couple of tables are required to be set up to control which timer/counter will be used to generate a tone and to keep a record of all the pins that are currently generating. This code is shown in Listing 3-9.

As with other listings in this book, I have removed any code that is not relevant to the ATmega328P.

Listing 3-9. Variables used by the tone() function

```
#define AVAILABLE_TONE_PINS 1      ①
#define USE_TIMER2                 ②

const uint8_t PROGMEM tone_pin_to_timer_PGM[] =
    { 2 /*, 1, 0 */ };                            ③

static uint8_t tone_pins[AVAILABLE_TONE_PINS] =
    { 255 /*, 255, 255 */ };                      ④
```

① This shows that the ATmega328 family has only one pin that can play at any one time – at least on the version of the code included with the Arduino IDE version 1.8.5.

② This tells the code, later on, which interrupt routine to use, to do the actual tone generation.

③ This array, which is created in the AVR microcontroller's flash memory, holds a list of the various timer/counters that can be used to generate tones. As the tone() function is a cut-down version of Brett's library, only a single timer/counter is used; currently, this is Timer/counter 2.

④ This array, which is created in the AVR microcontroller's Static RAM, holds a list of all the pin numbers that are currently playing a tone, or 255 if nothing is playing. There is one entry in the table for each timer/counter that can be used to generate tones. That means there is one entry in total for the ATmega328P boards. *There can be only one* (www.imdb.com/title/tt0091203/ – well, I *am* a Highlander!).

As you can see from the preceding text, the ATmega328P-based boards only have a single timer/counter in use to generate tones, this being Timer/counter 2.

In addition to the tables listed in Listing 3-9, the variables in Listing 3-10 are also required by the tone() function, specifically, in the interrupt service routine (ISR) which does the actual sound generation.

Listing 3-10. Variables used by the tone() function ISR

```
volatile long timer2_toggle_count;
volatile uint8_t *timer2_pin_port;
volatile uint8_t timer2_pin_mask;
```

⚠ You will note that all of these are declared `volatile`. This is because they will be used in an interrupt service routine (ISR), and *any* variable you wish to read or write during an interrupt *must* be declared as being `volatile`. If you forget, your code may not work because the compiler optimized the variable away.

The variable timer2_toggle_count holds the number of times that the interrupt routine will be called, if a duration for the tone is requested. If no duration is requested, this is unused.

Timer2_pin_port is related to the internal register to be used for the PORTx port for the pin which will be generating the sound, while timer2_pin_mask is a bitmask with a single bit, corresponding to the required pin, set to one. This indicates which bit in the PORTx register is being used to generate the sound.

The tone() function works by working out a suitable prescaler for the timer/counter clock so that the number of ticks to be counted per transition (LOW to HIGH or HIGH to LOW) of the pin falls into the range 0–255. This is required because Timer/counter 2 is only 8 bits wide and can only count within this range.

If the frequency chosen is such that even with a prescaler of 1024 in use the value still cannot fall in the range required, the code simply attempts to carry on regardless. This may render the tone generated to be the wrong frequency.

The first part of the source code for the tone() function is shown in Listing 3-11, and the code continues in Listing 3-12. Sections which are not relevant to ATmega328P devices have been removed for clarity.

Listing 3-11. The tone() function

```
// frequency (in hertz) and duration (in milliseconds).

void tone(uint8_t _pin,
          unsigned int frequency,
          unsigned long duration)
{
uint8_t prescalarbits = 0b001;
long toggle_count = 0;
uint32_t ocr = 0;
int8_t _timer;
```

```
_timer = toneBegin(_pin);        ①

if (_timer >= 0)
{
  // Set the pinMode as OUTPUT
  pinMode(_pin, OUTPUT);

  // if we are using an 8 bit timer, scan through prescalars
  // to find the best fit
  if (_timer == 0 || _timer == 2)
  {
    ocr = F_CPU / frequency / 2 - 1;                        ②
    prescalarbits = 0b001;  // ck/1: same for both timers
    if (ocr > 255)
    {
      ocr = F_CPU / frequency / 2 / 8 - 1;
      prescalarbits = 0b010;  // ck/8: same for both timers

      if (_timer == 2 && ocr > 255)
      {
        ocr = F_CPU / frequency / 2 / 32 - 1;
        prescalarbits = 0b011;
      }

      if (ocr > 255)
      {
        ocr = F_CPU / frequency / 2 / 64 - 1;
        prescalarbits = _timer == 0 ? 0b011 : 0b100;

        if (_timer == 2 && ocr > 255)
        {
          ocr = F_CPU / frequency / 2 / 128 - 1;
          prescalarbits = 0b101;
        }
```

```
      if (ocr > 255)
      {
        ocr = F_CPU / frequency / 2 / 256 - 1;
        prescalarbits = _timer == 0 ? 0b100 : 0b110;
        if (ocr > 255)
        {
          // can't do any better than /1024
          ocr = F_CPU / frequency / 2 / 1024 - 1;        ③
          prescalarbits = _timer == 0 ? 0b101 : 0b111;
        }
      }
    }
  }
...

  TCCR2B = (TCCR2B & 0b11111000) | prescalarbits;        ④
}
```

① The call to toneBegin() returns a timer/counter number. On the standard Arduino boards, based around the ATmega328 family of AVR microcontrollers, this will be Timer/counter 2. The toneBegin() function is discussed in Listing 3-13.

② These lines onward attempt to fit the required frequency into the range 0–255 using any of the available Timer/counter 2 prescaler values.

The frequency of the system clock, 16 MHz, is divided by *twice* the required frequency – because in order to make a tone, the pin must be raised and lowered – LOW ➤ HIGH ➤ LOW. This is then divided by the prescaler value being considered. The subtraction of one from the result is because the AVR microcontroller counts from zero.

If the result fits into an 8-bit value, then the current prescaler value will be used.

③ This is the last resort at fitting the frequency into range. If the prescaler set to divide by 1024 still cannot fit, then the code simply carries on regardless. This could result in the frequency being a tad wrong.

④ After the call to toneBegin() – see in the following – Timer/counter 2 is set up to run with *no prescaling*, so the calculated prescaler bits must be set up in the TCCR2B register, in bits CS22–CS20. See Chapter 8 for a full description of prescalers.

These bits will be set to whatever is in the lowest 3 bits of the prescalarbits variable. This sets the timer/counter to the correct prescaler value for the frequency that is required to be generated.

For example, if we assume that the system clock is 16 MHz and we wish to produce a tone of 440 Hz for the note A4 above middle C, then the repeated tests earlier will result in the following:

- With a prescaler of 1, the value calculated is 18,180 which cannot be used in an 8-bit timer/counter.

- With a prescaler of 8, the value calculated is 2,271 which cannot be used in an 8-bit timer/counter.

- With a prescaler of 32, the value calculated is 567 which cannot be used in an 8-bit timer/counter.

- With a prescaler of 64, the value calculated is 283 which cannot be used in an 8-bit timer/counter.

- With a prescaler of 128, the value calculated is 141 which *can* be used in an 8-bit timer/counter.

- With a prescaler of 256, the value calculated is 70 which *could* be used but won't be as prescaler 128 was found to fit.

- With a prescaler of 1024, the value calculated is 16 which *could* be used but won't be as prescaler 128 was found to fit.

Of these, the first one to fit into the range 0–255 is a prescaler of 128. So the ocr variable is set to 141, and the prescalarbits variable is set to 101_{binary} to select a divide-by-128 prescaler.

The source code for tone() continues in the following.

Listing 3-12. The tone() function, continued

```
...

// Calculate the toggle count
if (duration > 0)
{
   toggle_count = 2 * frequency * duration / 1000;    ①
}
else
{
   toggle_count = -1;
}

// Set the OCR for the given timer,
// set the toggle count,
// then turn on the interrupts
switch (_timer)
{
```

```
    ...

#if defined(OCR2A) && defined(TIMSK2) && defined(OCIE2A)
        case 2:
            OCR2A = ocr;                                        ②
            timer2_toggle_count = toggle_count;                 ③
            bitWrite(TIMSK2, OCIE2A, 1);                        ④
            break;
#endif

    ...

    }   // end switch (_timer)
  }       // End if (_timer >= 0)

}
```

① The duration is checked, and if it is specified, then the tone must only be generated for that length of time. The duration supplied to tone() is specified in milliseconds; however, as frequency is measured in cycles per second, the value is converted to seconds.

Continuing the preceding example of a 440 Hz tone, if the duration is required to be 1.5 seconds, then the toggle_count variable is set to $2 * 440 * 1.5$ or 1320. This is the number of times in 1.5 seconds that the pin must be toggled, to ensure that a 440 Hz tone is generated.

② The ocr value is the maximum count that the timer/counter counts up to before it clears to zero and causes an interrupt. Unlike the millis() interrupt routine, which counts from 0 to 255 (on Timer/counter 0), the maximum value for this timer/counter, when generating tones, is based on the frequency and the calculated prescaler value.

Once more, with the current example, the timer/
counter will count from 0 to 141 and toggle the pin,
then again from 0 to 141 and again toggle the pin,
and so on, for the desired duration.

③ If a duration was specified, the number of times
the pin must be toggled is written to the timer2_
toggle_count variable which will be used to disable
the tone, in the interrupt routine, when the duration
has passed. This is -1 if no duration was requested.

④ The setting of the bit OCIE2A in register TIMSK2
enables the Timer/counter 2 Compare Match A
interrupt. That interrupt routine is the code that
actually toggles the pin to cause the sound to be
generated and is discussed in Listing 3-14.

The tone() function begins by calling toneBegin() to obtain a timer/
counter number to use. Listing 3-13 shows the relevant parts of the
toneBegin() function. As before, parts of the code that are not relevant to
ATmega328P devices have been removed for clarity.

Listing 3-13. The toneBegin() function

```
static int8_t toneBegin(uint8_t _pin)
{
  int8_t _timer = -1;

  // if we're already using the pin, the timer
  //   should be configured.

  for (int i = 0; i < AVAILABLE_TONE_PINS; i++) {          ①
    if (tone_pins[i] == _pin) {
      return pgm_read_byte(tone_pin_to_timer_PGM + i);
    }
  }
```

```
// search for an unused timer.
for (int i = 0; i < AVAILABLE_TONE_PINS; i++) {              ②
  if (tone_pins[i] == 255) {
    tone_pins[i] = _pin;
    _timer = pgm_read_byte(tone_pin_to_timer_PGM + i);
    break;
  }
}

if (_timer != -1)                                           ③
{
  // Set timer specific stuff
  // All timers in CTC mode
  // 8 bit timers will require changing prescalar values,
  // whereas 16 bit timers are set to either ck/1
  // or ck/64 prescalar

  switch (_timer)
  {
    // Code removed - not relevant.

    #if defined(TCCR2A) && defined(TCCR2B)
    case 2:                                                 ④
      // 8  bit timer
      TCCR2A = 0;
      TCCR2B = 0;
      bitWrite(TCCR2A, WGM21, 1);
      bitWrite(TCCR2B, CS20, 1);
      timer2_pin_port =
          portOutputRegister(digitalPinToPort(_pin));
      timer2_pin_mask =
          digitalPinToBitMask(_pin);
      break;
    #endif
```

```
    // Code removed - not relevant.

  }   // End switch (_timer)
}       // End if (_timer != -1)

  return _timer;
}
```

① The toneBegin() code starts by checking the tone_
  pin_to_timer_PGM array to see if the requested pin
  is currently generating a tone. If it is, the code simply
  returns the timer/counter number to tone() – on an
  ATmega328P-based Arduino board, this is always
  Timer/counter 2.

② The tone_pins array is searched for an unused pin.
  If an entry is found, the tone_pin_to_timer_PGM
  array is read to determine the timer/counter
  number that can be used. There's only one timer/
  counter on Arduino boards, Timer/counter 2.

③ If there were no free slot(s) in the tone_pins array,
  toneBegin() exits, returning -1 to the calling code in
  tone().

④ Much bit twiddling then ensues to initialize Timer/
  counter 2 with

  • Bit WGM21 set in register TCCR2A to put the timer/
    counter into "Clear Timer on Compare" mode. The
    counter value will reset to zero whenever it reaches
    the value in OCR2A.

  • Bit CS20 set in register TCCR2B to put the timer/
    counter into "no prescaling" mode – the timer/
    counter's clock will run at the system clock speed,

16 MHz. This will be amended on return to tone()
when the frequency-dependent prescaler value is
calculated.

- The variable timer_pin_port is determined next.
  This is based on the pin requested and will be
  PORTB, PORTC, or PORTD on the ATmega328P.

- The required pin's bitmask, in timer2_pin_mask,
  is calculated next. This will be an 8-bit value, with
  a single bit set to indicate the required pin, on the
  just calculated PORTx register.

Most of the setup for tone() is now complete. All that is required is an
interrupt service routine to do the actual tone generation. The interrupt
in use is the "Timer/counter 2 Compare Match A" interrupt, which is
discussed in Listing 3-14.

Listing 3-14. The ISR for the tone() function

```
#ifdef USE_TIMER2
ISR(TIMER2_COMPA_vect)
{
  if (timer2_toggle_count != 0)                    ①
  {
    // toggle the pin
    *timer2_pin_port ^= timer2_pin_mask;           ②

    if (timer2_toggle_count > 0)                    ③
      timer2_toggle_count--;
  }
  else
  {
```

```
// need to call noTone() so that the tone_pins[]
// entry is reset, so the timer gets initialized
// next time we call tone().
// XXX: this assumes timer 2 is always the first
// one used.

  noTone(tone_pins[0]);                          ④
//  disableTimer(2);
//  *timer2_pin_port &= ~(timer2_pin_mask);
  }
}
#endif
```

① If there are still toggles to be done, then the pin must be toggled.

② The appropriate PORTx register has its bits XORd with the pin's bitmask. This toggles just the bit that is set to indicate which pin is being used to generate a tone. If the bit is currently a one, then XORing with the 1 bit in the mask will set the PORTx register's bit to a zero and vice versa. This sets the physical pin HIGH or LOW accordingly.

③ The number of toggles remaining for the required duration is reduced.

④ If there were no more toggles to be done, then a call is made to the noTone() function to silence the sound.

The old code following this line has been commented out. This is now because noTone() disables the timer/counter and sets the pin to LOW.

The Arduino Reference web site, `www.arduino.cc/reference/en/` `language/functions/advanced-io/tone/`, has the following to say about `tone()`:

> *If you want to play different pitches on multiple pins, you need to call* noTone() *on one pin before calling* tone() *on the next pin.*
>
> *It is not possible to generate tones lower than 31Hz. For technical details, see Brett Hagman's notes.* (`https://github.com/bhagman/Tone#ugly-details`)
>
> *Use of the* tone() *function will interfere with PWM output on pins 3 and 11 (on boards other than the Mega).*

3.3.2. Function noTone()

The code for the `noTone()` function is found in the file `$ARDINC/Tone.cpp`.

The `noTone()` function, as discussed in Listing 3-15, should be called to stop the generation of a square wave triggered by the `tone()` function. When the function is called, it turns off tone generation on the supplied pin, assuming that it was generating a tone, and then sets the pin's state to LOW *regardless* of whether or not it was previously generating a tone.

Listing 3-15. The noTone() function

```
void noTone(uint8_t _pin)
{
  int8_t _timer = -1;

  for (int i = 0; i < AVAILABLE_TONE_PINS; i++) {
    if (tone_pins[i] == _pin) {
      _timer = pgm_read_byte(tone_pin_to_timer_PGM + i);      ①
      tone_pins[i] = 255;                    ②
      break;
    }
  }
```

```
    disableTimer(_timer);                    ③

    digitalWrite(_pin, 0);                   ④
}
```

①   If the pin number supplied is currently generating a tone, then it is converted to a timer/counter number. In ATmega328P variants of the Arduino board, this will always be Timer/counter 2 – that's the only timer/counter currently used for tone generation.

②   This indicates that no pins are generating a tone.

③   If the pin was not generating a tone, the _timer variable will be set to -1, and that will have no effect in disableTimer(). Otherwise, Timer/counter 2 will be disabled, stopping the generation.

④   The pin is set LOW, *regardless* of whether it was generating a tone or not. This contradicts the documentation for noTone() at www.arduino.cc/reference/en/language/functions/advanced-io/notone/ where it states that this *has no effect if no tone is being generated on the specified pin when called*. This is definitely *not* the case if the pin was actually HIGH when noTone() was called on it.

The disableTimer() function, called from noTone(), is discussed in Listing 3-16. As with other listings, those parts of the code not relevant to the ATmega328P have been removed.

Listing 3-16. The disableTimer() function

```
// XXX: this function only works properly for timer 2 (the only
   one we use
// currently).  for the others, it should end the tone, but
   won't restore
// proper PWM functionality for the timer.

void disableTimer(uint8_t _timer)
{
  switch (_timer)
  {
    ...

    case 2:                                    ①
        #if defined(TIMSK2) && defined(OCIE2A)
            bitWrite(TIMSK2, OCIE2A, 0);
        #endif

        #if defined(TCCR2A) && defined(WGM20)  ②
            TCCR2A = (1 << WGM20);
        #endif

        #if defined(TCCR2B) && defined(CS22)   ③
            TCCR2B = (TCCR2B & 0b11111000) | (1 << CS22);
        #endif

        #if defined(OCR2A)                     ④
            OCR2A = 0;
        #endif

        break;

    ...
  }
}
```

① Setting bit OCIE2A in register PIMSK2 turns off the "Timer/counter 2 Compare Match A" interrupt which had been turned on by the toneBegin() function, itself called from the tone() function.

② This resets Timer/counter 2 into "Phase Correct PWM" mode originally set up in init() but which was changed to "Clear Timer on Compare" mode by the toneBegin() function, called from tone().

③ This resets the prescaler back to divide by 64 for Timer/counter 2. The tone() function changed that setting according to the frequency of the tone that was requested.

④ This resets the "Output Compare A" value for the timer/counter.

The effect of the preceding code is to restore the state of Timer/counter 2, its interrupts and so on, back to those configured in the initial setup within the init() function as described in Chapter 2, Section 2.9, "*The init() Function*."

The Arduino Reference web site at www.arduino.cc/reference/en/language/functions/advanced-io/notone/ has the following to say on noTone():

> *If you want to play different pitches on multiple pins, you need to call* noTone() *on one pin before calling* tone() *on the next pin.*

3.3.3. Function pulseIn()

The pulseIn() function, found in the file $ARDINC/wiring_pulse.c, is used to measure the period of a pulse on any pin. There is an alternative function, pulseInLong(), which is discussed later, which is better at handling long-duration pulses than pulseIn(); however, pulseIn() can be used in sketches where interrupts are disabled.

The function reads a pulse – HIGH or LOW – on any pin and returns the length of the pulse in microseconds. There are two methods of calling this function as shown in Listing 3-17.

Listing 3-17. Calling the pulseIn() function

```
unsigned long microSeconds = 0;

microSeconds = pulseIn(pin, state, timeout);

// or

microSeconds = pulseIn(pin, state);  // Timeout defaults to 1 second
```

The return value is an unsigned long.

If no timeout is specified, the default is one second. The timeout is specified in microseconds – millionths of a second.

If the function is called with a LOW state to be measured, it will

- Wait for the pin in question to become HIGH if it currently is LOW. If the timeout expires before the pin goes HIGH, the function returns zero. Thus, the code is waiting for the current pulse to end.

- Wait for the pin to go LOW again – this is the *start* of the pulse to be measured. Once more, if the *remaining* time left in the timeout expires, the function returns zero.

- Wait for the pin to go HIGH again – this is the *end* of the pulse to be measured. If the *remaining* time left in the timeout expires, then the function again returns zero; otherwise, it returns the time, in microseconds, that the pin remained LOW.

> **ⓘ** To be absolutely clear, the timeout you pass to the function is
> used for *all* of the function – waiting for the current pulse to finish,
> waiting for the new pulse to start, and then waiting for the new pulse
> to complete – one timeout to rule them all.

Similar, but opposite, actions take place when `pulseIn()` is called with
a state of `HIGH`.

Unlike the function `pulseInLong()`, `pulseIn()` *can* be executed when
interrupts are disabled as it does not require the `micros()` function.

It measures the pulse length by calling an assembly language function,
`countPulseASM()`, which can be seen in the file `$ARDINC/wiring_pulse.S`
and, according to the source code, it started life as a C routine, similar to
that shown in Listing 3-18. I will not be discussing the assembly language
version of `countPulseASM()` here – looking at compiler output is quite
tedious it has to be said.

Listing 3-18. C code version of countPulseASM()

```
unsigned long pulseInSimpl(volatile uint8_t *port,
                           uint8_t bit,
                           uint8_t stateMask,
                           unsigned long maxloops)
{
    unsigned long width = 0;                        ①

    // wait for any previous pulse to end
    while ((*port & bit) == stateMask)
        if (--maxloops == 0)
            return 0;                               ②
```

```
    // wait for the pulse to start
    while ((*port & bit) != stateMask)
        if (--maxloops == 0)
            return 0;                            ③

    // wait for the pulse to stop
    while ((*port & bit) == stateMask) {
        if (++width == maxloops)
            return 0;                            ④
    }

    return width;                                ⑤
}
```

① The pulse length will be returned in the width variable; here, it is initialized to zero.

② The function returns zero if the timeout expired while waiting for the current pulse to end.

③ The function returns zero if the timeout remaining expired while waiting for the new pulse to begin.

④ The function returns zero if the timeout remaining expired while the new pulse was being measured.

⑤ The pulse has been successfully measured, and the variable width holds its width as the number of while loops which were executed while measuring the pulse length.

Listing 3-19 shows the source code for the current version of the pulseIn().

Listing 3-19. The pulseIn() function

```
/* Measures the length (in microseconds) of a pulse on the pin;
   state is HIGH
 * or LOW, the type of pulse to measure.  Works on pulses from
   2-3 microseconds
 * to 3 minutes in length, but must be called at least a few
   dozen microseconds
 * before the start of the pulse.
 *
 * This function performs better with short pulses in
   noInterrupt() context
 */

unsigned long pulseIn(uint8_t pin,
                      uint8_t state,
                      unsigned long timeout)
{
    // cache the port and bit of the pin in order to speed
    // up the pulse width measuring loop and achieve finer
    // resolution.  calling digitalRead() instead yields
    // much coarser resolution.
    uint8_t bit = digitalPinToBitMask(pin);          ①
    uint8_t port = digitalPinToPort(pin);            ②
    uint8_t stateMask = (state ? bit : 0);           ③

    // convert the timeout from microseconds to a number
    // of times through the initial loop; it takes
    // approximately 16 clock cycles per iteration

    unsigned long maxloops =
        microsecondsToClockCycles(timeout)/16;       ④
```

```
unsigned long width =
    countPulseASM(portInputRegister(port),
    bit, stateMask, maxloops);                          ⑤

// prevent clockCyclesToMicroseconds to return
// bogus values if countPulseASM timed out

if (width)                                              ⑥
    return clockCyclesToMicroseconds(width * 16 + 16);
else
    return 0;
}
```

① The supplied pin number is converted to a bitmask. As with all calls to digitalPinToBitMask(), the bitmask returned is an 8-bit binary value, with a single bit set to one. This bit represents the desired physical pin on the AVR microcontroller and its appropriate position in the PORTx and PINx registers.

② The appropriate port (PB, PC, or PD) is obtained from the pin number.

③ The stateMask variable is set to zero for LOW or to the pin's bitmask for HIGH.

④ The timeout counter is initialized to the required number of microseconds multiplied by 16 as the assembly code will loop in system clock cycles as opposed to microseconds.

⑤ The assembly language code is called to

  • Wait for the current pulse on the pin to end or the timeout to expire.

- Wait for the pin to begin a new pulse or the timeout to expire.

- Wait for the pulse to end or the timeout to expire.

The call to portInputRegister() will convert the pin's port number, PB, PC, or PD, to the appropriate PINx register in the AVR microcontroller; and this will be passed to the assembly code.

⑥ The width value is converted from the number of while loops executed while measuring the pulse to microseconds. Each loop takes 16 microseconds, so width is multiplied by 16. It now holds the number of clock cycles it spent in the loop. An additional 16 is added for the overhead of calling and returning from the countPulseASM() function. These clock cycles are then converted to microseconds by the clockCyclesToMicroseconds() function.

ⓘ The reason that the code calls out to an assembly language routine is at first a little mysterious, especially as the assembly code was, it appears, created from C code originally. Why not just call the C code again?

Well, what happens to the timings in the C code if, somehow, a compiler version that is later used by the IDE implements a new optimization that makes the generated code run much more quickly? The timings will be off somewhat.

Running a standard assembly language routine, where the actual timings of each and every instruction are known, means that no matter what improvements are made in the compiler, the existing countPulseASM() function will continue to run at exactly the same speed, thus keeping the results of pulseIn() consistent.

The Arduino Reference web site (www.arduino.cc/reference/en/language/functions/advanced-io/pulsein/) gives the following notes about the pulseIn() function:

> *The timing of this function has been determined empirically and will probably show errors in longer pulses. Works on pulses from 10 microseconds to 3 minutes in length.*

There is also an example of the function's use on the web site, as shown in Listing 3-20.

Listing 3-20. Example usage of pulseIn()

```
int pin = 7;
unsigned long duration;

void setup()
{
    pinMode(pin, INPUT);
}

void loop()
{
    duration = pulseIn(pin, HIGH);
}
```

However, the example code doesn't do *anything* with the returned result!

3.3.4. Function `pulseInLong()`

The `pulseInLong()` function is found in the file `$ARDINC/wiring_pulse.c`. It is an alternative to the `pulseIn()` function previously described and is better at handling long-duration pulses. It cannot, however, be used in sketches where interrupts are disabled.

The function reads a pulse – `HIGH` or `LOW` – on any pin and returns the length of the pulse in microseconds. There are two methods of calling this function as shown in Listing 3-21.

Listing 3-21. Calling the pulseInLong() function

```
unsigned long microSeconds = 0;

microSeconds = pulseInLong(pin, state, timeout);

// or

microSeconds = pulseInLong(pin, state);    // Timeout defaults
                                           to 1 second
```

The return value is an `unsigned long`.

If no timeout is specified, the default is one second. The timeout should be specified in microseconds – millionths of a second.

If the function is called with a `HIGH` state to be measured, it will

- Wait for the pin in question to become `LOW` if it currently is `HIGH`. If the timeout expires before the pin goes `LOW`, the function returns zero. Thus, the code is waiting for the current pulse to end.

- Wait for the pin to go `HIGH` again – this is the *start* of the pulse to be measured. Once more, if the *remaining* time left in the timeout expires, the function returns zero.

- Wait for the pin to go LOW again – this is the *end* of the pulse to be measured. If the *remaining* time left in the timeout expires, then the function again returns zero; otherwise, it returns the time, in microseconds, that the pin remained HIGH.

Similar, but opposite, actions take place when called with a state of LOW.

The source code for the pulseinLong() function is discussed in Listing 3-22, which has been slightly reformatted so that it can fit on the page.

Listing 3-22. The pulseInLong() function

```
/* Measures the length (in microseconds) of a pulse on the
 * pin; state is HIGH or LOW, the type of pulse to measure.
 * Works on pulses from 2-3 microseconds to 3 minutes in
 * length, but must be called at least a few dozen
 * microseconds before the start of the pulse.
 *
 * ATTENTION:                                       ①
 * this function relies on micros() so cannot be
 * used in noInterrupt() context
 */

unsigned long pulseInLong(uint8_t pin,
                          uint8_t state,
                          unsigned long timeout)
{
    // cache the port and bit of the pin in order to speed
    // up the pulse width measuring loop and achieve finer
    // resolution. Calling digitalRead() instead yields much
    // coarser resolution.
```

```
    uint8_t bit = digitalPinToBitMask(pin);      ②
    uint8_t port = digitalPinToPort(pin);        ③
    uint8_t stateMask = (state ? bit : 0);

    unsigned long startMicros = micros();        ④

    // wait for any previous pulse to end        ⑤
    while ((*portInputRegister(port) & bit) == stateMask) {
        if (micros() - startMicros > timeout)
            return 0;
    }

    // wait for the pulse to start                ⑥
    while ((*portInputRegister(port) & bit) != stateMask) {
        if (micros() - startMicros > timeout)
            return 0;
    }

    unsigned long start = micros();              ⑦
    // wait for the pulse to stop                 ⑧
    while ((*portInputRegister(port) & bit) == stateMask) {
        if (micros() - startMicros > timeout)
            return 0;
    }

    return micros() - start;                     ⑨
}
```

① Your attention is drawn to this comment. Because the code uses the `micros()` function, it cannot be used if the global interrupts have been turned off, as the call to `micros()` will not change without interrupts, specifically, the Timer/counter 0 Overflow interrupt. The `micros()` function is discussed in Section 3.4.3, "*The micros() Function.*"

② The supplied pin number is converted to a bitmask.

③ The appropriate port (PB, PC, or PD) is obtained from the pin number.

④ The timeout counter is initialized. Because this uses micros(), interrupts *must* be enabled, and the default interrupt handler for the Timer/counter 0 Overflow interrupt must be configured. (This is done at startup in the init() function as discussed in Chapter 2.)

⑤ The wait for the pin to *stop* being in the state we are considering happens here. If the timeout expires during the wait, the function returns zero. The pulse did not occur.

The call to portInputRegister() will convert the pin's port number, PB, PC, or PD, to the appropriate PINx register in the AVR microcontroller.

⑥ The wait for the pin to start the next pulse happens here. If the remaining timeout expires during the wait, the function returns zero. The pulse did not occur.

⑦ A new pulse has started, so the time that it started is recorded in start.

⑧ The function waits while the pulse continues. If the timeout expires while waiting, the function will once again return zero to indicate that the pulse did not get measured completely within the timeout period.

⑨ If the pulse did complete before the timeout expired, the function returns the time that the pin was in the state that the sketch was interested in.

The description of pulseinLong() at www.arduino.cc/reference/
en/language/functions/advanced-io/pulseinlong/ gives the following
notes about the function:

> *The timing of this function has been determined empirically
> and will probably show errors in shorter pulses. Works on
> pulses from 10 microseconds to 3 minutes in length. This rou-
> tine can be used only if interrupts are activated. Furthermore
> the highest resolution is obtained with large intervals.*

> *This function relies on* micros() *so cannot be used in the*
> noInterrupts() *context.*

There is also an example of the function's use on the Arduino web site,
reproduced in Listing 3-23.

Listing 3-23. Example usage of pulseInLong()

```
int pin = 7;
unsigned long duration;

void setup() {
    pinMode(pin, INPUT);
}
void loop() {
    duration = pulseInLong(pin, HIGH);
}
```

However, the example doesn't do *anything* with the returned result!

3.3.5. Function shiftIn()

The code for the shiftIn() function is found in the file $ARDINC/wiring_
shift.c.

The shiftIn() function is used to read an 8-bit data value, 1 bit at a
time, from an external device, for example, a shift register.

The operation may be carried out with the most significant bit (MSB) being shifted in first, or with the least significant bit (LSB) first, according to how the external device sending the data is sending it.

The Arduino only requires two pins and can read 8 bits or more, depending on the number of bits the device wishes to send to the Arduino. The pins required are

- A data pin, which is the pin that the bits in the external device will be presented on, ready to be read by the Arduino.

- A clock pin, which is set HIGH to signal the external device that the Arduino is ready to receive a single bit of data and held LOW when the Arduino doesn't wish to read the data or has just finished reading a bit.

The source code for the shiftIn() function is shown in Listing 3-24.

Listing 3-24. The shiftIn() function

```
uint8_t shiftIn(uint8_t dataPin,
                uint8_t clockPin,
                uint8_t bitOrder) {

    uint8_t value = 0;
    uint8_t i;

    for (i = 0; i < 8; ++i) {
        digitalWrite(clockPin, HIGH);                  ①
        if (bitOrder == LSBFIRST)                       ②
            value |= digitalRead(dataPin) << i;         ③
        else
            value |= digitalRead(dataPin) << (7 - i);   ③
        digitalWrite(clockPin,  LOW);                   ④
    }
    return value;                                       ⑤
}
```

The function works by reading 8 separate bits, one at a time, by

①   Raising the clock pin HIGH to signal the external device that the Arduino is ready to receive data.

②   Reading a one or zero from the data pin. The external device should have placed its data bit on the pin when the clock pin was raised.

③   Accumulating the newly read bit into the value variable. Yes, there *are* two places where this happens – it depends on whether the code is being called with LSBFIRST or MSBFIRST and which of the two lines is actually executed.

④   Bringing the clock pin LOW to end the reading of this 1 bit.

⑤   The data is returned as a single 8-bit, unsigned value.

The documentation for the shiftIn() function, at www.arduino.cc/reference/en/language/functions/advanced-io/shiftin/, has the following to say about shiftIn():

If you are interfacing with a device that is clocked by rising edges, you'll need to make sure that the clock pin is LOW *before the first call to* shiftIn()*, e.g. with a call to* digitalWrite (clockPin, LOW)*.*

This is a software implementation; see also the Arduino SPI library that uses a hardware implementation, which is faster but only works on specific pins.

3.3.6. Function `shiftOut()`

The code for the `shiftOut()` function is found in the file `$ARDINC/wiring_shift.c`.

The `shiftOut()` function is used to pass an 8-bit data value, 1 bit at a time, from the AVR microcontroller to an external device such as a shift register. This is carried out in software so that any Arduino pin can be used for the data pin. There is also the ability to use the hardware of the AVR microcontroller itself, which uses the Arduino's SPI library, but can only be used with certain pins on the ATmega328P.

The operation can be carried out with the most significant bit (MSB) being shifted out first, or with the least significant bit (LSB) shifting first, according to how the device receiving the data desires it.

Shift registers, for example, are useful devices for reducing the number of pins required by the Arduino board for certain purposes. For example, to flash eight LEDs would require eight data pins on the Arduino, but with a shift register in place, this is reduced to two, possibly three, depending on the shift register type. The pins required are

- A data pin, which is the pin that the bits in the data to be shifted out are sent on.

- A clock pin, which is toggled `HIGH` and then `LOW` to latch the data bit into the external device.

- Optionally, but not used in `shiftOut()`, some shift register devices have an enable pin, so that the output pins on the shift registers are all set to the desired state at once, when all the bits have been received, and not as and when each bit is latched into the device.

💡 A benefit of shift registers is that they can be cascaded together. With two in a circuit, 16 LEDs can be flashed, for only two or three data pins on the Arduino. This can be extended up to 24, 32, and so on for as many shift registers, and LEDs, as you have handy.

I have also seen shift registers being used to reduce the number of Arduino pins required to drive a pair of stepper motors (www. youtube.com/watch?v=OeqQPlD3mNA&index=16&list=PLyE5 6WXwO_5QrkEwXZ2AXwh6A-sOiQoVl).

There are tutorials on using the shiftOut() function, with a shift register, on the Arduino Tutorials web site at https://arduino.cc/en/ Tutorial/ShiftOut.

The function works by looking at each individual bit in the value to be shifted out, starting at the appropriate end, and raising the data pin HIGH if the bit is a one or LOW if it is a zero.

Once the bit has been presented on the data pin, the clock pin is toggled HIGH and then LOW to signal the external device that the data bit is valid and should be "clocked in" to the device.

On some devices, this will have the side effect of changing the output state, not always a good thing. On others, the data are buffered internally by the devices until they receive an "enable" signal, and then all the data are presented on the devices' output pins simultaneously. This version of shiftOut() does not have this ability.

The source code for the shiftOut() function is as shown in Listing 3-25.

Listing 3-25. The shiftOut() function

```
void shiftOut(uint8_t dataPin,
              uint8_t clockPin,
              uint8_t bitOrder,
              uint8_t  val)
{
    uint8_t i;

    for (i = 0; i < 8; i++)   {
        if (bitOrder == LSBFIRST)
            digitalWrite(dataPin, !!(val & (1 << i)));
        else
            digitalWrite(dataPin, !!(val & (1 << (7 - i))));

        digitalWrite(clockPin, HIGH);
        digitalWrite(clockPin, LOW);
    }
}
```

The preceding code shows the use of an interesting technique, one that I had never come across previously. Let's take the following line as the example:

```
digitalWrite(dataPin, !!(val & (1 << i)));
```

The (val & (1 << i)) part isolates a single bit of val and returns its value as the appropriate power of two. For example, if i is 5 and val is 250, then (val & (1 << i)) returns 2^5 which is 32.

In binary, this is

```
250 = 11111010
 32 = 00100000
AND = 00100000
```

The interesting part is the !! part, which means, for this example, not not 32. To my initial eye, that simply means 32, which confused me. However, in C, it's a little different:

```
  32 = 32
 !32 = 0
!!32 = 1
```

Try it and see! You get a one or a zero according to whether the bit is set or not. In the past, I've only ever seen this style of code:

```
(val & (1 << i)) >> i;
```

This does give the same answer, one or zero. However, this variant requires a shift right operation in addition to the bitwise AND operation, and I suspect that the !! variant is a little quicker. I need to do some testing!

The shiftOut() reference at www.arduino.cc/reference/en/language/functions/advanced-io/shiftout/ has the following to say:

> *If you are interfacing with a device that's clocked by rising edges, you'll need to make sure that the clock pin is LOW before the call to* shiftOut()*, e.g. with a call to* digitalWrite (clockPin, LOW)*.*
>
> *This is a software implementation; see also the SPI library, which provides a hardware implementation that is faster but works only on specific pins.*

3.4. Time

This section looks into those functions which deal with timings on the Arduino. Here, we investigate the delay() function which holds up processing for a few milliseconds, delayMicroseconds() which delays for a few microseconds, and the two functions which return details of how long the sketch has been running since power on, reset, or upload time – micros() and millis().

3.4.1. Function `delay()`

This function causes the sketch to pause, and do almost nothing, for a certain number of milliseconds. According to the reference guide at www. arduino.cc/reference/en/language/functions/time/delay/, while the `delay()` function is running, you cannot:

- Call `digitalRead()`, `digitalWrite()`, `pinMode()`, `analogRead()`, `analogWrite()`, etc., to manipulate the board's pins, to read sensors and so on.

- Carry out any calculations.

- *Transmit* data to `Serial`.

ℹ️ I'm interested in that last point. Transmission of data to the USART (the Serial interface) is carried out under an interrupt service routine, just like the receipt of serial data, so *should* still work. I assume – always a bad idea – that what they are meaning is simply that while `delay()` is running, your sketch cannot call the `Serial. print()` functions.

You can be sure, however, that the following *will* still work:

- *Receipt* of data from `Serial`, which will be saved for later use.

- Values written to PWM pins with `analogWrite()` will be *maintained*, but cannot be *changed*. Motors attached to PWM pins will still run, and LEDs will remain lit; however, their speed and/or brightness during the `delay()` will remain constant.

141

- Interrupt routines will work. This includes the Timer/counter 0 Overflow interrupt which keeps the millis counter up to date. Calls to `millis()` or `micros()`, after a call to `delay()`, will accurately reflect the passage of time for the sketch.

⚠️ Interestingly, `delay()` calls `micros()` to measure the delay period. The `micros()` function *does* disable interrupts while it reads `timer0_overflow_count` which is updated every time that Timer/counter 0's 8-bit counter overflows (every 1024 microseconds). So, technically, while `delay()` itself doesn't disable interrupts, it does cause interrupts to be disabled and enabled quite frequently within the delay loop.

The maximum delay period that can be requested is $2^{32} - 1$ milliseconds, or 4,294,967.295 seconds. This is *almost* 50 days – 49 days, 17 hours, 2 minutes, 47 seconds, and 294.87424 milliseconds! I imagine a sketch that delays for that long should really consider being put to sleep – see Chapter 7, Section 7.3.8, "*Putting the AVR to Sleep,*" for details.

Listing 3-26 shows the source code for the `delay()` function which has been extracted from the file `$ARDINC/wiring.c`.

Listing 3-26. The delay() function

```
void delay(unsigned long ms)
{
    uint32_t start = micros();

    while (ms > 0) {
        yield();                                               ①

        while ( ms > 0 && (micros() - start) >= 1000) {
```

```
        ms--;
        start += 1000;
    }
  }
}
```

① The call to the `yield()` function, as shown in
Listing 3-27, is interesting.

All that `delay()` is doing is fetching the current `micros()` value and then
entering a *busy loop* to waste time until the required number of milliseconds
have elapsed. This is why you are almost unable to carry out anything else
in your sketch while there is a `delay()` – because the call to `delay()` uses *all*
the time and CPU cycles until the delay period has finished.

In the ATmega328P-based versions of Arduino boards, this doesn't do
much; in fact, it's defined as an empty function in the file `$ARDINC/hooks.c`.

Listing 3-27. The yield() function

```
/**
 * Empty yield() hook.
 *
 * This function is intended to be used by library writers to
 * build libraries or sketches that support cooperative
 * threads.
 *
 * Its defined as a weak symbol and it can be redefined to
 * implement a real cooperative scheduler.
 */
static void __empty() {
    // Empty
}
void yield(void) __attribute__ ((weak, alias("__empty")));
```

So, in these boards, calling delay() has an overhead of calling this empty function, but the calculation in the delay() function's loop takes this into account.

Other boards that can use the Arduino IDE and language, such as those based around the ESP8266, have internal schedulers that *must* be kept active during long-running code; otherwise, the microcontroller may reset itself, assuming that something has hung. The AVR microcontroller has a similar feature known as the Watchdog Timer which will be discussed later, in Chapter 7, Section 7.3, "*The Watchdog Timer.*"

Because the delay() function could take too long and starve these devices of scheduler time, the yield() function is defined as weak, and this allows the developers to define their own yield() function in sketches so that the processor doesn't suffer from random or strange resets.

I presume that a maker could, if they were so inclined, write a yield() function in an AVR microcontroller–based Arduino board and do some processing during the delay; however, it would need to be carefully considered, and whatever was being executed in the yield() function should be kept as short and quick as possible to avoid affecting any delay() loops that require reasonably accurate delay periods.

The Arduino Reference web site (www.arduino.cc/reference/en/ language/functions/time/delay/) gives the following notes about the delay() function:

> *While it is easy to create a blinking LED with the* delay() *function, and many sketches use short delays for such tasks as switch debouncing, the use of* delay() *in a sketch has signifi-cant drawbacks.*
>
> *No other reading of sensors, mathematical calculations, or pin manipulation can go on during the* delay() *function, so in effect, it brings most other activity to a halt.*
>
> *For alternative approaches to controlling timing see the* mil-lis() *function and the sketch listed below (in Listing 3-28).*

More knowledgeable programmers usually avoid the use of delay() *for timing of events longer than 10's of milliseconds unless the Arduino sketch is very simple.*

Certain things do go on while the delay() *function is controlling the Atmega chip however, because the* delay() *function does not disable interrupts. Serial communication that appears at the RX pin is recorded, PWM* (analogWrite()) *values and pin states are maintained, and interrupts will work as they should.*

Listing 3-28 is the sketch mentioned in the notes. It uses the millis() function to time the blinking of the LED, rather than calling the delay() function.

ℹ️ Please note I have removed most comments and wrapped longer lines of code in Listing 3-28 to preserve space on the page and to avoid the code running off the edge of the page. The original code on the Web is very well commented.

Listing 3-28. Blink without using delay()

```
/*
  Blink without  Delay
  created 2005          by David A. Mellis
  modified  8 Feb 2010 by Paul Stoffregen
  modified 11 Nov 2013 by Scott Fitzgerald
  modified  9 Jan 2017 by Arturo Guadalupi

  This example code is in the public domain.

  http://www.arduino.cc/en/Tutorial/BlinkWithoutDelay
*/
```

```
const int ledPin = LED_BUILTIN;  // the number of the LED pin
int ledState = LOW;              // ledState used to set the LED
unsigned long previousMillis = 0;                              ①
const long interval = 1000;                                    ②
void setup() {
  pinMode(ledPin,  OUTPUT);
}
void loop() {
  unsigned long currentMillis = millis();                      ③
  if (currentMillis - previousMillis >= interval) {            ④
    previousMillis = currentMillis;                            ⑤
    if (ledState == LOW) {                                     ⑥
      ledState = HIGH;
    } else {
      ledState = LOW;
    }
    digitalWrite(ledPin, ledState);                            ⑦
  }
}
```

① The variable previousMillis holds the previous time that the LED was toggled.

② The delay between blinks is set here, in interval.

③ The current time is obtained into currentMillis.

④ Check here to see if the required interval has passed.

⑤ If the LED is to be toggled, record the current time.

⑥ Calculate the LED's new state – HIGH or LOW.

⑦ Finally, toggle the LED.

3.4.2. Function `delayMicroseconds()`

This function, like the `delay()` function, causes your sketch to pause, and do almost nothing, for a certain number of microseconds – millionths of a second. While the `delayMicroseconds()` function is running, you cannot

- Call `digitalRead()`, `digitalWrite()`, `pinMode()`, `analogRead()`, `analogWrite()`, etc., to manipulate the board's pins.

- Carry out any calculations.

- *Transmit* data to `Serial`.

The following will still work while the function is delaying:

- *Receipt* of data from `Serial`, which will be saved for later use.

- Values written to PWM pins with `analogWrite()` will be *maintained*, but cannot be *changed*. Motors attached to PWM pins will still run, and LEDs will remain lit; however, their speed and/or brightness during the `delayMicroseconds()` will remain constant.

- Interrupt routines will work. This includes the Timer/ counter 0 Interrupt which keeps the `millis()` counter up to date. Calls to `millis()` or `micros()`, after a call to `delayMicroseconds()`, will accurately reflect the passage of time for the sketch.

Unlike the `delay()` function, `delayMicroseconds()` has no call to `yield()` as the delay period is most likely far too short to cause those Arduino boards, with potential scheduler problems, resulting in a reset. It is assumed that this function will only be used for fairly small delays; otherwise, the developer would be advised to call `delay()` instead.

As with `delay()`, this function simply burns CPU cycles, time, and power until the required delay period has passed; however, unlike `delay()` which allows a delay period of up to nearly 50 days, `delayMicroseconds()` takes an `unsigned int` parameter for the delay period. This is only a 16-bit variable (`delay()` uses 32 bits) so the maximum delay period is 65,536 microseconds, or 0.065536 seconds.

Listing 3-29 shows most of the source code for the `delayMicroseconds()` function which has been extracted from the file `$ARDINC/wiring.c`. Similarly to other listings, I have removed some (large) comments and all the parts of the code which are not relevant to the ATmega328P on standard Arduino boards.

Listing 3-29. The delayMicroseconds() function

```
/*
 * Delay for the given number of microseconds.
 * Assumes a 1, 8, 12, 16, 20 or 24 MHz clock.
 */

void delayMicroseconds(unsigned int us)
{
    // call = 4 cycles + 2 to 4 cycles to init us
    // (2 for constant delay, 4 for variable)

    // calling avrlib's delay_us() function with low
    // values (e.g. 1 or 2 microseconds) gives delays
    // longer than desired.
    //delay_us(us);                                     ①

#if F_CPU >= 24000000L

    ....

#elif F_CPU >= 16000000L
    // for the 16 MHz clock on most Arduino boards
```

```
    if (us <= 1) return; // = 3 cycles, (4 when true)    ②
    us <<= 2; // x4 us, = 4 cycles                         ③
    us -= 5; // = 2 cycles,                                ④

    ...

#endif
    // busy wait
    __asm__ __volatile__ (                                ⑤ ⑥
        "1: sbiw %0,1" "\n\t" // 2 cycles
        "brne 1b" : "=w" (us) : "0" (us) // 2 cycles
    );
    // return = 4 cycles
}
```

① Interesting! It appears, from this comment, that
the delayMicroseconds() function *used* to call the
delay_us() function in the AVRLib. It's therefore
worth noting that the comment matches *exactly*
with a warning on www.arduino.cc/reference/en/
language/functions/time/delaymicroseconds/
about inaccuracies when called with low values for
the delay.

I rather suspect that the problem with periods below
3 microseconds only applies to the old versions of
the Arduino Language where that call to delay_us()
is still being made.

The warnings from the Arduino Reference site are
reproduced in the following for your information.

② The function begins by returning if the delay
is 1 microsecond, or less, as that period will
have elapsed by the time it gets to that point

in the function. Calling the function takes one
microsecond, so there's nothing more to be done.

③ Because the actual delay is carried out by an
assembly language routine, and as each iteration
of the loop takes only a quarter of a microsecond,
the delay period, in the variable us, needs to
be multiplied by 4 to get the correct delay in
microseconds.

④ The us variable now needs to be adjusted to take
account of the time that has passed doing all the
preceding checks. As either 19 or 21 cycles (19
or 21 quarters of a microsecond) have gone by, 5
(microseconds) is subtracted from us to account for
those values. This is *almost* correct as it equates to
20 cycles rather than the observed 19 or 21.

⑤ The adjusted value in us is then passed to the
assembly code and the loop executed us times. All
that the assembly function does is to subtract one
from the value in a register pair, which started off
with the us variable's value, and then loop around
doing that subtraction over and over until the us
value reduces to zero. The compiler will pick a
suitable register pair to hold the initial us value and
to be decremented in the code.

⑥ The assembly routine is declared volatile to
prevent the compiler from optimizing the routine
away completely – as it appears to do nothing.

The following notes about the delayMicroseconds() function can be
found online at www.arduino.cc/reference/en/language/functions/
time/delaymicroseconds/:

This function works very accurately in the range 3 microseconds and up. We cannot assure that delayMicroseconds() *will perform precisely for smaller delay-times.*

As of Arduino 0018, delayMicroseconds() *no longer disables interrupts.*

ⓘ I am certain that the preceding warning about very small delays is no longer applicable and only applied to previous versions of the function which called delay_us() – which the current version no longer does.

3.4.3. Function micros()

The micros() function returns the number of microseconds since

- The Arduino board was powered on.

- The board was reset.

- The board was reprogrammed with a new sketch and began execution.

The return value, an unsigned long, can hold up to 32 bits and will overflow to zero after approximately 70 minutes according to the reference notes for this function. On 16 MHz Arduino boards, the value returned by the micros() function is always a multiple of four microseconds. On 8 MHz Arduinos, the result is always a multiple of eight microseconds.

I wonder how *approximate* that 70-minute overflow period is. We know that the variable m can hold up to $2^{32} - 1$ microseconds, so

```
2^32 - 1    = 4,294,967,295 microseconds
/ 1,000,000 = 4,294.967295 Seconds
/ 60        = 71.58278827 Minutes
            = 71 minutes 34 seconds 967295 microseconds.
```

So the counter has a wee bit more than 70 minutes before it overflows on standard Arduinos.

Listing 3-30 shows the source code for the `micros()` function which has been extracted from the file $ARDINC/`wiring.c`.

Listing 3-30. The micros() function

```
unsigned long micros() {
    unsigned long m;
    uint8_t oldSREG = SREG, t;                        ①

    cli();                                            ②
    m = timer0_overflow_count;                        ③

#if defined(TCNT0)
    t = TCNT0;                                        ④

    ...
#endif

#ifdef TIFR0
    if ((TIFR0 & _BV(TOV0)) && (t < 255))             ⑤
        m++;

    ...
#endif

    SREG = oldSREG;                                   ⑥

    return ((m << 8) + t)
        * (64 / clockCyclesPerMicrosecond());         ⑦
}
```

①   The status register is copied to preserve the current
     state of the interrupts and other flag bits.

② Global interrupts are disabled. This stops the
    interrupt routine that calculates millis() from
    executing and updating the variable timer0_
    overflow_count while it is being copied.

③ The current Timer/counter 0 overflow count is
    copied from timer0_overflow_count into the
    variable m. There are 256 timer clock ticks per
    overflow, so there is one overflow every 1024
    microseconds.

④ The current count for Timer/counter 0 is read from
    the register TCNT0 into variable t. This register is
    incremented once every 16,000,000/64 system clock
    ticks, or every 4 microseconds.

⑤ If Timer/counter 0 has *just* overflowed from 255 to 0,
    the TOV0 bit will be set unless the interrupt handler
    has completed, so the copy of timer0_overflow_
    count is incremented because the timer/counter
    has just overflowed again while we were messing
    about with the current values.

⑥ The status register is restored, thus re-enabling
    interrupts if they were running previously.

⑦ The return value is calculated by multiplying the
    timer0_overflow_count by 256, adding the fraction,
    and multiplying that result by 4, the number of
    microseconds in each timer clock tick. See the
    following for the actual calculation. (I had to wrap
    this line to fit the page.)

The result is required to be the number of microseconds since the time began for the sketch, so we have the following:

- The value in variable m is the count of Timer/counter 0 overflows, which we already know from init() occurs every 256 *system* clock ticks.

- The value in variable t is the count of the Timer/counter 0 clock ticks since the last overflow.

- The total number of clock ticks since the sketch began is therefore $(256 * m) + t$. Shifting m left by eight places is the same as multiplying by 2^8 which is 256.

- The prescaler, 64, is the number of system clock ticks which occur for each timer clock tick.

- The function clockCyclesPerMicrosecond(), defined in the file $ARDINC/Arduino.h as F_CPU / 1000000, returns 16; and the 64 is the system clock prescaler amount. This calculation gives us 4 microseconds per timer clock tick.

So we need to return the value equivalent to $((m * 256) + t) * 4$ microseconds, and that's exactly what the final line does. For a standard Arduino at 16 MHz, the function clockCyclesPerMicrosecond() returns 16. The clockCyclesPerMicrosecond() function is based on the board's F_CPU (system clock speed) and will return the correct result for micros() regardless of the actual speed of the board this code is running on.

3.4.4. Function millis()

This function returns the number of milliseconds since

- The Arduino board was powered on.

- The board was reset.

- The board was reprogrammed with a new sketch and began execution.

The source code for the function can be seen in Listing 3-31 or, if you wish, by examining the file $ARDINC/wiring.c on your system.

The init() function, which is executed at the start of any sketch, initializes the ATmega328P's Timer/counter 0 so that every time it overflows from 255 to 0, it executes an interrupt routine to count up the milliseconds. When a sketch calls the millis() function, it simply reads the return value from a global variable named timer0_millis.

Listing 3-31. The millis() function

```
unsigned long millis()
{
    unsigned long m;
    uint8_t oldSREG = SREG;        ①

    // disable interrupts while we read timer0_millis or
    // we might get an inconsistent value (e.g. in the
    // middle of a write to timer0_millis)

    cli();                         ②
    m = timer0_millis;             ③
    SREG = oldSREG;                ④

    return m;                      ⑤
}
```

①   A copy of the status register is taken to preserve the current interrupt flag, plus other flags, stored there.

②   Global interrupts must be disabled – see the comment in the code for the reason.

③   The current value of the millis counter is read.

④   The status register is restored, turning interrupts back on, if they were originally on.

⑤   The result of the millis() function is returned.

The code must disable global interrupts before reading the value from `timer0_millis`. This is to prevent the counter being incremented while this code is in the middle of reading the current value. As disabling the interrupts changes the status register in the AVR microcontroller, a copy is taken so that it can be restored later. After retrieving the current value, the status register is restored, and the value is returned to the calling code. This minimizes the time that interrupts are disabled.

You should be aware that whenever the interrupts are disabled, and other functions such as `digitalRead()` will disable interrupts, then the `millis()` count will stop incrementing. This implies that some normal Arduino code can affect the `millis()` and `micros()` function results, however briefly.

For further information, you can read about the `init()` function in Chapter 2, Section 2.9, "*The init() Function*."

ⓘ According to the Arduino Reference for `millis()` at www.arduino.cc/reference/en/language/functions/time/millis/, the value returned from `millis()` will roll over to zero if the Arduino has been running for approximately 50 days. You may need to be aware of this if you are using `millis()` for anything important and make sure that your code handles situations where the value read from `millis()` at the start of something is greater than the value at the end. This would indicate a rollover has taken place.

Remember it is only when the Arduino has been powered on or a sketch has been running for around 50 days, not a particular part of your sketch's code.

How *approximate* is the value 50 days quoted?

An unsigned long stores data in 32 bits and so has a maximum value of 2^{32} – 1 or 4,294,967,295 milliseconds. Divide that by the number of milliseconds in one day (24 ∗ 60 ∗ 60 ∗ 1000 = 86,400,000); and the result is 49.71026962 days, which works out at 49 days, 17 hours, 2 minutes, and 47.29487424 seconds (plus one solitary millisecond to cause the rollover).

So it appears that the rollover isn't quite as long as 50 days; it's *short* by 7 hours, 22 minutes, and 53.0819328 seconds.

A warning from www.arduino.cc/reference/en/language/ functions/time/millis/:

> *Please note that the return value for* millis() *is an* unsigned long. *Logic errors may occur if a programmer tries to do arithmetic with smaller data types such as* ints. *Even* signed long *may encounter errors as its maximum value is half that of its unsigned counterpart.*

3.5. Interrupts

The Arduino Language allows your sketches to set up functions which will be called automatically, whenever a certain type of event happens.

These are called interrupt service routines, or ISRs, and there are some functions in the Arduino Language which help you in setting up and using these ISRs. These are interrupts() and noInterrupts() to enable and disable interrupts for the whole board and attachInterrupt() and detachInterrupt() to link and unlink your sketch's functions to the interrupt handling system of the ATmega328P.

3.5.1. Function interrupts()

The interrupts() function is defined in the file $ARDINC/Arduino.h as per Listing 3-32.

Listing 3-32. The interrupts() function

```
#define interrupts() sei()
```

Its purpose is to enable global interrupts which is done by calling the sei() function. This itself is defined in $AVRINC/interrupt.h as the assembly language instruction sei, which sets the interrupt flag in the status register, thus enabling interrupts.

3.5.2. Function noInterrupts()

The noInterrupts() function is defined in the file $ARDINC/Arduino.h as per Listing 3-33.

Listing 3-33. The interrupts() function

```
#define noInterrupts() cli()
```

Its purpose is to disable global interrupts which it does by calling the cli() function. This itself is defined in $AVRINC/interrupt.h as the assembly language instruction cli, which clears the interrupt flag in the status register and, thus, disables global interrupts.

3.5.3. Function attachInterrupt()

The code for the attachInterrupt() function is found in the file $ARDINC/WInterrupts.c and also extracted in Listing 3-34.

This function is used to attach an *external interrupt* to a function within a sketch. Each time the interrupt fires, the function will be called. The function *must* be defined as shown in Listing 3-34.

Listing 3-34. A skeleton interrupt handling function

```
void myInterruptRoutine() {
    ...
}
```

The function must not return any value, nor does it receive any parameters. The processing it carries out should be kept as short as possible. If it requires to access any variables in the main part of the sketch, then these *must* be defined as volatile, as follows:

```
volatile int interruptFlag = 0;
```

External interrupts are limited in number on some AVR microcontrollers, and on the ATmega328P family, there are only two of these. The two pins that can be used on the ATmega328P are Arduino pins D2 and D3 only. These pins, corresponding to ATmega328P pins PD2 and PD3, are the physical pins 4 and 5 on the device. They are able to respond to external *stimulus* even if they are configured as OUTPUT. In addition, if they are OUTPUT pins, and a sketch changes the state of the pin, then the change *may* cause the interrupt to be fired.

Arduino pin D2 is connected to the AVR microcontroller's INT0 interrupt, and Arduino pin D3 is connected to the INT1 interrupt. These are high-priority interrupts, only a RESET is higher, and INT0 takes priority if two arrive together.

The documentation states that the function should be called as shown in Listing 3-35.

Listing 3-35. Example usage of attachInterrupt()

```
attachInterrupt(digitalPinToInterrupt(pin), ISR, mode);
```

However, attachInterrupt() takes the first parameter, the interrupt, as an unsigned 8-bit value, but digitalPinToInterrupt() returns a signed value when the pin passed to it is not D2 or D3. In this case, it returns -1 which is defined as NOT_AN_INTERRUPT. Passing -1 to an unsigned will convert it to 255.

This is not a major bug or problem. It's just inconsistent and, as purists would probably say, wrong! (And I tend to agree, this time, with the purists.)

The parameters required are as follows:

- Pin must be either 2 for D2 or 3 for D3 and should be passed via digitalPinToInterrupt() and not passed directly to attachInterrupt() on the ATmega328P-based boards.

- ISR is the name of a void function, taking no parameters, to be called when the interrupt fires.

- mode is the definition of the external stimulus which will cause the interrupt to fire. It can be one of the following:

  - LOW to trigger the interrupt *whenever* the pin is low, which will fire constantly for *as long as the pin is held* LOW. Also, if a sketch sets the pin LOW, then the interrupt routine will keep firing until the pin is taken HIGH again.

  - CHANGE to trigger the interrupt whenever the pin changes value from HIGH to LOW or from LOW to HIGH. This can be in response to an external device or to a sketch changing the state of the pin with digitalWrite(), for example.

  - RISING to trigger the interrupt whenever the pin goes from LOW to HIGH.

  - FALLING to trigger the interrupt whenever the pin goes from HIGH to LOW.

If the function is called with a pin value other than 2 or 3, nothing will happen. It is advisable to use the helper function digitalPinToInterrupt(), because not all boards have the same pins connected to the same external interrupts. Using the helper function in this way ensures that the sketch could be run, with the code unchanged, on other boards with different AVR microcontrollers. Some other wiring changes may be necessary of course.

The helper function digitalPinToInterrupt() is defined in $ARDINST/variants/standard/pins_arduino.h as follows in Listing 3-36.

Listing 3-36. The digitalPinToInterrupt() function

```
#define digitalPinToInterrupt(p)  \
   ((p) == 2 ? 0 : ((p) == 3 ? 1 : NOT_AN_INTERRUPT))
```

It can be seen that passing pin 2 will return zero, passing pin 3 will return one, and any other value will return NOT_AN_INTERRUPT which is -1 – thus, INT0 for pin 2 and INT1 for pin 3 (Arduino pin numbering).

NOT_AN_INTERRUPT is defined in $ARDINC/Arduino.h as

```
#define NOT_AN_INTERRUPT -1
```

An example from the Arduino Reference web site on the use of the attachInterrupt() function is shown in Listing 3-37, while Figure 3-2 shows one possible breadboard circuit to use the sketch. It's a simple circuit to turn an LED on when a switch is pressed and off again when it is released.

Listing 3-37. Example sketch using attachInterrupt()

```
const byte ledPin = 13;
const byte interruptPin = 2;
volatile byte state = LOW;

void setup() {
  pinMode(ledPin, OUTPUT);
  pinMode(interruptPin, INPUT_PULLUP);                     ①
  attachInterrupt(digitalPinToInterrupt(interruptPin),
                  blink, CHANGE);
}
```

```
void loop() {
  digitalWrite(ledPin, state);                              ②
}

void blink() {
  state = !state;                                           ③
}
```

① The pin, which the switch and interrupt are attached to, is pulled HIGH by the internal pullup resistor.

② The main loop simply sets the built-in LED to the current value of state. This will be LOW until the switch is pressed *once*, whereupon it will toggle.

③ The interrupt service routine (ISR) changes the value of state from LOW to HIGH or from HIGH to LOW each time that pin D2 changes its state. The state variable is always the opposite of the state on pin D2.

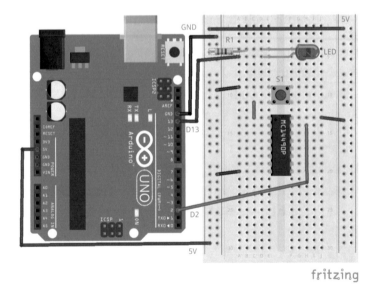

Figure 3-2. *Breadboard layout for the attachInterrupt() sketch*

In Figure 3-2, the resistor R1 is 330 Ohms and is there to limit the current drawn by the LED and is connected from the cathode to ground. The anode (the longest lead) is attached to D13 as the built-in LED is not very bright.

Given that switches bounce quite a lot, I suspected that Listing 3-37 was unlikely to work correctly, and indeed, it did not. The LED's state is at best described as "random," regardless of what you do with the switch.

In theory, when the switch is pressed or held down, it connects D2 to ground. This registers as a change in state for D2, and the ISR fires to change the state variable to HIGH. After the ISR has finished executing, the loop() code then turns the LED on. When the switch is released, the internal pullup resistors pull pin D2 HIGH again, which registers as a change of state, so the ISR executes again and the state variable toggles to LOW. This then results in the loop() code turning off the LED.

In practice, I have tested this code, and it's very difficult to get it to be consistent due to switch bounce. It makes and breaks numerous times before settling to a steady state. I've seen the LED remain lit while the switch was released and go out when it was pressed. This code needs a good debouncing routine; or, if necessary, a couple of extra components need to be added to the breadboard to debounce the switch in hardware.

I used a hardware solution and added the "MC14490 Hex Contact Bounce Eliminator" chip you can see in Figure 3-2. I connected the switch's output pin to pin 1, the Ain pin, on the MC14490, and pin 15, the Aout pin, to Arduino pin D2. Once the circuit was debounced, the code worked perfectly. The fully debounced circuit is shown in Figure 3-2. The MC14490 allows up to six switches to be debounced, and they are very cheap on eBay – plus, they debounce on "make" as well as "break."

Without debouncing of some kind, problems would occur if, for example, the switch changed state only *once*, so the ISR was called. While the ISR was executing, however short a time that was, interrupts were disabled and, thus, *no further interrupts were able to be actioned*. However, if other interrupts were received, a flag bit was set each time to show that one or more interrupts had occurred during the execution of the ISR. When the ISR finishes executing and returns to the main code, one instruction would be executed, and then the ISR would be executed again due to the flag bit being set. Regardless of how many interrupts were received during the first ISR's execution, it would only be executed again *once*.

If state was LOW and the switch was pressed, then the ISR would change the value of state to HIGH, and the LED would come on. However, if any number of bounces, let's say 4, occurred while the ISR was executing, then state *should* have changed four more times, so from HIGH – as currently set by the ISR – to LOW ➤ HIGH ➤ LOW ➤ HIGH, and the LED should remain on.

Unfortunately, those four changes only got recorded as having occurred *at least once*, not how many actually occurred, so the ISR would execute once and change state from HIGH to LOW and the LED would go off even though the button was still being pressed.

In order for the LED to follow the state of the switch, there must be no bouncing, or the ISR must be executed an even number of times, hence the requirement for a good debouncing function, or my solution in hardware, as it's almost impossible for a switch to only bounce an even number of times!

After all that excitement, the source code for the attachInterrupt() function follows in Listing 3-38. As with most other listings, large comment blocks and sections of code have been removed if they are not relevant to the ATmega328P devices. I have also wrapped some of the longer code lines to fit on the page.

Listing 3-38. The attachInterrupt() function

```
void attachInterrupt(uint8_t interruptNum,
                     void (*userFunc)(void), int mode) {
  if(interruptNum < EXTERNAL_NUM_INTERRUPTS) {      ①

    intFunc[interruptNum] = userFunc;               ②
```

```
switch (interruptNum) {

...

case 0:                                        ③

#if defined(EICRA) && defined(ISC00) && defined(EIMSK)
    EICRA = (EICRA &
            ~((1 << ISC00) | (1 << ISC01))) |
            (mode << ISC00);

    EIMSK |= (1 << INT0);

    ...

#endif
    break;

case 1:    ④
#if defined(EICRA) && defined(ISC10) && \
    defined(ISC11) && defined(EIMSK)

    EICRA = (EICRA &
            ~((1 << ISC10) | (1 << ISC11))) |
            (mode << ISC10);

    EIMSK |= (1 << INT1);
#endif

    ...

    break;

    ...

  }   // End switch (interruptNum)
 }      // End if(interruptNum ...
}
```

① EXTERNAL_NUM_INTERRUPTS is defined as 2, in $ARDINC/wiring_private.h, and is the total number of external interrupts available on an ATmega328P. You should note that interruptNum is unsigned here; however, digitalPinToInterrupt() can, if passed an invalid pin number, return NOT_AN_INTERRUPT which is *negative*. However, this code will still work correctly as NOT_AN_INTERRUPT converts to 255 when passed as -1 to an unsigned variable.

② The supplied pointer to the interrupt function in the sketch is saved in a table. There are EXTERNAL_NUM_INTERRUPTS slots in the table.

③ This sets up the INT0 external interrupt and enables it.

④ This sets up the INT1 external interrupt and enables it.

The attachInterrupt() function is quite simple in operation. It saves the sketch's function addresses in a table, set up for just this reason, and then, depending on the interrupt requested, sets the bits in the EICRA and EIMSK registers so that the interrupt will fire on the appropriate stimulus.

You should be aware that the functions passed to attachInterrupt() are *not* interrupt service routines. They are merely a function that will be called from the actual ISR. The real ISR is set up as per the source code in Listing 3-39, extracted from the file $ARDINC/WInterrupts.c.

Listing 3-39. The real ISR for attachInterrupt()

```
#define IMPLEMENT_ISR(vect, interrupt) \
  ISR(vect) { \
    intFunc[interrupt](); \
  }
```

```
IMPLEMENT_ISR(INT0_vect, EXTERNAL_INT_0)
IMPLEMENT_ISR(INT1_vect, EXTERNAL_INT_1)
```

This code connects the function INT0_vect with INT0 and INT1_vect with INT1. It is *these* two functions that get called when the appropriate interrupt fires. The brief snippet of code in Listing 3-40 is that generated for the INT0 interrupt handler.

Listing 3-40. ISR for the INT0 interrupt

```
ISR(INT0_vect) {
    intFunc[0]();        ①
}
```

  ①   This one line accesses the user-supplied ISR
     function in the table and executes it.

The documentation for attachInterrupt() at www.arduino.cc/ reference/en/language/functions/external-interrupts/attachinterrupt/ on the Arduino Reference web site has the following to say:

> *The first parameter to attachInterrupt is an interrupt number. Normally you should use* digitalPinToInterrupt(pin) *to translate the actual digital pin to the specific interrupt number. For example, if you connect to pin 3, use* digitalPinToInterrupt(3) *as the first parameter to* attachInterrupt().

> *Inside the attached function,* delay() *won't work and the value returned by* millis() *will not increment as* millis() *relies on interrupts to count, so it will never increment inside an ISR. Since* delay() *also requires interrupts to work, it will not work if called inside an ISR – because interrupts are disabled while processing an ISR.*

> *The* micros() *function will work initially, but will start behaving erratically after 1-2 milliseconds.*

However, the `delayMicroseconds()` *function does not use any counter/interrupt, so it will work as normal.*

Serial data received while in the function may be lost.

You should declare as `volatile` *any variables that you modify within the attached function. Typically global variables are used to pass data between an ISR and the main program. To make sure variables shared between an ISR and the main program are updated correctly, declare them as volatile.*

Generally, an ISR should be as short and fast as possible. If your sketch uses multiple ISRs, only one can run at a time, other interrupts will be executed after the current one finishes in an order that depends on the priority they have.

Regarding the potential loss of serial data received, you should be aware that serial data is copied from the USART to the serial receive buffer under control of an interrupt handler. Obviously, when processing your interrupt function, interrupts are off, but the USART still runs in the background as it is not controlled by the main CPU. There is room in the USART for 2 bytes only, so if your interrupt function takes too long and data are being received by the USART, it will buffer up the first 2 bytes and then suffer a buffer overrun error. Subsequent bytes received will be lost.

You must always remember the following when dealing with interrupts either in your own interrupt functions or in an ISR to handle interrupts that the Arduino Language doesn't:

- Keep the ISR or interrupt functions physically as short as possible. If you must do work as a result of an interrupt, use the ISR or function to simply set a flag, a variable value or similar, and have the main `loop()` code check it and execute the desired actions.

- Do not call `delay()` or any of the `Serial.print()` functions from inside an ISR or interrupt function. That way, dragons lie!

- All variables you wish to share with the main code should be declared volatile and, if necessary, when being accessed, may require to be wrapped in a "critical section" which means calling noInterrupts() before accessing the shared data and calling interrupts() afterwards This, obviously, is required within the main code, not in the interrupt function.

- Finally, don't enable interrupts within an ISR or interrupt function *unless* you *really, really* know what you are doing.

3.5.4. Function detachInterrupt()

The code for the detachInterrupt() function is found in the file $ARDINC/WInterrupts.c and also in Listing 3-41.

This function detaches an interrupt function, in a sketch, from an external interrupt. The function will have been previously attached to the interrupt by a call to the attachInterrupt() function. There isn't always a need to call detachInterrupt() unless your sketch is finished with the ability to process the appropriate interrupt and wants to prevent any further processing of the interrupt function from taking place.

This function works by disabling the INT0 and/or INT1 interrupt bits in the EIMSK register and blanks out the entry for the function in the function pointer table populated in attachInterrupt().

The source code for detachInterrupt() is shown in Listing 3-41, and, as with previous listings, sections of the source that are not relevant to the standard Arduino boards have been omitted for clarity.

Listing 3-41. The detachInterrupt() function

```
void detachInterrupt(uint8_t interruptNum) {

  if(interruptNum < EXTERNAL_NUM_INTERRUPTS) {        ①

    switch (interruptNum) {
        ...
    case 0:
        EIMSK &= ~(1 << INT0);                        ②
        break;

    case 1:
        EIMSK &= ~(1 << INT1);                        ③
        break;
        ...
    }

    intFunc[interruptNum] = nothing;                  ④
  }
}
```

① Passing an invalid pin number to digitalPinToInterrupt() will return NOT_AN_INTERRUPT (-1) which is a signed value, as previously discussed. The detachInterrupt() function will still act correctly in that case and do nothing at all.

② Disable the INT0 interrupt handler from Arduino pin D2.

③ Disable the INT1 interrupt handler from Arduino pin D3.

④ The sketch's interrupt function pointer is removed from the array of interrupt functions.

The value nothing is defined in $ARDINC/WInterrupts.c as shown in Listing 3-42 and defines an empty interrupt function so that its address can be used in the interrupt function table as an "empty" value. NULL *could* have been used, but in that case detaching an interrupt function would have caused the NULL pointer to be dereferenced if a subsequent interrupt occurred on the appropriate pin. Dereferencing a NULL pointer is a bad thing to do!

Listing 3-42. The nothing() interrupt handler function

```
static void nothing(void) {
}
```

The documentation for detachInterrupt() at www.arduino.cc/reference/en/language/functions/external-interrupts/detachinterrupt/*incorrectly* states that this function should be called as

```
detachInterrupt();
```

However, this is a bug, as it should be called as follows:

```
detachInterrupt(interruptNumber);
```

This is where the interruptNumber parameter is the one returned from digitalPinToInterrupt() when called previously when calling attachInterrupt() for this pin.

3.6. Bits and Bobs

This section deals with a few "bits and bobs" – macros which allow you to do bit handling at the lowest level.

3.6.1. Macro bit()

The bit() macro is defined in the file $ARDINC/Arduino.h as follows:

```
#define bit(b) (1UL << (b))
```

It returns the value of 2^b where b is the bit number. For example, calling bit(5) will return 32 as 2^5 is 32. You will hopefully notice that the returned value is an unsigned long from the initializer 1UL, so there are 32 bits to play with, but remember to number the bits from 0 through to 31.

Listing 3-43 shows an example of how to use the bit() macro.

Listing 3-43. Example usage of the bit() macro

```
...
Serial.print("2 to the power 10 is: ");
Serial.println(bit(10));
...
```

This will display "2 to the power 10 is: 1024" on the Serial Monitor.

Table 3-3 lists the powers of two corresponding to an unsigned long variable, and these are the values that the bit() function will return.

Table 3-3. *Bits and their values*

Bit	Value Returned	Bit	Value Returned	Bit	Value Returned	Bit	Value Returned
0	1	1	2	2	4	3	8
4	16	5	32	6	64	7	128
8	256	9	512	10	1,024	11	2,048
12	4,096	13	8,192	14	16,384	15	32,768
16	65,536	17	131,072	18	262,144	19	524,288
20	1,048,576	21	2,097,152	22	4,194,304	23	8,388,608
24	16,777,216	25	33,554,432	26	67,108,864	27	143,217,728
28	268,435,456	29	536,870,912	30	1,073,741,824	31	2,147,483,648

3.6.2. Macro `bitClear()`

The `bitClear()` macro is defined in the file `$ARDINC/Arduino.h` as follows:

```
#define bitClear(value, bit) ((value) &= ~(1UL << (bit)))
```

The macro simply clears the requested `bit`, in the `value` passed, to zero and returns the resulting new `value`. For example, you could lowercase a character by clearing bit 5, as shown in Listing 3-44.

Listing 3-44. Example usage of the bitClear() macro

```
char lowerCaseA = bitClear('A', 5);
```

However, there are probably much better ways to achieve this!

3.6.3. Macro `bitRead()`

The `bitRead()` macro is defined in the file `$ARDINC/Arduino.h` as follows:

```
#define bitRead(value, bit) (((value) >> (bit)) & 0x01)
```

This macro returns a one or a zero depending on the state of the bit requested in the value passed. Listing 3-45 continues the rather absurd example from the preceding text.

Listing 3-45. Example usage of the bitRead() macro

```
char upperCaseA = 'A';
char lowerCaseA;

if (bitRead(upperCaseA, 5)) {
    lowerCaseA = bitClear('A', 5);
}
```

3.6.4. Macro `bitSet()`

The `bitSet()` macro is defined in the file `$ARDINC/Arduino.h` as follows:

```
#define bitSet(value, bit) ((value) |= (1UL << (bit)))
```

This macro can be called to set a specific bit in a variable or value to a one. Listing 3-46 is an example of the use of `bitSet()`.

Listing 3-46. Example usage of the bitSet() macro

```
char lowerCaseA = 'a';
char upperCaseA;

upperCaseA = bitSet(lowerCaseA, 5);
```

3.6.5. Macro `bitWrite()`

The `bitWrite()` macro is defined in the file `$ARDINC/Arduino.h` as follows:

```
#define bitWrite(value, bit, bitvalue) \
    (bitvalue ? bitSet(value, bit) : bitClear(value, bit))
```

The purpose of this macro is to call either `bitSet()` or `bitClear()` for the appropriate bit, in a value or variable, depending on whether it is to be set to a one or a zero. An example is shown in Listing 3-47.

Listing 3-47. Example usage of the bitWrite() macro

```
char someCharacter = 'H';

char lowerCase = bitWrite(someCharacter, 5, 0);
char upperCase = bitWrite(someCharacter, 5, 1);
```

3.6.6. Macro `highByte()`

The `highByte()` macro is defined in the file `$ARDINC/Arduino.h` as follows:

```
#define highByte(w) ((uint8_t) ((w) >> 8))
```

This macro returns the value in the higher 8 bits of a value or variable. It returns a `uint8_t` which is guaranteed to be an unsigned, 8-bit value. Listing 3-48 shows how to use the `highByte()` macro to extract the top 8 bits from the value 513.

Listing 3-48. Example usage of the highByte() macro

```
Serial.println(highByte(513));
```

The code in Listing 3-48 will print "2" on the Serial Monitor. $513_{decimal}$ is 201_{hex} which converts to $0000\ 0010\ 0000\ 0001_{binary}$. The high 8 bits are $0000\ 0010_{binary}$ which is 2 in decimal.

3.6.7. Macro `lowByte()`

The `lowByte()` macro is defined in the file `$ARDINC/Arduino.h` as follows:

```
#define lowByte(w) ((uint8_t) ((w) & 0xff))
```

This macro returns the value in the lower 8 bits of a value or variable. It returns a `uint8_t` which is guaranteed to be an unsigned, 8-bit value. Listing 3-49 shows how to use the `lowByte()` macro to extract the bottom 8 bits from the value 513.

Listing 3-49. Example usage of the lowByte() macro

```
Serial.println(lowByte(513));
```

The code in Listing 3-49 will print "1" on the Serial Monitor. $513_{decimal}$ is 201_{hex} which converts to $0000\ 0010\ 0000\ 0001_{binary}$. The low 8 bits are $0000\ 0001_{binary}$ which is 2 in decimal.

3.6.8. Macro sbi()

The sbi() macro is defined in the file $ARDINC/wiring_private.h as
follows:

```
#ifndef sbi
#define sbi(sfr, bit) (_SFR_BYTE(sfr) |= _BV(bit))
#endif
```

In order to use this macro, you must include the header file wiring_
private.h, as shown in Listing 3-50.

The macro sets the requested bit, in the *register*, to one. You cannot call
this with a value or a variable; it *must* be one of the lowest 32 I/O registers,
as defined in the file $AVRINC/iom328p.h which is included automatically
for you by $AVRINC/io.h, itself included by $ARDINC/Arduino.h.

For example, to ensure that Arduino pin D13, the built-in LED pin, was
set to OUTPUT, but without using pinMode(), you would do this in a sketch
as shown in Listing 3-50, given that Arduino pin D13 is AVR pin PB5 which
corresponds to bit PORTB5 in register PORTB.

Listing 3-50. Example sbi() macro call

```
#include <wiring_private.h>

void setup() {
    // Avoid pinMode() and make D13 OUTPUT.
    sbi(PORTB, PORTB5);
    ...
}
```

⚠ The two macros described here, the preceding `sbi()` and the following `cbi()`, should *probably* not be used as they may fail to do what is required in some circumstances. This is because the ATmega328P has some of its I/O registers outside the range of addresses that these two instructions can access. Both `sbi()` and `cbi()` can only access the lowest 32 of the various I/O registers in the ATmega328P.

You *might* get away with it, but then again, you might not. You have been warned. It is especially galling that the compiler doesn't give any error messages if you do try to access a register that is out of range. Be careful.

3.6.9. Macro `cbi()`

The `cbi()` macro is defined in the file $ARDINC/wiring_private.h as follows:

```
#ifndef cbi
#define cbi(sfr, bit) (_SFR_BYTE(sfr) &= ~_BV(bit))
#endif
```

In order to use this macro, you must include the header file, as shown in Listing 3-51.

The macro clears the requested bit, in the *register*, to zero. You cannot call this with a value or a variable; it *must* be a register, as defined in the file $AVRINC/iom328p.h which is included automatically for you by $AVRINC/io.h, itself included by $ARDINC/Arduino.h.

For example, to ensure that Arduino pin D13, the built-in LED pin, was set to INPUT, but without using pinMode(), you would do this as shown in Listing 3-51, given that Arduino pin D13 is actually AVR pin PB5 which is PORTB5 on register PORTB.

Listing 3-51. Example cbi() macro call

```
#include <wiring_private.h>

void setup() {
    // Avoid pinMode() and make D13 INPUT.
    cbi(PORTB, PORTB5);

    ...
}
```

The definition of PORTB5 (and others from PORTB0 to PORTB7) allows you to refer to the individual bits in the PORTB register. Similar definitions exist for PORTC and PORTD, as well as the three DDRx and PINx registers. All the bits in all the registers are predefined for you when you compile a sketch. This means that you don't have to use the Arduino Language all the time, especially if there is an ATmega328P feature that isn't available from the Arduino Language. The Analogue Comparator, for example, as discussed in Chapter 9, must be accessed using the registers directly.

CHAPTER 4

Arduino Classes

This chapter investigates the various C++ `classes` supplied as part of the Arduino Language and which help, in most cases, to make the programmer's life easier when using features of the Arduino board (and the ATmega328P) such as the Serial interface.

ℹ️ In the remainder of this chapter, I will not be showing *all* the source code for the various Arduino classes. Some of these classes have a large amount of code, and the book would become very large and unwieldy as a result. I will be explaining the important parts though.

4.1. The `Print` Class

The `Print` class is found in the two files `Print.h` and `Print.cpp` both located in the `$ARDINC` directory. A tutorial on implementing your own classes which inherit from `Print` can be found online at `https://playground.arduino.cc/Code/Printclass/`.

The `Print` class will be inherited by descendant classes and provides the ability to call `print()` and `println()` in those classes. It is used by, among others, the `Serial` interface and the `Printable` class. By far, the vast majority of the functions exposed by this class boil down to internal calls to a `virtual` function named `write()` which has to be provided by the descendant class as it is declared `pure virtual` in the `Print` class.

© Norman Dunbar 2020
N. Dunbar, *Arduino Software Internals*, https://doi.org/10.1007/978-1-4842-5790-6_4

Descendants of the `Print` class inherit from `Print` the ability to call `print()` and `println()` to "print" some information from within the descendant class. The `Print` class allows the following data types to be "printed" using `print()`:

- `String` class variables
- Data stored in flash memory
- `char` variables and `char` arrays
- `int` variables
- `long` variables
- `double` variables
- Class variables descending from the `Printable` class

The `println()` function allows all of the preceding data types, plus `void` parameters, which simply means a call to `println()` without passing any parameters. This simply "prints" a linefeed to the interface. A linefeed in this case is a Windows-style linefeed consisting of a carriage return and a linefeed – ASCII characters 13 and 10.

ℹ️ I use "prints" in quotes as the descendant class in the hierarchy will output the bytes as appropriate. The `Serial` interface, for example, "prints" bytes to a buffer which will then be sent to the USART for transmission, while the `LiquidCrystal` library class displays the characters on screen. Other interfaces will most likely have their own manner of "printing," which could mean sending the data down the network cable to the Internet, to a file on an SD card and so on.

Listing 4-1 shows the four `virtual` functions defined in the Print class.

Listing 4-1. The Print class virtual functions

```
virtual size_t write(uint8_t) = 0;                              ①

virtual size_t write(const uint8_t *buffer, size_t size);       ②
virtual int availableForWrite() { return 0; }                   ③
virtual void flush() { /* Empty */ }                            ④
```

① Only the write(uint8_t) is a pure virtual
    function and, as such, must be implemented
    by a descendant class. In the file $ARDINC/
    HardwareSerial.cpp, for example, the
    write(uint8_t) function sends a single unsigned
    char to the USART. The Serial interface descends
    from the Stream class, which itself descends from
    the Print class; and as long as at least one class
    in the hierarchy implements the write(uint8_t)
    function, the code should compile.

② If required, descendant classes may implement
    this function which should be called to provide a
    manner of "printing" entire char arrays. The Print
    class provides a default implementation of this
    function, which simply sends each character in the
    array to the write(uint8_t) function.

③ This function defaults to returning zero to indicate
    that a single call to write() may block. This
    obviously depends on the interface in use. The
    descendant classes may wish to reimplement
    this function if, for example, they use some form
    of buffering which helps prevent blocking. Other

non-zero values indicate that the call to write()
may not block. The Serial class has done this in
file $ARDINC/HardwareSerial.cpp as it buffers data
for transmission, and also for receipt, and uses
interrupts to transmit and receive data from/to the
buffers.

④ The flush() function is provided for backward
compatibility with older versions of the Arduino
Language. In the current version, 1.8.5, it is an
empty function which does nothing. Classes may
reimplement this function if necessary – as the
Serial class does.

4.1.1. Class Members

The Print class defines the following public members. They are used
when outputting numeric data in bases other than the default, base 10.

- BIN – Defined as the value 2 and used when outputting
data in binary, or base 2

- OCT – Defined as the value 8 and used when outputting
data in octal, or base 8

- DEC – Defined as the value 10 and used when
outputting data in decimal, or base 10, the default

- HEX – Defined as the value 16 and used when
outputting data in hexadecimal, or base 16

The following functions are exposed by this class:

- `Print()` – Constructor. This does very little other than setting the error flag to show that, so far, no errors have occurred.

- `size_t print()` – Sends data to the output without a trailing newline. It can be used to "print" many different data types.

- `size_t println()` – Similar to `print()` but terminates the output with a Windows-style carriage return and linefeed.

- `int getWriteError()` – Returns any error code from a `write()` function call.

- `void clearWriteError()` – Clears any existing write error code.

- `size_t write(const char *str)` – May be overridden by descendant classes. This is the default function to "print" a character array.

- `size_t write(const uint8_t *buffer, size_t size)` – May be overridden by descendant classes. This function "prints" an array, of known size, of unsigned characters.

- `size_t write(const char *buffer, size_t size)` – Calls the `write(const uint8_t *buffer, size_t size)` function to "print" a signed character array.

- `int availableForWrite()` – May be overridden by descendant classes. This function returns zero if the descendent class's `write()` function will, or may, block.

- void flush() – May be overridden by descendant classes. This function flushes the output buffer to ensure that all data are correctly written.

If your own class which inherits from the Print class has defined, as it must, the pure virtual function write(), then your class can send bytes to whatever it needs to. If your class header file includes

using Print::write;

it will be also able to use the Print class's functions which write other data types. As these all call down to the virtual write() function eventually, it will call your class's own write() function, so you get the ability to "print" data types other than a single unsigned char, for free.

4.1.2. Using the Print Class

An example of the use of the Print class is in the library for the LiquidCrystal display as supplied with the Arduino IDE. The library can be found in the two files LiquidCrystal.h and LiquidCrystal.cpp located in the $ARDBASE/libraries/LiquidCrystal/src directory. The following description includes only the relevant parts of the code – those which show the use of the Print class by the LiquidCrystal library.

In the header file LiquidCrystal.h, we see the code shown in Listing 4-2.

Listing 4-2. LiquidCrystal.h

```
#include <Print.h>                          ①

    ...

class LiquidCrystal : public Print {        ②
public:
    ...
    virtual size_t write(uint8_t);          ③
    ...
    using Print::write;                      ④
    ...
}
```

①   When writing a library, *you* are responsible for including all the required header files. The IDE doesn't do this for you anymore! The `Print.h` file is required as we are inheriting from the `Print` class.

②   The `LiquidCrystal` class inherits from the `Print` class. This gives objects of the `LiquidCrystal` class the ability to call `print()` and `println()` which are member functions in the base class, `Print`.

③   Descendant classes, inheriting from `Print`, must define the `write()` function as it is declared as `pure virtual` in the `Print` class.

④   Descendant classes don't need to redefine all the other `write()` functions which "print" different data types if they use this line of code. This gives access to all the functions in the `Print` class, but each will call out to the descendant class's `write()` function.

We now need to look into the LiquidCrystal.cpp file to see how this class has implemented the requirements of the Print class. Listings 4-3, 4-4, and 4-5 show the relevant extracts from the source code.

Listing 4-3. LiquidCrystal's write() function

```
inline size_t LiquidCrystal::write(uint8_t value) {
  send(value, HIGH);
  return 1; // assume success
}
```

This is the function that all of Print's descendant classes must implement themselves. In the LiquidCrystal class, this simply makes a call to the send() function – see Listing 4-4, which is declared as private in the header file LiquidCrystal.h. I note from the comment that this function always assumes that nothing went wrong. Hmmm.

Listing 4-4. LiquidCrystal's send() function

```
void LiquidCrystal::send(uint8_t value, uint8_t mode) {
  digitalWrite(_rs_pin,  mode);

  // if there is a RW pin indicated, set it low to Write
  if (_rw_pin != 255) {
    digitalWrite(_rw_pin,  LOW);
  }

  if (_displayfunction & LCD_8BITMODE) {
    write8bits(value);
  } else {
    write4bits(value>>4);
    write4bits(value);
  }
}
```

If we ignore the code that's setting up the pins to enable the sketch to write to the display, we eventually end up at the calls to `write8bits()` and `write4bits()`. LiquidCrystal displays can be configured to receive 8 bits of data from the Arduino, or just 4 bits – some displays only cope with 4 bits. For this explanation, I shall concentrate on 8-bit displays – the main difference being that 4-bit displays need two data writes to receive a character, while 8-bit displays get the whole character in one write.

We can easily see from Listing 4-4 that the `send()` function sets the display to receive data and then calls out to the `write8bits()` function, passing over the data which is to be displayed. Listing 4-5 shows the full code for the called `write8bits()` function.

Listing 4-5. LiquidCrystal's write8bits() function

```
void LiquidCrystal::write8bits(uint8_t value) {
  for (int i = 0; i < 8; i++) {
    digitalWrite(_data_pins[i], (value >> i) & 0x01);
  }

  pulseEnable();
}
```

That's all there is to it! The passed data, in parameter `value`, is used to set the bits on the eight data lines for the display. (Other displays can use the I^{2}C interface which uses a lot fewer data lines; see the LiquidCrystal_I2C library for details.)

The preceding code sets a data pin `HIGH` if the corresponding bit in `value` is a 1_{binary} and `LOW` if it is a 0_{binary}. Once all eight data pins have been set correctly, `pulseEnable()` is called to, ahem, pulse the enable pin for the display and latch the data into the display whereupon it will be "printed" to the screen.

The LiquidCrystal library provides an example. Go to File ➤ Examples ➤ LiquidCrystal ➤ HelloWorld in the Arduino IDE to load the example sketch which is shown, in full but minus all comments, in Listing 4-6

and also online with circuit diagrams at www.arduino.cc/en/Tutorial/
HelloWorld.

Listing 4-6. The HelloWorld example sketch

```
#include <LiquidCrystal.h>                        ①

const int rs = 12, en = 11,
          d4 = 5, d5 = 4,
          d6 = 3, d7 = 2;                          ②

LiquidCrystal lcd(rs, en, d4, d5, d6, d7);         ③

void setup() {
  lcd.begin(16, 2);                                ④
  lcd.print("hello, world!");                      ⑤
}

void loop() {
  lcd.setCursor(0, 1);                             ⑥
  lcd.print(millis() / 1000);
}
```

   ①   We must include the library's header file; normally
this is done with the Sketch ➤ Include Library ➤
LiquidCrystal menu option. In my case, this line was
included twice by the menu. I removed the extra line.

   ②   Here, some constants are defined for the various
pins that the LiquidCrystal objects require. In this
case, we are only using 4 bits of data, not 8. The
rs pin is the display's register select pin, en is the
enable pin – used to latch data onto the display –
and d4, d5, d6, and d7 are the four data pins.

③ An object of type LiquidCrystal is declared and initialized here. The various pins to be used are passed in the constructor. On return, lcd is our object through which we can manipulate the display.

④ The display is further initialized to two rows of 16 characters. Other options are available. My own display has four rows.

⑤ This is what we have been working up to. The lcd object can call the Print class's print() function. Within the Print class, the function which prints an array of char will be called, and that will pass each character to the LiquidCrystal class's write() function. The characters in the array are then printed to the display using the code in Listings 4-3 through 4-5.

⑥ The loop() code just sets the cursor to the start of the second line (rows number from 0) and uses the print() function to print the number of millis() that have passed since the sketch began. Here the value to be printed is an unsigned long, and within the Print base class, that call will work its way down to the LiquidCrystal class's write() function in the manner described earlier.

4.2. The **Printable** Class

The Printable class can be used by your own classes, using inheritance, so that they can print themselves using the Print class functions print() and println(), to interfaces which themselves inherit from the Print class, for example, the Serial interface. This is different from calling the print() or println() function as we saw in the previous chapter, for example

```
lcd.print(12345);
```

where you pass a data value to be "printed." The Printable class allows the entire object to be "printed" with a single call:

```
Serial.print(aPerson);
```

In this case, the PrintTo() function would handle the streaming of the aPerson object's data. For example, it might print the name, address, and phone numbers of the specific person. We are, of course, assuming that aPerson is an object of some class that describes a person.

The Printable class has no implementation, or cpp file, only the header file, $ARDINC/Printable.h, which can be seen in Listing 4-7 and which is all that is required to make it possible for your own classes to print themselves. The code in Listing 4-7 is the entire source code of the header file, but as usual, I have removed a few comments for brevity.

Listing 4-7. The Printable.h header file

```
#ifndef Printable_h
#define Printable_h

#include <stdlib.h>

class Print;                              ①

class Printable
{
  public:
    virtual size_t printTo(Print& p) const = 0;    ②
};

#endif
```

① This is a forward declaration of the `Print` class. It can be done without including the `Print.h` header file as we don't need anything from it within this file, other than the fact that it exists and is a class named `Print`. In the case being examined here, the `print.h` header isn't that large, so the time saved by not having to read it in is insignificant. Other class header files may not be so forgiving.

② The `Printable` class cannot be instantiated by itself as it has only pure virtual members. It must be used as an ancestor class, and the descendant classes must implement the `printTo()` function. To use the `Printable` class, therefore, your classes have to

- Include the `Printable.h` header file

- Inherit from the `Printable` class

- Implement a function named `printTo` which takes a reference to a `Print` class and returns a `size_t` value which is the number of bytes printed

That's all there is to it. Your class can now be printed over the `Serial` interface, or similar, provided that the specific interface inherits from the `Print` class.

4.2.1. An Example **Printable** Class

The source code shown in Listings 4-8 and 4-9 is that of a very simple class which has been set up to allow itself to be sent over, for example, the `Serial` interface. For a more useful, but more complicated, example, have a look at the files `$ARDINC/IPAddress.h` and `$ARDINC/IPAddress.cpp` which are used by Arduino boards that have, for example, Ethernet interfaces built in.

Listing 4-8 is the header file `Person.h`, for a simple class named Person, which has `Printable` as an ancestor class. You can clearly see that it has included the `Printable.h` header file, as required, and declares a public member function `printTo()`.

Listing 4-8. Printable example class header

```
#ifndef Person_h
#define Person_h

#include <Printable.h>

class Person : public Printable {

    private:
        String _foreName;
        String _surName;

    public:
        // Constructors:
        Person(const String foreName, const String surName);
        Person(const char *foreName, const char *surName);
        Person();

        // Printable requires this:
        virtual size_t printTo(Print& p) const;
};

#endif // Person_h
```

I've given this simple class a set of three constructors so that objects of this type can be instantiated by passing char arrays or String values. If nothing is passed, then a default will be used. This is explained in Listing 4-9 which shows the file `Person.cpp` which implements the new class. It simply copies any supplied parameters, String or char arrays, into the class member Strings and implements the code to facilitate the mandatory printTo() function. If nothing is passed to the constructor, you will get my name as the default.

Listing 4-9. Printable example class implementation

```
#include <Print.h>
#include "Person.h"

// Constructor 1:
Person::Person(const String foreName, const String surName) :
    _foreName(foreName),
    _surName(surName) {
};

// Constructor 2:
Person::Person(const char *foreName, const char *surName) :
    _foreName(String(foreName)),
    _surName(String(surName)) {
};

// Constructor 3:
Person::Person() :
    _foreName("Norman"),
    _surName("Dunbar") {
};
// This is for Printable:
size_t Person::printTo(Print &p) const {
    size_t bytesPrinted = 0;

    bytesPrinted += p.print(_surName);
    bytesPrinted += p.print(", ");
    bytesPrinted += p.print(_foreName);

    return bytesPrinted;
}
```

💡 In the preceding constructors, the initialization of the member variables might look strange; however, I'm reliably informed by those in the know about C++ that this is deemed the correct way to initialize member variables. Who am I to argue?

We can see from the preceding code that the `printTo()` function accepts a `Print` class object, which is required to be a descendant of a `Print` class, and calls its `print()` function three times passing over data from the `private` members of the class. The function returns the number of bytes printed, which is a requirement.

Now that the class has been defined, it can be used as shown in Listing 4-10. This is a brief sketch showing how `Printable` class descendants can stream themselves over the interface to any `Print` class descendants. In this case, I'm using the `Serial` interface. In the example in Listing 4-10, the `Serial` object is passed to the `me` and `wife` objects' `printTo()` function as the `Print` class descendant. C++ can at times mess with your head! This line of code

```
Serial.println(me);
```

is effectively equivalent to this line:

```
me.printTo(Serial);
```

However, the first version is how it should be done.

Listing 4-10. Printable example class usage

```
#include "Person.h"

// Declare a class object.
Person me;
Person wife("Alison",  "Dunbar");
```

```
void setup() {
    Serial.begin(9600);
}

void loop() {
    Serial.print(me);
    Serial.print(" + ");
    Serial.println(wife);
    delay(1000);
}
```

If you upload the preceding code to an Arduino board, then you should see "Dunbar, Norman + Dunbar, Alison" written back to the serial monitor – over and over again. You can, if you wish, substitute your own name in the code shown in Listing 4-10.

It is not mandatory to use `Serial`. Any ancestor of a `Print` class will suffice. In the previous discussions, we saw how the LiquidCrystal library descended from `Print` which means that the `me` and `wife` objects in the preceding code could be passed to a `LiquidCrystal` class object, such as `lcd`.

4.3. The **Stream** Class

The `Stream` class is the base class which defines the data reading functions (e.g., `Serial.read()`). `Stream` supplies the *reading* features complementary to the `Print` class's *writing* features.

The `Stream` class, like `Printable`, is designed to be used as a base class and allows character, or binary, "streaming" of data into a descendant class's variables and so on. It cannot be instantiated on its own. The descendent classes are expected to implement the three pure virtual functions detailed in Listing 4-11.

Listing 4-11. The Stream class's pure virtual functions

```
virtual int available() = 0;      ①
virtual int read() = 0;           ②
virtual int peek() = 0;           ③
```

① The available() function is required to inform the descendant class, Serial, for example, that the underlying stream has data available to be read. The function returns the number of bytes that have already been *received* by the underlying stream but which have yet to be *read* by the sketch.

② The read() function is implemented to allow the descendant classes to physically read the available data. This function will remove the data it reads from the input stream.

③ The peek() function is implemented to allow the descendant classes to take a sneaky peek at the available data, but in a nondestructive manner. The data may subsequently be read by the read() function.

As Stream descends from the Print class, any class that inherits from Stream also inherits the features of the Print class. This will require the descendant class to implement the pure virtual function write() from the Print class, in addition to the requirements of the Stream class.

Examples of Arduino classes which descend from Stream are as follows:

- HardwareSerial – The standard Serial interface.

- USBAPI – Serial interface for the Leonardo boards. These use USB serial as opposed to the ATmega328P's TX and RX pins.

- Client – Part of the software for the various Ethernet shields.

- Ethernet – A networking library.

- SD – A third-party library for accessing SD cards.

4.3.1. Class Members

Listing 4-12 shows how the Stream class defines the LookaheadEnum enumeration, which is used in some of the following functions, when scanning for numeric values.

Listing 4-12. The Stream class's LookaheadMode enumeration

```
enum LookaheadMode{
    // All invalid characters are ignored.
    SKIP_ALL,

    // Nothing is skipped, and the stream is not
    // touched unless the first waiting character is valid.
    SKIP_NONE,

    // Only tabs, spaces, line feeds & carriage returns
    //are skipped.
    SKIP_WHITESPACE
};
```

The class also defines the following public functions, in addition to the definitions and functions exposed by the Print class, from which it inherits.

- Stream() – Constructor. It sets the default timeout to one second (1000 milliseconds). The timeout is used in many of the following functions to limit the scanning process – to prevent code hangups or blocking if the data in the stream, for example, has not fully arrived.

- `void setTimeout(unsigned long timeout)` – Sets the maximum timeout, in milliseconds, to wait for stream data.

- `unsigned long getTimeout(void)` – Returns the current timeout for the stream.

- `int available()` – This function must be overridden in descendant classes. It returns the number of bytes which have been received by the stream, but which have yet to be read by the sketch.

The following Stream functions return TRUE if the required target was found and FALSE if not, or if the scan timed out. The scan is destructive in that it removes data from the stream's internal buffers while scanning:

- `bool find(char *target)`
- `bool find(uint8_t *target)`
- `bool find(char *target, size_t length)`
- `bool find(uint8_t *target, size_t length)`
- `bool find(char target)`

The following Stream functions return TRUE if the required target was found and FALSE if not, or if the scan timed out. The scan is destructive in that it removes data from the stream's internal buffers while scanning; however, these scans end at the first occurrence of the terminator string. Characters beyond the terminating string will be safe, for now!

- `bool findUntil(char *target, char *terminator)`
- `bool findUntil(uint8_t *target, char *terminator)`
- `bool findUntil(char *target, size_t targetLen, char *terminate, size_t termLen)`

- `bool findUntil(uint8_t *target, size_t targetLen, char *terminate, size_t termLen)`

The following `Stream` functions return numeric values from the stream:

- `long parseInt(LookaheadMode lookahead = SKIP_ALL, char ignore = NO_IGNORE_CHAR)`
- `float parseFloat(LookaheadMode lookahead = SKIP_ALL, char ignore = NO_IGNORE_CHAR)`

The following `Stream` functions return -1 if there was a timeout, or they return a single character from the stream. Both of these functions are required to be implemented in a `Stream`'s descendant class:

- `int peek()` – Returns characters from the stream without removing them from the internal buffer for the stream.
- `int read()` – Returns characters from the stream and removes them from the internal buffer for the stream.

The following functions return the number of characters read from the stream while copying the data read into a buffer. If a timeout occurs, -1 will be returned, and the contents of the buffer will be undefined. Only `length` characters maximum will be copied into the buffer. If no valid data are found, then zero will be returned.

The `until` versions of the functions stop scanning the stream's buffer when the terminator *character* is read:

- `size_t readBytes( char *buffer, size_t length)`
- `size_t readBytes( uint8_t *buffer, size_t length)`

- size_t readBytesUntil(char terminator, char *buffer, size_t length)

- size_t readBytesUntil(char terminator, uint8_t *buffer, size_t length)

The following two functions read an Arduino String class variable from the stream. The until version stops scanning the stream's buffer when the terminator *character* is read:

- String readString()

- String readStringUntil(char terminator)

In the Stream class, the vast majority of the public functions eventually find their way down to the descendant class's read(), peek(), or available() function. For this reason, I will not be describing all of the preceding functions – I suspect you would get bored very quickly – only the ones which do the actual work.

Most of these functions are simply wrappers around a slightly lower-level function which does a similar thing or takes slightly different parameters. For example, Listing 4-13 shows the two separate find() functions.

Listing 4-13. Various Stream class cascading find() functions

```
// find returns true if the target string is found
bool  Stream::find(char *target)
{
  return findUntil(target, strlen(target), NULL, 0);        ①
}

// reads data from the stream until the target string of
// given length is found returns true if target string is
//  found, false if timed out
bool Stream::find(char *target, size_t length)
```

```
{
  return findUntil(target, length, NULL, 0);                    ②
}
```

① Starting with a simple find() with a single char array parameter, it does nothing except call down to findUntil() passing a few more parameters. FindUntil() is shown in Listing 4-14.

② This is a different find() function which takes an additional length parameter to limit the search to that number of characters. Again, it passes control down the ladder to the same findUntil() as noted earlier.

So far, so good. The called findUntil() functions from the preceding code are listed in Listing 4-14. We are not done climbing the ladder yet!

Listing 4-14. Various Stream class cascading findUntil() functions

```
// as find but search ends if the terminator string is found
bool  Stream::findUntil(char *target, char *terminator)
{
  return findUntil(target, strlen(target),
                   terminator, strlen(terminator));          ①
}

// reads data from the stream until the target string of
// the given length is found search terminated if the
// terminator string is found.
// returns true if target string is found, false if terminated
// or timed out
bool Stream::findUntil(char *target, size_t targetLen,       ②
                       char *terminator, size_t termLen)
```

```
{
  if (terminator == NULL) {                                      ③
    MultiTarget t[1] = {{target, targetLen, 0}};
    return findMulti(t, 1) == 0 ? true : false;
  } else {                                                       ④
    MultiTarget t[2] = {{target, targetLen, 0},
                        {terminator, termLen, 0}};
    return findMulti(t, 2) == 0 ? true : false;
  }
}
```

① This version of findUntil() accepts a pair of parameters, so is not called from the find() functions in Listing 4-14. It does, however, pass control down to the same findUntil() as the find() functions do. Nearly there! This variant ends the search at the given terminator character or string.

② Here we are, finally – perhaps. We have reached the findUntil() function that everyone eventually gets to. Regardless of which find() or findUntil() we originally called, here is where we arrive.

③ If the terminator is NULL, then we have arrived from find() (or perhaps the first findUntil()). In this case, we create a MultiTarget array in variable t, with a single entry, and call yet another function, findMulti(), to do the actual searching.

④ If the `terminator` is not NULL, we have been passed some text to use as the end of search marker. In this case, we create a `MultiTarget` array in variable t, with a pair of entries, and again call `findMulti()` to do the actual searching.

The `MultiTarget` structure is defined in `Stream.h` as a `protected` structure, alongside the `findMulti()` function; and so, as internal-only helpers, they are not described here.

The various `read()` functions are quite simple in that they call down to a `protected` `timedRead()` function as shown by the example in Listing 4-15, which shows the `readBytes( char *buffer, size_t length)`.

Listing 4-15. One of the readBytes() functions

```
// read characters from stream into buffer
// terminates if length characters have been read, or
// timeout (see setTimeout)
// returns the number of characters placed in the buffer
// the buffer is NOT null terminated.
//
size_t Stream::readBytes(char *buffer, size_t length)
{
  size_t count = 0;
  while (count < length) {
    int c = timedRead();                    ①
    if (c < 0) break;
    *buffer++ = (char)c;
    count++;
  }
  return count;
}
```

① All of the various read() functions call out to the protected function timedRead(). That function, although protected, is quite small and is discussed in Listing 4-16 as it does require more investigation as it uses timeouts and it is where your Stream descendant class finally gets accessed! The purpose is to return a single character from the underlying stream within a given timeout period.

Listing 4-16. The protected timedRead() function

```
// protected method to read stream with timeout
int Stream::timedRead()
{
  int c;
  _startMillis = millis();                           ①
  do {                                               ②
    c = read();                                      ③
    if (c >= 0) return c;                            ④
  } while(millis() - _startMillis < _timeout);       ⑤
  return -1;     // -1 indicates timeout             ⑥
}
```

① The function has to use the millis() counter because calling delay() would not act as a timeout, but more of a block on any processing. The timeout is required to prevent the sketch hanging up, or blocking, because the underlying stream hasn't sent enough data or is running too slowly. The error code passed back can be used to loop around, if necessary, and try reading data again.

② This do loop will execute for as long as the timeout has not expired.

③ This is where your class gets to earn a living. The Stream class is now, finally, calling down to the descendant class's implementation of the read() function to fetch a single character from the stream.

④ We have received a valid character, so we can exit the do loop and return the character to the calling function.

⑤ On return from the descendant class's read() function, if nothing was retrieved, the tail end of the loop checks that the timeout has not yet expired and, if not, will resume the do loop for another iteration.

⑥ If the timeout expired and we fell through the bottom of the do loop, -1 is returned to indicate the fact that we couldn't read any data from the underlying stream within the current timeout period.

4.4. The **HardwareSerial** Class

The Serial interface, in the Arduino Language, is an instance of a class known as HardwareSerial and provides the ability to read and write from the hardware serial port built into the ATmega328P. Other AVR microcontrollers such as the Mega 2560 have more than one hardware serial port, up to four in some devices. Only the codc relating to the Uno's Serial port will be discussed here as the others are very similar.

Other devices have serial ports that connect directly to the USB port – the Leonardo, for example. These boards are not discussed here.

The HardwareSerial class is defined in $ARDINC/HardwareSerial.h and implemented in

- $ARDINC/HardwareSerial_private.h where the constructor and the *USART Receive Complete* interrupt handler helper function _rx_complete_irq() can be found.

- $ARDINC/HardwareSerial.cpp where most of the public functions are implemented, alongside the *USART Data Register Empty* interrupt handler helper function _tx_udr_empty_irq().

- $ARDINC/HardwareSerial0.cpp where the *actual* interrupt handlers USART_RX_vect() and USART_UDRE_vect() are found. These two, when fired, call out to _rx_complete_irq() and _tx_udr_empty_irq(), respectively, to do the actual work. This is also the file where the instantiation of Serial as an instance of the HardwareSerial class is carried out.

The HardwareSerial class inherits from the Stream class and from Stream's ancestor class, Print, and this inheritance is the reason that the Serial object can read from and write to the ATmega328P's USART device. The USART is described in detail in Chapter 9, Section 9.3, "*USART.*"

4.4.1. Interrupt Handlers

The HardwareSerial class has two interrupt handlers, one of which will be fired whenever the USART receives a single byte, the "USART Receive Complete interrupt." The other will fire whenever the USART's transmit buffer is empty and ready to be reloaded with the next byte to be transmitted. This is the "<<"USART Data Register Empty interrupt."

The two interrupt handlers are created simply to call the two helper routines. Both are implemented in the file $ARDINC/HardwareSerial0.cpp as the functions _rx_complete_irq() and _tx_udr_empty_irq().

In the code listings that follow, only those parts relevant to the ATmega328P are listed.

4.4.1.1. USART Receive Complete Interrupt

The source code for the USART Receive Complete interrupt is as per Listing 4-17, and that listing is extracted from the file $ARDINC/HardwareSerial0.cpp.

Listing 4-17. USART Receive Data interrupt handler

```
ISR(USART_RX_vect)
{
    Serial._rx_complete_irq();
}
```

As can be seen, it simply calls out to the appropriate helper function. That function, _rx_complete_irq(), is found in $ARDINC/HardwareSerial_private.h and is extracted in Listing 4-18. I've slightly massaged the code to get it to fit on the page.

Listing 4-18. USART Receive Data interrupt helper

```
void HardwareSerial::_rx_complete_irq(void)
{
    if (bit_is_clear(*_ucsra, UPE0)) {              ①
        unsigned char c = *_udr;                    ②

        rx_buffer_index_t i =                       ③
```

```
        (unsigned int)(_rx_buffer_head + 1) %
        SERIAL_RX_BUFFER_SIZE;

    if (i != _rx_buffer_tail) {                          ④
      _rx_buffer[_rx_buffer_head] = c;
      _rx_buffer_head = i;
    }
  } else {
    // Parity error, read byte but discard it
    *_udr;                                               ⑤
  };
}
```

① This line of code checks to see if the character
   received had a parity error. If not, processing will be
   allowed to continue.

② The received byte is read from the USART Data
   Register UDR0. This clears the data received flag,
   RXC0 in register UCSR0A, and readies the USART
   to receive the next byte. The USART has a 2-byte
   internal buffer which, if it fills and another character
   is received, causes an error.

③ The receive buffer head pointer is advanced by 1
   byte. This might cause it to wrap around to the start
   again as this is a circular buffer. This new position is
   where the just received byte will be stored.

④ If the new receive buffer head pointer is not yet the
   same as the current tail pointer, the byte received
   can be stored and the head pointer updated to the
   most recently stored byte in the receive buffer. If, on

the other hand, the two pointers are equal, the byte
just received is quietly lost.

⑤   If there was a parity error, then the byte must still be
read from the USART Data Register UDR0. This will
clear the data received flag, RXC0 in register UCSR0A.
The character read is discarded and not written to
the buffer.

ⓘ The head pointer is the first free location in the buffer where
new received data will be stored. The tail pointer is the next data byte
to be read by the sketch. If the head pointer equals the tail pointer,
then the buffer must be full, and there is nowhere to store any further
data without overwriting currently unread data.

4.4.1.2. USART Data Register Empty Interrupt

The source code for the USART Data Register Empty interrupt is as per
Listing 4-19, which is extracted from $ARDINC/HardwareSerial0.cpp.

Listing 4-19. USART Data Register Empty interrupt handler

```
ISR(USART_UDRE_vect)
{
    Serial._tx_udr_empty_irq();
}
```

As with the preceding receive handling code, it calls out to the
appropriate helper function. That function, _tx_udr_empty_irq(), is
located in the file $ARDINC/HardwareSerial.cpp and can be seen in
Listing 4-20. I have reformatted the code slightly to fit on the page.

Listing 4-20. USART Data Register Empty interrupt helper

```
void HardwareSerial::_tx_udr_empty_irq(void)
{
  unsigned char c = _tx_buffer[_tx_buffer_tail];      ①
  _tx_buffer_tail = (_tx_buffer_tail + 1) %           ②
                    SERIAL_TX_BUFFER_SIZE;

  *_udr = c;                                          ③

  *_ucsra = ((*_ucsra) & ((1 << U2X0) |               ④
                          (1 << MPCM0))) |
                          (1 << TXC0);

  if (_tx_buffer_head == _tx_buffer_tail) {           ⑤
    cbi(*_ucsrb, UDRIE0);
  }
}
```

① The next byte to be transmitted is retrieved from the tail end of the transmit buffer. As this is an interrupt handler, then interrupts must be enabled which is only true when there are data in the transmit buffer ready to be sent through the USART.

② The buffer tail pointer is updated to point at the next character in the buffer. This may cause it to wrap around to the start again.

③ The next byte to be transmitted is stored in the USART Data Register UDR0, in the case of the ATmega328P. Storing a byte here automatically starts the transmission – when the previous byte has been transmitted.

④   The Transmit Complete (TXC0) flag is cleared in register UCSR0A. This bit is automatically cleared when the *USART Transmit Complete interrupt* fires, but the Arduino doesn't use that interrupt – it uses the *USART Data Register Empty interrupt* instead, so the code must clear it manually. This line of code also preserves the U2X0 and the MPCM0 flags – the USART Double Speed and Multi-processor Communications flags. (See the ATmega328P data sheet for details.)

The clearing of the TXC0 bit looks strange. It is already set to a 1_{binary}; so if it is ANDed with another 1_{binary}, it will remain as it is. Then when written back to UCSR0A, it will clear it to zero. Weird? Really weird?

The other bits and flags in the UCSR0A register will be cleared to 0_{binary} by this line of code, unless they too need to be cleared – by writing a 1_{binary} of course. You should note that the bits for Frame Error, FE0; Data Overrun, DOR0; and Parity Error, UPE0, *must all* be 0_{binary} when writing any value to the UCSR0A register. See the data sheet for details.

⑤   If the transmit buffer's head and tail pointers are the same, then it is empty, interrupts are disabled, and this stops transmission attempts.

The choice of interrupt handler is interesting here. Why not use the USART Transmit Complete interrupt rather than the USART Data Register Empty interrupt? There is much confusion about this it seems; however, the answer is relatively simple.

The UDR0 register can be empty while the transmission is still in progress. The register contains a single byte, or 8 bits. The USART has to transmit a *frame* of more than 8 bits – there are the start and stop bits, the parity bit if required, as well as the 8 bits of data – so the USART Data Register Empty interrupt will fire and allow the next byte to be loaded into UDR0 while the previous byte is still in the process of being transmitted. This should increase performance a tiny bit, depending on how many actual bits are in a frame.

4.4.2. Class Functions and Macros

The HardwareSerial class defines the following in the file $ARDINC/ HardwareSerial.h.

4.4.2.1. Macro **SERIAL_TX_BUFFER_SIZE**

This is the number of bytes to be used in the transmit buffer for the Serial interface. It is defined, provided it doesn't already have a definition, as in Listing 4-21. The buffer is set to be 16 bytes if there is less than 1 Kb of Static RAM in the AVR microcontroller or 64 bytes if there is more. The Arduino boards with the ATmega328P will use 64-byte buffers for both transmit and receive.

Listing 4-21. Definition of SERIAL_TX_BUFFER_SIZE

```
#if !defined(SERIAL_TX_BUFFER_SIZE)
    #if ((RAMEND - RAMSTART) < 1023)
        #define SERIAL_TX_BUFFER_SIZE 16
    #else
        #define SERIAL_TX_BUFFER_SIZE 64
    #endif
#endif
```

If you need to change the buffer size, there is no simple way – currently at least – to do this. You will need to edit the file $ARDINC/ HardwareSerial.h and add your new buffer size *above* the lines shown in Listing 4-21, as follows:

```
#define SERIAL_TX_BUFFER_SIZE 128
```

Remember to make the new value a power of two.

4.4.2.2. Macro **SERIAL_RX_BUFFER_SIZE**

This is the number of bytes to be used in the receive buffer for the Serial interface. It is defined, provided it doesn't already have a definition, as per the code in Listing 4-22. The buffer is set to be 16 bytes if there is less than 1 Kb of Static RAM in the AVR microcontroller or 64 bytes if there is more.

Listing 4-22. Definition of SERIAL_RX_BUFFER_SIZE

```
#if !defined(SERIAL_RX_BUFFER_SIZE)
    #if ((RAMEND - RAMSTART) < 1023)
        #define SERIAL_RX_BUFFER_SIZE 16
    #else
        #define SERIAL_RX_BUFFER_SIZE 64
    #endif
#endif
```

If you need to change the buffer size, there is no simple way – currently at least – to do this. You will need to edit the file $ARDINC/ HardwareSerial.h and add your new buffer size *above* the lines shown in Listing 4-22, as follows:

```
#define SERIAL_RX_BUFFER_SIZE 128
```

Don't forget, the new value needs to be a power of two.

4.4.2.3. Typedefs **tx_buffer_index_t** and **rx_buffer_index_t**

These are typedefs for the data type of the head and tail pointers into the transmit and receive buffers. By default these are 8 bits wide (uint8_t); however, if the appropriate buffer is larger than 256 bytes, then the index data types are increased to 16 bits (uint16_t) to cope with the larger-sized buffer. The definition of the transmit buffer index type is shown in Listing 4-23, while the receive buffer definition is shown in Listing 4-24.

Listing 4-23. Definition of tx_buffer_index_t

```
#if (SERIAL_TX_BUFFER_SIZE>256)
    typedef uint16_t tx_buffer_index_t;
#else
    typedef uint8_t tx_buffer_index_t;
#endif
```

Listing 4-24. Definition of rx_buffer_index_t

```
#if  (SERIAL_RX_BUFFER_SIZE>256)
    typedef uint16_t rx_buffer_index_t;
#else
    typedef uint8_t rx_buffer_index_t;
#endif
```

4.4.2.4. Serial Communications Parameters

There are numerous configuration definitions for Serial.begin(). These are named "SERIAL_bps" where "b" is the number of bits , 5, 6, 7, or 8; "p" is "N," "O," or "E" for none, odd, or even parity; and "s" is the number of stop bits which can be 1 or 2. The complete set of config options is listed in Table 4-1.

Table 4-1. *Configuration parameters for the Serial.begin() function*

Define	Value	Description
SERIAL_5N1	0x00	5 bits, no parity, 1 stop bit
SERIAL_6N1	0x02	6 bits, no parity, 1 stop bit
SERIAL_7N1	0x04	7 bits, no parity, 1 stop bit
SERIAL_8N1	0x06	8 bits, no parity, 1 stop bit (Default)
SERIAL_5N2	0x08	5 bits, no parity, 2 stop bits
SERIAL_6N2	0x0A	6 bits, no parity, 2 stop bits
SERIAL_7N2	0x0C	7 bits, no parity, 2 stop bits
SERIAL_8N2	0x0E	8 bits, no parity, 2 stop bits
SERIAL_5E1	0x20	5 bits, even parity, 1 stop bit
SERIAL_6E1	0x22	6 bits, even parity, 1 stop bit
SERIAL_7E1	0x24	7 bits, even parity, 1 stop bit
SERIAL_8E1	0x26	8 bits, even parity, 1 stop bit
SERIAL_5E2	0x28	5 bits, even parity, 1 stop bit
SERIAL_6E2	0x2A	6 bits, even parity, 1 stop bit
SERIAL_7E2	0x2C	7 bits, even parity, 1 stop bit
SERIAL_8E2	0x2E	8 bits, even parity, 1 stop bit
SERIAL_5O1	0x30	5 bits, odd parity, 1 stop bit
SERIAL_6O1	0x32	6 bits, odd parity, 1 stop bit
SERIAL_7O1	0x34	7 bits, odd parity, 1 stop bit
SERIAL_8O1	0x36	8 bits, odd parity, 1 stop bit
SERIAL_5O2	0x38	5 bits, odd parity, 2 stop bits

(*continued*)

Table 4-1. (*continued*)

Define	Value	Description
SERIAL_602	0x3A	6 bits, odd parity, 2 stop bits
SERIAL_702	0x3C	7 bits, odd parity, 2 stop bits
SERIAL_802	0x3E	8 bits, odd parity, 2 stop bits

If Serial.begin() is called with no config, only a baud rate, then the default is 8 bits, no parity, and 1 stop bit (SERIAL_8N1). There are two versions of the begin() function in the file $ARDINC/HardwareSerial.h. The default variant is shown in Listing 4-25, while Listing 4-29 shows the actual begin() function which does the hard work of initializing the Serial interface.

Listing 4-25. Default Serial.begin() function

```
void begin(unsigned long baud) { begin(baud, SERIAL_8N1); }
```

You can see it simply calls the overloaded begin() function – see Listing 4-29 – with the required two parameters.

4.4.2.5. Macro HAVE_HWSERIAL0

In the case of the standard Arduino board, this will always be defined. There are up to three additional serial interfaces that may exist, on the Mega boards, for example, but these are not discussed here. HAVE_HWSERIALn defines are able to be used in code to determine whether or not the microcontroller has the specific serial port as numbered. The ATmega328P has only one serial port, so HAVE_HWSERIAL0 will return true. The Mega 2560 Arduino boards have four serial ports, so all of HAVE_HWSERIAL0 through HAVE_HWSERIAL3 will return true.

Listing 4-26. Defining `Serial` as `extern`.

```
#if defined(UBRRH) || defined(UBRR0H)
  extern HardwareSerial Serial;
  #define HAVE_HWSERIAL0
#endif
```

Listing 4-26 shows how the first serial port on the Atmega328P is defined, and also, the actual `Serial` interface (actually, an instance of a HardwareSerial object) is declared `extern`. This is required as `Serial` is actually declared as an object in the file `$ARDINC/HardwareSerial0.cpp`, shown in Listing 4-27.

Listing 4-27. Actual definition of `Serial`

```
#if defined(UBRRH) && defined(UBRRL)
  ...
#else
  HardwareSerial Serial(&UBRR0H,
                        &UBRR0L,
                        &UCSR0A,
                        &UCSR0B,
                        &UCSR0C,
                        &UDR0);
#endif
```

The `Serial` variable is an object of type `HardwareSerial`. The following functions are exposed by this class.

4.4.2.6. Constructor `HardwareSerial()`

This is the class constructor. Because of the different internal AVR microcontroller register names on different boards and microcontrollers, the constructor takes *pointers* to the registers required for serial

communications. Listing 4-28 is extracted from the file $ARDINC/
HardwareSerial_private.h and shows the constructor.

Listing 4-28. HardwareSerial constructor()

```
HardwareSerial::HardwareSerial(
  volatile uint8_t *ubrrh, volatile uint8_t *ubrrl,
  volatile uint8_t *ucsra, volatile uint8_t *ucsrb,
  volatile uint8_t *ucsrc, volatile uint8_t *udr) :      ①
    _ubrrh(ubrrh), _ubrrl(ubrrl),
    _ucsra(ucsra), _ucsrb(ucsrb), _ucsrc(ucsrc),
    _udr(udr),
    _rx_buffer_head(0), _rx_buffer_tail(0),
    _tx_buffer_head(0), _tx_buffer_tail(0)
{                                                        ②
}
```

① This constructor is using the "colon" manner
of initializing the member variables from the
parameters passed to the constructor.

② All the initialization has been done; the body of the
constructor is empty.

This manner of initializing an object in the constructor is considered
the correct method in modern versions of the C++ standards.

4.4.2.7. Function begin(unsigned long baud)

This function is called to commence serial communications at the
specified baud rate, with a config of SERIAL_8N1 for 8-bit, no parity,
and 1 stop bit communications. This function calls the overridden
begin(unsigned long, uint8_t) function in Listing 4-29, passing the
desired baud rate and SERIAL_8N1.

4.4.2.8. Function `begin(unsigned long, uint8_t)`

The `begin()` function is called to initialize serial communications at the desired baud rate and configuration. Listing 4-29 shows the code that performs the actual initialization. There are other overloaded versions of the `begin()` function which take fewer parameters; however, they all eventually arrive at the following code.

The code in Listing 4-29 has been massaged slightly to fit the page.

Listing 4-29. The HardwareSerial::begin() function

```
void HardwareSerial::begin(unsigned long baud, byte config)
{
  // Try u2x mode first                              ①
  uint16_t baud_setting = (F_CPU / 4 / baud - 1) / 2;
  *_ucsra = 1 << U2X0;

  if (((F_CPU == 16000000UL) &&                      ②
      (baud == 57600)) || (baud_setting > 4095))
  {
    *_ucsra = 0;
    baud_setting = (F_CPU / 8 / baud - 1) / 2;
  }

  *_ubrrh = baud_setting >> 8;        ③
  *_ubrrl = baud_setting;

  _written = false;                   ④

  *_ucsrc = config;                   ⑤

  sbi(*_ucsrb, RXEN0);                ⑥
  sbi(*_ucsrb, TXEN0);
```

```
  sbi(*_ucsrb, RXCIE0);                        ⑦
  cbi(*_ucsrb, UDRIE0);
}
```

① This assumes that high-speed communications *will* be used and sets bit U2X0 in the UCSR0A register to enable high-speed communications mode. All other bits are cleared. The baud_setting variable here is *not* the actual baud rate desired – that's in baud. The calculation here is working out a value for the USART Baud Rate Register 0 or UBRR0, which *will* define the actual baud rate for communications.

② If an older board is in use, with a clock speed of 16 MHz, and a baud rate of 57600 is chosen, or if the baud_setting calculated above is 4096 or higher on *any* board, then the high-speed mode is disabled and baud_setting recalculated for the low-speed mode. There is a comment in the code which states that this line is a

Hardcoded exception for 57600 for compatibility with the bootloader shipped with the Duemilanove and previous boards and the firmware on the 8U2 on the Uno and Mega 2560. Also, The baud_setting *cannot be > 4095, so switch back to non-u2x mode if the baud rate is too low.*

③ UBRR0 is a 12-bit register – well, it's a 16-bit register, but the top 4 bits of the high byte are ignored. It is used as a counter for the serial clock generator. Every time that it counts down to zero, it will be reset to the value calculated in baud_setting. This is the baud rate generator for the USART. The calculated baud_setting is split into two parts and loaded into the high and low bytes of the UBRR0 register. 16-bit registers in the ATmega328P must, usually, be loaded high byte first and then low byte.

④   The _written flag is set whenever a byte is transmitted. This is used as a simple shortcut, so that calls to flush() can return quickly if no actual transmissions have taken place.

⑤   The desired data width, parity, and stop bits are set up here. The default is 8 bits, no parity, and 1 stop bit.

⑥   These two lines enable data receipt and transmission. This has the effect of removing Arduino pins D0 and D1 from general use – they are now in the care of the USART.

⑦   The final two lines enable the interrupts for receiving and transmitting data. This is why the Serial interface cannot be used within an interrupt handler because interrupt handlers disable interrupts while executing. The interrupts enabled are the USART Receive Complete interrupt and the USART Data Register Empty interrupt.

i The Arduino code calculates the UBRRO value (in `baud_setting`) *differently* from the data sheet. In the data sheet, the formula for high-speed communications is given as this:

```
  (F_CPU / (8 * baud)) -1
= (F_CPU / 8 / baud) -1
```

while the Arduino code calculates the "minus 1" as *part* of the division, not *after* the division, which it performs in two parts, as follows:

```
F_CPU / 4 / (baud -1) / 2
```

However, both the Arduino and the data sheet *usually* agree on the final, integer, result. This applies to both low- and high-speed communications calculations. Figures 4-1 and 4-2 show the calculated values and error rates.

In addition to the slightly different calculation, the Arduino code works with unsigned integers, `unsigned long` and `uint16_t`, while the data sheet appears to calculate using floating point arithmetic with rounding up or down carried out at the very end. At least, that's the only way I could get the same answers as the data sheet. I am therefore of the opinion that the data sheet is incorrect!

A similar discrepancy exists between how the Arduino and the data sheet calculate low-speed UBBRO settings and also error rates for the various settings. (See in the following.)

4.4.2.8.1. Notes on Baud Rate Calculations

The images in Figures 4-1 and 4-2 show the required values for the UBRR0 register as calculated by the data sheet and by the Arduino code. There are separate images for the low-speed and high-speed modes. Both images are from a spreadsheet which I used to perform the calculations.

Low Speed

FCPU	BAUD	Data Sheet			Arduino Code		
		UBRR	BAUD	ERROR	UBRR	BAUD	ERROR
16000000	2400	416	2398	-0.1	416	2398	-0.1
	4800	207	4808	0.2	207	4807	0.1
	9600	103	9615	0.2	103	9615	0.2
	14400	68	14493	0.6	68	14492	0.6
	19200	51	19231	0.2	51	19230	0.2
	28800	34	28571	-0.8	34	28571	-0.8
	38400	25	38462	0.2	25	38461	0.2
	57600	16	58824	2.1	16	58823	2.1
	76800	12	76923	0.2	12	76923	0.2
	115200	8	111111	-3.5	8	111111	-3.5
	230400	3	250000	8.5	3	250000	8.5
	250000	3	250000	0	3	250000	0
	500000	1	500000	0	1	500000	0
	1000000	0	1000000	0	0	1000000	0

Figure 4-1. *Low-speed baud rate calculations*

High Speed

		Data Sheet			Arduino Code		
FCPU	BAUD	UBRR	BAUD	ERROR	UBRR	BAUD	ERROR
16000000	2400	832	2401	0	832	2400	0
	4800	416	4796	-0.1	416	4796	-0.1
	9600	207	9615	0.2	207	9615	0.2
	14400	138	14388	-0.1	138	14388	-0.1
	19200	103	19231	0.2	103	19230	0.2
	28800	68	28986	0.6	68	28985	0.6
	38400	51	38462	0.2	51	38461	0.2
	57600	34	57143	-0.8	34	57142	-0.8
	76800	25	76923	0.2	25	76923	0.2
	115200	16	117647	2.1	16	117647	2.1
	230400	8	222222	-3.5	8	222222	-3.5
	250000	7	250000	0	7	250000	0
	500000	3	500000	0	3	500000	0
	1000000	1	1000000	0	1	1000000	0

Figure 4-2. High-speed baud rate calculations

The areas highlighted show discrepancies between what the data sheet calculates and the Arduino's result for the same calculation due to rounding. In the figures, the following apply:

- The clock speed for the AVR microcontroller is 16 MHz.

- The data sheet figures use floating point calculations and are rounded at the very end. Rounding is up or down according to where the fractional parts are in relation to 0.5 – equal or higher rounds up and lower down.

- The data sheet baud rates are again calculated from the floating point values with rounding at the end. This, to my mind at least, is incorrect as the value in UBRR0 *cannot* possibly be a floating point value!

- The Arduino figures use unsigned integer values throughout with truncation downward as opposed to rounding up or down as appropriate.

- The difference between floats with fractions and unsigned integers accounts for the variances highlighted – even when it appears that the data sheet and the Arduino code have the same UBRR0 figures.

The low-speed baud rates are calculated as

```
F_CPU / 16 * (UBRR0 + 1)
```

This means that the baud rate, in low-speed mode, ranges from 16 MHz/(16 * (0 + 1)) which is 1,000,000 baud down to 16 MHz/(16 * (4,095 + 1)) which equals 244 baud.

The high-speed baud rate is calculated as

```
F_CPU / 8 * (UBRR0 + 1)
```

This means that the baud rate, in high-speed mode, ranges from 16 MHz/(8 * (0 + 1)) which is 2,000,000 baud down to 16 MHz/(8 * (4,095 + 1)) which equals 488 baud.

---

i You should be aware that you are not limited to the baud rates in the preceding images. The Arduino code will accept any value for the requested baud rate and attempt to calculate a suitable value for UBRR0.

The value written to UBRR0 is used as a divider of the system clock and can be anything between 0 and 4095. It is *not* the baud rate. It is used to calculate the correct timings to give the required baud rate by prescaling the system clock.

4.4.2.8.2. **Notes on Baud Rate Errors**

Just about all desired baud rates are not quite *exactly* achievable. This is because calculating the UBRR0 value loses accuracy when the fractional parts are lost – registers don't have room for fractions after all. This means that the USART may not quite be running at exactly the baud rate requested by the sketch.

Because the UBRR0 value may not always be exactly as calculated, then the actual baud rate calculation will not match up to the baud rate requested. The preceding spreadsheet images show error rates using the calculation from the data sheet, which is

```
Error% = (Actual Baud/Desired Baud - 1) * 100
```

⚠ The *new* ATmega328P data sheet from Microchip appears to have a bug in the calculation. It states that the error rate is "Error% = (Actual Baud / Desired Baud -1)^2 100."

In this formula, instead of a multiplication by 100, the 100 just sits there by itself while the result of preceding division is squared. The superscripted "2" in the data sheet *could* be a footnote number, but as there is only a single footnote on the page, this doesn't look likely. The old Atmel data sheet has the correct formula.

The data sheet figures for the error rate appear to be rounded to a single decimal place at the end of the calculation.

The data sheet advises avoiding those baud rates where the calculated error rate is plus or minus 0.5% or higher.

The data sheet figures should be taken with a pinch of salt! You cannot count with register values holding floating point values – unless you are using a floating point unit (FPU) of course, but the AVR microcontroller doesn't have one.

4.4.2.8.3. Notes on Low- and High-Speed Communications

According to the data sheet, setting U2X0 in register UCSR0A to 1_{binary} will *reduce the divisor of the baud rate divider from 16 to 8 effectively doubling the transfer rate for asynchronous communication.*

It goes on to state that

> *Setting this bit will reduce the divisor of the baud rate divider from 16 to 8, effectively doubling the transfer rate for asynchronous communication. Note however that the Receiver will in this case only use half the number of samples (reduced from 16 to 8) for data sampling and clock recovery, and therefore a more accurate baud rate setting and system clock are required when this mode is used. For the Transmitter, there are no downsides.*

So it appears that this bit may affect data receipt while not affecting data transmission.

4.4.2.9. Function end()

Calling the serial.end() function disables serial communication and flushes the transmission buffer so that any bytes which were in the process of being transmitted will be allowed to complete. Interrupts for transmission and receipt of data are then disabled, and finally, Arduino pins D0 and D1 are disconnected from the USART and can now be used for normal input/output operations. The code for the end() function is as shown in Listing 4-30.

Listing 4-30. The HardwareSerial::end() function

```
void HardwareSerial::end()
{
  // wait for transmission of outgoing data
  flush();                                        ①
```

```
  cbi(*_ucsrb, RXENO);                                      ②
  cbi(*_ucsrb, TXENO);
  cbi(*_ucsrb, RXCIEO);                                     ③
  cbi(*_ucsrb, UDRIEO);

  // clear any received data
  _rx_buffer_head = _rx_buffer_tail;                        ④
}
```

① Any data currently in the transmission buffer is allowed to complete its transmission.

② The USART transmit and receive functions are disabled. Pins D0 and D1 return to normal Arduino input/output mode.

③ Transmit and Receive interrupts are disabled.

④ The receive buffer is emptied ready for subsequent receipt of data. The data may not have been read by the sketch yet, but it is now gone.

4.4.2.10. Operator `bool()`

The bool() function, in Listing 4-31, will return true if the specified serial port is available. It is called, for example, as in if (Serial) ..., and will only ever return false if called in a sketch which is running on a Leonardo board, for example, and the USB CDC serial connection is not yet ready.

On the standard Arduino boards, the function always returns true which can clearly be seen in Listing 4-31.

Listing 4-31. The HardwareSerial::operator bool() function

```
operator bool() {
    return true;
}
```

The preceding code is from a standard Arduino, obviously!

4.4.2.11. Function `available(void)`

This function overrides the virtual one in the ancestor class Stream and returns the number of bytes available, in the receive buffer, which have yet to be read by the sketch. Listing 4-32 shows the full code for the available() function, and it was reformatted slightly to fit on the page.

Listing 4-32. The HardwareSerial::available() function

```
int HardwareSerial::available(void)
{
  return ((unsigned int)(SERIAL_RX_BUFFER_SIZE +
                        _rx_buffer_head - _rx_buffer_tail)) %
                        SERIAL_RX_BUFFER_SIZE;
}
```

The head is where the next byte received by the USART will be placed; the tail is the next byte to be read into the sketch. The difference between the two is the number of bytes available. The preceding calculation accounts for any wraparound that takes place when the addition of new bytes to the buffer by the USART causes the head pointer to point back at the start of the buffer while the tail pointer is still at a (now) higher address.

If, for example, the buffer was 64 bytes long at address 100 and the head pointer has wrapped around and is now pointing at address 105, while the tail pointer is pointing at address 155, the amount of data available to read is

```
    (64 + head - tail) % 64
=> (64 + 105 - 155) %  64
=> (169 - 155) % 64
=> 14 %  64
=   14
```

So there are 14 bytes of data not yet read by the sketch. These are in the buffer at addresses 155–163 and bytes 100–105, which, if you use your fingers like I just did, is exactly 14 bytes. Remember the tail pointer is the first byte to be read from the buffer and passed to the sketch, while the head pointer is where the next byte read in from the USART will be stored – it is the first free location in the sketch's receive buffer.

4.4.2.12. Function peek(void)

Listing 4-33 shows the peek() function. This function overrides the virtual one in the ancestor class Stream and returns the next character that *will* be returned when the read() function – see Listing 4-34 – is called. The character remains in the buffer, so this is a nondestructive read. If there are no characters in the buffer, -1 is returned.

Listing 4-33. The HardwareSerial::peek() function

```
int HardwareSerial::peek(void)
{
  if (_rx_buffer_head == _rx_buffer_tail) {     ①
    return -1;
```

```
  } else {
    return _rx_buffer[_rx_buffer_tail];            ②
  }
}
```

① If the head and tail are equal, there's nothing in the buffer. An invalid character code, -1, is returned.

② The character at the tail end of the buffer is returned, without changing the tail pointer.

4.4.2.13. Function `read(void)`

The function read(), as shown in Listing 4-34, overrides the virtual function in the ancestor class Stream and returns the next character from the receive buffer and adjusts the tail pointer to remove the character read from the buffer. If there are no characters in the buffer, -1 is returned. Listing 4-34 has had to be reformatted slightly to fit on the page.

Listing 4-34. The HardwareSerial::read() function

```
int HardwareSerial::read(void)
{
  if (_rx_buffer_head == _rx_buffer_tail) {          ①
    return -1;
  } else {
    unsigned char c = _rx_buffer[_rx_buffer_tail];   ②
    _rx_buffer_tail = (rx_buffer_index_t)
                     (_rx_buffer_tail + 1) %          ③
        SERIAL_RX_BUFFER_SIZE;
    return c;                                          ④
  }
}
```

① If the head and tail are equal, there's nothing in the buffer. An invalid character code, -1, is returned.

② The next, unread, character is extracted from the buffer.

③ The tail pointer is adjusted to the next character in the buffer, which may cause the tail pointer to wrap around to the first character in the buffer.

④ The extracted character is returned to the sketch.

4.4.2.14. Function `availableForWrite(void)`

This function, shown in Listing 4-35, overrides the virtual one in the `Print` ancestor class and returns the number of bytes of free space remaining in the `Serial` interface's transmit buffer.

Listing 4-35. The HardwareSerial::availableForWrite() function

```
int HardwareSerial::availableForWrite(void)
{
  tx_buffer_index_t head;                                 ①
  tx_buffer_index_t tail;

  TX_BUFFER_ATOMIC {                                      ②
    head = _tx_buffer_head;
    tail = _tx_buffer_tail;
  }

  if (head >= tail)
    return SERIAL_TX_BUFFER_SIZE - 1 - head + tail;       ③

  return tail - head - 1;                                 ④
}
```

① The transmit buffer's head and tail pointers will be copied to these two variables, so they are declared with the same data type as the actual head and tail pointers for the buffer.

② Wrapping these two lines in `TX_BUFFER_ATOMIC` is necessary if the buffer size is bigger than 256 bytes as reading an 8-bit value is atomic – cannot be interrupted – but reading a 16-bit value could be interrupted, and the value may be updated in between reading the low and high bytes. The `TX_BUFFER_ATOMIC` macro is defined as shown in Listing 4-36.

The protected code block simply copies the current values for the head and tail pointers into the two local variables. The `tail` pointer is the next location in the sketch's transmit buffer that will be copied to the USART's transmit register, while the `head` pointer is where the sketch will store the next byte sent from the sketch.

③ If the `head` is ahead of the `tail`, this calculation returns the bytes between `head` and `tail`. If `head` equals `tail,` then the buffer is empty, and this calculation returns `SERIAL_TX_BUFFER_SIZE - 1`.

④ If the `head` has wrapped back to the start of the buffer and is now behind the `tail`, this calculation returns the difference between them accounting for the wraparound.

The `TX_BUFFER_ATOMIC` macro is defined as shown in Listing 4-36.

Listing 4-36. The TX_BUFFER_ATOMIC macro

```
#if (SERIAL_TX_BUFFER_SIZE>256)
#define TX_BUFFER_ATOMIC  ATOMIC_BLOCK(ATOMIC_RESTORESTATE)
#else
#define TX_BUFFER_ATOMIC
#endif
```

ATOMIC_BLOCK(ATOMIC_RESTORESTATE) is from the AVRLib and means that whatever state the interrupts were before this block, they should be restored after the block. The block will disable interrupts for the duration.

If the buffer size is less than 256 bytes, the TX_BUFFER_ATOMIC macro expands to nothing as no special handling is required for transferring 8-bit values – they cannot be interrupted.

4.4.2.15. Function `flush(void)`

The flush() function in Listing 4-37 overrides the virtual function in the ancestor class Print and ensures that any data currently in the process of being transmitted is allowed to continue until completion. This empties the sketch's transmit buffer and ensures that the entire contents are, indeed, transmitted.

Listing 4-37 has been slightly reformatted to fit on the page.

Listing 4-37. The HardwareSerial::flush() function

```
void HardwareSerial::flush()
{
  if (!_written)                             ①
    return;

  while (bit_is_set(*_ucsrb, UDRIE0) ||      ②
         bit_is_clear(*_ucsra, TXC0)) {

    if (bit_is_clear(SREG, SREG_I) &&        ③
        bit_is_set(*_ucsrb, UDRIE0))
```

```
    // Interrupts are globally disabled, but the DR
    // empty interrupt should be enabled, so poll the
    // DR empty flag to prevent deadlock

    if (bit_is_set(*_ucsra, UDRE0))              ④
    _tx_udr_empty_irq();
  }

// If we get here, nothing is queued anymore (DRIE is
// disabled) and the hardware finished transmission
// (TXC is set).
}
```

① If we have never transmitted a byte, since Serial.
begin(), then there is no need to flush. This special
check is needed since there is no way to force the
TXC0 – transmit complete – bit to 1_{binary} during
initialization of the USART which could cause
flush() to block forever if called when no data had
ever been transmitted.

② The while loop will execute as long as the USART
Data Register Empty interrupt remains enabled
or if data is currently being transmitted by the
USART. The comment at the bottom of the function
shows the conditions that will be in force when the
while loop exits:

- The sketch's transmit buffer is empty.

- The transmit complete bit, TXC0, in the UCSR0A
register has been set.

- The UDRIE bit in UCSR0B is clear to disable the
USART Data Register Empty interrupt.

③ If global interrupts are currently disabled but
the USART Data Register Empty interrupt is still
enabled, then we must still have data in the transmit
buffer waiting to be sent.

④ This line explicitly calls the helper function for the
USART Data Register Empty interrupt handler if
the UDR0 register is currently empty and waiting for
another byte.

In other words, the preceding code ensures that even if global
interrupts are not enabled, as long as data remains to be transmitted to the
USART and beyond, it will indeed be transmitted.

4.4.2.16. Function `write(uint8_t)`

This function overrides the virtual one in the ancestor class `Print` and
defines how a single `unsigned char` will be transmitted to the `Serial`
interface. The `write()` function is split into two separate parts. The first
part, the code which follows in Listing 4-38, deals with those occasions
when both the transmit buffer in the sketch and the USART Data Register,
UDR0, are also empty.

Rather than adding the byte to be transmitted to the sketch's transmit
buffer and waiting for the interrupt handler to forward it to the USART, the
code in Listing 4-38 cuts out the middleman and writes the byte directly
into the USART Data Register for transmission. The function then returns
the number of bytes written – which will always be one.

The code in Listings 4-38 and 4-38 have been reformatted to fit the page.

Listing 4-38. The HardwareSerial::write() function

```
size_t HardwareSerial::write(uint8_t c)
{
  _written = true;                              ①

  if (_tx_buffer_head == _tx_buffer_tail &&     ②
      bit_is_set(*_ucsra, UDRE0)) {
    // If TXC is cleared before writing UDR and the
    // previous byte completes before writing to UDR,
    // TXC will be set but a byte is still being
    // transmitted causing flush() to return too soon.
    // So  writing UDR must happen first.

    // Writing UDR and clearing TC must be done atomically,
    // otherwise interrupts might delay the TXC clear so the
    // byte written to UDR is transmitted (setting TXC)
    // before clearing TXC. Then TXC will be cleared when
    // no bytes are left, causing flush() to hang.

    ATOMIC_BLOCK(ATOMIC_RESTORESTATE) {         ③
      *_udr = c;                                ④
      *_ucsra = ((*_ucsra) & ((1 << U2X0) |
                              (1 << MPCM0))
              ) | (1 << TXC0);                  ⑤
    }

    return 1;                                   ⑥
}
```

    ①   This flag is used by flush() to determine if anything
          has been written yet, so it must be set any time a
          byte is supplied to be transmitted. In flush() – see
          Listing 4-37 – this flag is used as a "quick exit" as it
          tells flush() whether or not it has work to do.

② This is a performance shortcut to load the passed byte directly into the USART Data Register if the sketch's transmit buffer is empty – `_tx_buffer_head` equals `_tx_buffer_tail` – and the USART Data Register is also currently empty. This reduces overhead and makes higher baud rates more reliable.

③ The comment above this line explains it all. The code must be careful to not get interrupted, so is wrapped in an atomic block which will disable interrupts if necessary, make the required changes, and re-enable interrupts if they were previously enabled. The `ATOMIC_BLOCK` and `ATOMIC_RESTORESTATE` macros are defined in the depths of the AVRLib code.

④ The code here simply writes the data byte to the USART Data Register ready to be transmitted.

⑤ This line updates the USCR0A register to preserve the state of the high-speed (U2X0) and Multi-processor (MPCM0) flags while clearing the Transmit Complete flag (TXC0) by writing a 1_{binary} to its location. If it was not set, this change would have no effect; if it was previously set, then ANDing it with a 1_{binary} would cause a new 1_{binary} to be written back, thus clearing the flag. This is required because with an empty transmit buffer, USART interrupts are disabled so this bit will not be cleared automatically.

⑥ The function exits, returning the number of bytes written to the buffer, always one, which is not quite true as the code has completely bypassed the sketch's transmit buffer.

The write() function continues in Listing 4-39 if the sketch's transmit buffer and the USART's UDR0 register were not both found to be empty on entry to the write() function.

Listing 4-39. The HardwareSerial::write() function – continued

```
tx_buffer_index_t i =
  (_tx_buffer_head + 1) % SERIAL_TX_BUFFER_SIZE;        ①

// If the output buffer is full, there's nothing
// for it other than to wait for the interrupt
// handler to empty it a bit

while (i == _tx_buffer_tail) {                          ②
  if (bit_is_clear(SREG, SREG_I)) {

    // Interrupts are disabled, so we'll have to poll
    // the data register empty flag ourselves. If it is
    // set, pretend an interrupt has happened and call
    // the handler to free up space for us.

    if(bit_is_set(*_ucsra, UDRE0))
      _tx_udr_empty_irq();                              ③

  } else {                                              ④
    // nop, the interrupt handler will free up
    // space for us
  }
}

_tx_buffer[_tx_buffer_head] = c;                        ⑤

// make atomic to prevent execution of ISR between
// setting the head pointer and setting the interrupt
// flag resulting in buffer retransmission.
```

```
ATOMIC_BLOCK(ATOMIC_RESTORESTATE) {        ⑥
  _tx_buffer_head = i;
  sbi(*_ucsrb, UDRIE0);        ⑦
}

return 1;
}
```

① The first free location in the sketch's transmit buffer is found. This will be used later to update the head pointer and also to determine if the buffer is currently full up. The head pointer is the first free byte in the transmit buffer.

② The while loop will execute for as long as the buffer remains full. Obviously, the variable i will never be updated, so the code depends on the sketch's transmit buffer tail pointer – the location in the buffer where bytes are removed and copied to the USART – to change, as it will be when the buffer is being emptied by the interrupt handler; if the interrupt and global interrupts are enabled.

③ The helper function for the USART's transmission code is called manually here as interrupts are not enabled so the transmit buffer will not empty under interrupt control.

④ If global interrupts are enabled, so the buffer will eventually empty by itself (no, actually, by the interrupt handler) – so there is nothing that needs to be done here.

⑤ The new data byte is stored in the buffer at the current head location as there is finally some space in the buffer to do so.

⑥ This block of code is wrapped in an atomic block to ensure that interrupts do not adjust the head pointer while this block is doing so. This could cause the same byte to be transmitted twice. Whenever there are data in the buffer, then the USART's transmit interrupt is enabled to ensure that they are written out to the Serial interface. The interrupt is disabled when end() is called or when the interrupt handler's helper, _tx_udr_ empty_irq, has emptied the buffer.

⑦ This sets the USART Data Register Empty interrupt enable bit to configure the USART to send bytes over the serial link while there are some left to transmit. It will be disabled when no more bytes are left in the sketch's transmit buffer.

The following functions facilitate the transmission of different numeric data types:

- write(unsigned long n)
- write(long n)
- write(unsigned int n)
- write(int n)

The following using call allows the Serial interface to transmit String class variables:

- using Print::write;

The various write() functions will all eventually call down to the write() function in Listings 4-38 and 4-39 to do the actual transmission via the USART.

4.4.2.17. Function _rx_complete_irq(void)

This is the receive data interrupt helper function. It is not to be called from sketches directly.

4.4.2.18. Function _tx_udr_empty_irq(void)

This is the transmit data interrupt helper. It is not to be called from sketches directly.

The two interrupt handler helper functions are visible as they are declared public, but are most definitely *not* intended to be called by sketch code, only by the interrupt ISRs themselves or other internal code in the HardwareSerial class.

4.5. The String Class

The String class provides a simple C++ method of creating C++ strings, as opposed to C's *old-fashioned* char arrays. Strings can be added together, converted to and from numbers and so on. They are quite useful in this respect. However, they do use a lot of dynamic memory allocation and reallocation, and this has certain drawbacks – mainly the ability to use up your scarce Static RAM causing all sorts of possible corruptions and hard to find crashes.

⚠️ The String class uses a lot of dynamic memory allocation. This means that there could be runtime errors when used on AVR microcontrollers with minimal available RAM. The author of the Arduino JSON library, Benoit Blanchon, has a few warnings and pointers as to why you should *never* use the String class. You can read the article, or at least the "Disclaimer," at https://blog. benoitblanchon.fr/arduino-json-v5-0/#disclaimer and then, if you so wish, avoid the use of the String class in your Arduino code.

As a simple example, when making a string longer, there must be enough free Static RAM to allocate the existing allocated space plus the new amount that is required – this can, briefly, double the amount of Static RAM required and, under certain circumstances, exceed the amount available, leading to corruption.

Just because it compiles okay doesn't mean that it will (always) run okay. Beware.

Interestingly enough, I don't know of anyone who uses this class in their sketches. I've never seen one used either – but that doesn't mean there are no sketches out there in the wild which use String variables of course.

In this chapter, when describing the Printable class, I showed how a class, named Person, could be streamed by inheriting from the Printable class. That particular example *did* use the String class (because it was easier to type in!); however, it did take up a lot more Flash RAM than had I written the class to use char arrays rather than Strings. However, I did a quick experiment and created another class using plain old-fashioned char arrays instead of Strings.

With `Strings`, the example consumed 3,222 bytes of Flash and 234 bytes of Static RAM. When converted to use plain `char` buffers, the Flash RAM usage dropped to 1,808 bytes, and Static RAM usage dropped to 232 bytes. This was for a pair of `char[10]` buffers instead of the `String` variables, and Flash RAM usage was only 56% that of the `String` version for the same features. Obviously, bigger buffers will result in more Static RAM usage.

Given the simplicity of the `Person` class, `String` variables were a valid option. Apart from streaming them, nothing else was done with them at all. With only that sort of usage, `String` variables are perfectly acceptable. Had I perhaps written the class in such a way that it was required to manipulate those `String` variables, for example, changing data within them, adding extra characters, or other changes, then those actions would each be a potential source of random crashes if and when the various dynamic allocations and copying of `String` data around in Static RAM exceeded the amount of RAM available.

The ATmega328P has 32 Kb of Flash RAM, but only a paltry 2 Kb (2024 bytes) of Static RAM. Static RAM is where your sketch's variables get kept, while the sketch code goes into the Flash RAM. You see the memory used in each area at the end of a compilation and upload.

💡 Because the use of `String` variables is fraught with potential danger, I strongly advise against their usage. However, should you wish to use them, so be it. The Arduino Reference web site has all the details that you will need to create `Strings` from various other data types, and there is a full explanation of the various functions and methods that are available to operate on `Strings` there too. You can find all the documentation at `www.arduino.cc/reference/en/language/variables/data-types/stringobject/`.

CHAPTER 5

Converting to the AVR Language

This chapter briefly explains how you can begin to wean yourself off of the helpful features of the Arduino Language and write code that is in the AVR's own variant of C/C++ which can greatly reduce the size of your compiled code and could make the difference in fitting your project into an ATtiny85, for example, rather than needing a full-blown ATmega328P.

Writing AVR C/C++ also turns off all the hand holding that the Arduino gives you. You are talking directly to the device, rather than having your needs and wishes interpreted by an intermediary and passed along to the device, eventually.

You should be warned, writing in AVR C/C++ will entail frequent reading of the data sheet for the AVR microcontroller in your Arduino board and writing code that is – initially at least – a lot harder to understand than the Arduino Language that you are used to. However, you will find yourself writing small code libraries that get used frequently in your own code, which make life easier again. In addition, these libraries will be written in AVR C/C++ and will be far more efficient than the Arduino equivalent.

This chapter covers the *simple* things that you can do right now, even within your existing sketches to save a bit of Flash RAM, time, and battery power for those projects you want to power from batteries. Chapters 7, 8,

© Norman Dunbar 2020
N. Dunbar, *Arduino Software Internals*, https://doi.org/10.1007/978-1-4842-5790-6_5

and 9 of this book delve a lot deeper into the hardware of the ATmega328P, and in those chapters, there's a lot more low-level information.

5.1. Introduction

In this chapter, I will be looking at how you can convert, fairly easily, some of the Arduino Language features to AVR-specific C++. AVR-specific C++ is actually what the Arduino Language maps down on to anyway – as you will see later in Chapters 7, 8, and 9. Using AVR C++, the "middleman" gets cut out and things become smaller and faster, with less power required too. The information in this chapter should give you ideas on how to *start* migrating from the Arduino Language to talking directly to the microcontroller.

Having said that it is "fairly easy," you should also be reminded that the Arduino Language is very *readable* and this is extremely helpful for beginners and experienced makers alike. Plain AVR C/C++ is, how shall I put it, not *quite* so user-friendly. It's not impossible, but you should be aware that commenting your code is probably a must from now on.

Later on, in Chapter 6, I shall introduce you to an application named PlatformIO which allows you to code in pure AVR C/C++ without needing the Arduino Language or IDE. This really allows you to get down and dirty in the code. It also allows you to continue to create Arduino Language sketches, if you so desire, and can be used as an alternative to the Arduino IDE. PlatformIO allows you to use your preferred editor to write Arduino code.

PlatformIO is cross-platform and runs on Windows, Linux, and Mac, just like the Arduino IDE. It is also able to write and compile code for numerous different development boards, not just Arduino.

However, I shall start gently and continue using the Arduino IDE.

The rest of this chapter assumes that you

- Have a reasonable level of understanding of C/C++ code. I'll try to keep things as simple as I can though.

- Know about binary and hexadecimal number systems.

- Understand logical operations on binary values, AND, OR, NOT, and XOR specifically.

Just in case, here's a recap.

5.2. Numbering Systems

Writing code involves knowing a little about various numbering systems. It's not all decimal – although that's the one we are most used to, having ten digits on our hands and feet. Computers and microcontrollers work in binary, base 2, where something is on or off, or a 1 or a 0. There is nothing else. I'll start this chapter with a recap of the various numbering systems.

5.2.1. Decimal Numbering

It makes sense to start with something familiar!

In decimal, a digit's position in the number represents the count of the power of 10 at that point, counting from zero upward and from right to left. The third digit from the right is 10^2, the second is 10^1, the first is 10^0, and so on, for example, thinking back to my primary school days:

```
100 10 1
--------
  1  2 3
```

This number counts the number of 100s that we have, plus the number of 10s, plus the number of 1s. That's $(1 * 100) + (2 * 10)$ plus $(3 * 1)$ giving 123. Simple? Too easy? Let's move on.

5.2.2. Binary Numbering

Binary numbers use only the digits 0 and 1. This is another positional numbering system, similar to decimal, in that the rightmost digit, or bit, represents the units or 2^0, the next the 2^1, then the 2^2, and so on, doubling each time. Again, we see increasing powers of two as we move right to left.

In binary, the value $0111\ 1011_{binary}$ is therefore

```
128 64 32 16 8 4 2 1
--------------------
  0   1  1  1 1 0 1 1
```

This is $(1*64)+(1*32)+(1*16)+(1*8)+(1*2)+(1*1)$, which is $123_{decimal}$.

The problem with binary is that it easily gets unwieldy. Up to about 255 is fine – there are 8 bits (binary digits) to cope with. After that, it tends to get a bit hard to follow. Hexadecimal is a good way to keep things easily understandable, but reduces the number of digits required by a factor of 4 compared with binary.

5.2.3. Hexadecimal Numbering

Hexadecimal is based on powers of 16. And straight away, we can see a problem as we only have ten digits, 0–9. To get around this, hexadecimal uses all the digits, plus the letters A–F so that there are 16 hexadecimal digits in use to represent hexadecimal numbers. The digits represent themselves, as they do in decimal, and the letters A–F represent 10–15.

As with decimal, this is a positional numbering system, where the columns show multiples of 16, starting on the far right with 1s, then 16s, then 256s, then 4096s, and so on. Once again, each column is a power of 16 greater than the one to the right.

For the value $7B_{hex}$, we have

```
16 1
-----
 7 B
```

This value represents $(7 * 16)$ plus $(11 * 1)$ and is, once again, exactly $123_{decimal}$.

Hexadecimal is extremely useful when there are lots of binary digits to deal with. Binary can be confusing and has far too many bits to be visually useful, except in a few cases. Hexadecimal is a good way to represent binary values, with fewer digits, and is simple to convert to and from.

To represent 16 in binary requires only 4 bits = 8, 4, 2, and 1. There are 16 different values that can be created using just those bits, 0–15. If then the binary number is split into groups of 4, starting at the right, each of those groups can be converted to a hexadecimal digit using Table 5-1.

Table 5-1. *Binary, hexadecimal, and decimal conversion*

Binary	Hex	Decimal	Binary	Hex	Decimal
0000	0	0	1000	8	8
0001	1	1	1001	9	9
0010	2	2	1010	A	10
0011	3	3	1011	B	11
0100	4	4	1100	C	12
0101	5	5	1101	D	13
0110	6	6	1110	E	14
0111	7	7	1111	F	15

Using the preceding example, we can split the 8 bits of 0111 1011$_{binary}$ into two groups of 4 bits – this is 0111$_{binary}$ and 1011$_{binary}$. Converting to hexadecimal using the preceding table results in 7$_{hex}$ and B$_{hex}$, or 7B$_{hex}$. Instead of requiring a table to convert, it's easy to convert the binary bits in each 4-bit group into a decimal number and then make that into hexadecimal by adjusting the digits if the result is 10 or more.

0111$_{binary}$ is $(0 * 8) + (1 * 4) + (1 * 2) + 1$ and gives the answer 7. 1011$_{binary}$ is $(1 * 8) + (0 * 4) + (1 * 2) + 1$ and gives the answer 11. 11 is not a valid hexadecimal digit, but its equivalent is B$_{hex}$. Once more, the result is 7B$_{hex}$.

That's about all there is to it. Hexadecimal is a much better way to represent values in computer registers, memory, etc., rather than binary. Decimal could be used but, for some reason, isn't often.

5.3. Binary Logical Operations

Computers use binary. The various digital logic gates that computers and microcontrollers are built from rely on logic to work. There are only a few basic gates known or used, and many of them are actually made up from something called a NAND gate, or sometimes a NOR gate. The following sections deal with the most used gates in microcontroller construction.

Now you might be wondering what this has to do with the Arduino. Fear not. The following truth tables for hardware gates are exactly the same as the truth tables for those bitwise operations done in a sketch. There will be more on this later on in this chapter, so for now, consider the following a short reminder.

5.4. NOT

The NOT operation takes a single binary bit as input and results in its opposite value as the output. It inverts the bit, in other words.

The truth table for the NOT operation is thus

```
A Output
0   1
1   0
```

5.5. AND

Given any two, or more, binary digits, or bits, they can be ANDed together to give a result which depends on the two (or more) inputs. AND works as follows:

- If *all* inputs are 1_{binary}, then the result will also be 1_{binary}.

- Otherwise, the result will be 0_{binary}.

The truth table for the AND operation, with two inputs, is thus

```
A B Output
0 0   0
0 1   0
1 0   0
1 1   1
```

5.6. OR

Given any two, or more, binary digits, or bits, they can be ORd together to give a result which operates as follows:

- If *any* of the inputs are 1_{binary}, then the result will also be 1_{binary}.

- Otherwise, the result will be 0_{binary}.

The truth table for the OR operation, with two inputs, is thus

```
A B Output
0 0   0
0 1   1
1 0   1
1 1   1
```

5.7. XOR

Given any two, or more, binary digits, or bits, they can be XORd together to give a result which operates as follows:

- If *all* the inputs are 1_{binary}, then the result will be 0_{binary}.

- If *all* the inputs are 0_{binary}, then, again, the result will be 0_{binary}.

- Otherwise, the result will be 1_{binary}.

The truth table for the XOR operation, with two inputs, is thus

```
A B Output
0 0   0
0 1   1
1 0   1
1 1   0
```

The remainder of this chapter will require you to be at least slightly familiar with the truth tables listed here. Panic not. It will be explained as required. Now we are about ready to start looking at losing the Arduino Language hand holding, but in a gentle manner.

5.8. Replacing the Arduino Language

As I introduced in Chapter 2, the Arduino IDE does a fair amount of hand holding to make life easy for the beginner. It sets up various *stuff* in the background, it provides easy to understand function names and so on in the language, and you never *need* to see what's happening. If you wish to carry on in this manner, then I'm afraid that this section of the book is not for you!

Still here? Good!

Read on, and prepare to cast off the shackles of an easy life!

5.8.1. The ATmega328P Pins and Ports

On the ATmega328P, there are numerous pins, as you are aware, and these pins live in three different "banks" – each bank consisting of *up to* a maximum of eight pins. The pins in each bank are named, by Atmel/Microchip, "Pxn" where "x" is the bank and "n" is the pin number on that bank – PB5, for example, which corresponds to the Arduino D13 pin. On the ATmega328P, the banks are not all the same – not all have the full complement of eight pins:

- Bank B has eight pins, PB0–PB7. Most of the pins in this bank are usable on an Arduino board apart from pins PB6 and PB7 as these are used for the 16 MHz crystal oscillator, so there are only six available pins on Bank B.

- Bank C only has seven pins, PC0–PC6. Pin PC6 is special in that normally it is used as the RESET pin. It can also be used as an additional I/O pin if the appropriate fuse bit (see Chapter 7, Section 7.1, *"ATmega328P Fuses,"* for details), RSTDISBL, is programmed. Doing this, however, prevents the device from being programmed (or reset); and if further programming is required, a special high voltage or a parallel programmer must be used instead. In normal use, Bank C therefore has six pins available.

- Bank D has all eight pins, PD0–PD7, available for use on the Arduino.

See Figure 5-1 for a pinout diagram of the ATmega328P. You will find the Arduino and AVR pin labeling names on the diagram.

ALT	Arduino	PCInt	AVR	Pin		Pin	AVR	PCInt	Arduino	ALT
RESET		PCINT14	PC6	1	U	28	PC5	PCINT13	D19/A5	SCL
RX	D0	PCINT16	PD0	2		27	PC4	PCINT12	D18/A4	SDA
TX	D1	PCINT17	PD1	3		26	PC3	PCINT11	D17/A3	
INT0	D2	PCINT18	PD2	4		25	PC2	PCINT10	D16/A2	
OC2B/INT1	D3/PWM	PCINT19	PD3	5		24	PC1	PCINT9	D15/A1	
XCK/T0	D4	PCINT20	PD4	6		23	PC0	PCINT8	D14/A0	
			VCC	7		22	GND			
			GND	8		21	AREF			
XTAL1/OSC1		PCINT6	PB6	9		20	AVCC			
XTAL2/OSC2		PCINT7	PB7	10		19	PB5	PCINT5	D13	SCK
OC0B/T1	D5/PWM	PCINT21	PD5	11		18	PB4	PCINT4	D12	MISO
OC0A/AIN0	D6/PWM	PCINT22	PD6	12		17	PB3	PCINT3	D11/PWM	OC2A/MOSI
AIN1	D7	PCINT23	PD7	13		16	PB2	PCINT2	D10/PWM	OC1B/SS
ICP1/CLKO	D8	PCINT0	PB0	14		15	PB1	PCINT1	D9/PWM	OC1A
ALT	Arduino	PCInt	AVR	Pin		Pin	AVR	PCInt	Arduino	ALT

Figure 5-1. *Atmega328P pinout*

To summarize, the following pins are the only ones available to us on an ATmega328P-based Arduino board:

- PB0–PB5. Pins PB6 and PB7 are used for the 16 MHz crystal oscillator and so are unavailable on Arduino boards.

- PC0–PC5. Pin PC6 is the RESET pin and should *really* be left well alone!

- PD0–PD7.

ℹ️ Regarding pins PB6 and PB7, you can configure the ATmega328P to use its own internal 8 MHz oscillator rather than the external one and free up these two pins for general I/O use. Sadly, this cannot easily be done when the device is embedded in an Arduino board as there are no headers on an Arduino board that connect these pins to the outside world.

This works best if the microcontroller is used in a breadboard or in a circuit board of your own design, for example. See Appendix H for a breadboarded Arduino doing exactly that – running at 8 MHz without a crystal and able to use PB6 and PB7 as extra pins.

Figure 5-1 shows the location of the various banks of pins. The numbers in the columns labeled "Pin" are the physical pin numbers. The columns labeled "AVR" are the Atmel/Microchip pin names. The "PCInt" columns list the names used when processing Pin Change Interrupts, and next to those are the "Arduino" pin names like D3 and so on. Finally, on the outermost columns, we have the "ALT" or alternative functions for the pins as some pins can be configured for multiple – but separate – tasks.

You can see from Figure 5-1 that all the pins in a bank are not necessarily located adjacent to each other. Look at where PB6 and PB7 (physical pins 9 and 10) are to be found, slap bang within the pins of Bank D.

There are three ATmega328P registers which control the numerous pins in the three banks. These are

- The Data Direction Register, DDRx, which is used to configure a pin as either an INPUT, the default, or an OUTPUT. Each bank of pins has its own DDRx, and "x" is the bank name. DDRB for Bank B, for example.

- The bank's Data Register, PORTx, which is used to set the associated pins HIGH or LOW when configured as an OUTPUT. Each bank of pins has its own PORTx, and "x" is again the bank name. PORTC for Bank C, for example. The PORTx register *can* also be used with INPUT pins but only for one specific reason which is covered in the next section on replacing the pinMode() function.

- The bank's Input Pin Register, PINx, which is used to read the state of a pin that has been configured for INPUT. Each bank of pins has its own PINx where "x" is the bank name. PIND for Bank D, for example. As with the PORTx registers, the PINx registers *can* be used with pins configured as OUTPUT; and again, this is for one specific reason only. This will be discussed in the section dealing with replacing digitalWrite().

⚠ Each pin in a bank corresponds to a single bit in the preceding three registers. Pin PD0, for example, is bit zero in the DDRD, PORTD, and PIND registers. It might have been nice if Atmel/Microchip had allowed code to use the same name as the pins, but no, they didn't. Instead of setting bit PD5 in the DDRD register, for example, you have to set bit DDD5. The other two registers have their own names too; the same bit in PORTD is named PORTD5, and in the PIND register, it is PIND5.

5.9. Replacing `pinMode()`

One of the first things any sketch does, usually, is to set up pins for input or output as required. In the Arduino Language, this is accomplished using the `pinMode()` function, similar to the example in Listing 5-1.

Listing 5-1. Using pinMode() in a sketch

```
#define LED LED_BUILTIN
#define BUTTON 2
#define SENSOR 3
#define RELAY 7

void setup() {
    pinMode(LED, OUTPUT);
    pinMode(RELAY, OUTPUT);
    pinMode(BUTTON, INPUT_PULLUP);
    pinMode(SENSOR, INPUT);
}
```

Here we can see the three different modes that an Arduino pin can be configured, `INPUT`, `OUTPUT`, and `INPUT_PULLUP`.

In the end, after much processing and checks, the prime purpose of `pinMode()` is simply to set or clear one single bit in the DDRx register for the bank that the pin is located on.

If the bit in the DDRx register is a zero, the corresponding pin is an INPUT pin. A 1_{binary} bit in the DDRx register configures the pin as an OUTPUT.

When an AVR microcontroller is reset, or powered on, all pins are configured internally as input pins. Alternatively, you can be 100% certain that a pin is correctly configured as input if you explicitly do it yourself – just write a zero to the appropriate bit in the DDRx register to make it an input pin.

Because input is the default state for all the pins, you are not required to *explicitly* configure any pins as input. It is helpful, from a code readability point of view, to do so. Bear in mind, however, that doing so will use up some additional space in the flash area on the microcontroller. If program space is *really* at a premium, you could omit configuring the input pins and save a little space. The ATmega328P has 32 Kb of Flash RAM, so there should be ample. The Arduino bootloader takes around 2 Kb of that – on my Duemilanove – but only 512 bytes on my Uno.

💡 When you are *really* stuck for space in a sketch, you might be surprised at how many bytes of Flash RAM you can save by omitting the pinMode() calls and writing directly to the DDRx registers instead.

💡 When an Arduino resets or powers up, all the pins are configured as INPUT. The init() function described way back in Chapter 2 does not change this configuration.

Setting pins as OUTPUT, on the other hand, must be explicitly specified. This requires writing a 1_{binary} to the appropriate bit in the DDRx register.

The example in Listing 5-2 shows how all of Bank D, PD0–PD7, could be set as input pins, while four pins on bank C, PC0–PC3, could be set as output pins.

Listing 5-2. Replacing pinMode()

```
#include <avr/io.h>

#define ALL_INPUT 0
#define HALF_OUTPUT 0x0F
```

```
void setup() {
    DDRD = ALL_INPUT;
    DDRC = HALF_OUTPUT;
}
```

Now, it should be obvious from the preceding code, that setting multiple bits in DDRx can easily be done in a *single* instruction, rather than having to set each pin individually using pinMode(). To perform the equivalent of this in Arduino code would require a minimum of four pinMode() calls to configure D14–D17 as OUTPUT and, optionally, a further eight calls to configure D0–D7 as INPUT followed by a further two pinMode() calls to configure the D18 and D19 as INPUT pins. Fourteen pinMode() calls in total – that's a lot of overhead.

From Figure 5-1 you will realize, I hope, that pins PC0–PC5 are Arduino pins A0–A5 which can be used as digital pins if necessary. These are pins D14–D19. Likewise, pins PD0–PD7 are Arduino pins D0–D7.

There are three different states that a pin can be configured as, INPUT and OUTPUT we now know about, but what about INPUT_PULLUP? The Arduino allows this mode, so what does the DDRx register do as it only has two states for a bit?

Given that a single bit in the DDR registers can only be a one or a zero, does this mean that we have a problem with INPUT_PULLUP? There's no other value that can be written to the DDRx register to make the pin take on the desired mode. How then is it possible to set up a pin as INPUT_PULLUP? In the previous section, I mentioned that when a pin is an INPUT pin, we can still use the corresponding PORTx register for a special purpose – this is that purpose.

It appears that the designers of the ATmega328P decided that as the PORTx register has no use normally with input pins, it could be used to enable the internal pullup resistors for the pin. If you write a 1_{binary} to any of the PORTx register bits, then input pins will be configured with pullups.

💡 I have seen it advised, in examples in books, on the Web, and in the data sheets, to set the PORTx bits to pullup *before* configuring the DDRx register to set the pins as input. I'm not 100% convinced to be honest. If the microcontroller has been reset, the pins are already input pins by default, so just the pullup is required. If the pins have already been used as outputs, writing a 1_{binary} to the PORTx register will set the pins HIGH and *might*, briefly, enable some feature of the project into a dangerous state. If the Arduino (or the microcontroller) is running a high-power laser cutter, enabling something, however briefly, is not always going to be a safe option.

That's just my opinion.

In my sketches, I configure the pins as INPUT and then write to the PORTx register to enable the pullups which is also what the Arduino Language does deep in the code for pinMode().

5.10. Replacing `digitalWrite()`

The digitalWrite() function, as described in Chapter 3, and much loved by users of the *Blink* sketch, is used to set a physical pin on the Arduino board to either supply voltage, when set HIGH, or to ground, when set LOW. The function does a lot of checking and so on before getting down to the real purpose of its existence. This is, quite simply, setting or clearing a bit in one of the PORTx registers.

One of the failings of digitalWrite() is that it can only be applied to a single pin at a time, so if you wanted to *simultaneously* set a number of pins – perhaps connected to LEDs – to HIGH, then you cannot do that with digitalWrite() as it affects a single pin.

When using AVR C/C++ and avoiding the helpfulness of the Arduino Language, you *can* set a number of pins to a given state at the same time. This relies rely on the pins all being on the same bank. Bank D, for example, allows up to eight separate pins to be set high together, using the AVR C/C++ language, whereas this would require eight separate calls to the digitalWrite() function and, obviously, would not set all eight pins at *exactly* the same instant.

---

 i Although I said earlier that "you *can* set a number of pins to a high state at the same time," that obviously applies to all the pins on the same *bank*. It would not be possible to set all pins on bank C *and* also those on bank D to high, together; it would have to be one bank's pins first and then the other bank.

To set an output pin HIGH, simply set the appropriate bit in the PORTx register corresponding to the bank that the pin is in, to a 1_{binary}. To set the pin LOW instead, the bit should be cleared to a 0_{binary}. If you need to set multiple pins high or low, set or clear the appropriate bits – perhaps in an 8-bit variable, such as a uint8_t – and write the variable's resulting value to the PORTx register. Some examples follow in Listing 5-3.

Listing 5-3. Replacing digitalWrite() examples

```
#define ALL_OUTPUT 0xFF    // All pins are output pins
#define ALL_ON 0xFF        // 11111111 Binary
#define ALL_OFF 0          // 00000000 Binary

void setup() {
    // Set banks B, C and D to all outputs.
    DDRB = ALL_OUTPUT;
```

```
    DDRC = ALL_OUTPUT;
    DDRD = ALL_OUTPUT;

    ...
}

void loop() {
...
    // Set all pins on Bank B to low.
    PORTB = ALL_OFF;                                       ①

    // Set all pins on Bank D to high.
    PORTD = ALL_ON;                                        ②

    // Set pin PC5 to high.
    // Leave all other Bank C pins unchanged.
    PORTC |= (1 << PORTC5);                                ③

    // Now, turn pin PD0 low.
    // Leave all other Bank D pins unchanged.
    PORTD &= ~(1 << PORTD0);                               ④
...
}
```

① This turns off all pins in Bank B. Pins in the bank which are nonfunctional, or not present, are simply ignored. PB6 and PB7, used for the crystal oscillator, would not be affected.

② This turns on all pins in Bank D.

③ This turns on pin PC5 (Arduino D19 also known as A5) in Bank C, but without affecting any other pin in that bank.

④ This turns off pin PD0 (Arduino D0) in Bank D without affecting any other pin in that bank.

In normal circumstances, you may wish to set a pin high or low without affecting any other pins in the same bank, as per the preceding third example. This is where binary bit twiddling comes to the fore.

5.10.1. Enabling Internal Pullup Resistors

I previously mentioned the use of the PORTx register with pins configured as inputs which was described in Section 5.9, *"Replacing pinMode()."* I'm including it here as it is relevant to the PORTx registers. If you write a 1_{binary} to a bit in the PORTx register for a pin configured as input, then you will enable that pin's pullup resistor.

5.10.2. Bit Twiddling

The introductory section in this chapter discussed various binary logic operations. When using PORTs, PINs, and DDRs, a certain amount of binary logic is required. It is considered impolite, and sometimes dangerous, to simply set all the bits in a register when you only need to change one. To that end, the following will explain how individual bits can be turned on or off at will.

To turn on a single bit in a value or register, use the bitwise OR operator, "|", with a mask holding the appropriate bit set to 1_{binary}, and only that single bit will be affected. You can see this in the preceding third example PORTC |= (1 << PORTC5).

If you need more than one bit, then just keep adding bits in. For example, to turn on bits PC1–PC3, simply use ((1 << PORTC3) | (1 << PORTC2) | (1 << PORTC1)) as the mask and OR that with the current contents of the PORTC register.

To turn off a single bit in a value, use the bitwise AND operator, "&", with a mask holding the appropriate bit cleared to 0_{binary}, and only that single bit will be affected. To set a single bit to zero easily, create a mask with the required bit set to a 1_{binary} initially, and then invert it with the "~" operator.

That creates the desired mask. This is what is done in the final example –
`PORTD &= ~(1 << PORTD0);`.

If you need more than one bit, then as in the preceding text, just keep adding bits in. For example, to turn off bits PC1–PC3, simply use `~((1 << PORTC3) | (1 << PORTC2) | (1 << PORTC1))` as the mask and AND that with the current contents of the PORTC register.

So much typing, so much to get wrong! If you are setting up some multibit bitmasks, you may wish to `#define` them, similar to Listing 5-4.

Listing 5-4. Defining and using multibit bitmasks

```
#define PORTC_1_2_3_ON ((1 << PORTC3) | \
                        (1 << PORTC2) | \
                        (1 << PORTC1))

#define PORTC_1_2_3_OFF ~(PORTC1TO3_ON)

...
    // Pins PC1 - PC3 go high.
    // Other pins unchanged.
    PORTC |= PORTC_1_2_3_ON;

    // Pins PC1 - PC3 go low.
    // Other pins unchanged.
    PORTC &= PORTC_1_2_3_OFF;
...
```

When using these types of shifts and inverts, the *compiler* does all the work, so any bit shifting and/or inverting is done once at compile time and not frequently at runtime.

When you are getting down and dirty in some of the internals of the ATmega328P, or looking at code which does so, you might see code that shifts a 0 bit such as

```
PORTC |= ((1 << PORTC0) | (0 << PORTC2) ... );
```

This is quite a good idea as it explicitly shows the state of all the bits. It's perhaps not so useful in the PORTx register as all the bits have pretty much the same meaning, but in Timer/counter control registers, for example, where each bit has vastly different functions, and there are numerous configuration options, it can be a lot more useful to see all the bits.

It's also a lot easier later when you realize that you got it wrong first time and have to add in a bit or two extra!

5.11. Replacing `digitalRead()`

The `digitalRead()` function is used to read the voltage present on a physical pin on the Arduino board. It will return either a HIGH or a LOW depending on the voltage on the pin. When a pin is left floating, then the value returned will be untrustworthy to say the least.

 Never, ever let input pins float. You have been warned!

When you wish to read the state of a pin, or pins, you read the PINx register for the bank appropriate to those pins. You can only read the state of multiple pins when they are on the same bank. If a specific bit in the PINx register is a 1_{binary}, then the pin is HIGH; otherwise, it is LOW. There is a PINx register for each bank of pins on the ATmega328P.

As with `digitalWrite()`, you can only `digitalRead()` a single pin at a time in the Arduino Language.

When you are talking directly with the ATmega328P, bypassing the Arduino's "hand holding," you can read up to eight pins simultaneously. They do have to be on the same bank of course. For example, Listing 5-5 shows how to read eight pin states in a single instruction.

Listing 5-5. Reading multiple pin states simultaneously

```
void setup() {
    DDRD = 0; // All of bank D are inputs.
    ...
}
void loop() {
    ...
    uint8_t bankD = PIND;
    ...
}
```

That's it. You just read the state of all eight pins in Bank D in one operation, by reading the PINx register for the bank in question. Reading the register returns an unsigned 8-bit value (`uint8_t`) which has a 0_{binary} for every LOW pin and a 1_{binary} for every HIGH pin. If you only need to read a single pin, or perhaps a few, you can set up a bitmask with a 1_{binary} in the positions representing the pins you wish to interrogate. Then read the PINx register and use the bitwise AND operator (`&`) to mask out the unwanted bits, as shown in Listing 5-6.

Listing 5-6. Reading a single pin's state

```
// I'm interested in Pin PD1 only (Arduino D1).
#define PIN_D1 (1 << PIND1)

void setup() {
    DDRD = 0; // All of bank D are inputs.
    ...
}
void loop() {
    ...
    // Read PIND and extract PD1 only.
    uint8_t pin_d1 = (PIND & PIN_D1);
```

```
    if (pin_d1) {
        // PD1 was HIGH.
        ...
    } else {
        // PD1 was LOW.
        ...
    }
    ...
}
```

You can also extract the values for more than one pin by ANDing the PINx value with a suitable bitmask.

5.11.1. Toggling Output Pins

Back in the introduction to this chapter, I promised to tell you about the special use of the PINx register with pins configured as outputs. If you write, yes, write, a 1_{binary} to a bit in the PINx register for an output pin, then whatever state the pin is currently in will *toggle*. Given how simple this is, I'm mildly surprised that the Arduino Language doesn't include a digitalToggle() function, especially as the Blink sketch appears to be extremely popular! Listing 5-7 would work for digitalToggle() and uses the features of writing to the PINx register to toggle an output pin.

Listing 5-7. The digitalToggle() function

```
void digitalToggle(uint8_t pin)
{
    uint8_t timer = digitalPinToTimer(pin);          ①
    uint8_t bit = digitalPinToBitMask(pin);
    uint8_t port = digitalPinToPort(pin);
    volatile uint8_t *in;
```

```
    if (port == NOT_A_PIN) return;

    // If the pin supports PWM output, we need to turn it off
    // before doing a digital write.
    if (timer != NOT_ON_TIMER) turnOffPWM(timer);

in = portInputRegister(port);                              ②

    uint8_t oldSREG = SREG;                                ③
    cli();
    *in |= bit;                                            ④
    SREG = oldSREG;                                        ⑤
}
```

① The code begins by converting the pin number, in the usual Arduino manner, to a timer/counter number, a bitmask with a single bit set representing the pin, and a port name. The function quietly exits if the pin turns out to be invalid. This is in keeping with the actions of digitalRead() and digitalWrite().

② This is where we get the PINx register for the pin in question.

③ From here, the code saves the status register and disables interrupts. Is this actually necessary? In digitalWrite() it *is* required because the operation to change the bit is not atomic and could be interrupted, so I am playing safe here too. See issue 146 at https://github.com/arduino/Arduino/issues/146 which appears to be why it was added to the digitalWrite() function.

④   Writing a 1_{binary} to the bit in the PINx register will toggle the pin, regardless of the current state.

⑤   Restore the status register and, by implication, turn interrupts back on – if they were previously on.

5.11.2. Installing `digitalToggle()`

You unfortunately cannot simply add the preceding code to any sketch you write that needs to toggle a pin, either in the sketch itself or in a separate tab in the IDE. This is down to the fact that the function `turnOffPWM()` is declared static in the file `wiring_digital.c` and, as such, cannot be called from anywhere outside that file. If you wish to use the `digitalToggle()` function I've described in Listing 5-7, you will have to add it to that very same file.

To install the function, proceed as follows:

- Close the Arduino IDE.

- Add the code in Listing 5-8 to `Arduino.h`.

Listing 5-8. Adding digitalToggle() to Arduino.h

```
void digitalToggle(uint8_t);
```

- Save the file.

- Add the code for `digitalToggle()` in Listing 5-7 to the file `wiring_digital.c`.

- Save the file.

⚠️ If you do decide to go ahead and install this function, be aware that you will have to reinstall it every time you upgrade the Arduino IDE and software. Maybe, just maybe, I'll submit this as a patch and see if it can be included in the official releases.

Once installed, you can test it with a sketch containing the code shown in Listing 5-9.

Listing 5-9. Example `digitalToggle()` sketch

```
void setup() {
  pinMode(LED_BUILTIN, OUTPUT);

}

void loop() {
  digitalToggle(LED_BUILTIN);
  delay(1000);
}
```

After compiling and uploading the preceding sketch, the built-in LED is yet again flashing every second, and as a bonus, it was only 890 bytes compiled rather than the standard blink sketch's 928 bytes. That's 96% of the standard blink, which doesn't sound much, but it could be the difference between getting a sketch to upload and not.

As we are considering casting off some parts of the Arduino Language to save on resources and potentially increase performance, we can do even better than Listing 5-9. As we all now know all about the DDRx, PORTx, and PINx registers, we can rewrite the Blink sketch in a much more precise way, as shown in Listing 5-10.

Listing 5-10. Hard-core Blink sketch

```
void setup() {
    DDRB = (1 << DDB5);
}

void loop() {
    PINB |= (1 << PINB5);
    delay(1000);
}
```

This version compiled down to a size of only 598 bytes, or 64% of the original. Yes, *I know*, blink isn't representative, but you get the idea – the hand holding and helpfulness of the Arduino Language can lead to *slightly* bloated programs.

That's a very brief introduction to replacing some of the Arduino Language with less resource-intensive (but less readable) code. You can carry on using the Arduino IDE and simply replace your pinMode(), digitalRead(), and digitalWrite() calls with code similar to that shown earlier and reap the benefits of losing a bit of weight from your sketches and gaining a few milliseconds of better performance.

In order to start replacing functions like analogRead() or analogWrite(), for example, you need a better understanding of the Atmega328P's internals. That comes in Chapters 7, 8, and 9 of this book. Before that, however, I thought I would introduce you to a couple of alternatives to the Arduino IDE. Chapter 6 is next and covers a couple of replacements – should you be interested.

CHAPTER 6

Alternatives to the Arduino IDE

A number of alternatives to the Arduino IDE exist. Some are massive overkill such as the Atmel Studio 7 (`www.microchip.com/mplab/avr-support/atmel-studio-7`), based on Microsoft Visual Studio and which only runs on Windows, and MPLAB-X (`www.microchip.com/mplab/mplab-x-ide`). Others such as the AVR Eclipse Plugin (`http://avr-eclipse.sourceforge.net/wiki/index.php/The_AVR_Eclipse_Plugin`) are plugins for the Eclipse IDE, a Java-based IDE *on steroids,* and again quite large. This chapter looks at two other, smaller, alternatives and the two which I will be investigating here are

- PlatformIO (`https://platformio.org/`), which is both a command-line version and can be used to convert your favorite text editor into an IDE to develop Arduino software – if your favorite editor is Atom or VSCode/VSCodium, that is, but fear not. It can also be used to create project files for a number of popular IDEs.

- The all-new Arduino CLI, (`https://github.com/arduino/arduino-cli`), which is still in its alpha release status but which is available and surprisingly usable. This is proposed as a compilation replacement for the current Java-based IDE in a forthcoming version, but is specifically designed to be used in make files.

© Norman Dunbar 2020
N. Dunbar, *Arduino Software Internals*, https://doi.org/10.1007/978-1-4842-5790-6_6

Bear in mind that the latter is in its alpha release status, so is likely to change as time passes.

6.1. PlatformIO

PlatformIO is a system which allows you to write, compile, and upload programs to your Arduino board, either in plain Arduino format – as you are used to in the Arduino IDE – or in plain vanilla AVR C/C++ format, which removes the hand holding that you get from the Arduino IDE and only sets up and runs the code that you write. There is no `millis()` function, for example – you are on your own.

The PlatformIO package comes in two flavors:

- PlatformIO Core – Which installs command-line utilities.

- PlatformIO IDE – Which installs an IDE-style plugin for the `Atom` editor and also for the `Visual Studio Code` editor. Other IDE systems, Eclipse or Code::Blocks, for example, don't have plugins as such, but the `pio` command can generate project files for those IDEs to allow you to develop AVR code in a familiar IDE environment.

6.1.1. Installing PlatformIO Core

PlatformIO Core runs in a bash shell, but don't panic. There are IDE versions if you wish to use one; however, I think it's better to understand what is happening before heading off to a GUI tool – you never know when you will be without a GUI.

This requires Python 2.7 as, currently, no other versions are able to be used. If you have Linux, as I do, the chances are that Python 2.7 is already installed alongside Python 3.

> ⓘ The following instructions apply to Debian-based systems such as Debian itself, Ubuntu, or Linux Mint, which I'm using.

```
python --version
```

The response needs to be something like Python 2.7.x; Python3 does not yet work.

If this gives something like python not found, then install it:

```
sudo apt install python
```

Don't worry if you already have Python version 3.x installed. This command shouldn't overwrite your Python 3 installation as, on all the systems I've looked at, it is known as python3 when installing and when executing code written in version 3 syntax.

Next, make sure that pip is installed:

```
pip --version
```

The response should print the text pip 9.0.1 from /usr/lib/ python2.7/dist-packages (python 2.7) or similar. Look for python 2.7 in the text. If pip is not installed, install it as follows:

```
sudo apt install python-pip
```

Then install the setuptools package using pip:

```
pip install -U setuptools
```

Now, install platformio:

```
pip install -U platformio
```

⚠ You might see warnings informing you that the `bottle` and/or `symantic-version` wheels cannot be built. Don't worry about this. As long as you see the following, or something remarkably similar at the end, you are good to go:

```
Successfully installed bottle-0.12.13 certifi-
2018.8.24chardet-3.0.4 click-5.1 colorama-0.3.9
idna-2.7platformio-3.6.0 pyserial-3.4 requests-
2.19.1semantic-version-2.6.0 urllib3-1.23
```

You can see that both `bottle` and `symantic-version` were installed, regardless of the errors listed.

6.1.2. Testing PlatformIO Core

The commands `pio` and `platformio` are now installed, in my case to `/home/norman/.local/bin`, and both are actually the same thing. Because I'm lazy, I use the shorter version, `pio`. Feel free to use the longer version if this appeals to you.

6.1.2.1. Set Up Your Environment

On Linux, in order for your user to upload code to the Arduino, they must be a member of the `dialout` group. On Debian-based Linux systems, it appears that you may require to be in the group `plugdev` too if you wish to use an ICSP device. These rules apply to the PlatformIO system as well, so first of all, check that you do indeed have membership of the group(s). You must do this while logged in as your normal account:

```
groups
```

In my case, I received the following response:

```
norman adm dialout cdrom sudo dip plugdev lpadmin sambashare vboxsf
```

I am already a member of `dialout` and `plugdev` as I've been using the Arduino IDE and an ICSP device previously. If your account shows that you are not a member of one or the other of the two groups, then run the following commands, as appropriate, making sure to enter the "G" in upper case and substitute your login name where indicated:

```
sudo usermod -a -G dialout your_user_name
sudo usermod -a -G plugdev your_user_name
```

This will add you to the desired group *when you next log in*, so log out and log back in again. This isn't Windows, so you don't have to reboot! Once logged in, make sure you are now a member of `dialout` as mentioned.

Using an ICSP Programming Device

If you intend to use an ICSP device, rather than the Arduino bootloader, then you will need to download the appropriate udev rules file from `https://github.com/platformio/platformio-core/blob/develop/scripts/99-platformio-udev.rules` and copy it, as root with sudo, to `/etc/udev/rules.d` so that the programmer will be recognized and permissions given to allow your user (any user actually) to upload programs to the Arduino board.

In my setup, I originally had a few difficulties with the ICSP device, both in the Arduino IDE and using PlatformIO, so I had to edit the downloaded rules file as follows for my USBtiny ICSP device.

The original line for my device was this, all on one line:

```
# USBtiny
SUBSYSTEMS=="usb", ATTRS{idProduct}=="0c9f",
    ATTRS{idVendor}=="1781", MODE="0666"
```

I changed it to the following, again, all on one line:

```
# USBtiny
SUBSYSTEMS=="usb", ATTRS{idProduct}=="0c9f",
    ATTRS{idVendor}=="1781", MODE="0666", GROUP="plugdev"
```

Setting the group to plugdev allows anyone in that group to use the device. I could have set it to dialout I suppose, but I'm sure that the relevant document outlining the solution to my (long forgotten) problem said to use plugdev.

ℹ️ It is a minor annoyance that if you have to make changes to this file, every time that you compile some code with PlatformIO, it will warn you that the file is missing or out of date and must be reinstalled. This appears in the output for the compilation and not, thankfully, as a pop-up.

Once the file is installed, you may be required to restart the udev service – I didn't – however, just in case, other systems do require this:

```
sudo service udev restart
```

If that gives errors because systemd is not in use, then these commands should suffice:

```
sudo udevadm control --reload-rules
sudo udevadm trigger
```

Now, if your Arduino board is connected to the computer, you must unplug it and plug it back in to pick up the changes.

ℹ️ None of this is necessary if you *only* intend to use the bootloader built in to the Arduino.

If you do intend to use a programmer, then you must be aware that any time you program the Arduino with such a device, the AVR microcontroller will be erased completely and *you can no longer use the bootloader* as it has been overwritten.

You can, thankfully, restore the bootloader, either with PlatformIO (see in the following) or with the Arduino IDE – just pick your board and programmer in the normal manner and then go to Tools ➤ Burn Bootloader, and it will be restored. You will, of course, have to use the ICSP device to burn the bootloader, for obvious reasons!

6.1.2.2. Set Up a New Project

Find out where PlatformIO expects to find your projects. The default will be displayed using the following command which displays *all* the current settings:

```
pio settings get
```

A more specific command, to display only the `projects_dir` setting, is the following:

```
pio settings get projects_dir
```

On my Linux system, it returns the following:

```
Name            Value [Default]
------------------------------------------------------------
projects_dir    /home/norman/Documents/PlatformIO/Projects
```

> ℹ️ In order to save wrapping text around, I've trimmed the excess from the preceding output. The output also lists a description of the setting name, which is useful.

If you don't like the default location, you can easily change it:

```
mkdir -p ~/SourceCode/PlatformIO/Projects
pio settings set projects_dir ~/SourceCode/PlatformIO/Projects
```

The result of executing this command is

```
The new value for the setting has been set!
Name            Value [Default]
------------------------------------------------------------
projects_dir    /home/norman/SourceCode/PlatformIO/Projects
```

The previous setting is listed, at the end of the line, in square brackets, but is not shown here.

> ℹ️ PlatformIO has the idea of a default location for projects, but strangely, *it is not used* except in PlatformIO Home which is a browser-based pseudo-IDE, which is discussed later on in Section 6.1.5, "*PlatformIO Home.*"
>
> When creating new projects, you must be located in the folder or directory where you wish to create the new project. The pio   init command creates all its files *right where you are currently located –* so beware.

Change to the project directory, as listed, and create a new folder to house the project:

```
cd ~/SourceCode/PlatformIO/Projects
mkdir TestProject
cd TestProject
```

Determine the name to be used for your specific board. In my case, it's a Duemilanove:

```
pio  boards  duemil
```

This gives me two options:

```
Platform: atmelavr
----------------------------------------------------------------
ID                      MCU         ...  Name
----------------------------------------------------------------
diecimilaatmega168      ATMEGA168   ...  Arduino Duemilanove ...
diecimilaatmega328      ATMEGA328P  ...  Arduino Duemilanove ...
```

The output text has a lot more information – but it's far too wide for the page, so I've trimmed it of irrelevant detail.

As I'm using the latter version with the ATmega328P, I need to initialize the new project with the `diecimilaatmega328` board name. If you have an Arduino Uno, the process is similar, but has many more results. You should be looking under the `Platform: atmelavr` for your Uno, which will be called uno.

ℹ️ There is no need to install any tools, compilers, etc. for the various boards as PlatformIO will do this automatically for you if it detects that you are using a board for which no tools yet exist.

Unfortunately, it doesn't use the existing tools that were installed by the Arduino IDE, so you may end up with two separate versions of the AVR compiler and so on. This is not a major problem and does mean that when you decide to continue writing Arduino code using PlatformIO, instead of the Arduino IDE, you can simply uninstall the Arduino *stuff* and still be able to compile with PlatformIO.

6.1.2.3. Initialize the Project

The following example sets up a new project for the Duemilanove board which I'm using. You can also create the same project for numerous boards. To show how this can be done, I'll create the project for an Arduino Uno as well as my Duemilanove.

> **ℹ** If you accidentally forget to initialize a second or subsequent board, you can easily do it by making another call to `pio init --board` with the additional board(s). Those new boards will be added to the current project.

```
pio init --board diecimilaatmega328 --board uno
```

After a very short delay, the screen will be filled with useful information about the new project and a list of commands to compile, upload, and clean the project files.

As the messages indicate, some files and directories have been created. These are as follows:

- `platformio.ini` is a file that holds all the configuration for the project. Any changes you make to this file will only affect the project in the current directory – but all environments *may* be involved. The file itself contains settings for all the boards with which the project was initialized. Listing 6-1 shows the default file in full.

- include is a folder expected to be used for any header files for your project. These are the *.h files.

- src is a folder where you are expected to save all the C/C++ files that make up the project.

- lib is a folder where any libraries, private to this project, should be saved or copied. A readme.txt file is also created within this directory explaining how it should be used.

Some commands are displayed as examples of how to build and upload sketches to the board. However, these assume that you will be using the normal Arduino bootloader to do the uploading.

You can edit platformio.ini and change the long-winded name, if necessary, to something more memorable. I changed mine to the following as I couldn't be bothered to have to type "diecimilaatmega328" all the time ("2009" is what "duemilanove" means in Italian):

```
...
[env:2009]
platform = atmelavr
board = diecimilaatmega328
framework = arduino

[env:uno]
...
```

Now I can compile for the Duemilanove with the name 2009 instead. It's easier to remember and less typing too.

If, like me, you have an ICSP device, then you need to edit the platformio.ini file, or programming the board will not work. In my case, I added a new environment so that I could use either the bootloader or the ICSP device. The new environment is simply a copy of the existing one, with a couple of lines added as shown in Listing 6-1. I did edit the Uno environment as well, but that's not shown in the listing.

Listing 6-1. Example platformio.ini file

```
...
[env:2009]
platform = atmelavr
board = dieimilaatmega328
framework = arduino

[env:uno]
...

; Code below added by NDunbar to allow use of
; my USBtiny for programming.

[env:2009_programmer]
platform = atmelavr
board = dieimilaatmega328
framework = arduino
;uploader = usbtinyisp
upload_protocol = usbtiny

[env:uno_programmer]
...
```

The PlatformIO Documentation at `https://docs.platformio.org/en/latest/platforms/atmelavr.html` has details of what is required by each known ICSP device. In my case, I have a USBtiny clone, so I used these two lines from Listing 6-1:

```
;uploader = usbtinyisp
upload_protocol = usbtiny
```

💡 From version 4.1.0 onward, it appears that the `uploader` line is no longer required, just the `upload_protocol` line. I assume (always a bad idea) that the protocol gives PlatformIO all the detail it needs to determine the uploader device.

It does no harm to leave the line in; however, you will receive a warning at upload time if you do. I've simply commented mine out with a leading semicolon to disable the warning message.

Also available in recent versions is the ability to extract common lines to a separate section and just add in the specific lines for the environments in your file. This is not shown here.

The command to use to upload a sketch using the programmer is

```
pio run -e 2009_programmer -t program
```

You can now run `pio run -e 2009 -t upload` to upload using the bootloader or the preceding command to use the ICSP device. Be aware that once you have used the programmer, you no longer have a bootloader and cannot then use `pio run -t -e 2009 upload` to upload. You must always use `pio run -t -e 2009_programmer program` – until you recreate the bootloader of course.

I suppose we need to create the ubiquitous *Blink* sketch now?

6.1.2.4. Arduino-Style Projects

As mentioned earlier, PlatformIO allows you to continue using the Arduino Language in your projects. This section will explain how the Blink sketch can be converted and compiled in the new environment.

Create a new file, src/main.cpp (or whatever name you wish – I called mine Blink.cpp), and add the code in Listing 6-2 to it.

Listing 6-2. Arduino blink sketch

```
#include "Arduino.h"                                    ①

// Is the built in LED already named?
#ifndef LED_BUILTIN                                     ②
#define LED_BUILTIN 13
#endif

// This runs once, in the usual Arduino manner.
void setup()
{
    // Make sure the LED is an output pin.
    pinMode(LED_BUILTIN, OUTPUT);
}

void loop()
{
    // LED on, then wait 1,000 milliSeconds.
    digitalWrite(LED_BUILTIN, HIGH);
    delay(1000);

    // LED off, then wait another 1,000 milliSeconds.
    digitalWrite(LED_BUILTIN, LOW);
    delay(1000);
}
```

① You normally do not need to do this in the Arduino
   IDE, but in PlatformIO, you must.

② This is just a safety check to ensure that the built-in
   LED has been given a name in the Arduino.h file.
   In most cases, it has been done, but it's always best
   to check and avoid any compilation errors that may
   arise.

As you see, apart from adding one line, nothing has changed. You can
now use your favorite text editor to write code for your Arduino.

6.1.2.4.1. Compiling Arduino Projects

Compile the preceding code by first making sure that you are located in
the directory where the file platformio.ini exists. If you have changed
into the src directory to edit the file as in the preceding text, then please
change back up one level.

Now run this command:

```
pio run -e 2009
```

The -e option relates to the environment (or board) that you wish
to compile the code for. As I created two, I need to inform PlatformIO
which board I wish to compile for. In this case, it's the Duemilanove
(which I renamed to "2009") and not the Uno. If you omit this option, *all*
environments in the platformio.ini file will be compiled, as follows:

```
pio run
```

Compile, but do not upload, the code – in case there are errors:

```
pio run -e 2009
```

The compilation produced the following (slightly abridged) output:

```
...
PLATFORM: Atmel AVR > Arduino Duemilanove ... ATmega328       ①
SYSTEM: ATMEGA328P 16MHz 2KB RAM (30KB Flash)                 ②

Library Dependency Finder ... [URL removed for brevity]      ③
LDF MODES: FINDER(chain) COMPATIBILITY(soft)
Collected 24 compatible libraries                            ④

Scanning dependencies...                                     ⑤
No dependencies

Compiling .pioenvs/2009/src/blink.cpp.o                      ⑥

Archiving .pioenvs/2009/libFrameworkArduinoVariant.a         ⑦
Indexing .pioenvs/2009/libFrameworkArduinoVariant.a
Compiling .pioenvs/2009/FrameworkArduino/CDC.cpp.o
...
Archiving .pioenvs/2009/libFrameworkArduino.a                ⑧
Indexing .pioenvs/2009/libFrameworkArduino.a
Linking .pioenvs/2009/firmware.elf

Checking size .pioenvs/2009/firmware.elf
Building .pioenvs/2009/firmware.hex                          ⑨

Memory Usage -> http://bit.ly/pio-memory-usage              ⑩
DATA:    [            ]   0.4% (used 9 bytes from 2048 bytes)
PROGRAM: [            ]   3.0% (used 928 bytes from 30720 bytes)
============ [SUCCESS] Took 1.06 seconds ============

============ [SUMMARY] ============                          ⑪
Environment 2009    [SUCCESS]
Environment uno     [SKIP]
============ [SUCCESS] Took 1.06 seconds ============
```

①   This line summarizes the platform and board in use. In this case, the platform is Atmel AVR, and the board is a Duemilanove (even though I renamed it to 2009 in the `platformio.ini` file).

②   This line summarizes the capacity of the chosen device.

③   The PlatformIO dependency finder goes hunting for anything that it thinks needs to be included in this compilation. I removed the URL that's normally listed here to get the line on the page.

④   This is the number of files and others that the finder thinks are required.

⑤   The system is looking for any dependencies here. It decided that there were none.

⑥   This is where my source file got compiled. Your file name should appear here too.

⑦   Do you recognize these file names? They are all the files that are included by default when you compile an Arduino sketch in the Arduino IDE.

⑧   All the Arduino code is statically linked to the elf file. This will be converted to a hex file for uploading.

⑨   The hex file is the one that will be uploaded to the Arduino board. It has only been compiled at present, not yet uploaded.

⑩   The memory usage section shows that this Arduino sketch used 9 bytes of RAM and 928 bytes of flash program memory. This is standard for the default Arduino Blink sketch. The blank spaces between the square brackets here look pointless; however, when you compile large sketches, this shows a histogram of the amounts of Static and Flash RAM used.

① The "SUMMARY" shows that this compilation only affected the 2009 environment/board and that the uno was not touched.

ⓘ On the first compilation of any target device, PlatformIO will download the required toolchain. In my example, it downloaded the gcc-avr compiler toolset. This already exists under my Arduino IDE installation, but is sadly not found or used by PlatformIO.

6.1.2.4.2. Uploading Arduino Projects

Uploading compiled sketches to an Arduino board is carried out with a bootloader or with an ICSP device. In the former case:

```
pio run -e 2009 -t upload
```

Or with an ICSP device:

```
pio run -e 2009_programmer -t program
```

Don't forget that you need to edit the platformio.ini file if you want to use a programmer instead of the bootloader – see preceding text.

You should note that in the absence of an -e option, all environments/boards in the current project will be compiled and uploaded. This is best avoided as you could end up with Uno code uploaded to your Duemilanove, which may not work correctly – it depends on which board is attached to the USB at the time.

You could see something similar to the following when uploading:

```
...
Configuring upload protocol...
AVAILABLE: arduino
CURRENT: upload_protocol = arduino
Looking for upload port...
...
Auto-detected: /dev/ttyUSB0
Uploading .pioenvs/2009/firmware.hex

avrdude: AVR device initialized, ready to accept instructions

Reading | ################################### | 100% 0.01s

avrdude: Device signature = 0x1e950f (probably m328p)
avrdude: reading input file ".pioenvs/2009/firmware.hex"
avrdude: writing flash (928 bytes):

Writing | ################################### | 100% 0.51s

avrdude: 928 bytes of flash written
avrdude: verifying flash memory ...
avrdude: load data flash data from input file ...
avrdude: input file ... contains 928 bytes
avrdude: reading on-chip flash data:

Reading | ################################### | 100% 0.44s

avrdude: verifying ...
avrdude: 928 bytes of flash verified

avrdude: safemode: Fuses OK (E:00, H:00, L:00)

avrdude done. Thank you.

============ [SUCCESS] Took 3.33 seconds ============
```

⚠ It appears that you will always see the following message until you install the requested file or if it has been installed but has been modified from the released file:

Warning! Please install `99-platformio-udev.rules` and check that your board's PID and VID are listed in the rules. `http://docs.platformio.org/en/latest/faq.html#platformio-udev-rules`

This can be a little irritating, but if anything goes wrong with the upload, at least you have a couple of clues as to what to check. It's especially irritating as the file is *only* required for ICSP devices. Using a bootloader only requires that your user be in the `dialout` group.

You should be able to see the built-in LED flashing away merrily in the usual manner.

So that's how easy it is to create Arduino-style projects using the command-line versions of the PlatformIO Core code. I admit that it would be nice to have an IDE, even one as simple as the Arduino IDE, so later on, in Section 6.1.4, "*PlatformIO in an IDE*," I'll explain how easy it is to add PlatformIO features to one of a number of existing IDEs.

In the meantime, the next section shows how to create the Blink sketch as a plain AVR C/C++ program.

ⓘ You can use PlatformIO to import existing Arduino sketches. This is not really possible from the command line, yet. You have to use the `pio home` command, which is discussed later. If you need to do it manually, then

- Create a new project in the usual manner.

- Edit the `platform.ini` file and make sure that the Arduino framework is listed.

- Copy the existing Arduino project's `ino` file into the `src` folder.

- Edit the ino file and add the line `#include "Arduino.h"` at the top.

6.1.2.5. AVR-Style Projects

The preceding project used the standard Arduino Language and compiled down to a hex file the same size as you would have seen if the Arduino IDE had been used instead. You can, however, *go commando* and bypass the entire Arduino system, as shown in the following. Remember, however, that it is your responsibility to make all the decisions about ports, pins, and so on.

If you are still in the `TestProject` directory, change back up one level to the standard location for PlatformIO projects. Then create a new project similar to the previous one. I'm not using an additional uno variant this time, but there's no reason that you cannot use "uno," for example.

Remember this is no longer an Arduino board; it's a plain vanilla Atmel AVR development board – it just happens to look like an Arduino!

You should find a suitable board as follows, specifying the "atmega328" device name:

```
pio boards atmega328 | grep 16
```

If you are on Windows, then use this command instead:

```
pio boards atmega328 | find "16"
```

There are quite a few occurrences of the text "atmega328," so the additional filtering with grep or find helps narrow it down to 16 MHz versions. I picked the 328p16m variant, but anything which matches your setup should do:

```
mkdir TestProjectAVR
cd TestProjectAVR
pio init --board 328p16m
```

Once again, if you wish to upload using a programmer, then edit the platformio.ini file and add a new environment which is a copy of the one just created, with the additional lines for your particular programmer. Mine will be as per Listing 6-3, with the comments removed for brevity.

Listing 6-3. The new platform.ini file

```
[env:328p16m]
platform = atmelavr
board = 328p16m

[env:328p16m_programmer]
platform = atmelavr
board = 328p16m
;uploader = usbtinyisp
upload_protocol = usbtiny
```

You can hopefully see that I've also deleted the line `framework = arduino` as this is no longer required for plain AVR programming. Leaving it in will cause all the Arduino files to be compiled regardless of the fact that they are not used.

Yes, the actual physical board *is* an Arduino of some kind, but it is now being used as an AVR development board instead of an Arduino.

Create `src/Blink.cpp` containing the code in Listing 6-4.

Listing 6-4. Another blink sketch

```
#include <avr/io.h>            ①
#include <util/delay.h>        ②

int main(void)
```

```
{
    // D13 is actually PortB Pin 5. Configure
    // that pin as an output.
    // This equates to the Arduino setup() function.
    DDRB = (1 << DDB5);                              ③

    // This equates to the Arduino loop() function.
    while (1)
    {
        _delay_ms(1000);                             ④

        // Toggle the LED by writing to PINB.
        PINB = (1 << PINB5);                         ⑤
    }

    return 0;                                        ⑥
}
```

① This brings in the correct settings, register names, pin numbers and other definitions for the particular AVR microcontroller in use.

② We need this to enable us to call the _delay_ms() function (delay in milliseconds).

③ This is effectively pinMode(13, OUTPUT). Digital pin 13 is on PORTB and is bit 5 of that port.

④ This delays for 1 second.

⑤ Pin toggling is carried out by writing a 1_{binary} to the appropriate bit in the PIN register for the pin to be toggled.

⑥ We never get here, but because main() is always declared as returning an int, then the compiler complains if we leave this off. There are other ways to silence the compiler, but this is the easiest, in my opinion.

6.1.2.5.1. Compiling AVR Projects

Compiling an AVR-style program is exactly the same as before:

```
pio run -e 328p16m
```

The -e option can be omitted if there is only a single board in the project. The output from the command will be as follows, and no Arduino files will have been included in the compilation. The following has been slightly abridged to fit on the page:

```
...
PLATFORM: Atmel AVR > Microduino Core (Atmega328P@16M,5V) ①
SYSTEM: ATMEGA328P 16MHz 2KB RAM (31.50KB Flash)         ②

Library Dependency Finder ...                            ③
LDF MODES: FINDER(chain) COMPATIBILITY(soft)
Collected 0 compatible libraries                         ④

Scanning dependencies...                                 ⑤
No dependencies

Compiling .pioenvs/328p16m/src/Blink.o                   ⑥
Linking .pioenvs/328p16m/firmware.elf                    ⑦
Checking size .pioenvs/328p16m/firmware.elf
Building .pioenvs/328p16m/firmware.hex                   ⑧

Memory Usage -> http://bit.ly/pio-memory-usage           ⑨
DATA:    [            ]    0.0% (used 0 bytes from 2048 bytes)
PROGRAM: [            ]    0.5% (used 158 bytes from 32256 bytes)
============ [SUCCESS] Took 0.36 seconds ============
```

① This line summarizes the platform and board in use.

② This line summarizes the capacity of the chosen device. You may notice that it appears to have an extra 1.5 Kb of flash over the Duemilanove that I used previously. This is using the Uno bootloader which is smaller, by 1.5 Kb.

③ The PlatformIO dependency finder goes hunting for anything that it thinks needs to be included in this compilation. The URL (not shown) that would normally be on this line is that of the documentation for the Library Dependency Finder. I removed it to fit the page width.

④ This is the number of libraries that the finder thinks are required. It says nothing else will be required.

⑤ The system is looking for any dependencies here. It decided that there were none.

⑥ This is where my source file got compiled. Your file name should appear here too.

⑦ The code is first compiled into an elf file. This will be converted to a hex file later.

⑧ The hex file is the one that will be uploaded to the Arduino board. It has only been compiled at present, not yet uploaded.

⑨ The memory usage section shows that this Arduino sketch used no RAM and only 158 bytes of flash program memory.

In bare-bones AVR code, the standard blink sketch takes 158 bytes of flash program memory rather than the Arduino's 928. It also does not create any variables in RAM.

6.1.2.5.2. Uploading AVR Projects

There's no difference in uploading the compiled AVR C/C++ code to the AVR microcontroller than previously. It is done with a bootloader or with an ICSP device as normal. In the former case:

```
pio  run  -e  328p16m  -t upload
```

Or with an ICSP device:

```
pio run -e 328p16m_programmer -t program
```

Remember to edit the platformio.ini file if you want to use a programmer instead of, or as well as, the bootloader – see preceding text.

The output from the upload is very similar to that when an Arduino-style project is uploaded, so has not been reproduced here.

The plain AVR style of programming takes less time to compile as it is not required to compile all the Arduino support code – what you see in the program is what you get.

💡 Those readers who are slightly ahead of me here will realize that this means that you don't get things like millis() and micros(),Timer/counter 0 Overflow interrupts, or even interrupts enabled when you compile an AVR-style project. Everything you need, *you* have to enable. The Arduino does a heck of a lot of stuff in the background to make your life easy.

I wish I had £1.00 (about $1.28 currently) for every project that didn't work initially because I forgot to enable interrupts!

You should now be able to see the built-in LED flashing away merrily in the usual manner, but this time, using far fewer bytes of flash – 158 as opposed to 928 – and even better 0 bytes of scarce Static RAM for variables, as opposed to 9 bytes previously.

6.1.3. Burning Bootloaders

The PlatformIO software has the ability to burn a bootloader for your device. When you have initialized the board in a project, you need to simply do the following:

- Edit the `platformio.ini` file and add the lines required to use an ICSP device, rather than the bootloader, to do the uploading.

- Run the command `pio run --target bootloader` to do the burn.

As mentioned, you will have to use an ICSP device, or a spare Arduino to use as an ISP, but it does work and is simple. The current version of the `arduino-cli`, 0.6.0 (see Section 6.2), does not yet have the ability to burn a bootloader.

So that's a very brief introduction to the PlatformIO system on the command line. As promised, I shall now demonstrate how you can install PlatformIO so that you can use an existing IDE to develop code for your Arduino boards – be that in Arduino Language or plain AVR C/C++ – the choice is yours.

6.1.4. PlatformIO in an IDE

You have seen how PlatformIO can be used in the command line, but let's face it. It's not an easy task switching from the editor back to the command line to compile, then back to the editor to fix, and so on. Some Linux editors do allow you to open a terminal within the editor, so that's handy. However, wouldn't it be nice to add PlatformIO to our current favorite development IDE?

There is a variant of PlatformIO which is named *PlatformIO IDE* and this is used as a plugin for, among others, the Atom editor (`https://atom.io/`) or the VSCode editor (`https://code.visualstudio.com/`).

💡 The VSCode editor apparently feeds some data back to Microsoft. People are upset about this, and as the code for VSCode is open source, a variant of VSCode without the telemetry has been created. This is named VSCodium and can be obtained from `https://github.com/VSCodium/vscodium/releases/latest` if you don't want data fed back to Microsoft.

Having said that, the PlatformIO IDE Integration page at `https://docs.platformio.org/en/latest/ide.html` gives details on using PlatformIO Core (yes, Core, not IDE) to create project files for various IDEs. For the rest of the PlatformIO section of the book, I'll be looking at Code::Blocks (`http://codeblocks.org/`) as that's an IDE that I use on Windows (at work) and on Linux.

Run the following in a command-line session:

```
pio init --help
```

The output is as follows with the current version:

```
Usage: pio init [OPTIONS]

Options:
  -d, --project-dir DIRECTORY
  -b, --board ID
  --ide [atom|clion|codeblocks|eclipse|emacs|netbeans|
        qtcreator|sublimetext|vim|visualstudio|vscode]
  -O, --project-option TEXT
  --env-prefix TEXT
  -s, --silent
  -h, --help                      Show this message and exit.
```

These are the various options that the command accepts. Look at the --ide options. There are facilities for PlatformIO to create project files for a number of IDEs such as Eclipse, QT Creator, Code::Blocks, etc. I'm a big fan of QT Creator and Code::Blocks, so let's set up a project for Code::Blocks.

! I have recently noticed that QT Creator projects don't compile properly. This is due to the AVR version of the g++ compiler not being correctly configured into the project file. Unlike Code::Blocks, which does include the compiler in the project settings, QT Creator doesn't. You have to pick it manually in the settings to use the AVR version of g++.

There's no other software that you need to install. The PlatformIO Core software has everything you need to integrate into one of the many supported IDEs.

6.1.4.1. Set Up a New Code::Blocks Arduino Project

If you are not already there, change your working directory back to the default location for PlatformIO projects as before and initialize a new Arduino-style project as follows. Adjust the board to match your specific setup of course:

```
mkdir CodeBlocks
cd CodeBlocks
pio init --ide codeblocks --board diecimilaatmega328
```

Once the command has completed, you will be able to find the usual files and folders as previously; however, in addition, there will be a platformio.cbp file – a Code::Blocks project file.

Open the Code::Blocks IDE as usual and select File ➤ Open, navigate to the directory where the project was just initialized within, and open the project file platformio.cbp in the normal manner.

Open the platformio.ini file within the IDE. You may be asked to select which editor to use – simply scroll down the list and allow it to be opened within Code::Blocks itself. The file looks like the following:

```
[env:diecimilaatmega328]
platform = atmelavr
board = diecimilaatmega328
framework = arduino
```

This time, it doesn't matter that the environment has such a long-winded name. I'll never be referring to it again. Please also note that in this case I'm not intending to use the programmer – I'll be using the normal Arduino bootloader to program my board this time, but the process of setting up the ICSP is as before.

Click File ➤ New to add a new file. Select "Blank File" when prompted, and then choose to add it to the project. You will have to save the file first, so make sure that you select the src directory and save the file as Blink.cpp as usual.

When saved, you can accept the option to add the file to both the release and debug projects. The file will now be opened in the editor. Add the code in Listing 6-5 to the new file. This is a comment-free version of the standard Arduino Blink sketch that we created previously.

Listing 6-5. Code::Blocks blink sketch

```
#include "Arduino.h"

#ifndef LED_BUILTIN
#define LED_BUILTIN 13
#endif
```

```
void setup()
{
    pinMode(LED_BUILTIN, OUTPUT);
}

void loop()
{
    digitalWrite(LED_BUILTIN, HIGH);
    delay(1000);
    digitalWrite(LED_BUILTIN, LOW);
    delay(1000);
}
```

Now click the build button – it looks like a cogwheel – or click Build ➤ Build or press Ctrl+F9 to compile the code. The build log tab at the bottom should fill with the usual text.

When it compiles cleanly, it's ready to be uploaded. This is done by clicking the run button (the green arrow), clicking Build ➤ Run, or pressing Ctrl+F10.

A new window will open, and the normal PlatformIO text that we are by now used to will scroll up the screen. Your Arduino board has now been programmed and should once more be blinking. Press Enter in the newly opened window to close it and return to the IDE.

6.1.4.2. Set Up a New Code::Blocks AVR Project

It is just as simple to create a new project to code in plain AVR C/C++.

Change directory back to the default location for PlatformIO projects as before and then initialize a new AVR-style project as follows:

```
mkdir CodeBlocksAVR
cd CodeBlocksAVR
pio init --ide codeblocks --board 328p16m
```

Open the platformio.ini file within the Code::Blocks IDE as normal and delete the last line that says framework = arduino – we don't need it. You may also add the lines to use your programmer, if necessary. I'm again using a bootloader in this example.

As before, click File ➤ New to add a new file. Select "Blank File" when prompted, and then choose to add it to the project. You will have to save the file first, so make sure that you select the src directory and save the file as Blink.cpp as usual.

When saved, accept the option to add the file to both the release and debug projects. The file will now be opened in the editor. Add the following code – which is a comment-free version of the standard AVR Blink sketch which we created previously and is shown in Listing 6-6.

Listing 6-6. Another blink sketch.

```
#include<avr/io.h>
#include<util/delay.h>

int main(void)
{
    DDRB = (1 << DDB5);

    while (1)
    {
        _delay_ms(1000);
        PINB = (1 << PINB5);
    }

    return 0;
}
```

Now click the build button, click Build ➤ Build, or press Ctrl+F9 to compile the code. When it compiles cleanly, it's ready to be uploaded. This is done by clicking the run button (the green arrow), clicking Build ➤ Run, or pressing Ctrl+F10.

A new window will open, and the normal PlatformIO text that we are by now used to will scroll up the screen. Your Arduino board has now been programmed and should once more be blinking. Press Enter in the newly opened window to close it and return to the IDE.

---

i You should be aware that there isn't, apparently, an option to determine the environment/board to be compiled and programmed when using the IDE in this manner. At least, I've not been able to find one! So don't go adding numerous boards to your project file at creation time.

Also, as before, when programming your device with an ICSP device, you will need to edit the platformio.ini file to suit your programmer.

6.1.5. PlatformIO Home

This is an *interesting* development in the PlatformIO system. Running the command for the first time will download some files, and then this text will appear on the screen:

```
   __I_
 /\-_--\      PlatformIO Home
/  \_-__\
|[]| [] |     http://127.0.0.1:8008
|_|___|_____
```

After a short delay, the default browser on your system should open at the page http://localhost:8008, and an IDE-alike screen will be waiting for you.

> ⓘ The `pio` home command will hang up the session it was opened in until closed by pressing Ctrl+C. If you do this while the browser is open, then the browser will stop responding as the HTML server has just been "crashed."
>
> When you are finished in the "pio home" page, close it in the browser and then shut down the server by pressing Ctrl+C in the session you typed the `pio` home command.

On this browser screen, you can search for boards, libraries, etc. and install them. You can add new or update existing platforms and so on. However, this is where you can create new projects without needing to remember all those `pio init` commands and options.

6.1.5.1. Creating Projects

Click the "New Project" button, and on the following dialogue, give the project a name and choose a board and a framework – if there are options available for the chosen board, the framework will usually be automatically selected based on the board you have chosen. When choosing a board, start typing, and the list will be filtered according to your typed text.

This is where the `pio settings get projects_dir` is used. As you may have noticed, although you set this way back when installing PlatformIO, it was never apparently used for new projects – you always had to be in the desired location to create a new project. So leaving the box ticked to "use the default location," the project will be created there. Hover over the "?" to see where the default location will be. You can also click the "custom" link to define where you want to create the new project.

Click the "Finish" button, and after a small delay, a message will appear telling you that the project has been created and will be found wherever you chose and that you can process it with the command `platformio run`. Hmmm – and there was me thinking I could use PIO Home to edit projects. No such luck I'm afraid.

6.1.5.2. Opening Projects

It's useful to create projects, but the option to "Open Project" simply tells you to go to the location where the project is and open it in your favorite IDE. However, maybe the future will be different, and we can edit and so on within the browser. That would be fun!

So, after creating the project, you are pretty much back in your favorite IDE or editor, editing and running `pio run` commands to compile the code and `pio run -t upload` to upload with the bootloader.

6.1.5.3. Importing Arduino Sketches

Another useful feature of PIO Home is that existing Arduino projects can be imported from the PIO Home main screen. To do this, you simply click "Import Arduino Project" and follow the on-screen prompts to

- Choose a board.

- Select the existing Arduino project.

Then click the "Import" button.

A new folder will be created in your default PlatformIO project directory. It will *not* be named in a meaningful manner, so renaming it might be helpful and wise. Within that directory, you will find the usual PlatformIO directories and files, and, finally, the original sketch will be found in the `src` directory, with its original `*.ino` name.

To compile the imported project, simply execute the command `pio run` within the project's top-level directory where the file `platformio.ini` is to be found.

> 💡 To be honest, `pio` home doesn't appear to be of much use as described earlier, other than as an easy way to import existing Arduino sketches. However, when you use the PlatformIO IDE variant, coming next, that home screen is much more useful in that environment.

6.1.6. PlatformIO IDE

This section of the book will concentrate on the PlatformIO IDE variant using the VSCode editor or, in my case, the VSCodium version which is slightly different from the original in that it doesn't "phone home" to Microsoft with details of what you might have been doing.

What's the difference between PlatformIO Core and PlatformIO IDE?

PlatformIO Core, as discussed, installs a number of command-line tools to allow you to use your favorite editor, or programming IDE, to develop software for the Arduino board, either in Arduino Language or in the AVR's native C++ format. You normally edit the code in your editor and compile it from the command line.

PlatformIO IDE is simply an extension or plugin to the Atom and the VSCode editors which effectively turns those two editors into an IDE to develop Arduino software. In this variant, you develop the code in the editor and then compile and upload it also from within the editor.

> 💡 Don't get confused. PlatformIO IDE isn't necessary to generate project files for a number of IDEs.
>
> The "IDE" part of the name comes from the fact that this version of PlatformIO turns your favorite editor into an IDE for generating code for your embedded devices. This assumes that your favorite editor is Atom or VSCode/VSCodium, that is!

I use VSCodium as my editor, so the remainder of this chapter will look at installing PlatformIO into that specific editor; however, the process is almost identical if you are using Atom.

With Atom, there is a toolbar with big chunky buttons down the left side where you can compile and upload projects. With VSCode/VSCodium, there is an *alien's head* icon added to the left toolbar, which opens the Project Tasks list, from where you can click any of the activated options to run compilations and so on. There does appear to be more options in VSCode/VSCodium than in Atom.

6.1.6.1. Installation

To install PlatformIO IDE in VSCodium, either

- Open the extensions view on the left side.

- Press Ctrl+Shift+X.

- Click View ➤ Extensions.

The extensions search should now open on the left side of the editor window.

In the search box at the top, type in "PlatformIO" and choose to install the option which appears, probably at the top of the list, "PlatformIO IDE."

After it installs, a window at the bottom of the editor window will open, and a few tools will be installed to enable PlatformIO IDE. Do not close the window or move to another editor tab until you are advised that the installation is complete.

To start using the new plugin, you have to restart the editor, so click the button helpfully displayed by the PlatformIO installation process.

After restarting, you will notice the following:

- A new editor tab appears named "PIO Home," with an alien's head as an icon.

- The command palette (View ➤ Command Palette
  or Ctrl+Shift+P) has a number of new PlatformIO
  commands listed.

6.1.6.2. PIO Home Tab

On the PIO Home tab in the editor, you have a new toolbar on the left and
some options on the main display area. On the toolbar, there are icons for
the following:

- Home – Takes you back to the PIO Home page, if you
  happen to have chosen one of the following options.

- Inspect – Allows various details of an existing project to
  be inspected and displayed. The code is analyzed as in
  memory usage and so on.

- Libraries – Allows you to search for and install libraries
  that may be required by some Arduino and AVR
  projects.

- Boards – Allows you to search for a board. Try entering
  "Duemilanove" and clicking the search icon. The two
  variants of the board will be shown alongside some
  important details of the boards such as the platform
  and framework required, the memory sizes, etc.

- Platforms – Displays any installed platforms and
  allows you to uninstall them or to install any new
  requirements for a new board.

- Devices – Assuming you have an Arduino board
  attached, this option will display details of the board(s),
  the type of communications chip, and the port it is
  attached to. Similarly to the `arduino-cli`, this option
  will not detect an ICSP device.

While on the main page itself, we can see these options:

- New Project – This should be fairly obvious. It allows you to create a new project and pick as many boards for it as you wish.

- Import Arduino Project – This option lets you navigate to an existing Arduino project and import it into PlatformIO's favored format.

- Open Project – Opens an existing project within the editor and allows you to continue developing it.

- Example Projects – Displays a few example projects and allows you to import them into PlatformIO for inspection or learning. You can, of course, compile the example projects.

At the bottom of the screen is a couple of items of recent PlatformIO news and a list of your most recent projects. If this is a new install, you probably don't have any listed. If you did, you have options here to hide the projects from this list or to open it. Clicking the "open" link opens the VSCode/VSCodium explorer on the left side of the screen to the top-level directory for the project. From there you can open files for editing in the usual manner.

6.1.6.3. Creating a New Project

A new project is created from the PIO Home screen. If it is not already being displayed, then click the PlatformIO icon in the left-side toolbar to open the PlatformIO menu. Under quick access, open the list of options under "PIO Home" and click "Open." A new tab appears named "PIO Home."

On this tab, click the new project option. Then fill in (or select) the appropriate options for the project name, the board you want to use, and the location for the project. You can supply a custom location or simply accept the default, which will be displayed if you hover over the "?".

If you wish to use the same source code for numerous different boards, simply keep adding new ones until you have everything set up as you wish.

Click the "Finish" button to create the project. After a short delay, the PIO Home tab will close. This never used to happen prior to version 4.1.0, so was a little disconcerting! On the left, the explorer will open with the various files and directories of the new project on display. The PIO Home tab will then reopen, after another short delay. I usually keep it closed as it is of little use during development.

You can now edit your files in the usual manner.

6.1.6.4. Opening Existing Projects

If your project already exists, then you can use the PIO Home tab to open it. As in the preceding text, make sure the tab is visible in the editor, then click the "Open Project" option, navigate to the project's location, and click the "Open <project name>" button.

As before, the PIO Home tab will close, and the explorer on the left will open at the project's location. The project can now be edited as required.

6.1.6.5. Editing the Project

The PlatformIO system expects to find header files within the `include` directory and source files in the `src` directory under the project's home. To test a new project, open the dummy `src/main.cpp` file and type in the code from Listing 6-7.

Listing 6-7. Yet another blink sketch!

```
#include <avr/io.h>
#include <util/delay.h>

int main(void)
{
    // D13 is actually PortB Pin 5. Configure
    // that pin as an output.
    // This equates to the Arduino setup() function.
    DDRB = (1 << DDB5);

    // This equates to the Arduino loop() function.
    while (1)
    {
        _delay_ms(250);

        // Toggle the LED by writing to PINB.
        PINB |= (1 << PINB5);
    }

    return 0;
}
```

6.1.6.6. Compiling a Project

Once editing is done, you can compile the project either from the left-side toolbar or from a terminal which can be opened in the editor (Terminal ➤ New Terminal or Ctrl+Shift+#). If you use the terminal, it opens into the project's location, and you can run any of the usual PlatformIO commands already described in Section 6.1.2, "*Testing PlatformIO Core.*"

To compile from the toolbar, you need to open the PlatformIO window on the left by clicking the icon. Then, under the "Project Tasks" list, select

"Build" to build the project. You can also press Ctrl+Alt+B to build it from within one of the project's files open in the editor.

A new terminal will open, and progress will be displayed. You are requested to close this terminal when finished with it, by pressing any key. This will only work if the terminal has focus. (Ask me how I know this.)

If all looks okay with the compilation, we are ready to upload or program the board.

6.1.6.7. Upload or Program a Project

In the Project Tasks list, click "Upload" to upload using a bootloader or "Upload using programmer" to use an ICSP device. This latter option requires that you have added the device's details to the platformio.ini file in the usual manner:

```
;uploader = usbtinyisp
upload_protocol = usbtiny
```

ℹ️ From PlatformIO 4.1.0 onward, the preceding first line is no longer required and has been commented out.

Another new terminal will open, and progress messages will be displayed as appropriate. Then when it completes, your Arduino board should be blinking happily again.

That's a very quick and high-level overview of something that's becoming very popular in the Arduino world, especially with users of 3D printers running the Marlin Firmware as Marlin 2.0 onward uses PlatformIO to build and upload the firmware.

I personally have swapped over from the Arduino IDE to PlatformIO for most of my projects and experimenting with AVRs and Arduinos. I find it a lot faster to develop software using PlatformIO, and I'm more comfortable in the editor than in the Arduino IDE.

Coming up next, I'll be taking a look at the new, but still under development, Arduino CLI – a command-line version of the Arduino IDE which allows you to use your own favorite editor and make files to create and build your Arduino projects.

6.2. Arduino Command Line

The Arduino IDE has always had a sort of command-line version, at least on Linux. Windows had a separate version due to the way that Windows GUI and command-line applications are so different. However, in August 2018, a new Arduino command-line application, `arduino-cli`, came out in alpha test.

It is possible that what is explained here might be likely subject to some changes as time goes by.

When I first started looking into the `arduino-cli`, it was September 2018, and the latest release at that time was 0.2.1-alpha. It had quite a few bug and foibles, but hey, it's an alpha release so it's expected. The version I'm looking at here is a much later release, 0.6.0 (it's November 2019 now), and many of the original bugs and foibles have been sorted. As more releases are, ahem, released, things can only get better.

The use of the Arduino CLI is to help in getting code built using make files, for incorporating into other IDEs and, *most likely*, as the basis for whatever IDE changes appear in version 2 of the Arduino IDE itself. It has been noted on the Arduino Developers Google Group (`https://groups.google.com/a/arduino.cc/forum/#!forum/developers`) that visually impaired users have great difficulty with IDEs and that command-line versions are much better, so this can only be helpful.

6.2.1. Obtaining the Arduino CLI

Stable releases are available for download from the project's main release page at `https://github.com/arduino/arduino-cli/releases` which has links to the all binary releases for numerous platforms – there are 32- and 64-bit versions for Linux and a version for Linux on ARM chips – Raspberry Pi, for example. Users with Windows or Macs are not left out either. Click the link to download the appropriate version for your system.

You can always get to the most up-to-date release using the URL `https://github.com/arduino/arduinocli/releases/latest`.

On the main project page, there are additional links to various nightly builds. These can be used if you want the latest, bleeding-edge release; however, you are advised to stick with the stable releases.

Failing all this, you can, if you are so inclined, build your own from the source code. Links are on the preceding home page with the details. I'm avoiding this option as I'd want to look at the source and I'm not a Go (Golang) developer, yet.

6.2.2. Installing

There are details on the home page which hint that you can download and install the `arduino-cli` with a single `curl` command. While I'm sure that this will work perfectly well, I would be blindly allowing a script, downloaded from the Internet, to be executed without checking what it might do. I'm going with the latest release from the preceding URL instead.

Pick the file that's appropriate for your system. I'm on 64-bit Linux Mint, so my file is `arduino-cli_0.6.0_Linux_64bit.tar.gz`.

After downloading, simply `unzip` (Windows users) or use `tar` on Linux and MacOS, as shown in the following Linux example:

```
tar -zvjf arduino-cli_0.6.0_Linux_64bit.tar.gz
```

On Windows, right-click the file and "extract," or in the command line, the following will suffice:

```
unzip  arduino-cli_0.6.0_Windows_64bit.zip
```

The current version, 0.6.0, expands to three files:

- `arduino-cli` which is the utility itself.

- `License.txt` which is the license.

- `readme.md` which is a markdown file used on the project's main GitHub page. This is a good place to start reading.

If the location you unzipped/untarred the download isn't on your path, you can either add it to the path or copy the `arduino-cli` file to a directory that *is* on your path:

```
cp arduino-cli ~/bin/
```

Test that the downloaded file works with this command:

```
arduino-cli version

arduino-cli Version: 0.6.0 Commit: 3a08b07
```

You can get a feel for the various commands and options available in the latest version with the following command:

```
arduino-cli help
```

The 0.6.0 version returns the following output:

```
Arduino Command Line Interface (arduino-cli).

Usage:
  arduino-cli [command]

Examples:
  arduino-cli <command> [flags...]
```

```
Available Commands:
  board           Arduino board commands.
  compile         Compiles Arduino sketches.
  config          Arduino Configuration Commands.
  core            Arduino Core operations.
  daemon          Run as a daemon on port :50051
  help            Help about any command
  lib             Arduino commands about libraries.
  sketch          Arduino CLI Sketch Commands.
  upload          Upload Arduino sketches.
  version         Shows version number of arduino CLI.

... Lots more output omitted here ...

Use "arduino-cli [command] --help" for more information.
```

6.2.3. Configuring the CLI

By default, the configuration assumes a number of details about your system. It's best we find those out before we dive in and start creating sketches:

```
arduino-cli  config  dump
```

There's not much to see though:

```
proxy_type: auto
sketchbook_path: /home/norman/Arduino
arduino_data: /home/norman/.arduino15
board_manager: {}
```

Unfortunately, we cannot change these settings from the command line yet as there are no options to the config command other than dump or init. If you need to make changes, then the following will be required:

```
arduino-cli config init
```

```
Config file PATH: /home/norman/.arduino15/arduino-cli.yaml
```

You now have all the default config stored in the file name listed earlier. You may edit the file and change the configuration as desired. Currently, there's not much to change, but the readme file that came with the download does have some information of uses for this file, which may be of interest, but are not covered here.

Things are changing with regard to configuration, even as I type! I raised issue 503 (`https://github.com/arduino/arduino-cli/issues/503`) on GitHub, because the `sketch new` command no longer created sketches in the sketchbook location. I was advised that:

- If a sketch name only is passed as parameter, assume that the sketch directory is the current directory.

- If a relative path for the sketch is passed, join it with the current directory path.

- If an absolute path for the sketch is passed, simply use it.

This is to be applied to the `sketch new` command in addition to `compile` and `upload` commands.

So, no reference at all to the sketchbook , so I would consider leaving the configuration well alone until the application settles down to at least release candidate or release level.

6.2.4. Creating Sketches

As the readme advises, the first task is to create a new sketch. This is done with the `arduino-cli sketch new <name>` command:

```
arduino-cli  sketch  new  MyFirstSketch

Sketch created in: /home/norman/MyFirstSketch
```

That was easy, and it has created a blank sketch, `MyFirstSketch.ino`, with the content in Listing 6-8.

Listing 6-8. A brand-new sketch

```
void setup() {
}

void loop() {
}
```

As noted earlier, version 0.6.0 is not using the default sketchbook location from the `config dump` – previous versions did. The sketch is created within the *current directory*. For now, let's move it to the proper place:

```
mv  ~/MyFirstSketch/  ~/Arduino/

cd  ~/Arduino/MyFirstSketch
```

You can see from the preceding code that there's not much to a new sketch, but it's a start on developing your next great project. The almost obligatory Blink sketch is obviously required at this point, so edit the generated `MyFirstSketch.ino` file with your favorite editor with the code in Listing 6-9.

Listing 6-9. MyFirstSketch.ino

```
void setup() {
    pinMode(LED_BUILTIN, OUTPUT);
}

void loop() {
    for (short x = 0; x < 4; x++) {
        digitalWrite(LED_BUILTIN, HIGH);
        delay(150);
        digitalWrite(LED_BUILTIN, LOW);
        delay(150);
    }

    delay(500);
}
```

Well, I can't just keep using the *same* blink sketch all the time, can I? I need a bit of variety!

We are now ready to compile the sketch, but as this is a new installation, we have a bit of preliminary work to do. First, we should update the system to make sure we have the latest package index file:

```
arduino-cli core update-index
```

```
Updating index: package_index.json downloaded
```

Now, connect your Arduino to the USB port in the normal manner. Leave a few seconds for it to initialize, and search to see what you have. I have a genuine Duemilanove and a non-genuine Mega 2560 attached. Let's see what the system recognizes:

```
arduino-cli board list
```

After a short delay, I see the information relating to my two boards displayed. Unfortunately, the lines of text are far too wide for this page, so I shall have to summarize.

For my Mega 2560 clone, I see that it

- Is attached to port */dev/ttyACM0* which is a *Serial Port (USB)* type of port

- Has a board name of *Arduino/Genuino Mega 2560*

- Uses the *arduino:avr* core

- Has *arduino:avr:mega* as its FQBN

The board's FBQN is its "Fully Qualified Board Name" and is required, later, to compile and upload sketches.

For my genuine Duemilanove, I see the following:

- Attached to port */dev/ttyUSB0* which is a *Serial Port (USB)* port type

- Has a board name of *Unknown*

- Apparently, has no known core

- Apparently, has no FQBN

💡 The readme advises that boards will be listed as "unknown" if they are connected via an FTDI adaptor. I'm using the Arduino-supplied USB cable on my Duemilanove, but on that board there is an FTDI chip, so I see the board listed as unknown.

Boards are detected based on a vendor and product ID, VID/PID. On boards with FTDI, these identifiers are generic, so the actual board cannot be determined. This is not a major problem here, however, as both my boards have at least been identified as being present.

> ℹ️ Boards will not be detected if they are connected to your computer with an ICSP device.

Now we need to install a core (aka platform) for the boards. The Mega is easy as it lists its core as "arduino:avr" which is useful. The Duemilanove, on the other hand, doesn't list a core, so how do we determine the correct core?

Well, given that it too is an Arduino and has an AVR ATmega328P on board, I'm certain that it has the same core. However, we can search

```
arduino-cli board listall | grep -i duemilanove

Arduino Duemilanove or Diecimila    arduino:avr:diecimila
```

This is useful as it lists the board's name followed by its FQBN. The Fully Qualified Board Name is required when compiling or uploading sketches to the board. It also starts with the appropriate platform/core name, "arduino:avr".

6.2.5. Installing Platforms

At the moment, you only have the command-line tool itself. In order to compile code for Arduino boards with AVR microcontrollers, you must first install a "core" or "platform." In my own case, I need the arduino:avr core for both my boards:

```
arduino-cli core install arduino:avr

Downloading packages...
arduino:avr-gcc@7.3.0-atmel3.6.1-arduino5 downloaded
arduino:avrdude@6.3.0-arduino17 downloaded
arduino:arduinoOTA@1.3.0 downloaded
arduino:avr@1.8.1 downloaded
```

```
Installing arduino:avr-gcc@7.3.0-atmel3.6.1-arduino5...
arduino:avr-gcc@7.3.0-atmel3.6.1-arduino5 installed
Installing arduino:avrdude@6.3.0-arduino17...
arduino:avrdude@6.3.0-arduino17 installed
Installing arduino:arduinoOTA@1.3.0...
arduino:arduinoOTA@1.3.0 installed
Updating arduino:avr@1.6.23 with arduino:avr@1.8.1...
arduino:avr@1.8.1 installed
```

We can check what we have now with the following:

```
arduino-cli core list
```

```
ID              Installed Latest Name
arduino:avr     1.8.1     1.8.1  Arduino AVR Boards
```

Those numbers seem to match up with the list of downloaded "stuff," so we should be good to go.

ℹ️ Don't worry. You don't need to jump through all these hoops every time you want to compile with the `arduino-cli`, just the first time, or when you add a new board that had a different core of course.

6.2.6. Compiling Sketches

The time has arrived. We are now ready to compile our first sketch. You should still be located within the sketch's directory. In my case, that's /home/norman/Arduino/MyFirstSketch, so let's compile it, first for my Mega 2560:

```
arduino-cli compile --fqbn arduino:avr:mega MyFirstSketch
```

```
Error during build: build failed: unable to stat Sketch
     location: stat /home/norman/Arduino/MyFirstSketch/
     MyFirstSketch: no such file or directory
```

Oh well, that didn't go well. Why not?

- If you are located in the parent directory of the sketch, /home/norman/Arduino in my case, the preceding command works fine.

- If you are located elsewhere on the system, perhaps in /home/norman, then you need to supply the full path to the sketch's top-level directory – /home/norman/ Arduino/MyFirstSketch or, the short version, ~/ Arduino/MyFirstSketch.

Let's try another compilation, from the sketch's parent directory instead:

```
cd ..
```

```
arduino-cli compile --fqbn arduino:avr:mega MyFirstSketch
```

When compiling a sketch, you must supply the board's FQBN. If the compilation succeeds, the usual details about the RAM usage will be displayed. If you need verbose output, simply add the -v command-line option to the preceding compile command.

Now, let's compile the same source code for the Duemilanove:

```
arduino-cli compile \
          --fqbn arduino:avr:diecimila \
          MyFirstSketch
```

💡 Yes, on Linux, you can split a long command over a number of lines if it makes it more readable. Each line, except the last, must end with the backslash character and an immediate linefeed – there are no spaces between those characters.

You will see other occasions in this book where I do this. It helps keep things on the page.

Sometimes, when compiling, you might see an error like this:

```
avr-g++: error: missing device or architecture after '-mmcu='
Error: exit status 1
Compilation failed.
```

This is a compiler error, and it is telling you that the command line passed to the compiler was missing an option telling it the microcontroller in use on the board in question.

In older versions of arduino-cli, this used to happen for my Duemilanove and my Nano, so I had to update the board's FQBN at compile and upload time, to specify the appropriate AVR microcontroller. This actually makes sense as some early boards have an ATmega168, while later boards, mine, for example, have an ATmega328.

The following should resolve the issue if you suffer from these errors:

```
arduino-cli compile \
            --fqbn arduino:avr:diecimila:cpu=atmega328 \
            MyFirstSketch
```

Adding the cpu to the FQBN gets rid of the error, and the sketch compiles.

If, like me, you have a Duemilanove or a Nano, then either of these can use the ATmega168 or the Atmega328 family of microcontrollers. While you might not need to, you can always specify the cpu option and be absolutely certain that the compiler will compile the code for the correct CPU. Doing this is the equivalent of selecting the correct board option from the Tools ➤ Boards menu in the IDE.

You can use the -v option on the compile command to see the full, verbose, compilation text. This is similar to what is produced in the Arduino IDE when you have the verbose compilation option enabled.

6.2.7. Uploading Sketches

Uploading a sketch uses a similar command to compiling, and you must remember to always use the same FQBN, or it will ask you to compile the sketch first. The port name is always required when uploading. If you forget the port, then the arduino-cli board list command is your friend.

Uploading to my Duemilanove is carried out as follows:

```
arduino-cli upload \
          --fqbn arduino:avr:diecimila \
          --port /dev/ttyUSB0 \
          MyFirstSketch
```

If you left the cpu=atmega328 parameter attached to the FQBN, it will be ignored.

There will be no output displayed on screen if all went well with the upload. If you wish to see the upload details, just add -v to the command, and you will get the same verbose output as you would have seen in the IDE.

If you see something like the following error message, change up into the parent directory – you are inside the sketch directory:

```
Error during Upload: compiled sketch
    MyFirstSketch/MyFirstSketch.arduino.avr.diecimila.hex
    not found
```

It is possible that you might encounter the following upload error, at least, on Linux:

```
ser_open(): can't open "/dev/ttyUSB0": Permission denied
Error: exit status 1
Error during upload
```

This is simply because the user that you are logged in as is not a member of the group which owns the port that the upload command was trying to use to communicate with the board. You can check, and fix the problem, as follows:

```
ls -l /dev/ttyUSB0
crw-rw-rw- 1 root dialout 188, 0 Nov 30 19:09 /dev/ttyUSB0

groups
norman: norman adm cdrom sudo dip lpadmin sambashare

usermod -a -G dialout your_user
```

Unfortunately, you will need to log out and back in again to pick up the new group. This is mildly irritating, so here's a quick tip on temporarily working around the need to log out.

💡 Instead of logging out and back in again, just, from the command-line session that you are in, run this:

```
su - your_name
```

You will be asked for your password and will start a new shell with the new group assigned. Test it by running the `groups` command again, and note that now you do have `dialout` present.

Now you can upload to your Arduino board.

6.2.8. Uploading Sketches with an ICSP

At present, uploading is only possible when you are using an Arduino board which still has a bootloader present. In-Circuit System Programmers (ICSPs) are not yet supported. If you have a board connected using an ICSP, then the `arduino-cli board list` command will not see it.

There is a workaround, but it's not completely ideal, but it does work.

If you open a sketch in the Arduino IDE, then go to File ➤ Preferences and set the upload option to verbose. Now, compile and upload the sketch to the board with the ICSP device you want to use with `arduino-cli`. Any sketch will do, even an empty one.

In the output area, look for and highlight (or select) the line which mentions "avrdude." It will look something like this exceedingly long line:

```
/home/norman/.arduino15/packages/arduino/tools/avrdude/
6.3.0-arduino17/bin/avrdude -C/home/norman/.arduino15/packages/
arduino/tools/avrdude/6.3.0-arduino17/etc/avrdude.conf -v
-patmega328p -cusbtiny -Uflash:w:/tmp/arduino_build_760389/
sketch_nov30a.ino.hex:i
```

Now, in my case, that is an upload to a Duemilanove using my USBtiny programmer. From this, I can see the various parameters on the command line and can write a shell script to do the required work after compiling with `arduino-cli`. You can see what I created in Listing 6-10 where the code for `upload.sh` is shown.

Listing 6-10. The upload.sh shell script for Linux

```bash
#!/bin/bash
#
# a script to program a Duemilanove with a compiled sketch
# created by the Arduino CLI utility. Currently, version 0.6.0
# does not have the ability to upload by any means except a
# bootloader.
#
# The following command is slightly adapted from that used in
# the Arduino IDE to program a Duemilanove with the USBtiny
# programmer. It requires a filename on the command line,
# which is the name of the compiled hex file to be uploaded.
#

# Devices and ports etc.
#
# AVR device:
AVR=atmega328p                                    ①

# ICSP device:
ICSP=usbtiny                                      ②

# programs and config files
#
# Where everything lives:                         ③
ARDUINO_HOME="${HOME}"/.arduino15
AVRDUDE_TOOLS="${ARDUINO_HOME}"/packages/arduino/tools
AVRDUDE_HOME="${AVRDUDE_TOOLS}"/avrdude/6.3.0-arduino17

# Avrdude executable:                             ④
AVRDUDE="${AVRDUDE_HOME}"/bin/avrdude

# Avrdude configuration file:                     ⑤
```

```
AVRDUDECONF="${AVRDUDE_HOME}"/etc/avrdude.conf

# Leave blank if you don't want all the output.
# Otherwise, use -v
VERBOSE=-v                                    ⑥

# Get hex file.
HEXFILE="${1}"                                ⑦

# Did we get a parameter?
if [ "${HEXFILE}" == "" ]
then
    echo A hex filename must be passed.
    exit 1
fi

# Does the file exist?
if ([ ! -f "${HEXFILE}" ])
then
    echo "${HEXFILE}" is not a filename.
    exit 1
fi

# Does the file have the 'hex' extension? ⑧
EXTENSION="${HEXFILE##*.}"
if [ "${EXTENSION}" != "hex" ]
then
    echo "${HEXFILE}" is not a valid compiled Arduino sketch
    exit 1
fi

# Upload via the ICSP device.            ⑨
"${AVRDUDE}" -C "${AVRDUDECONF}" "${VERBOSE}" \
    -p "${AVR}" -c "${ICSP}" -Uflash:w:"${HEXFILE}":i
```

① This is a copy of the device name extracted from the upload command line displayed by the IDE.

② This is a copy of the uploading device name, again, extracted from the IDE's command line for the upload.

③ This is the parent directory where the avrdude applications, bin directories, etc. are to be found. No trailing "/" is required. As before, this path is extracted from the IDE output.

④ This is where we find the avrdude file, relative to $AVRDUDE_HOME.

⑤ This is where we find the avrdude.conf file, relative to $AVRDUDE_HOME.

⑥ We want verbose output. If you don't want all the chatter from avrdude, remove the -v and you will get less output when uploading.

⑦ From here down, we do a bit of validation. Did we get a file name passed to us? Is it actually a file name for a file that physically exists? Does it have an extension of "hex" on the file name?

⑧ Nobody said that bash coding was easy! This extracts the file name's extension. We are looking for "hex."

⑨ The upload happens here. Of course, this will overwrite your Arduino's bootloader, so from now on, you will have to continue using the ICSP device or burn a new bootloader.

Your will need to check and maybe replace my directory names to those appropriate to your system.

> If you decide to follow my example and create an
> upload.sh script, beware when using the Arduino
> IDE if it asks to update your boards or libraries. This
> can have the effect of changing the names of some
> of the directories I've used in the following in my
> script. If you suddenly start getting upload errors,
> check what's been updated and amend the script.

> This script also doesn't upload any data to the
> ATmega328P's EEPROM. I did say that this wasn't an
> ideal solution.

So I hear you ask, "How do I find out where the compiled hex file is?"
Simple. Once your sketch compiles correctly, with no errors or warnings,
you will be able to find the required .hex file in the sketch's directory:

```
ls -1 MyFirstSketch      # That's a one, not an ell.

MyFirstSketch.arduino.avr.diecimila.elf MyFirstSketch.
arduino.avr.diecimila.hex MyFirstSketch.arduino.avr.mega.elf
MyFirstSketch.arduino.avr.mega.hex MyFirstSketch.ino
```

We can see from the preceding code that different boards have
different files. The cpu that we may have needed to use when compiling,
however, is not part of the output file name – only the FQBN is used.

You can now pass the required file name to the upload.sh script as a
parameter, and the sketch will be uploaded via the ICSP device instead of
using the bootloader.

6.2.9. Burning Bootloaders

As of version 0.6.0, the latest version available at the time I wrote this, it is
still not possible to burn a bootloader with the arduino-cli utility. So, if you
have managed to either corrupt or overwrite the bootloader, what can you do?

In a manner similar to that described earlier to enable uploads using an ICSP device, there is a workaround – and again, the Arduino IDE is required.

💡 Obviously, if you have the Arduino IDE installed, you can burn a bootloader for your device at any time you like using Tools ➤ Burn Bootloader.

The process is very similar to that described earlier to upload a sketch with an ICSP. We use the Arduino IDE, in verbose mode, to extract the required command lines used when burning a bootloader and then simply create a shell script with just about everything parameterized, ready to be run on the command line.

Extracting was easy. I burned a bootloader to my Duemilanove with my USBtiny device and copied the two calls to avrdude from the verbose output. You will see them at the bottom of Listing 6-11, my burnBootloader.sh script.

If you are writing the script for a different device or board, you will need to change the device and board names and locations to match your system.

Listing 6-11. The burnBootloader.sh shell script for Linux

```
#!/bin/bash
#
# A script to program a Duemilanove with the default Arduino
# bootloader and fuses. The script assumes that the device
# is indeed a Duemilanove, that the default bootloader hex
# file exists and that a USBtiny programmer will be used.
#
# You CANNOT burn a bootloader using the current bootloader!
```

```
#
# Run the "burn bootloader" command in the IDE, for your
# device, with verbose upload configured to see your command
# line, and change the necessary variables below.
#

# Devices and ports etc.
#
# AVR device:
AVR=atmega328p                              ①

# ICSP device:
ICSP=usbtiny                                ②

# programs and config files
#
# Where everything lives:                   ③
ARDUINO_HOME="${HOME}"/.arduino15
AVRDUDE_TOOLS="${ARDUINO_HOME}"/packages/arduino/tools
AVRDUDE_HOME="${AVRDUDE_TOOLS}"/avrdude/6.3.0-arduino17

# The following long path is split on two lines. There
# are no leading or trailing spaces on each line.
BOOTLOADER_HOME="${ARDUINO_HOME}"/packages/arduino/\
hardware/avr/1.8.2/bootloaders/atmega

# Avrdude executable:                       ④
AVRDUDE="${AVRDUDE_HOME}"/bin/avrdude

# Avrdude configuration file:               ⑤
AVRDUDECONF="${AVRDUDE_HOME}"/etc/avrdude.conf

# Leave blank if you don't want all the output.
# Otherwise, use -v
VERBOSE=-v                                  ⑥
```

```
# Bootloader details:                          ⑦
BOOTLOADER="${BOOTLOADER_HOME}"/ATmegaBOOT_168_atmega328.hex

# Fuses:                                       ⑧
EFUSE=0xFD
HFUSE=0xDA
LFUSE=0xFF

LOCK=0x0F
UNLOCK=0x3F

# Does the bootloader file exist?              ⑨
if ([ ! -f "${BOOTLOADER}" ])
then
    echo "${BOOTLOADER}" is not a valid filename.
exit 1
fi

# Does the bootloader file have the 'hex' extension?
EXTENSION="${BOOTLOADER##*.}"
if [ "${EXTENSION}" != "hex" ]
then
    echo "${BOOTLOADER}" is not a valid bootloader file
    exit 1
fi

# Set the fuses for a Duemilanove.            ⑩
${AVRDUDE}" -C ${AVRDUDECONF}" "${VERBOSE}" \
-p "${AVR}" -c "${ICSP}" -e -Ulock:w:"${UNLOCK}":m \
-Uefuse:w:"${EFUSE}":m -Uhfuse:w:"${HFUSE}":m \
-Ulfuse:w:"${LFUSE}":m

# Burn the actual bootloader hex file.        ⑪
"${AVRDUDE}" -C "${AVRDUDECONF}" "${VERBOSE}" \
-p "${AVR}" -c "${ICSP}" -Uflash:w:"${BOOTLOADER}":i \
-Ulock:w:"${LOCK}":m
```

① This is a copy of the device name extracted from the upload command line displayed by the IDE.

② This is a copy of the uploading device name, again, extracted from the IDE's command line for the upload.

③ This is the parent directory where the avrdude applications, bin directories, etc. are to be found. No trailing "/" is required. As before, this path is extracted from the IDE output.

④ This is where we find the avrdude file, relative to $AVRDUDE_HOME.

⑤ This is where we find the avrdude.conf file, relative to $AVRDUDE_HOME.

⑥ We want verbose output. If you don't want all the chatter from avrdude, remove the -v and you will get less output when uploading.

⑦ This is where the bootloader used by the IDE is to be found. This is extracted from the command line passed from the IDE to avrdude.

⑧ We need to set three fuse bytes for the Duemilanove. These are defined here and are as per the IDE's command line. There are a couple of lock bytes also that we need.

⑨ From here down, we do a bit of validation. Is the bootloader file name a file that physically exists? Does it have an extension of "hex" on the file name?

⑩ This call to avrdude unlocks the device and sets the three fuse bytes as required for a Duemilanove.

The fuse settings can be extracted from the Arduino installation's `boards.txt` file, if you are stuck, but they are also able to be extracted from the command line used by the IDE to burn the bootloader.

(11) This call to `avrdude` burns the bootloader file, as supplied with the Arduino IDE software, and then locks the device again.

💡 If you decide to follow my example and create a `burnBootloader.sh` script, beware when subsequently using the Arduino IDE if it asks to update your boards or libraries. This can have the effect of changing the names of some of the directories I've used in the following in my script.

If you suddenly start getting upload errors, check what's been updated and amend the script. In my case, the BOOTLOADER_HOME location changed from version 1.8.1 to 1.8.2 and broke my script.

I did say that this wasn't an ideal solution, but at least it was a simple fix.

6.2.10. Serial Usage

If you need to monitor what the Arduino is sending to the serial device, you will not yet be able to do so with the current version of the `arduino-cli`. However, if you install the `screen` utility on Linux, you can see what the board is sending back as follows:

```
screen /dev/ttyUSB0 9600
```

Windows or, indeed, Linux users can use the freely available `putty` utility with the following command:

```
putty -serial COM4 -sercfg 9600
```

You would most likely replace `COM4` with the port you uploaded the sketch on. Linux users would use `/dev/ttyuUSB0` or similar.

After a short pause, the display should begin showing what the Arduino is sending. To exit from the `screen` session, press Ctrl+A followed by the letter "k" in upper- or lowercase. You will be asked to confirm your wish to kill the session. Press "y" to continue.

To exit from `putty`, just close the window and confirm your intention to do so when prompted.

Obviously, 9600 is the baud rate and must match that which you used in your call to `Serial.begin()`, and `/dev/ttyUSB0` is the same port that you uploaded the sketch to. Use the `arduino-cli board list` to see what it should be if necessary.

It's possible to send data from the `screen` session to the Arduino, but it doesn't echo on the display and seems to be quite slow for some reason. Further investigations appear to be required – there's probably an option when starting `screen` that resolves it.

If you *only* need to send data down to the Arduino, that's simple too:

```
echo [-n] "Hello World" > /dev/ttyUSB0
```

The `-n` may be required to flush the buffer and make sure that the data are sent to the Arduino.

That's a very quick overview of something that's to come soon in the Arduino world. It certainly looks interesting, and I'll be keeping an eye on it. It's not yet perfect, it is an alpha release after all, and I have not covered all the options and commands available – installing libraries, for example. I think it's best to wait a while for a proper release to see if anything changes, but hopefully, this will have whetted your appetite.

I've seen comments on the Arduino forums about this utility, and a lot of people seem to be very happy that they no longer require to install Java to develop Arduino code.

After that slight deviation, I think it's now time to look into the features of the ATmega328P that we need to know about in order to continue from where we were in Chapter 5 where we started replacing functions like `pinMode()`, `digitalWrite()`, and `digitalRead()` with plain AVR C++ variations.

CHAPTER 7

ATmega328P Configuration and Management

In these last three chapters, I'll dig deeper into the ATmega328P microcontroller itself and take a look at some very important features of the device, many of which are either ignored, unused, or just too confusing as you read through the data sheet.

This chapter looks at those features which allow the ATmega328P to be configured and which provide a certain amount of protection and power reduction for application code – this can help it run on battery power alone in some cases.

The following two chapters look deeper at the actual, usable hardware of the device.

The contents of Chapters 8 and 9 will, hopefully, assist you in developing projects using the AVR C++ rather than the Arduino Language – should that be your wish. Even if you have no wish to discard the Arduino Language, the source code for the numerous functions I discussed back in Chapters 2, 3, and 4 rely on the information you will find here.

© Norman Dunbar 2020
N. Dunbar, *Arduino Software Internals*, https://doi.org/10.1007/978-1-4842-5790-6_7

7.1. ATmega328P Fuses

Fuses are special areas of the AVR microcontroller by which the device can be configured with a number of different settings. The ATmega328 has three fuses – low, high, and extended – each of which has different responsibilities.

When a brand-new device is shipped from the factory, the fuses are set to a default configuration, and this default may not be as required for any specific purpose.

There are many online fuse calculators where you can select various options and be shown the commands and/or values with which to program your fuses. `www.engbedded.com/fusecalc` is a good one.

⚠️ It is easy to *brick* your device by setting incorrect fuses, so be *exceedingly* careful and don't go playing around with things you don't understand, yet! Ask me how I know!

ℹ️ You should also be very careful to remember that a fuse that is unprogrammed has a bit value of 1, while a programmed fuse has a bit value of 0. The online fuse calculators show programmed fuses with a ticked checkbox and an unprogrammed fuse with a clear checkbox. This is the opposite way round from what I consider normal, but that's how the AVR microcontroller works.

The three fuses are discussed in the following.

7.1.1. Low Fuse Bits

The interesting bits in the low fuse, at least of interest to Arduino users, are the SUT and CKSEL fuses and possibly CKDIV8. The latter simply divides the chosen clock source (see CKSEL) by 8 to obtain the final system clock speed.

The SUT and CKSEL fuse bits are discussed following Table 7-1 which describes the low fuse bits.

Table 7-1. *Atmega328P low fuse bits*

Bit	Fuse	Purpose	Default
7	CKDIV8	Divides clock by 8	Programmed
6	CKOUT	Clock output on pin PORTB0	Unprogrammed
5	SUT1	Selects startup time$_1$	Unprogrammed
4	SUT0	Selects startup time$_0$	Programmed
3	CKSEL3	Selects clock source$_3$	Programmed
2	CKSEL2	Selects clock source$_2$	Programmed
1	CKSEL1	Selects clock source$_1$	Unprogrammed
0	CKSEL0	Selects clock source$_0$	Programmed

7.1.1.1. SUT Fuse Bits

The SUT fuses comprise 2 bits in the high fuse byte. These determine how much of a delay there will be after the power is applied, or the system reset, in order to allow everything to settle down and become stable. Some power supplies, for example, need a bit more time than others to stabilize at the required voltage; and if the Arduino (or AVR microcontroller) was to start running too soon, it could "brown out" or otherwise not behave correctly. The startup and reset delays allow the oscillator to stabilize as well as the power supply.

As each different possible oscillator has different startup delays from power on or from a wake-up call during a Power Save sleep mode, you are advised to check the data sheet for your particular device as there are numerous variations in each of the settings for these two fuse bits for each particular oscillator.

7.1.1.2. CKSEL Fuse Bits

The CKSEL fuse bits, shown in Table 7-2, select the desired internal or external oscillator to be used as the system clock. On the Arduino boards, this is always an external crystal oscillator running at 16 MHz, so the other options are not of much use there, but can be used if you build your own boards and do away with the crystal.

Table 7-2. *Atmega328P CKSEL oscillator choice fuse*

CKSEL3–CKSEL0 Bits	Oscillator to Be Used
0000	External clock
0001	Reserved, do not use
0010	Internal calibrated 8 MHz RC oscillator
0011	Internal 128 KHz RC oscillator
0100–0101	Low-frequency crystal oscillator
0110–0111	Full-swing crystal oscillator
1000–1111	Low-power crystal oscillator

When using the low-power crystal oscillator, the CKSEL3:1 bits determine the frequency of the oscillator in use, as shown in Table 7-3. Our Arduinos with their 16 MHz oscillators will be using the 111_{binary} option.

Table 7-3. *Atmega328P CKSEL oscillator frequency ranges*

CKSEL3–CKSEL1	Frequency
100	0.4–0.9 MHz
101	0.9–3 MHz
110	3–8 MHz
111	8–16 MHz

If a low-power crystal oscillator is being used, then the SUT1:0 fuse bits can be used to specify differing power-on/wake-up delays as defined in the data sheet.

7.1.2. Low Fuse Factory Default

From the factory, the ATmega328P is shipped with this fuse set to 62_{hex} which is $0110\ 0010_{binary}$ and is configured as follows:

- CKDIV8 (bit 7) is programmed (zero) and causes the system clock to be divided by 8. See also CKSELn in the following.

- SUT0 (bit 4) is programmed and sets the default startup time, after a reset, to 14 clock cycles plus 65 milliseconds over and above that of the power-up time. From initial power-up or wake from Power Save sleep mode, the startup delay time is six clock cycles. These delays allow the device and power supply to settle down before anything important starts running.

- CKSEL3, CKSEL2, and CKSEL0 (bits 3, 2, and 0) are zero
  and cause the system clock to be defaulted to an
  internal 8 MHz oscillator. Given that the default also
  programs CKDIV8, then the device will only be running
  at 1 MHz. This does mean that while slower, it draws
  less current and can run from a lower supply voltage.

Fuses CKOUT (bit 6), SUT1 (bit 5), and CKSEL1 (bit 1) remain
unprogrammed by default; and this means that the system clock pulse
does not appear on PORTB, pin zero (CKOUT). SUT1 affects the startup time,
and CKSEL1 affects the default system clock.

7.1.3. Arduino Low Fuse Settings

The Arduino boards running with the ATmega328P microcontroller
set the low fuse to FF_{hex} or $1111\ 1111_{binary}$ – at least on the Nano with an
ATmega328P, the Duemilanove with an ATmega328P, the Diecimila, and
the Uno.

This disables everything covered by this fuse and means that,
according to the data sheet

- The chosen oscillator is *not* divided by 8 (CKDIV8
  unprogrammed), and an external crystal oscillator
  in the range 8–16 MHz is in use (CKSEL3:1
  unprogrammed) with a slow rising power supply
  (SUT1:0 unprogrammed alongside CKSEL0
  unprogrammed). This allows for 16,384 clock cycles
  of startup delay at power on or from a Power Save
  sleep wake-up call with an additional 14 clocks plus 65
  milliseconds from a reset.

- SUT1:0, which define the startup time for the device, are
  set to 11_{binary}; and this is a setting described as *reserved* in
  the ATmega328P data sheet. Hmmm, interesting.

7.1.4. High Fuse Bits

Table 7-4 lists the high fuse bits and their purpose.

Table 7-4. *Atmega328P high fuse bits*

Bit	Fuse	Purpose	Default
7	RSTDISBL	Disables RESET pin and use for I/O	Unprogrammed
6	DWEN	Debug wire enable	Unprogrammed
5	SPIEN	Enables serial programming (SPI) and data downloading	Programmed
4	WDTON	Watchdog Timer always on	Unprogrammed
3	EESAVE	Preserves EEPROM data during chip erasure	Unprogrammed
2	BOOTSZ1	Selects bootloader size bit 1	Programmed
1	BOOTSZ0	Selects bootloader size bit 0	Programmed
0	BOOTRST	Selects RESET vector	Unprogrammed

High fuse bits of interest to Arduino users are the BOOTSZ bits shown in Table 7-5 and the BOOTRST fuse bit shown in Table 7-6. It's probably not wise to play with the others!

Table 7-5. *Atmega328P BOOTSZ bootloader fuse*

BOOTSZ1–BOOTSZ0	Boot Area Size	Application Address Range	Bootloader Address Range
11	128 Words	$0-F7F_{hex}$	$F80_{hex}-FFF_{hex}$
10	256 Words	$0-EFF_{hex}$	$F00_{hex}-FFF_{hex}$
01	512 Words	$0-DFF_{hex}$	$E00_{hex}-FFF_{hex}$
00	1024 Words	$0-BFF_{hex}$	$C00_{hex}-FFF_{hex}$

⚠️ One word in the AVR is equivalent to 2 bytes, or is it 4 bytes? It depends on which memory you are discussing.

Given that the Uno has a 512-byte – that's an 8-bit byte – bootloader, its fuse settings define 128 words. If a word was 2 bytes, this would be only 256 bytes for the bootloader. It wouldn't fit. So it appears that here, a word must surely be 4 bytes.

There is much confusion all over the Internet about what exactly a word is in the data sheet. However, be aware that in Static RAM, addresses point to bytes. A word there would be 2 bytes or 16 bits. In the Flash RAM, an address points to a 16-bit-wide "byte," so a word of Flash RAM is two of those "bytes" given, in reality, 4 bytes.

Confused? The bootloader lives in Flash RAM, so each address is 16 bits wide, not 8, and still confusion reigns.

In Static RAM, address 0 points at the very first 8 bits in memory and address 1 the next 8 bits. In Flash RAM, address 0 points at the first 16 bits of flash and address 1 at the next 16 bits.

The Arduino Uno sets the BOOTSZ1:0 fuses to 11_{binary}, while the Duemilanove, Diecimila, and Nano use 01_{binary} resulting in a bootloader of 128 words and 512 (8-bit) bytes, for the Uno, and 512 words and 2048 (8-bit) bytes for the others.

The BOOTRST fuse has two possible values. The Arduino always sets this fuse to 0, meaning programmed. The possible values for this fuse are shown in Table 7-6. The ATmega328P's RESET vector can be configured to point either at the bootloader or at the application address space in Flash RAM.

Table 7-6. *Atmega328P BOOTRST reset vector fuse*

BOOTRST	Purpose
0	The RESET vector points to the bootloader address (see preceding table)
1	The RESET vector points at the application start address (address 0)

The Arduino therefore sets this fuse so that the RESET vector will start executing at the bootloader rather than the application code, which is a good thing as it means that you will be able to reprogram the Arduino as the bootloader watches for programming instructions before jumping into the application code if none are forthcoming.

7.1.5. High Fuse Factory Default

From the factory, this fuse defaults to $D9_{hex}$ or $1101\ 1001_{binary}$ and means that

- SPIEN (bit 5) is programmed so serial programming (SPI) and data downloading is enabled.

- BOOTSZ1:0 (bits 2 and 1) are programmed giving the device 2048 words of flash starting at address 3800_{hex} for use as the bootloader area.

The remaining fuses are not programmed. Therefore

- RSTDISBL (bit 7) being unprogrammed means that the RESET pin, pin 1, is not disabled and works as a RESET pin. If this fuse is programmed, you cannot program the AVR microcontroller unless you use a high-power programmer device. (This is the fuse setting that bricked one of my ATtiny85 devices when I managed to program it!)

- DWEN (bit 6) being unprogrammed results in the Debug Wire interface being disabled. This is beyond the scope of this book. (In other words, it's something I have not yet studied!)

- WDTON (bit 4) not being programmed means that the Watchdog Timer is not always running and unable to be disabled. This means that the Arduino can program the Watchdog on or off as required.

- EESAVE (bit 3) remaining unprogrammed results in the internal EEPROM being wiped clean each and every time the AVR microcontroller is programmed. If you need to save data in the EEPROM between program changes and uploads, then you should program this bit.

- BOOTRST (bit 0) being unprogrammed means that the device will not jump to the bootloader address at startup. On reset, the device will start execution at the normal reset vector at address 0.

7.1.6. Arduino High Fuse Settings

This fuse is set to DE_{hex}, 1101 1110$_{binary}$, on the Uno, but to DA_{hex}, 1101 1010$_{binary}$, on the Duemilanove, the Diecimila, and the Nano. This programs the following fuses:

- SPIEN (bit 5) is the same as the factory default and enables SPI.

- BOOTSZ1 (bit 2) is programmed (but unprogrammed on the Uno).

- BOOTRST (bit 0) is programmed.

As detailed earlier, the Uno is programmed with 128 words of bootloader space, while other boards based on the ATmega328P use 512 words. A reset causes execution to start from the bootloader address.

7.1.7. Extended Fuse Bits

The extended fuse byte controls the BOD or brown-out detector in the microcontroller. Not all of this fuse byte is used, and the relevant bits are described in Table 7-7.

Table 7-7. *Atmega328P extended fuse bits*

Bit	Fuse	Purpose	Default
2	BODLEVEL2	Brown-out detection trigger level$_2$	Unprogrammed
1	BODLEVEL1	Brown-out detection trigger level$_1$	Unprogrammed
0	BODLEVEL0	Brown-out detection trigger level$_0$	Unprogrammed

All other bits of the extended fuse are unused and should always be programmed as 1_{binary} to avoid possible problems. Table 7-8 shows how the BOD fuse bits can be configured.

Table 7-8. *Atmega328P BOD voltage ranges*

Bits 2–0	BOD V_{min}	BOD $V_{typical}$	BOD V_{max}
111	N/A	N/A	N/A
110	1.7 V	1.8 V	2.0 V
101	2.5 V	2.7 V	2.9 V
100	4.1 V	4.3 V	4.5 V

All other values for the BODLEVEL2:0 fuse bits are reserved and must not be used.

7.1.8. Extended Fuse Factory Default

From the factory, this fuse is set to FF_{hex} or $1111\ 1111_{binary}$ – so the brown-out detection is disabled. Only fuse bits 2–0 are used (BODLEVEL2:0); the rest should remain as 1_{binary}.

7.1.9. Arduino Extended Fuse Settings

The Arduino sets this fuse to FD_{hex} or $1111\ 1101_{binary}$ which sets the brown-out detection threshold voltage to 2.7 V as only BODLEVEL1 is programmed. This is *potentially* a bad idea as the Arduino boards are running with an external 16 MHz crystal and the data sheet advises that this will only be reliable between 4.0 V and 5.5 V – so this fuse should really be set to FC_{hex}, $1111\ 1100_{binary}$, to give a 4.1 V threshold.

7.2. Brown-Out Detection

A brown-out is a feature of electrical supplies when the supply voltage is not stable and varies up and down from the typical voltage that the supply *should* be.

Some electrical devices either don't run, don't run properly, get confused, or reset themselves if the supply voltage goes too low.

Brown-out detection, or BOD, is a means by which the AVR microcontroller keeps a watchful eye on the power supply (VCC) and, when it drops below a configured level, initiates a system shutdown by pulling, and holding, the RESET pin low, until the power rises back above the BOD level again.

The BOD is enabled and configured using the BODLEVEL2:0 fuses as described in Section 7.1.7, "*Extended Fuse Bits.*" Remember a fuse is not programmed when it has a value of 1_{binary}, but is programmed when it has the value 0_{binary}.

The Arduino boards using the ATmega328P microcontroller are fused so that the BOD is 2.7 V typical, while a brand-new ATmega328P, supplied from the factory, will have the fuses unprogrammed and, thus, BOD will be disabled (111_{binary}).

⚠️ Given that the data sheet for the ATmega328P shows that the minimum voltage for a 16 MHz AVR microcontroller is 4.0 V, the default setting for an Arduino Uno, in this case, is a little out of range!

The default fuse settings can be found in the $ARDINST/boards. txt file. For a Nano with the ATmega328p, Duemilanove, and Uno, the extended fuse is set to FD_{hex}. This is $1111\ 1101_{binary}$ which means that BODLEVEL2:0 is 101, and that sets the BOD threshold at 2.7 V which is way below what the data sheet says is safe for the Arduino setup.

The ATmega328P is stable, when running with an external 16 MHz crystal, with VCC between 4.0 V and 5.5 V. Above this and the AVR microcontroller will probably let the *magic blue smoke* out and stop working. Below this and the ATmega328P will *possibly* not work correctly, and this may affect any sensors that are attached especially if accurate timings are required.

ℹ️ It is a well-known fact that all electronic devices seem to run on magic blue smoke. The reason for this belief is that when you somehow let the smoke out, most electronic devices stop working!

The available BOD settings on an ATmega328P are shown in Table 7-9.

Table 7-9. *ATmega328 BOD voltage ranges*

BODLEVEL2–BODLEVEL0	BOD Minimum	BOD Typical	BOD Maximum
111	BOD is disabled		
110	1.7 V	1.8 V	2.0 V
101	2.5 V	2.7 V	2.9 V
100	4.1 V	4.3 V	4.5 V
0xx	Reserved. Don't use		

The typical value is what the BOD settings define.

The ATmega328P, as mentioned , can run safely at 16 MHz if it has power supplied at at least 4.0 V. Anything below 4.0 V means the chip is likely to misbehave. This would be a problem if the device were being used with sensors to take measurements or relied on accurate timings.

To prevent this possible problem, the BOD trigger threshold voltage *should* be set to the 4.3 V typical setting shown earlier, by setting the BODLEVEL2:0 fuses to 100_{binary}.

The trigger level has a built-in *hysteresis* to ensure that the BOD doesn't keep triggering and putting the AVR microcontroller into a BOD reset loop as the supply voltage fluctuates. This hysteresis allows the voltage to briefly drop below the threshold level; and, if it *quickly* rises back above it, no BOD reset will take place.

The hysteresis on the detection level should be interpreted as

Vbot+ = Vbot + Vhyst/2

and

Vbot- = Vbot - Vhyst/2

The data sheet for the ATmega328P lists the hysteresis as 50 milliVolts, which implies the typical $V_{BOT}+$ = 2.7V + 25mV $\Rightarrow$ 2.725V and V_{BOT^-} = 2.7V – 25mV $\Rightarrow$ 2.675V.

Some AVR microcontrollers allow the BOD to be disabled in software; others don't. The ATmega328P is one of the devices that can disable the BOD – this is useful when entering various sleep modes as the BOD uses power that may be scarce, but disabling the BOD could leave your project open to apparently random resets if the voltage isn't stable.

7.3. The Watchdog Timer

The Watchdog Timer (WDT) is an internal *safety switch* which can be used to prevent code hangups, runaways, etc. or which can be used to fire off an interrupt every so often. It runs off of a dedicated internal 128 KHz oscillator and can be programmed to fire at a number of preset intervals.

The Watchdog Timer interrupt can be used to wake the device from the bottom of a really deep sleep; this can be used to save power and preserve battery life. The AVR microcontroller can be put into a Power Down Sleep mode, and the interrupt will wake it periodically, do some essential processing, and then put it back to sleep again ready for its next wake-up call.

Sleep modes are discussed in Section 7.3.9, "*Sleep Modes.*"

7.3.1. Watchdog Timer Modes of Operation

The WDT has three separate modes of operation:

- Watchdog Reset (WDR) – If the Watchdog Timer has not been reset within the timeout period, the whole AVR microcontroller will be forced to a reset. On restarting after the reset, bit WDRF will be set to a 1_{binary} in the MCU Status Register, MCUSR. The WDRF bit can be interrogated to determine if the AVR microcontroller was reset by the Watchdog, or otherwise.

On waking from a Watchdog-induced reset, the Watchdog Timer is still enabled; however, it is now firing with the shortest timeout period – not what you originally configured.

- Watchdog Interrupt (WDI) – An interrupt will be fired at the end of every Watchdog Timer timeout period.

- Interrupt and Reset – The interrupt will fire on the *first* Watchdog Timer timeout, and on the next timeout, the system will be reset, unless WDIE is set again to prevent it. As long as the WDIE bit is constantly being set, the system reset will not fire, only the interrupt.

The data sheet has the following warning about the use of the Watchdog Timer:

If the Watchdog is accidentally enabled, for example by a runaway pointer or brown- out condition, the device will be reset and the Watchdog Timer will stay enabled. If the code is not set up to handle the Watchdog, this might lead to an eternal loop of time-out resets. To avoid this situation, the application software should always clear the Watchdog System Reset Flag (WDRF) and the WDE control bit in the initialization routine, even if the Watchdog is not in use.

It should be noted that the Arduino code *might* be making this check, but that depends on how the bootloader was compiled. It is therefore still possible that your code could lead to a constantly resetting AVR microcontroller under the circumstances mentioned in the data sheet.

The code shown in Listing 7-1 from the Uno bootloader shows the test being made and the Watchdog Timer disabled, if configured accordingly.

Listing 7-1. Arduino bootloader code to prevent Watchdog Timer reset loops

```
#ifdef WATCHDOG_MODS                                      ①
    ch = MCUSR;                                           ②
    MCUSR = 0;                                            ③

    WDTCSR |= _BV(WDCE) | _BV(WDE);                       ④
    WDTCSR = 0;                                           ⑤

    // Check if the WDT was used to reset, in which      ⑥
    // case we don't bootload and skip straight to
    // the code. woot.
    if (! (ch & _BV(EXTRF)))                              ⑦
        app_start();   // skip bootloader
#else
    asm volatile("nop\n\t");
#endif
```

① This code will *only* execute if the bootloader was compiled with `WATCHDOG_MODS` defined, either on the command line that did the compile with `... -DWATCHDOG_MODS ...` (see `https://forum.arduino.cc/index.php?topic=27162.0`), or in an appropriate make file. Otherwise, there is no check on the WDT restart status on boot, and Watchdog Timer reset loops *are* possible.

② This copies the MCU Status Register for later use.

③ This initializes the MCU Status Register.

④ Watchdog Timer timed sequence begins

⑤ This disables the Watchdog Timer completely.

⑥   Actually, this comment is wrong and misleading. It ignores the bootloader and jumps to the sketch code if the AVR microcontroller was reset by any means, other than bringing the RST pin low.

⑦   This checks that the reset was not caused by the RST pin being brought low by pressing the reset button, for example. Powering the board up, or a restart following a Watchdog Timer reset, will not set this bit.

7.3.2. Amended Sketch **setup()** Function

Given that we currently do not know if the bootloader was compiled with WATCHDOG_MODS defined, perhaps the setup() code in Listing 7-2 could be added at the top of our sketches to ensure that potentially rogue Watchdog Timer reset loops can be avoided.

Listing 7-2. Amended setup() function to prevent Watchdog Timer reset loops

```
#include <avr/wdt.h>

void ensureWDTisOff() {
    // wdt_disable() will disable interrupts and
    // call wdt_reset first, then disable the WDT.
    wdt_disable();                                        ①

    // Reset the MCU Status Register.
    MCUSR=0;                                              ②
}

void setup() {
    // Ensure the WDT has not gone rogue!
    ensureWDTisOff();
```

```
// Do the sketch's own initialisation here.
pinMode(...);
...
}
```

① Calling wdt_disable() will turn off global interrupts to prevent them interfering with the timed sequence of instructions to disable/enable the Watchdog Timer, clear the Watchdog Timer counter, and then completely disable the Watchdog Timer. After disabling, interrupts will be enabled again if they were enabled when wdt_disable() was called.

② This resets the MCU Status Register to a known state.

The Watchdog Timer can now be enabled to a known and desired state, if required, in setup() and a call to wdt_reset() executed each time through the loop() and any other long-running processes.

7.3.3. Watchdog Timer Reset

To keep your code running, without the Watchdog Timer resetting the AVR microcontroller, your code must, periodically, clear the Watchdog Timer counter by executing the wdr assembly language instruction prior to the timeout period expiring. This instruction has been defined in the AVRLib code as follows:

```
#define wdt_reset() __asm__ __volatile__ ("wdr")
```

So, if you are using the Watchdog Timer, your code must include the file avr/wdt.h and call wdt_reset() at regular intervals. How regular? You must reset the Watchdog Timer within the configured timeout period.

i The call to wdt_reset() is *only* necessary when the Watchdog Timer is configured to run in "WDT Reset" and "Reset and Interrupt" modes. It is not necessary to call wdt_reset() when running in "WDT Interrupt" (WDI) mode as that mode does not cause the microcontroller to be reset.

7.3.4. The Watchdog Timer Control Register

The Watchdog Timer Control Register, WDTCSR, is 8 bits wide; and the individual bits have their usages defined in Table 7-10.

Table 7-10. *Watchdog Control Register*

Bit	Name	Comments
7	WDIF	Watchdog Interrupt Flag
6	WDIE	Watchdog Interrupt Enable
5	WDP3	Watchdog Timer Prescaler 3
4	WDCE	Watchdog Change Enable
3	WDE	Watchdog Reset Enable
2	WDP2	Watchdog Timer Prescaler 2
1	WDP1	Watchdog Timer Prescaler 1
0	WDP0	Watchdog Timer Prescaler 0

The bits are used as follows:

- WDIF is set when the Watchdog Timer times out and the Watchdog Timer interrupt is enabled. If global interrupts are also enabled, then the Watchdog Timer interrupt ISR fires, and this bit will be cleared automatically.

  User code may, if desired, clear this bit by writing a 1_{binary} to it when global interrupts are off. If it is not cleared, then the Watchdog Timer interrupt ISR will execute as soon as the global interrupts are subsequently re-enabled.

- WDIE, if set, enables Watchdog Timer Interrupt mode (WDI).

  Depending on the setting of the WDE bit – see in the following – then

  - If WDE is also set, the WDT is now in Reset and Interrupt mode. The first timeout will execute the Watchdog Timer interrupt ISR, clear WDIF as in the preceding text, clear WDIE to disable WDI, and leave WDE set to ensure WDR mode. The second timeout will cause a system reset.

  - If WDE is clear, then the mode is Watchdog Timer Interrupt or WDI. Each time the timeout expires, the Watchdog Timer interrupt ISR will be executed. No system reset will occur.

- WDCE is used in the timing sequence that allows the Watchdog Timer to be configured. The configuration allows for

  - Setting or clearing the WDE bit

  - Setting or clearing the prescaler bits, WDP3:0

- WDE enables the Watchdog Timer in Watchdog Reset (WDR) mode. If the Watchdog Timer is not reset before the timeout period expires, the AVR microcontroller will be reset, and on restarting, bit WDRF (Watchdog Timer Reset Flag) in MCUSR will be set to 1_{binary} showing that the reset occurred due to the Watchdog Timer.

  If WDIE see earlier – is also set, then the Reset and Interrupt mode is active. The first timeout will cause the interrupt to fire and execute the ISR, will clear WDIE to disable the Watchdog Timer interrupt, and will enable Watchdog Reset (WDR) mode. The second timeout will reset the system, unless WDIE was again set to enable the Watchdog Timer interrupt.

- WDP3:0 set the Watchdog Timer prescaler to give the desired timeout period. If the Watchdog Timer counter is not cleared within this period, then the system will be reset, or the interrupt will be fired, depending on the settings on WDE and WDIE.

Given the preceding discussion, we can pick and choose the Watchdog Timer modes that we wish to configure in our code as follows:

- Watchdog Reset (WDR) mode – WDE is set and WDIE is clear. The system will reset if the Watchdog Timer counter is not itself cleared within the timeout period. No interrupts will fire.

- Watchdog Interrupt (WDI) mode – WDE is clear and WDIE is set. The system will set WDIF on the timeout occurring and then fire the appropriate ISR if global interrupts are enabled.

- Watchdog Reset and Watchdog Interrupt mode – WDE and WDIE are both set.

In this mode of operation, if the Watchdog Timer was initialized at time T with timeout period P, then the interrupt will fire at time T + P (assuming global interrupts are enabled of course).

If WDIE is again set to 1_{binary} after the first P timeout, but before the second P timeout, then the system reset will *not* occur at time T + P + P. The Watchdog interrupt ISR will fire again instead.

If, on the other hand, WDIE is not set to 1_{binary} prior to the end of the next timeout period, P, then the system will be reset. This will occur at T + P + P.

This sequence allows for such things as using the ISR to save any data that must be updated between restarts; shutting down any peripherals, motors, laser cutters, etc. to a safe state before the restart occurs; and so on. Until the system has restarted, and fully initialized, the state of various pins is potentially unknown; and a runaway laser cutter, for example, is not a good thing to have close by!

⚠ If the WDTON fuse has been programmed (i.e., has value 0_{binary}) then you are unable to ever change bits WDE and WDIE in WDTCSR. The Arduino default is that this fuse bit is not programmed, so the Watchdog Timer can be enabled or disabled as you might wish.

With this fuse programmed, WDE is always 1_{binary}, while WDIE is always 0_{binary}, so the Watchdog Timer is *always* running in Watchdog Timer Reset (WDR) mode, and you cannot use the Watchdog Timer interrupt.

When the system is reset by the Watchdog Timer, on restarting, the Watchdog Timer is *still* enabled; however, it is now enabled at the *smallest possible timeout setting*, 16 milliseconds, and not perhaps as you configured it prior to the reset. This could cause Watchdog Timer reset loops. The Arduino bootloader *should* be checking and disabling the Watchdog Timer, but this depends on how the bootloader was compiled and cannot be relied upon. See Listing 7-2 for details on how to possibly prevent this from occuring.

7.3.5. Enabling the Watchdog Timer

In order that rogue programs don't cause problems by accidentally setting the WDT, and to try and ensure that any changes are valid ones, there is a certain timed sequence of events that must be followed in order to configure WDTCSR when either WDE or the prescaler bits WDP3:0 are being changed:

- Disable global interrupts. This will prevent any existing interrupt handlers from firing during the critical timed sequence, thus preventing a valid change to WDTCSR if the ISR in question takes longer than four system clock cycles to execute – which it will!

- Reset the Watchdog Timer. It may already be running, and it should not be allowed to reset the AVR microcontroller while it is being reconfigured, especially when reducing the timeout period.

  If the prescaler is being changed to reduce the timeout, and the new timeout period has already expired since the previous reset of the Watchdog Timer counter, then the Watchdog Timer *will* timeout as soon as the configuration completes.

- To start changing WDTCSR, you must write a 1_{binary} to both WDCE and WDE *in the same instruction.* If WDE is already a 1_{binary}, you must still write a 1_{binary} to it.

- Within four *system* clock cycles, write the desired configuration bits for the prescaler (see below), interrupt enable and so on to WDTCSR and include a 0_{binary} in bit WDCE. All bits must be set and/or cleared in the *same instruction*.

- Enable global interrupts.

The AVRLib functions defined in avr/wdt.h take care of all this when you make calls to the function wdt_enable().

7.3.6. Setting the Watchdog Timer Timeout

The Watchdog Timer can be configured, as mentioned earlier, by setting bits WDP3:0 according to Table 7-11, to time out after an approximate set time.

Table 7-11. *Watchdog timeout settings*

Timeout	WDP3-WDP0	WDP3-WDP0	Comments
16 mS	0000_{bin}	0	Only if VCC is 5 V. 3.3 V will be a longer timeout
32 mS	0001_{bin}	1	Only if VCC is 5 V. 3.3 V will be a longer timeout
64 mS	0010_{bin}	2	Only if VCC is 5 V. 3.3 V will be a longer timeout
0.125 S	0011_{bin}	3	Only if VCC is 5 V. 3.3 V will be a longer timeout
0.25 S	0100_{bin}	4	Only if VCC is 5 V. 3.3 V will be a longer timeout
0.5 S	0101_{bin}	5	Only if VCC is 5 V. 3.3 V will be a longer timeout
1.0 S	0110_{bin}	6	Only if VCC is 5 V. 3.3 V will be a longer timeout
2.0 S	0111_{bin}	7	Only if VCC is 5 V. 3.3 V will be a longer timeout
4.0 S	1000_{bin}	8	Only if VCC is 5 V. 3.3 V will be a longer timeout
8.0 S	1001_{bin}	9	Only if VCC is 5 V. 3.3 V will be a longer timeout

All other WDP3:0 values from 10 (1010_{binary}) to 15 (1111_{binary}) are reserved and should not be used.

Listing 7-3 shows an example Arduino sketch to enable the Watchdog Timer, in Watchdog Timer Reset (WDR) mode.

Listing 7-3. Arduino code to enable the Watchdog Timer

```
#include "avr/wdt.h"

void setup() {
    wdt_reset();

    // Fire WDT every 8 seconds.
    wdt_enable(WDTO_8S);
}

void loop() {
    // Make sure we reset the WDT.
    wdt_reset();

    // Do our loopy stuff here. It must
    // complete in less time than the
    // WDT timeout period.
    ...
}
```

Unfortunately, the wdt_enable(WDTO_8S) instruction in Listing 7-3 only sets the WDE and prescaler bits; it does not set the interrupt enable bit, WDIE, for you. At present, the AVRLib doesn't have the ability to set the Watchdog Timer interrupt, so, if Watchdog Timer interrupts are required, you need to configure everything manually. Listing 7-4 is a function which will enable the Watchdog Timer Interrupt mode, *without* enabling the WDR mode. Your project can then use the Watchdog Timer interrupt handler to carry out some work periodically and not have to worry about calling wdt_reset() within the timeout period.

Listing 7-4. Arduino code to enable Watchdog Timer interrupt

```
#include <avr/wdt.h>

void wdt_interrupts(uint8_t value) {

    // Save existing interrupt state.
    uint8_t oldSREG = SREG;                                    ①

    // Set the WDP3-WDP0 bits for the prescaler.
    uint8_t wdt_setting;
    value = (value > 9) ? 9 : value;                           ②
    wdt_setting = (value > 7) ? (1 << WDP3) : 0;
    wdt_setting |= (value & 7);

    // Disable interrupts and reset WDT.                        ③
    noInterrupts();
    wdt_reset();

    // Clear WDT restarted flag.
    MCUSR &= ~(1 << WDRF);                                      ④

    // Do the timed sequence next.                              ⑤
    #if defined WDTCSR
        // ATmega168/328/2560 etc
        WDTCSR |= ((1 << WDCE) | (1 << WDE));
        WDTCSR = (wdt_setting | (1 << WDIE));

    #elif defined WDTCR
        // ATtiny25/45/85 etc
        WDTCR |= ((1 << WDCE) | (1 << WDE));
        WDTCR = (wdt_setting | (1 << WDIE));
    #else
        #error "Unknown WDT Control Register on your AVR."
    #endif
```

```
    // Put interrupts back as they were previously.
    SREG = oldSREG;                                    ⑥
}
```

① Saving the status register preserves the state of global interrupts.

② There are 4 bits available here, so up to 16 values; however, we can only have 9 as the maximum value. If it is 8 or 9, then we need to set WDP3.

③ Interrupts and the Watchdog Timer must be disabled if we are going to change the Watchdog Timer settings. This will prevent rogue resets partway through changing the settings.

④ The data sheet says we must clear WDRF.

⑤ This is the timed sequence of instructions that we must complete in order that the changes to the Watchdog Timer will be considered valid.

⑥ Restore the global interrupt bit in the status register to how it was on entry to this function.

That takes care of enabling the Watchdog Timer interrupt. To disable it, use the function in Listing 7-5.

Listing 7-5. Arduino code to disable the Watchdog Timer interrupt

```
#include "avr/wdt.h"

void wdt_noInterrupts() {
    // Disable WDT interrupts leaving
    // everything else untouched.
    #if defined WDTCSR
        // ATmega328 etc
        WDTCSR &= ~(1 << WDIE);                        ①
```

```
    #elif defined WDTCR
        // ATtiny85 etc
        WDTCR &= ~(1 << WDIE);                        ①

    #else
        #error "Unknown WDT Control Register on your AVR."
    #endif
}
```

    ①   This clears the WDIE bit and leaves the other bits unaffected. The WDE and WDP3:0 bits cannot be changed except under the terms and conditions of the previously mentioned timed sequence. The code here doesn't violate those rules. The code attempts to determine between the ATmega328P and ATtiny85 microcontrollers – both of which I use.

The preceding code could now be used to program yet another replacement Blink sketch. Listing 7-6 shows how a regular blink could be applied to an LED using nothing but the Watchdog Timer interrupt.

Listing 7-6. Using the Watchdog Timer interrupt in the Blink sketch

```
void setup() {
  wdt_interrupts(WDTO_1S);
  pinMode(LED_BUILTIN, OUTPUT);
}

void loop() {
  ; //Do nothing.
}

ISR(WDT_vect) {
  PINB |= (1 << PINB5);
}
```

The loop() function does nothing at all. All the blinking takes place in the ISR for the Watchdog Timer interrupt. In code like this, where an ISR is doing all the work, the main loop should really put the AVR microcontroller to sleep. And this is something we will deal with in Section 7.3.8, "*Putting the AVR to Sleep*."

7.3.7. Disabling the Watchdog Timer

The Watchdog Timer can be disabled by following the sequence of events as follows:

> ⚠ If the WDTON fuse has been programmed (i.e., has value 0_{binary}), then you will be unable to disable the Watchdog Timer. In this case, the Watchdog Timer is always running in Watchdog Reset (WDR) mode.

- Disable global interrupts. This will prevent any existing interrupt handlers from firing during the critical timed sequence, thus preventing a valid change to WDTCSR.

- Reset the Watchdog Timer. It may already be running, and it should not reset the AVR microcontroller while it is being reconfigured.

- Ensure that bit WDRF in MCUSR is cleared.

- To start changing WDTCSR, you must write a 1_{binary} to both WDCE and WDE *in the same instruction*. If WDE is already a 1_{binary}, you must still write a 1_{binary} to it. You are advised to preserve the existing state of bits WDP3:0 to prevent unintentional Watchdog Timer timeouts which *will* occur if the timeout period is being reduced, explicitly or implicitly, and the new timeout has already expired.

- Within four *system* clock cycles, write a 0_{binary} to bits WDCE and WDE. All bits must be set and/or cleared in the same instruction. The data sheet, surprisingly, advises clearing the entire register – which completely disagrees with its previous instruction to *preserve the state of bits* WDP3:0.

- Enable global interrupts.

The AVRLib functions defined in avr/wdt.h take care of all this when you make calls to the function wdt_disable().

Listing 7-7 is an example Arduino sketch to completely disable the Watchdog Timer.

Listing 7-7. Arduino code to disable the Watchdog Timer

```
#include "avr/wdt.h"

void setup() {
    wdt_reset();
    MCUSR &= ~(1 << WDRF);      ①
    wdt_disable();              ②
}
```

    ① This clears the flag in the MCU Status Register which indicates that the Watchdog Timer reset the AVR microcontroller.

    ② The function wdt_disable() is defined in the avr/wdt.h header file and carries out all the necessary instructions to disable the Watchdog Timer including disabling interrupts and enabling them afterward, if appropriate.

You could, obviously, extract the preceding code to a function of your own and call that whenever the Watchdog Timer needed to be disabled.

7.3.8. Putting the AVR to Sleep

The ATmega328P comes with six different sleep modes built in. These can be used to vastly reduce power requirements of the AVR microcontroller when it doesn't need to be polling for button presses and so on. When sleeping, interrupts must normally be used to wake the device and let it run the necessary processing as required.

In other words, if the code is written in such a way as to not require the processor to be constantly polling sensors and so on in the main loop, then it can be put to sleep which will save power and make batteries last much longer.

ℹ️ Chapter 9 of the data sheet, "Sleep Modes", has the following points of note:

When entering a sleep mode, all port pins should be configured to use minimum power. The most important is then to ensure that no pins drive resistive loads. In sleep modes where both the I/O clock (clkI/O) and the ADC clock (clkADC) are stopped, the input buffers of the device will be disabled. This ensures that no power is consumed by the input logic when not needed. In some cases, the input logic is needed for detecting wake-up conditions, and it will then be enabled.

If the input buffer is enabled and the input signal is left floating or have an analog signal level close to VCC/2, the input buffer will use excessive power.

For analog input pins, the digital input buffer should be disabled at all times. An analog signal level close to VCC/2 on an input pin can cause significant current even in active mode. Digital input buffers can be disabled by writing to the Digital Input Disable Registers (DIDR1 and DIDR0).

The "analogue input pins" referred to are those of the ADC and the Analogue Comparator. Chapter 9, Section 9.1.3, "*Digital Input*," and Section 9.2.1.6, "*Disable Digital Input*," describe how to disable the digital input buffers when using the Analogue Comparator or the ADC.

The following sleep modes are available:

- Idle

- ADC Noise Reduction

- Power Down

- Power Save

- Standby (only when there is an external crystal or ceramic resonator)

- Extended Standby

To put the AVR microcontroller to sleep, the code must

- Set bits SM2:0 in SMCR (Sleep Mode Control Register) to select the sleep mode required.

- Set bit SE (Sleep Enable) in SMCR to enable the desired sleep mode.

- Execute the sleep instruction.

The values defined for the various modes are as follows and can be found in the header file $ARDINC/avr/iom328p.h:

```
#define SLEEP_MODE_IDLE (0x00<<1)
#define SLEEP_MODE_ADC (0x01<<1)
#define SLEEP_MODE_PWR_DOWN (0x02<<1)
#define SLEEP_MODE_PWR_SAVE (0x03<<1)
#define SLEEP_MODE_STANDBY (0x06<<1)
#define SLEEP_MODE_EXT_STANDBY (0x07<<1)
```

> **i** The bits SM2:0 in the SMCR register are bits 3, 2, and 1, hence the use of the shift left instructions in the preceding definitions.

To put an AVR microcontroller to sleep in Idle mode, for example, you *could* execute code similar to that shown in Listings 7-8 to 7-10. You could, but I wouldn't bother myself because it *doesn't work* as expected with the code shown! Don't worry as all will be made clear soon.

Listing 7-8 is a simple function to flash the built-in LED a few times. It's called from setup() to show that we are indeed alive and from the loop() when it's doing "real" work.

Listing 7-8. Non-functioning sleep sketch, flashLED()

```
#include <avr/sleep.h>
#include <avr/interrupt.h>

void flashLED(byte flashes) {
    for (byte x = 0; x < flashes; x++) {
        digitalWrite(LED_BUILTIN, HIGH);
        delay(250);
        digitalWrite(LED_BUILTIN, LOW);
        delay(250);
    }
}
```

Listing 7-9 is the setup() function which sets the requirements for Idle sleep mode and then flashes the LED a couple of times to show we are alive and well, so far. Setting the sleep mode doesn't put the Arduino to sleep at that point – that comes later.

Listing 7-9. Non-functioning sleep sketch, setup()

```
void setup() {
    set_sleep_mode(SLEEP_MODE_IDLE);
    pinMode(LED_BUILTIN, OUTPUT);

    // Show we are alive
    delay(1500);
    flashLED(2);
}
```

In Listing 7-10, we can see the loop() function. This is where the code would normally be doing application work and then sleeping until some stimulus wakes it up for the next pass through the loop.

Listing 7-10. Non-functioning sleep sketch, loop()

```
void loop() {
    noInterrupts();                 ①

    // Enable sleep mode and disable Brown Out Detection.
    // BOD disable is permitted on ATmega328P.
    sleep_enable();                 ②
    sleep_bod_disable();

    // Enable interrupts and execute the sleep_cpu() -
    // Which guarantees that the sleep_cpu() will execute
    // before any new interrupts will be fired.
    interrupts();                   ③
    sleep_cpu();                    ④

    // When we wake up, on an interrupt, disable
    // sleep mode while processing.
    sleep_disable();                ⑤
```

```
// Do some application "stuff" here after waking up ...
flashLED(4);                        ⑥

// On the next pass of the loop, we will go back to sleep.
}
```

① It is recommended to disable interrupts when changing sleep modes.

② In setup() we configured Idle sleep mode with set_sleep_mode(). This function call enables sleep modes, but still doesn't put the device to sleep. Also here, we turn off the brown-out detector (BOD) while sleeping.

③ Sleep modes need an interrupt to wake the device. We need interrupts turning on, or we will simply sleep forever.

④ Finally, we put the device to sleep. The device will sleep in Idle mode until woken.

⑤ This is where the application does some work, after it wakes up from sleep. It should disable sleeping until ready to go back to sleep.

⑥ This is the "real" work that the application has to do!

If, while the device is asleep, an interrupt occurs, the device will wake up but will then halt itself for four clock cycles before executing the interrupt routine. Those four clock cycles are in addition to any startup time requirements.

Once the interrupt routine has been executed, control returns to the instruction after the sleep instruction that put the device to sleep previously. The sleep instruction is built in to the ATmega328P. Our C++ code can call it as it has been defined elsewhere. Normally, it is easier to use the various sleep functions in AVRLib.

"So what's wrong with the preceding sketch?" I hear you think. "Why is SLEEP_MODE_IDLE not the best sleep mode for this demonstration?" You will possibly have realized that while an Arduino is in this sleep mode, the Timer/counter 0, used to count millis() and so on, is running with its Overflow interrupt enabled. And an interrupt wakes the AVR microcontroller when it fires, so in SLEEP_MODE_IDLE the main loop just runs and runs – it does sleep, but only until the timer/counter overflows and that happens every 1024 microseconds.

If you were to recompile the preceding code, but use SLEEP_MODE_PWR_DOWN instead, once the LED flashes twice in setup(), you won't see it again until a proper interrupt occurs – but because I haven't enabled any particular interrupts, the Arduino will simply go to sleep and never wake up. There's a much better example in Section 7.3.10.

7.3.9. Sleep Modes

In the following discussions, regarding each different sleep mode, I give the sleep modes numbers; SLEEP_MODE_IDLE, for example, is sleep mode 0. I indicate the value in binary as well, in 3 bits. These are the 3 bits that need to be written to the SM2:0 bits in the Sleep Mode Control Register (SMCR). These 3 bits control which sleep mode the AVR microcontroller will enter when the Sleep Enable (SE) bit is set and a sleep instruction executed.

While there are 3 bits available, giving eight different sleep modes (000_{binary}–111_{binary}), sleep modes 4 (100_{binary}) and 5 (101_{binary}) are reserved and *should not be used*, leaving only six modes. Of these, one cannot be used on the Arduino as it requires Timer/counter 2 to be running in asynchronous mode, which is not possible on an Arduino, and another is dubious. We therefore have three good modes and two dubious ones left on our Arduinos.

To put the AVR microcontroller to sleep, the steps are as follows:

- Set the sleep mode required in bits SM2:0 of the SMCR. You can do this in a sketch by calling set_sleep_ mode() or directly in your own code. The examples in this section use the easy method – calling set_sleep_ mode() in AVRLib.

- Set the Sleep Enable bit, SE, to 1_{binary} in SMCR by calling sleep_enable() as part of the loop().

- Execute the sleep (assembly language) instruction by calling sleep_cpu() in the loop().

- On wake-up, the data sheet advises that you *immediately* clear the SE bit to 0_{binary}. You can do this simply by calling sleep_disable() before starting the code that is to be carried out upon waking from sleep.

The ATmega328P will be woken from sleep modes if an enabled interrupt occurs or if it is reset while asleep. The wake-up process is as follows, for an interrupt:

- The interrupt fires and the AVR microcontroller wakes up from sleep.

- The device is then halted for four clock cycles (over and above the device wake-up time).

- The interrupt service routine (ISR) is executed.

- Execution then continues from the instruction immediately following the sleep (or sleep_cpu()) instruction.

Table 7-12 shows a list of the various sleep modes available and whether they can be used on an Arduino.

Table 7-12. *Sleep modes*

Sleep Mode	Arduino	Comments
SLEEP_MODE_IDLE	Maybe	Only usable if Timer/counter 0 has the Overflow interrupt disabled
SLEEP_MODE_ADC	Yes	Could be used before an `analogRead()` call
SLEEP_MODE_PWR_DOWN	Yes	
SLEEP_MODE_PWR_SAVE	Maybe	On Arduinos, this is effectively identical to `SLEEP_MODE_PWR_DOWN` which should be used instead
SLEEP_MODE_STANDBY	Yes	This is just `SLEEP_MODE_PWR_DOWN` but with the main oscillator running
SLEEP_MODE_EXT_STANDBY	No	This is just `SLEEP_MODE_PWR_SAVE` but with the main oscillator running

7.3.9.1. Idle Sleep Mode

This is sleep mode 0 (000_{binary}) and is the lightest sleep mode, it saves power but not really a lot, and it's *almost* useless on an Arduino.

In Idle mode, CLK_{cpu} and CLK_{flash} are stopped while the remaining clocks continue to run. This means that the AVR microcontroller is unable to access the flash memory or actually run any instructions. Peripherals such as the USART, SPI, ADC, Two=Wire Interface (TWI), Analogue Comparator, the three timer/counters, and the Watchdog Timer *will* continue to run.

If the hardware is set up correctly, then the Asynchronous Timer/counter on Timer/counter 2 can also be used, but not on Arduinos.

To wake the device from Idle mode, one of the following stimuli will be required:

- External interrupts – INT0, INT1, and any Pin Change Interrupt

- Internal interrupts such as a Timer/counter Overflow, USART Transmit Complete, the Analogue Comparator interrupt, or the Watchdog Timer interrupt.

---

i As demonstrated earlier, this sleep mode is of very limited use on an Arduino as the Overflow interrupt for Timer/counter 0 is active when sketches are compiled. You would have to disable the Timer/counter 0 Overflow interrupt in your sketch to be able to use this sleep mode.

Please also note that the Analogue Comparator is definitely known to keep running in this sleep mode; this is an unknown quantity in the other sleep modes however.

A summary of this sleep mode is given in Table 7-13.

Table 7-13. *Idle sleep mode summary*

Sleep Mode 0 (Idle)

Clocks	CLK_{cpu} (Core, RAM)	Stopped	
	CLK_{flash} (Flash RAM, EEPROM)	Stopped	
	CLK_{io} (SPI, USART, TWI, GPIO pins, Timer/counters, external interrupts)	Running	
	CLK_{adc} (ADC)	Running	
	CLK_{asy} (Asynchronous Timer/counter 2)	Running (but not on an Arduino board)	
Oscillators	Main system oscillator	Running	
	Asynchronous Timer oscillator	Running (Not Arduino)	
Peripherals	ADC	Running	CLK_{adc}
	Analogue Comparator	Running	
	Core	Stopped	CLK_{cpu}
	RAM	Stopped	CLK_{cpu}
	EEPROM	Stopped	CLK_{flash}
	External interrupts	Running	CLK_{io}
	Flash RAM	Stopped	CLK_{flash}
	SPI	Running	CLK_{io}
	Timer/counters	Running	CLK_{io}
	TWI (address matching)	Running	CLK_{io}
	USART	Running	CLK_{io}
	Watchdog	Running	

(*continued*)

Table 7-13. (*continued*)

Sleep Mode 0 (Idle)

Wake on	External Reset
	INT0 interrupt
	INT1 interrupt
	Pin Change Interrupt
	TWI address match
	Timer/counter 2 interrupt
	SPM/EEPROM ready interrupt
	ADC Conversion Complete interrupt
	Watchdog Timer interrupt
	Other I/O interrupts
	Analogue Comparator interrupt

If wake-up from the Analogue Comparator interrupt is not required, the Analogue Comparator should be powered down by setting the ACD bit in the Analogue Comparator Control and Status Register – ACSR.

If the ADC is enabled, an ADC conversion will be started automatically when the Idle sleep mode begins after the sleep instruction's execution.

7.3.9.2. ADC Noise Reduction Sleep Mode

This is sleep mode 1 (001_{binary}) and is used when there is a need to reduce any noise coming from the AVR microcontroller itself, so that the ADC can take better analogue readings. This sleep mode is usable on Arduinos.

In ADC Noise Reduction mode, CLK_{cpu}, CLK_{io}, and CLK_{flash} are stopped while the remaining clocks continue to run. This means that while the AVR microcontroller is unable to access the flash memory, use the I/O pins (except for the analogue pins obviously), or actually run any instructions, peripherals such as the ADC, USART, SPI, ADC, TWI, Analogue Comparator, the three Timer/counters, and the Watchdog Timer will continue to run.

To wake the device from this mode, one of the following stimuli will be required:

- External (level) interrupts – INT0, INT1, and any Pin Change Interrupt

- Internal interrupts such as the ADC Conversion Complete interrupt, a Timer/counter 2 interrupt (if running in asynchronous mode), USART Transmit Complete, or the Watchdog Timer interrupt.

A summary of this sleep mode is given in Table 7-14.

Table 7-14. *ADC Noise Reduction sleep mode summary*

Sleep Mode 1 (ADC Noise Reduction)

Clocks	CLK$_{cpu}$ (Core, RAM)	Stopped
	CLK$_{flash}$ (Flash RAM, EEPROM)	Stopped
	CLK$_{io}$ (SPI, USART, TWI, GPIO pins, Timer/counters, external interrupts)	Stopped
	CLK$_{adc}$ (ADC)	Running
	CLK$_{asy}$ (Asynchronous Timer/ counter 2)	Running (but not on an Arduino board)
Oscillators	Main system oscillator	Running
	Asynchronous Timer oscillator	Running (not Arduino)

(*continued*)

Table 7-14. (*continued*)

Sleep Mode 1 (ADC Noise Reduction)

Peripherals	ADC	Running	CLK_{adc}
	Analogue Comparator	Unknown!	
	Core	Stopped	CLK_{cpu}
	RAM	Stopped	CLK_{cpu}
	EEPROM	Stopped	CLK_{flash}
	External interrupts	Stopped	CLK_{io}
	Flash RAM	Stopped	CLK_{flash}
	SPI	Stopped	CLK_{io}
	Timer/counters	Stopped	CLK_{io}
	TWI (address matching)	Stopped	CLK_{io}
	USART	Stopped	CLK_{io}
	Watchdog	Running	
Wake on	External Reset		
	INT0 LOW (level) interrupt		
	INT1 LOW (level) interrupt		
	Pin Change Interrupt		
	TWI address match		
	Timer/counter2 interrupt – only if Timer/counter2 is running in asynchronous mode, which is not possible on an Arduino		
	SPM/EEPROM ready interrupt		
	ADC Conversion Complete interrupt		
	Watchdog Timer interrupt		

When the SM2:0 bits in SMCR are written to 001_{binary}, the sleep instruction makes the MCU enter ADC Noise Reduction mode, stopping the CPU but allowing the ADC, the external interrupts, the two-wire Serial interface address watch, Timer/counter 2 (only in asynchronous mode), and the Watchdog to continue operating (if enabled). This sleep mode basically halts CLK_{io}, CLK_{cpu}, and CLK_{flash} while allowing the other clocks to run.

This improves the noise environment for the ADC, enabling higher-resolution measurements. If the ADC is enabled, a conversion starts automatically when this mode is entered.

Only an External Reset, a LOW level interrupt on the INT0 or INT1 pins, a Watchdog System Reset, a Watchdog Interrupt, a Brown Out Reset, a 2-wire Serial Interface address match, a Timer/counter 2 interrupt or an SPM/EEPROM ready interrupt will wake the AVR from this sleep mode.

7.3.9.3. Power Down Sleep Mode

This is sleep mode 2 (010_{binary}). This is a deep sleep and saves the most power. Consequently, it has fewer wake-up stimuli. This sleep mode is usable on Arduinos.

In Power Down mode, *all* clocks are stopped. This means that the AVR microcontroller is effectively powered off; however, the Watchdog Timer continues to run, a LOW level interrupt on the INT0 and INT1 pins or any of the Pin Change Interrupts will wake the device as will the TWI address match interrupt and the Brown Out Detector (BOD).

A summary of this sleep mode is given in Table 7-15.

Table 7-15. *Power Down sleep mode summary*

Sleep Mode 2 (Power Down)			
Clocks	CLK_{cpu} (Core, RAM)	Stopped	
	CLK_{flash} (Flash RAM, EEPROM)	Stopped	
	CLK_{io} (SPI, USART, TWI, GPIO pins, Timer/counters, external interrupts)	Stopped	
	CLK_{adc} (ADC)	Stopped	
	CLK_{asy} (Asynchronous Timer/counter 2)	Stopped	
Oscillators	Main system oscillator	Stopped	
	Asynchronous Timer oscillator	Stopped	
Peripherals	ADC	Stopped	CLK_{adc}
	Analogue Comparator	Unknown!	
	Core	Stopped	CLK_{cpu}
	RAM	Stopped	CLK_{cpu}
	EEPROM	Stopped	CLK_{flash}
	External interrupts	Running	CLK_{io}
	Flash RAM	Stopped	CLK_{flash}
	SPI	Stopped	CLK_{io}
	Timer/counters	Stopped	CLK_{io}
	TWI (address matching)	Running	CLK_{io}
	USART	Stopped	CLK_{io}
	Watchdog	Running	

(continued)

Table 7-15. (*continued*)

Sleep Mode 2 (Power Down)	
Wake on	External Reset
	INT0 interrupt (LOW level only)
	INT1 interrupt (LOW level only)
	Pin Change Interrupt
	TWI address match
	Watchdog Timer interrupt (or Reset)
	Brown-Out Reset

7.3.9.4. Power Save Sleep Mode

This is sleep mode 3 (011_{binary}). This is also a deep sleep and saves much power. However, it is slightly less a deep sleep than the preceding mode, Power Down. This sleep mode is possibly usable on Arduinos but not advised as the asynchronous mode for Timer/counter 2 is not enabled.

In Power Save mode, *all* clocks are stopped except CLK_{asy}. This is almost as deep a sleep as the preceding one, but on an Arduino board, the asynchronous mode of Timer/counter 2 cannot be used, so *effectively*, this too is a Power Save sleep. Once again, the AVR microcontroller is pretty much powered off; however, the Watchdog Timer continues to run, and the INT0 and INT1 level interrupts and any of the Pin Change Interrupts will wake the device as will the TWI address match interrupt and the BOD.

If this is not an Arduino board and Timer/counter 2 is configured in asynchronous mode, then Timer/counter 2 can also wake the device from this sleep mode with either an Overflow or a Compare Match interrupt. This isn't possible on an Arduino though as the pins required for the external crystal for that particular timer mode are used for the main oscillator which has a 16 MHz crystal attached.

On an Arduino, Timer/counter 2 will not therefore be enabled during this sleep mode and according to the data sheet, we should be using power down mode, rather than Power Save mode if Timer/counter 2 is not running asynchronously.

A summary of this sleep mode is given in Table 7-16.

Table 7-16. *Power Save sleep mode summary*

Sleep Mode 3 (Power Save)

Clocks	CLK_{cpu} (Core, RAM)	Stopped
	CLK_{flash} (Flash RAM, EEPROM)	Stopped
	CLK_{io} (SPI, USART, TWI, GPIO pins, Timer/counters, external interrupts)	Stopped
	CLK_{adc} (ADC)	Stopped
	CLK_{asy} (Asynchronous Timer/ counter 2)	Running (but not on an Arduino board)
Oscillators	Main system oscillator	Stopped
	Asynchronous Timer oscillator	Running (not Arduino)

(continued)

Table 7-16. (*continued*)

Sleep Mode 3 (Power Save)

Peripherals	ADC	Stopped	CLK$_{adc}$
	Analogue Comparator	Unknown!	
	Core	Stopped	CLK$_{cpu}$
	RAM	Stopped	CLK$_{cpu}$
	EEPROM	Stopped	CLK$_{flash}$
	External interrupts	Running	CLK$_{io}$
	Flash RAM	Stopped	CLK$_{flash}$
	SPI	Stopped	CLK$_{io}$
	Timer/counters	Stopped	CLK$_{io}$
	TWI (address matching)	Running	CLK$_{io}$
	USART	Stopped	CLK$_{io}$
	Watchdog	Running	
Wake on	External Reset		
	INT0 interrupt (LOW level only)		
	INT1 interrupt (LOW level only)		
	Pin Change Interrupt		
	TWI address match		
	Timer/counter2 interrupt		
	Watchdog Timer interrupt (or Reset)		
	Brown-Out Reset		

7.3.9.5. Standby Sleep Mode

This is sleep mode 6 (110_{binary}). The data sheet advises not to use this sleep mode unless there is an external crystal running the main clock. This is appropriate for Arduino boards due to the 16 MHz crystal which is used to run the main system oscillator.

This mode is identical to the Power Down mode described earlier, apart from the main oscillator running. This sleep mode is usable on Arduinos.

In Standby mode, *all* clocks are again stopped. This means, yet again, that the AVR microcontroller is effectively powered off; however, the Watchdog Timer continues to run, and the INT0 INT1 Level interrupts and any of the Pin Change Interrupts will wake the device as will the TWI address match interrupt and the BOD.

A summary of this sleep mode is given in Table 7-17.

Table 7-17. *Standby sleep mode summary*

Sleep Mode 6 (Standby)		
Clocks	CLK$_{cpu}$ (Core, RAM)	Stopped
	CLK$_{flash}$ (Flash RAM, EEPROM)	Stopped
	CLK$_{io}$ (SPI, USART, TWI, GPIO pins, Timer/counters, external interrupts)	Stopped
	CLK$_{adc}$ (ADC)	Stopped
	CLK$_{asy}$ (Asynchronous Timer/counter 2)	Stopped
Oscillators	Main system oscillator	Running
	Asynchronous Timer oscillator	Stopped

(*continued*)

Table 7-17. (*continued*)

Sleep Mode 6 (Standby)

Peripherals	ADC	Stopped	CLK_{adc}
	Analogue Comparator	Unknown!	
	Core	Stopped	CLK_{cpu}
	RAM	Stopped	CLK_{cpu}
	EEPROM	Stopped	CLK_{flash}
	External interrupts	Running	CLK_{io}
	Flash RAM	Stopped	CLK_{flash}
	SPI	Stopped	CLK_{io}
	Timer/counters	Stopped	CLK_{io}
	TWI (address matching)	Running	CLK_{io}
	USART	Stopped	CLK_{io}
	Watchdog	Running	
Wake on	External Reset		
	INT0 interrupt (LOW level only)		
	INT1 interrupt (LOW level only)		
	Pin Change Interrupt		
	TWI address match		
	Watchdog Timer interrupt (or Reset)		
	Brown-Out Reset		

On a wake-up call, when sleeping in this mode, the device is back up and running in six clock cycles.

7.3.9.6. Extended Standby Sleep Mode

This is sleep mode 7 (111_{binary}). The data sheet advises not to use this sleep mode unless there is an external crystal running the main clock.

This mode is identical to the Power Save mode described earlier, apart from the two main oscillators running. This sleep mode is best avoided on Arduinos as the asynchronous timer clock isn't running. Use Standby sleep mode instead.

In Extended Standby mode, *all* clocks are again stopped; and once more, the AVR microcontroller is powered off for all intents and purposes. The Watchdog Timer does continue to run, and the INT0 and INT1 Level interrupts and any of the Pin Change Interrupts will wake the device as will the TWI address match interrupt and the BOD.

A summary of this sleep mode is given in Table 7-18.

Table 7-18. *Extended Standby sleep mode summary*

Sleep Mode 7 (Extended Standby)		
Clocks	CLK_{cpu} (Core, RAM)	Stopped
	CLK_{flash} (Flash RAM, EEPROM)	Stopped
	CLK_{io} (SPI, USART, TWI, GPIO pins, Timer/counters, external interrupts)	Stopped
	CLK_{adc} (ADC)	Stopped
	CLK_{asy} (Asynchronous Timer/ counter 2)	Running (but not on an Arduino board)
Oscillators	Main system oscillator	Running
	Asynchronous Timer oscillator	Running (not Arduino)

(*continued*)

Table 7-18. (*continued*)

Sleep Mode 7 (Extended Standby)			
Peripherals	ADC	Stopped	CLK_{adc}
	Analogue Comparator	Unknown!	
	Core	Stopped	CLK_{cpu}
	RAM	Stopped	CLK_{cpu}
	EEPROM	Stopped	CLK_{flash}
	External interrupts	Running	CLK_{io}
	Flash RAM	Stopped	CLK_{flash}
	SPI	Stopped	CLK_{io}
	Timer/counters	Stopped	CLK_{io}
	TWI (address matching)	Running	CLK_{io}
	USART	Stopped	CLK_{io}
	Watchdog	Running	
Wake on	External Reset		
	INT0 interrupt (level only)		
	INT1 interrupt (level only)		
	Pin Change Interrupt		
	TWI address match		
	Timer/counter2 interrupt		
	Watchdog Timer interrupt (or Reset)		
	Brown-Out Reset		

On a wake-up call, when sleeping in this mode, the device is back up and running in six clock cycles.

7.3.10. Analogue Comparator

The data sheet is not very clear on whether or not the Analogue Comparator interrupt can be used to wake the device from some of the sleep modes. Believe me I searched in vain for the detail! To this end, I configured the various sleep modes and set up a circuit identical to the one described in Chapter 9 on the Analogue Comparator. There's a full description of the circuit and how it works in Chapter 9, Section 9.1, "*The Analogue Comparator.*"

In the code in Listings 7-11 to 7-14, I set the Arduino into various sleep modes in setup() and then tested to see if the comparator would wake the AVR microcontroller from its slumbers.

Listing 7-11 is the setupComparator() function which has not been changed from Chapter 9, other than to #include the avr/sleep.h and avr/interrupt.h header files at the top of the function.

Listing 7-11. Analogue Comparator wake-up, setupComparator()

```
//=======================================================
// The purpose of the sketch is to test the various sleep
// modes and to see if the AC will wake the Arduino.
//=======================================================

#include <avr/sleep.h>
#include <avr/interrupt.h>

// This function sets up the comparator to fire an interrupt
// each time the ACO bit toggles. It uses D6 as the reference
// voltage and D7 as the voltage to be compared.
void setupComparator() {
    ACSR &= ~(1 << ACIE);
    ACSR &= ~(1 << ACD);
    DIDR1 |= ((1 << AIN0D) | (1 << AIN1D));
```

```
    ACSR &= ~(1 << ACBG);
    ADCSRB &= ~(1 << ACME);
    ACSR |= ((1 << ACIS1) | (1 << ACIS0));
    ACSR |= (1 << ACIE);
}
```

Listing 7-12 is pretty much the same setup() function to that in Chapter 9, with the minor addition of the call to function set_sleep_mode(). It is here that I tested each and every valid sleep mode to see which, if any, would be interrupted by the Analogue Comparator's interrupt.

Listing 7-12. Analogue Comparator wake-up, setup()

```
void setup() {
    pinMode(LED_BUILTIN, OUTPUT);
    setupComparator();

    // Here is where I set the various sleep modes.
    set_sleep_mode(SLEEP_MODE_IDLE);
}
```

An interrupt is required to wake the ATmega328P, but we don't need to do any work inside the ISR. Listing 7-13 shows the code required for just such a purpose; it is an empty ISR to handle the Analogue Comparator interrupt.

Listing 7-13. Analogue Comparator wake-up, empty ISR

```
// Analogue Comparator Interrupt Handler. Simply used to
// wake up the device, so no code required.
EMPTY_INTERRUPT(ANALOG_COMP_vect);
```

Listing 7-14 is the main `loop()` function for the sketch. It puts the device to sleep in whatever mode I used in `setup()` and waits for a wake-up call. If one arrives, it will flash the built-in LED to show that it woke up. It will then go back to sleep.

Listing 7-14. Analogue Comparator wake-up, loop()

```
void loop() {
    noInterrupts();
    sleep_enable();
    sleep_bod_disable();

    // Kill timer 0 and its overflow interrupt otherwise
    // it will wake the AVR from SLEEP_MODE_IDLE thus
    // negating the test. I need the AC to do the wake
    // up call!
    TCCR0B &= ~((1 << CS02) | (1 << CS01) | (1 << CS00));

    interrupts();

    // Go to sleep now.
    sleep_cpu();

    sleep_disable();

    // Reset Timer 0 to divide by 64 or delay() doesn't!
    TCCR0B |= ((1 << CS01) | (1 << CS00));

    // Flash the LED on wake up.
    for (short x = 0; x < 4; x++) {
        digitalWrite(LED_BUILTIN, HIGH);
        delay(250);

        digitalWrite(LED_BUILTIN, LOW);
        delay(250);
    }
}
```

And the results? The Analogue Comparator does indeed wake up the Arduino when in SLEEP_MODE_IDLE but doesn't wake it up in any other mode which is as I *thought* would be the case, but at least I now *know*.

7.4. Power Reduction

Many AVR microcontrollers come with numerous different, potentially power-hungry, peripherals. If these are not being used by a sketch, then they can be disabled by setting a bit in the PRR or Power Reduction Register. This will shut them down and reduce overall power consumption by the AVR microcontroller, thus increasing battery life on battery-powered devices.

Numerous parts of the AVR microcontroller can be disconnected or shut down to save power, and it is recommended that this be done if those peripherals are not in use. The Arduino system cannot determine which parts you are not using, so it is up to you, the maker, to decide and disable accordingly.

Power consumption and the various sleep modes discussed in Section 7.3.9, "*Sleep Modes*," are a great way to reduce the power requirements of your project and can help – in some cases – to dramatically increase running time from battery power.

7.4.1. Power Consumption

The ATmega328P can be run at a number of supply voltages. On Arduino boards with a 16 MHz crystal or ceramic resonator, the supply voltage is limited to between 4.0 V and 5.5 V. The data sheet gives the figures shown in Table 7-19 for power consumption for each of those voltages, at 16 MHz, when the device is *idle* (in sleep mode Idle) and *active* or not sleeping.

Table 7-19. *ATmega328P power consumption*

VCC	Idle Current	Idle Power	Active Current	Active Power
4.0 V	1.75 milliAmps	7.0 milliWatts	7.0 milliAmps	28 milliWatts
4.5 V	2.1 milliAmps	9.45 milliWatts	8.2 milliAmps	36.9 milliWatts
5.0 V	2.4 milliAmps	12.0 milliWatts	9.6 milliAmps	48.0 milliWatts
5.5 V	2.8 milliAmps	15.4 milliWatts	11.0 milliAmps	60.5 milliWatts

ℹ️ You should note that these figures are for a bare-bones AVR microcontroller and *not* for the whole Arduino board, complete with power-hungry devices like the voltage regulator, the always-on power LED, and so on.

You may be surprised to find out exactly how few components you actually need to run a device with an ATmega328P as the microcontroller and even fewer if your device can be run using an ATtiny85!

From Table 7-19, it can be seen that an active ATmega328P, running at 16 MHz with a VCC of 4 V, uses half the power of the same device running with a VCC of 5.5 V. Sadly, our Arduino boards are fixed at 5.0 V for VCC, so we are not able to do much in that area to reduce power consumption. However, for a bare-bones AVR microcontroller on a breadboard or circuit board of our own design, we do have the option.

i While the Arduino boards themselves are excellent for prototyping, they are a tad expensive, and power hungry, to embed in the finished product. In the case where a device is deemed to be market-ready, the Arduino itself will normally be replaced by a minimal ATmega328P circuit, with far fewer resource requirements and a much lower cost.

Table 7-20 shows the power consumption of the various ATmega328P internal peripherals and is taken from the data sheet. It should be noted that the typical figures listed are those for an AVR microcontroller running with a VCC of 5 V and a clock frequency of 8 MHz. This will not be accurate for an Arduino at 16 MHz, but read on, as all will become clear.

Table 7-20. *ATmega328P peripherals' power consumption*

Peripheral	Typical Current	Active Extra	Idle Extra
ADC	295.38 microAmps	4.1%	22.1%
USART	100.25 microAmps	1.4%	7.8%
SPI	186.5 microAmps	2.9%	15.7%
Timer/counter 1	176.25 microAmps	2.7%	14.5%
Timer/counter 0	61.13 microAmps	0.9%	4.8%
Timer/counter 2	224.25 microAmps	3.3%	17.8%
TWI	199.25 microAmps	3.0%	16.6%

7.4.1.1. Calculating Power Requirements

As the data sheet explains, it is possible to calculate the power requirements for each of the preceding seven peripherals, based on the voltage and frequency of the crystal or ceramic oscillator in use. The preceding typical figures are based on a 5 V AVR microcontroller running at 8 MHz. The Arduino runs at 16 MHz, so we need to get the calculator out.

It's actually quite simple. Take the current drawn from Table 7-19 for the voltage your device is using, and then add the percentage for active or idle from Table 7-20 for the peripheral in question. If there are more than one peripherals, simply add each percentage.

If we consider the AVR microcontroller running on a 5 V supply at 16 MHz, with all peripherals enabled and running, what is the idle power required?

```
Idle power at 5V = 2.4 mA
Peripheral percentages = 22.1% + ... + 16.6% = 99.3%
99.3% of 2.4 mA = 2.3832 mA
Added to 2.4 mA = 4.7832 mA
Resulting power = 5V * 4.5432 mA = 22.916 mW.
```

The same calculation in active mode results in

```
Active power at 5V = 9.6 mA
Peripheral percentages = 4.1% + ... + 3.0% = 18.3%
18.3% of 9.6 mA = 1.7568 mA
Added to 9.6 mA = 11.3568 mA
Resulting power = 5V * 11.3568 mA = 56.784 mW.
```

7.4.2. Power Reduction Register

Not all AVR microcontrollers have the same set of peripherals, and the relevant ones in the ATmega328P are as follows:

- Analogue to Digital Converter (ADC)

- Universal Synchronous/Asynchronous Receiver/Transmitter (USART)

- Two-Wire Interface (TWI) aka I^{2}C interface

- Timer/counter 0

- Timer/counter 1

- Timer/counter 2

- Serial Peripheral Interface (SPI)

Those seven peripherals each have a single bit in the Power Reduction Register or PRR so that when set to a 1_{binary}, that particular peripheral is powered off. The bits in question are

- PRADC which enables or disables power to the ADC

- PRUSART0 which enables or disables power to the USART

- PRSPI which enables or disables power to the SPI

- PRTIM1 which enables or disables power to Timer/counter 1

- PRTIM0 which enables or disables power to Timer/counter 0

- PRTIM2 which enables or disables power to Timer/counter 2

- PRTWI which enables or disables power to the TWI

What these bits do is to stop the clock to the peripheral. Once the clock has been stopped, that peripheral is effectively suspended, and there is no ability to write to, or read from, the device's registers.

The data sheet warns that *Resources used by the peripheral when stopping the clock will remain occupied, hence the peripheral should in most cases be disabled before stopping the clock.*

What this means is that whatever peripheral you wish to power off should be disabled before powering it down. In the case of the ADC, for example, this would entail writing a 0_{binary} to ADEN in the ADCSRA register to disable the ADC and then writing a 1_{binary} to PRADC in the PRR to power it off.

The on-off switches for each preceding peripheral are listed in Table 7-21 and, unless otherwise noted, should be written with a zero$_{binary}$ to disable the appropriate peripheral.

Table 7-21. *Disabling ATmega328P peripherals*

Peripheral	Bit	Register	Comments
ADC	ADEN	ADCSRA	Shuts down the ADC
USART	RXENn	UCSRnB	Shuts down the USARTn Receiver
USART	TXENn	UCSRnB	Shuts down the USARTn Transmitter
SPI	SPE	SPCR	Shuts down the SPI
Timer/counter 1	CS12–CS10	TCCR1B	Shuts down Timer/counter 1 when written as 000_{binary}
Timer/counter 0	CS02–CS00	TCCR0B	Shuts down Timer/counter 0 when written as 000_{binary}
Timer/counter 2	CS22–CS20	TCCR2B	Shuts down Timer/counter 2 when written as 000_{binary}
TWI	TWEN	TWCR	Shuts down the TWI/I²C Interface
Analogue Comparator	ACD	ACSR	Shuts down the Analogue Comparator

To power up a peripheral from its powered-down state, simply write a 0_{binary} to the appropriate bit in the PRR. The peripheral will wake up again and will resume the state that it was in when powered down. You have to write a zero because that disables the power reduction for that peripheral.

ℹ The Analogue Comparator doesn't have a bit in the PRR. It does, however, have the ACD bit in the Analogue Comparator Control and Status Register – ACSR. Write a 1_{binary} to that bit to power off the Analogue Comparator.

7.4.3. Saving Arduino Power

Now you know what peripherals can be disabled and powered down, you are able to perhaps save a little of your device's power by using the setup() function to power off all those bits of the ATmega328P that you don't need for a sketch.

Taking the old favorite blink sketch, yet again, what does it *actually* need? Nothing more than the I/O pins and a timer/counter to work the delay() function. The delay() function and millis() and micros() all depend on Timer/counter 0. Listings 7-15 to 7-17 show an example blink sketch with unwanted peripherals turned off.

The AVRLib has some useful power maintenance functions, and these can be used to power off the peripherals we don't need in our blink sketch. There is a trade-off of course: adding code to setup() to disable and power off these peripherals will increase the code size of the final sketch.

In the case of the blink sketch, it's unlikely that this will be a problem, but for other sketches that might be pushing at the capacity of the AVR microcontroller, it could be a problem and you might have to revert to the direct manner of setting the registers in your code, rather than using the AVRLib functions.

The sketch in Listings 7-15, 7-16, and 7-17 could be used to enhance battery life for an Arduino device, running the blink sketch. Listing 7-15 is a function, `disable()`, which disables all the unwanted peripherals based on parameters passed to it, prior to powering them all off.

Listing 7-15. Low-power blink, disable() function

```
#include <avr/power.h>

void disable(bool ADCdisable, bool USARTdisable, bool
SPIdisable,
            bool TIMER0disable, bool TIMER1disable, bool
            TIMER2disable,
            bool TWIdisable, bool ACdisable)
{
    // Disable ADC.
    if (ADCdisable)
        ADCSRA &= ~(1 << ADEN);

    // Disable USART0 RX and TX.
    if (USARTdisable)
        UCSR0B &= ~((1 << RXEN0) | (1 << TXEN0));

    // Disable SPI.
    if (SPIdisable)
        SPCR &= ~(1 << SPE);

    // Disable Timer/Counter 0
    if (TIMER0disable)
        TCCR0B &= ~((1 << CS02) | (1 << CS01) | (1 << CS00));

    // Disable Timer/Counter 1.
    if (TIMER1disable)
        TCCR1B &= ~((1 << CS12) | (1 << CS11) | (1 << CS10));
```

```
    // Disable Timer/Counter 2.
    if (TIMER2disable)
        TCCR2B &= ~((1 << CS22) | (1 << CS21) | (1 << CS20));

    // Disable TWI.
    if (TWIdisable)
        TWCR &= ~(1 << TWEN);

    // Disable Analogue comparator.
    if (ACdisable)
        ACSR &= ~(1 << ACD);
}
```

The setup() function in Listing 7-16 calls disable() with a list of peripherals to disable and then calls the AVRLib's __power_all_disable() function which powers down all the peripherals. It then powers Timer/counter 0 back on to ensure that that is still working as it is needed by the sketch.

Listing 7-16. Low-power blink, setup() function

```
void setup() {
    // Disable the peripherals we don't want.
    disable(
    /* ADCdisable = */ true,
    /* USARTdisable = */ true,
    /* SPIdisable = */ true,
    /* TIMER0disable = */ false,
    /* TIMER1disable = */ true,
    /* TIMER2disable = */ true,
    /* TWIdisable = */ true,
    /* ACdisable = */ true);

    // Power down everything except Timer/Counter 0.
    // It's quicker this way, and less code bloat!
```

```
    __power_all_disable();
    power_timer0_enable();

    // Finally, do the sketch stuff.
    pinMode(LED_BUILTIN, OUTPUT);
}
```

The loop() in Listing 7-17 just blinks the LED as usual.

Listing 7-17. Low-power blink, loop() function

```
void loop() {
    digitalWrite(LED_BUILTIN, HIGH);
    delay(1000);
    digitalWrite(LED_BUILTIN, LOW);
    delay(1000);
}
```

The sketch uses 1006 bytes of Flash RAM now, which is obviously more than the standard blink sketch would use. In larger sketches, the overhead should be less.

7.4.4. The Power Functions

As mentioned earlier, there are useful power handling functions in the AVRLib. These are, for the ATmega328P, as shown in Table 7-22.

Table 7-22. *AVRLib power functions*

Function Name	Description
power_adc_enable()	Enables power to the ADC
power_adc_disable()	Disables power to the ADC
power_spi_enable()	Enables power to the SPI
power_spi_disable()	Disables power to the SPI
power_timer0_enable()	Enables power to Timer/counter 0
power_timer0_disable()	Disables power to Timer/counter 0
power_timer1_enable()	Enables power to the Timer/counter 1
power_timer1_disable()	Disables power to the Timer/counter 1
power_timer2_enable()	Enables power to the Timer/counter 2
power_timer2_disable()	Disables power to the Timer/counter 2
power_twi_enable()	Enables power to the TWI
power_twi_disable()	Disables power to the TWI
power_usart0_enable()	Enables power to USART0 (the only one on the ATmega328P)
power_usart0_disable()	Disables power to USART0 (the only one on the ATmega328P)
__power_all_enable()	Enables power to *all* peripherals
__power_all_disable()	Disables power to *all* peripherals

Not all devices have these functions; it's another one of those configuration things. The iom328p.h header file sets up the appropriate functions which are available for peripheral devices on the ATmega328P.

i You are required to manually turn off the Analogue Comparator if you do not need it. There doesn't appear to be a utility function to do so in the AVRLib code.

7.5. Bootloaders

The ATmega328P on an Arduino board is supplied already programmed with a bootloader. This is a small area of the Flash RAM set aside for a special program, and when the device is reset or powered on, a jump to the bootloader takes place.

The standard Uno bootloader delays startup of the ATmega320P for a brief period, to check that no programming commands are being received on the USART pins (D0 and D1). If there are no commands, the application code starts normally; and the blink sketch, or whatever you programmed last, starts executing.

If there are specific commands being read, then the bootloader starts running those commands and may, depending on what it is being commanded to do, overwrite the previously uploaded code with a new version or just upload a new sketch to the application area of the Flash RAM. The bootloader *cannot* update itself with a new version.

7.5.1. Flash Memory

The flash memory in the ATmega328P is divided into two sections:

- The application section – This is where your sketch code is written to by the bootloader or the ICSP device.

- The bootloader section, or BLS – This is where the bootloader lives.

There are fuses, BOOTSZ1:0 and BOOTRST, to determine the size and address of the bootloader sections; and, in the case of the BOOTRST fuse, it determines whether the device starts executing the bootloader or the application code on startup and/or reset.

---

i While it is possible and, indeed, permitted for the bootloader to write to the application section, the converse is not true. The application cannot access the bootloader section.

You should also note that the whole of Flash RAM can be used as the application section if no bootloader is required. This seems to be easily done simply by using an ICSP device to do the programming.

The sections are considered completely separate by the device, and they can have different protection levels. This protection is determined by special lock bits. Boot Loader Lock Bits 0 protect the application section, while Boot Loader Lock Bits 1 protect the bootloader section. There are two other lock bits that protect the entire ATmega328P from either being reprogrammed or having its Flash RAM read out.

7.5.2. Lock Bits

The lock bits can be set in software, in serial or parallel programming mode. To clear the *bootloader* lock bits, a full chip erase command must be given. It may not be possible, but I have not checked this on my own devices – for obvious reasons, to ever unlock the device for programming if the device lock bits have been set.

7.5.2.1. Device Lock Bits

The device lock bits prevent anyone from reading or changing the contents of the AVR microcontroller. Those are lock bits LB1 and LB2 and have the following modes and settings.

Table 7-23. *Device lock bits 0*

MODE	LB02	LB01	Description
1	1	1	The device is totally unprotected. It can be programmed or Flash and EEPROM contents read at will.
2	1	0	Programming the device – Flash or EEPROM – is disabled in serial or parallel mode. The fuse bits are also locked. Any code already programmed can still be read.
3	0	0	Programming and reading the device – Flash or EEPROM – is disabled in serial or parallel mode. The fuse bits are also locked.

The default is LB Mode 1 which allows the device to be programmed and verified (read back) as required.

> In case you are wondering, serial programming is when either an ICSP device or a high-voltage serial programmer is used and requires only a few pins; parallel, on the other hand, requires many more pins and is uncommon outside of large establishments which need to program many devices at once.
>
> There are very good descriptions and circuit diagrams of both methods at Nick Gammon's blog [www.gammon.com.au/forum/?id=12898] if you are interested.

> As with fuses, lock bits are considered programmed when at 0_{binary} and unprogrammed when 1_{binary}.

7.5.2.2. Bootloader Lock Bits

With the two sets of lock bits, the following options can be selected. Details follow for the BLBn modes mentioned:

- The entire Flash RAM can be protected from a software update – BLB0 Mode 2 plus BLB1 Mode 2.

- Only the bootloader section can be protected – BLB0 Mode 1 and BLB1 Mode 2 or 3.

- Only the application section can be protected – BLB0 Mode 2 or 3 and BLB1 Mode 1.

- The entire Flash RAM can be unprotected – BLB0 Mode 1 plus BLB1 Mode 1.

7.5.2.2. Bootloader Lock Bits 0

These bits protect the application section of the device. There are two bits here, BLB01 and BLB02; and these are set according to a mode, known as BLB0 Mode. Table 7-24 summarizes the different modes:

Table 7-24. *Bootloader lock bits 0*

MODE	BLB02	BLB01	Description
1	1	1	The application section is totally unprotected
2	1	0	The Store Program Memory (SPM) instruction is not allowed to write to the section. The application section is fully protected

(*continued*)

Table 7-24. (*continued*)

MODE	BLB02	BLB01	Description
3	0	0	The SPM instruction cannot write to the application section; and, at the same time, the Load Program Memory (LPM) instruction cannot read from it if executing from the bootloader. See Note in the following.
4	0	1	The LPM instruction, if executing from the bootloader, is not allowed to read from the application section. See Note in the following.

ⓘ If interrupt vectors are located in the bootloader section, interrupts will be disabled while code is executing from the application section.

7.5.2.2. Bootloader Lock Bits 1

These bits protect the bootloader section of the device. There are two bits here, BLB11 and BLB12; and these are set according to a mode, known as BLB1 Mode. Table 7-25 summarizes the different modes:

Table 7-25. *Bootloader lock bits 0*

MODE	BLB12	BLB11	Description
1	1	1	The bootloader section is unprotected and can be written to, but *not* by code running in the application section
2	1	0	The Store Program Memory (SPM) instruction is not allowed to write to the section. The bootloader section is fully protected
3	0	0	The SPM instruction cannot write to the bootloader section; and, at the same time, the Load Program Memory (LPM) instruction cannot read from it if executing from the application section. See Note in the following.
4	0	1	The LPM instruction, if executing from the application section, is not allowed to read from the bootloader section. See Note in the following.

ℹ️ If interrupt vectors are located in the application section, interrupts will be disabled while code is executing from the bootloader section.

7.5.3. Installing the Uno (Optiboot) Bootloader

The Uno bootloader is around 500 bytes in size, so takes up less of your precious Flash RAM when installed. It is found, should you wish to examine it in detail, in $ARDINST/bootloaders/optiboot/optiboot.c.

Although it's commonly referred as the *Uno bootloader*, it is, in fact, quite easily installable into other devices. The comments in the source code mention that it is compatible with both the Duemilanove and the Diecimila and other ATmega168- or AtMega328P-based devices.

If you wish to use a much smaller bootloader on your Duemilanove, for example, and save 1.5 Kb of Flash RAM for your own programs, it's easy:

- Close the IDE if it is open.

- Open the file $ARDINST/boards.txt in your favorite text editor.

- Find this line, for the ATmega328P variant:

  `diecimila.menu.cpu.atmega328.upload.maximum_size=30720`

- Change it to the following:

  `diecimila.menu.cpu.atmega328.upload.maximum_size=32256`

- Find this line – it's a single line which has wrapped around on this page:

  `diecimila.menu.cpu.atmega328.bootloader.file= atmega/`
  `ATmegaBOOT_168_atmega328.hex`

- Change it to the following *single* line, not wrapped as follows:

  `diecimila.menu.cpu.atmega328.bootloader.file= optiboot/`
  `optiboot_atmega328.hex`

- Save the file.

- Open the IDE again.

- Make sure that the correct board is selected under Tools ➤ Boards.

- Choose Tools ➤ Burn Bootloader.

You now have a smaller, faster bootloader and an additional 1.5 Kb of flash for your program – and all for free.

7.5.4. Optiboot Bootloader Operation

When the device is powered on, or reset, and if the BOOTRST fuse is set to enable the bootloader to be executed at startup, then the bootloader code for the device is executed.

One of the first tasks that the bootloader does is to check the MCUSR to determine if this was an External Reset or not. It does this by checking the EXTRF bit in the MCUSR. If that bit is set, then the device was reset by pulling pin 1, RST low, and not by a power-on, Watchdog, or BOD reset. This could have been done by the user pressing the reset button on the Arduino board or by the programming device using the DTR pin to pull the ATmega328P's RST pin low. In any case, bit EXTRF will have been set.

In the case when this bit is *not* set, the bootloader assumes that the device is not about to be reprogrammed and jumps immediately to the application code, bypassing the rest of the bootloader itself. If the bit is set, then the bootloader continues executing.

The Watchdog Timer is set to fire after 1 second, the onboard LED is flashed once to indicate that it is waiting, and an infinite loop is entered to wait for characters coming in over the USART. If nothing is received after the 1 second timeout by the Watchdog, then the device will reset again but this time by the Watchdog. On restarting from a Watchdog-induced reset, the EXTRF bit in the MCUSR will no longer be set – the WDRF bit, on the other hand, will be set – so the application code is immediately executed.

The bootloader, if it continues executing, must have read at least 1 byte from the USART. These bytes are assumed to be commands from a subset of the STK500 communications protocol – the Optiboot bootloader currently only implements a subset of the STK500 instructions – and these commands are used to communicate with, usually, avrdude.

It is beyond the scope of this book to delve into the various bootloader commands as they really have little to do with *application* programming. Suffice it to say that the bootloader sits in a loop, reading characters from the USART and acting upon them, in addition to resetting the Watchdog Timer to prevent the device being reset by the Watchdog and messing up the programming.

Should you *really* wish to examine the Optiboot bootloader, there is a compilation listing for the ATmega328P, in the location $ARDINST/ bootloaders/optiboot/optiboot_atmega328.lst – it does make interesting reading.

CHAPTER 8

ATmega328P Hardware: Timers and Counters

This chapter and the next look at the hardware features of the ATmega328P and should link up with the information presented in Chapters 2 and 3. You should, I hope, see how the Arduino Language talks to the hardware described in these chapters. This chapter starts by looking, long and hard, at the facilities of the ATmega's timer/counters, while the following chapter delves into the ADC and serial communications hardware, the USART.

8.1. Timer/Counters

The Atmega328P has a total of three timer/counters named Timer/counter 0, Timer/counter 1, and Timer/counter 2. The first and last of these are both 8-bit timer/counters and have a maximum value of 255, while Timer/Counter 1 is 16 bits and its maximum is 65,535.

At power on, or reset, all timer/counters are disabled and must be enabled in software. The Arduino's `init()` function does a lot of timer/counter initialization so that the `millis()`, `micros()`, and `analogWrite()` functions work.

© Norman Dunbar 2020
N. Dunbar, *Arduino Software Internals*, https://doi.org/10.1007/978-1-4842-5790-6_8

Timer/counters are so called because they have two separate functions. They can

- Count up and down depending on the mode, with a regular clock source based off of the AVR microcontroller's system clock. This is when it acts as a timer.

- Count up, and down, based on an external rising or falling edge attached to a specific pin. This is when it acts as a counter.

⚠️ The data sheet for the ATmega328P advises that when setting various timer/counter modes, any output pins affected should be set to OUTPUT *after* setting the required modes.

In much of what follows, you may see references to TOP, MAX, and/or BOTTOM. These are definitions that are used in the data sheet for the ATmega328P and refer to the following:

- BOTTOM is easy. It is always zero.

- MAX is also easy. It is always the maximum value that can be held in the timer/counter's TCNTn register according to however many bits the timer/counter is configured for. This is calculated as $2^{bits} - 1$.

  For Timer/counters 0 and 2, this is always 8 bits, and so MAX always equals 255. For Timer/counter 1, MAX varies as follows:

  - In 8-bit mode, MAX = 255.

  - In 9-bit mode, MAX = 511.

- In 10-bit mode, MAX = 1,023.

- In 16-bit mode, MAX = 65,535.

- TOP depends on the timer/counter's mode and is either MAX for some modes or as defined by various other timer/counter registers such as OCRnA, OCRnB, ICR1, etc.

8.1.1. Timer/Counter 0 (8 Bits)

This timer/counter has eight different modes of operation defined by the Waveform Generation bits WGM02:0 in the registers TCCR0A and TCCR0B (Timer/counter 0 Control Registers A and B). Bit WGM02 is found in TCCR0B, while WGM01 and WGM00 are in TCCR0A.

Table 8-1 shows the various settings for the modes available in Timer/counter 0.

Table 8-1. *Timer/counter 0 modes*

Mode	WGM02– WGM00	TOP	OCR0x Updated	TOV0 Set at	Mode of Operation
0	000	255	NOW	255	Normal
1	001	255	TOP	0	PWM, Phase Correct
2	010	OCR0A	NOW	255	CTC
3	011	255	0	255	PWM, Fast
5	101	OCR0A	TOP	0	PWM, Phase Correct
7	111	OCR0A	0	TOP	PWM, Fast

Modes 4 and 6 are reserved and should not be configured.

When you write a new value to register OCR0x, the value doesn't get written until the timer/counter's value TCNT0 reaches that shown in the preceding table, where "NOW" means that the new value is written as soon as your code executes it and any other value means that the new value will be written when TCNT0 reaches that given value.

The various timer/counter modes are explained later in this chapter.

8.1.2. Timer/Counter 1 (8, 9, 10, and/or 16 Bits)

This timer/counter has 16 different modes of operation defined by the Waveform Generation bits WGM13:0 in the registers TCCR1A and TCCR1B (Timer/counter 1 Control Registers A and B). Bits WG13 and WGM12 are found in TCCR1B, while WGM11 and WGM10 are in TCCR1A.

Table 8-2 shows the various settings for the modes available in Timer/counter 1.

Table 8-2. *Timer/counter 1 modes*

Mode	WGM13–WGM10	TOP	OCR1x Updated	TOV1 Set at	Mode of Operation
0	0000	65535	NOW	65535	Normal
1	0001	255	TOP	0	PWM, Phase Correct 8 bit
2	0010	511	TOP	0	PWM, Phase Correct 9 bit
3	0011	1023	TOP	0	PWM, Phase Correct 10 bit
4	0100	OCR1A	NOW	65535	CTC
5	0101	255	0	TOP	PWM, Fast 8 bit
6	0101	511	0	TOP	PWM, Fast 9 bit
7	0101	1023	0	TOP	PWM, Fast 10 bit
8	1000	ICR1	0	0	PWM, Phase and Frequency Correct

(continued)

Table 8-2. (*continued*)

Mode	WGM13–WGM10	TOP	OCR1x Updated	TOV1 Set at	Mode of Operation
9	1001	OCR1A	0	0	PWM, Phase and Frequency Correct
10	1010	ICR1	TOP	0	PWM, Phase Correct
11	1011	OCR1A	TOP	0	PWM, Phase Correct
12	1100	ICR1	NOW	65535	CTC
14	1110	ICR1	0	TOP	PWM, Fast
15	1111	OCR1A	0	TOP	PWM, Fast

Mode 13 is reserved and should not be configured.

When you write a new value to register OCR1x, the value doesn't get written until the timer/counter's value TCNT1 reaches that shown in the preceding table, where "NOW" means that the new value is written as soon as your code executes it and any other value means that the new value will be written when TCNT1 reaches that given value.

ℹ️ Timer/counter 1 has an extra control register, TCCR1C, which the other two timer/counters don't have.

The various timer/counter modes are explained later in this chapter.

8.1.3. Timer/Counter 2 (8 Bits)

This timer/counter has eight different modes of operation defined by the Waveform Generation bits WGM22:0 in the registers TCCR2A and TCCR2B (Timer/counter 2 Control Registers A and B). Bit WGM22 is found in TCCR2B, while WGM21 and WGM20 are in TCCR2A.

Table 8-3 shows the various settings for the modes available in Timer/counter 2.

Table 8-3. *Timer/counter 2 modes*

Mode	WGM22–WGM20	TOP	OCR2x Updated	TOV2 Set at	Mode of Operation
0	000	255	NOW	255	Normal
1	001	255	TOP	0	PWM, Phase Correct
2	010	OCR2A	NOW	255	CTC
3	011	255	0	255	PWM, Fast
5	101	OCR2A	TOP	0	PWM, Phase Correct
7	111	OCR2A	0	TOP	PWM, Fast

Modes 4 and 6 are reserved and should not be configured.

When you write a new value to register OCR2x, the value doesn't get written until the timer/counter's value TCNT2 reaches that shown in the preceding table, where "NOW" means that the new value is written as soon as your code executes it and any other value means that the new value will be written when TCNT2 reaches that given value.

The various timer/counter modes are explained later in this chapter.

8.1.4. Timer/Counter Clock Sources

The timer/counters all have their own clock sources, most of which are based on the system clock, and each timer/counter has its own dedicated prescaler and this can be set to various values, to divide the system clock giving the timer/counter's clock speed or, alternatively, to clock on an external pin's rising, or falling, edge.

While all three timer/counters have *mostly* the same prescaler settings, Timer/counter 2 does not have the ability to be externally clocked, but it does have the ability to run with divide-by-32 and divide-by-128 prescalers, which the others cannot. It can also be configured to run in *asynchronous* mode with a 32.768 KHz crystal attached to the TOSCn pins. This is beyond the scope of this book, however, as the Arduino uses those two pins for a 16 MHz crystal, thus rendering asynchronous mode unusable.

Table 8-4 shows the various clock sources for the three timer/counters.

Table 8-4. Timer/counter clock sources

Prescaler	Timer 0 CS02–CS0	Timer 1 CS12–CS0	Timer 2 CS22–CS0	Frequency	Period
Disabled	000	000	000	–	–
Divide by 1	001	001	001	16 MHz	0.0625 microseconds
Divide by 8	010	010	010	2 MHz	0.5 microseconds
Divide by 32	–	–	011	500 KHz (0.5 MHz)	2 microseconds
Divide by 64	011	011	100	250 KHz (0.25 MHz)	4 microseconds
Divide by 128	–	–	101	125 KHz (0.125 MHz)	8 microseconds
Divide by 256	100	100	110	62.5 KHz	16 microseconds
Divide by 1024	101	101	111	15.625 KHz	64 microseconds
External falling	110 pin T0	110 pin T1	–	–	–
External rising	111 pin T0	111 pin T1	–	–	–

ℹ The preceding Pin T0 is physical pin 6 on the ATmega328P, which is PD4 in AVR terminology or D4 in the Arduino Language. Pin T1 is physical pin 11, also known as PD5 in the AVR terminology, and corresponds to Arduino pin D5.

8.1.5. Timer/Counter Operating Modes

As you have seen earlier, the three timer/counters can operate in a number of different modes. Not all timer/counters have the same modes though. Tables 8-1 through 8-3 show the modes available for each timer/counter individually.

8.1.5.1. Timers Disabled

This is not really a timer/counter mode, but setting the CSn2, CSn1, and CSn0 bits to zero in register TCCRnB will disable the timer/counters. The preceding "n" refers to the timer/counter in question.

Disabling Timer/counter 0 will disable the ability to use the millis() and micros() functions if you are using the Arduino Language. It will also prevent the use of analogWrite() on pins D5 and D6.

Disabling Timer/counter 1 will prevent the use of analogWrite() on pins D9 and D10.

Disabling Timer/counter 2 will prevent the use of analogWrite() on pins D3 and D11 and will also affect the ability of the tone() function to be used as that needs Timer/counter 2.

Due to the usefulness of the various timer/counters, it is unlikely that they will ever be disabled. However, should your code not require any of the timer/counters, you can save a few microAmps of power consumption by disabling power to the timer/counters in the PRR, by setting the required bits PRTIMn, where, as ever, "n" refers to the timer/

counter number. Section 7.4.2, *"Power Reduction Register,"* in Chapter 7 discusses the PRR in some detail.

ℹ️ Should you decide do this, Timer/counter 2 must be running either in *synchronous* mode off of the internal oscillator or on a 16 MHz crystal as per the Arduino. If the timer is running in *asynchronous* mode with a 32 KHz or higher crystal, plus AS2 set in register ASSR, then writing a 1_{binary} to PRTIM2 in the PRR register will *not* stop Timer/counter 2.

This latter mode of operation is, of course, not possible on an Arduino board as the 16 MHz crystal is attached to the two pins that an external 32 KHz crystal needs to use for asynchronous mode. On a bare-bones AVR microcontroller though, this need not be the case.

8.1.5.1.1. Disabling the Timers

Table 8-5 shows the settings required to disable the timer/counters.

Table 8-5. *Disable timer/counter settings*

Timer	Mode	TTCRnB Bits	Value
0	0	CS02–CS00	000_{binary}
1	0	CS12–CS10	000_{binary}
2	0	CS22–CS20	000_{binary}

8.1.5.2. Normal Mode

In normal mode, a timer/counter starts at zero, but this can be changed by writing a new value to TCNTn, which counts upward by 1 every time its clock source ticks, until it reaches MAX – see preceding text for details of MAX, BOTTOM, and TOP in relation to the three timer/counters – which is 255 for Timer/counter 0 and 2 or 65,535 for Timer/counter 1 in this mode.

At MAX, the timer/counter's value, in TCNTn, will roll over from MAX to zero – BOTTOM – on the *following* tick of the timer/counter's clock.

A number of things happen when the timer/counter rolls over or overflows:

- The Timer Overflow bit, TOVn, is set in the Timer Interrupt Flag Register, TIFRn, on *the same clock tick* as the timer/counter's value became zero – after MAX + 1 counts – assuming that you didn't change TCNTn. This flag is only ever set unless your program uses the timer/counter's Overflow interrupt. It will remain set until manually cleared by your sketch by writing a 1_{binary} to it.

- The Timer Overflow interrupt will be fired, if the Timer Overflow interrupt enable bit, TOIEn, is set in the Timer Interrupt Mask Register TIMSKn *and* global interrupts are enabled. In this case, the TOVn bit *will* be cleared automatically when the interrupt service routine is entered.

- Pin OCnA will perform an action. The action depends on the values in the COMnA1:0 bits, as described in Table 8-6, when TCNTn matches with OCRnA.

427

Table 8-6. *COMnA1:0 settings in normal mode*

COMnA1-COMnA0	Description
00	No effect on pin OCnA
01	Pin OCnA toggles on match with OCRnA
10	Pin OCnA is cleared (LOW) on match with OCRnA
11	Pin OCnA is set (HIGH) on match with OCRnA

- Pin OCnB will perform an action. The action depends on the values in the COMnB1:0 bits, as described in Table 8-7, when TCNTn matches with OCRnB.

Table 8-7. *COMnB1:0 settings in normal mode*

COMnB1-COMnB0	Description
00	No effect on pin OCnB
01	Pin OCnB toggles on match with OCRnB
10	Pin OCnB is cleared (LOW) on match with OCRnB
11	Pin OCnB is set (HIGH) on match with OCRnB

While running in this mode, you can, if you wish, write a value to the timer/counter's TCNTn register, which can reduce the time it takes for the Overflow bit to be set or the interrupt to be fired.

8.1.5.2.1. Setting Normal Mode

Table 8-8 shows the settings required to put the timer/counters into normal mode.

Table 8-8. *Normal mode settings*

Timer	Mode	Bits	Value
0	0	WGM02–WGM00	000_{binary}
1	0	WGM13–WGM10	0000_{binary}
2	0	WGM22–WGM20	000_{binary}

Note that bits WGMn0 and WGMn1 are found in register TCCRnA, bit WGMn2 is found in TCCRnB and, for Timer/counter 1 only, WGM13 is also found in TCCR1B.

8.1.5.2.2. Example Sketch

Atmel/Microchip's data sheets advise that *the Output Compare unit can be used to generate interrupts at some given time, Using the Output Compare unit to generate waveforms in Normal mode is not recommended, since this will occupy too much of the CPU time.*

So it sounds like we should use Overflow interrupts for useful purposes, and this is what the Arduino uses for its millis() function and so on, but can we use OCR0A and OCR0B to generate interrupts as well? Well, Listings 8-1 to 8-3 tell all.

⚠ I did originally write this code using Timer/counter 0, but as the TIMER0_OVF handling routine in the Arduino library is already using that timer/counter's Overflow interrupt, I got linker errors due to there being two copies of the interrupt handler. Any Arduino code with this vector in use will not be able to be compiled with the IDE.

The sketch initializes Timer/counter 2 with three interrupts in `setup()`. The three interrupts are

- The Overflow interrupt which will toggle an LED on pin D13

- The Compare Match A interrupt which will toggle an LED on pin OC2A which is Arduino pin D12

- The Compare Match B interrupt which will toggle an LED on pin OC2B which is Arduino pin D11

Listings 8-1, 8-2, and 8-3 show the `setup()`, `loop()`, and interrupt handler code, respectively.

Listing 8-1. Normal timer/counter mode setup() function

```
//==========================================================
// This sketch uses the Timer/Counter 2 as follows:
//
// Overflow Interrupt to toggle LED_BUILTIN (D13)
// COMPA Interrupt to toggle D12
// COMPB Interrupt to toggle D11.
//==========================================================

void setup() {
    TCCR2A = 0;                              ①
    TIMSK2 = ((1 << OCIE2B) |                ②
              (1 << OCIE2A) |
              (1 << TOIE2));

    // Set up the compare values.            ③
    OCR2A = 8;
    OCR2B = 172;
```

```
TCCR2B = ((1 << CS22) |                    ④
          (1 << CS21) |
          (1 << CS20));

// D11, D12 and D13 are outputs.         ⑤
pinMode(13, OUTPUT);
pinMode(12, OUTPUT);
pinMode(11,  OUTPUT);
}
```

① This clears the timer register to a known starting configuration. This enables normal mode.

② This enables interrupts on Overflow and Compare Matches A and B.

③ This is a couple of random values to compare against, for the interrupts to trigger.

④ This sets the prescaler to 1024 and starts the timer.

⑤ This configures the LED pins as OUTPUT after setting the timer/counter configuration, as per the data sheet.

Listing 8-2. Normal timer/counter mode loop() function

```
void loop() {
    // Nothing happening here, move along now!
}
```

As you can see, the loop() function is empty – the timer/counter interrupts take care of flashing the LEDs without needing the loop() to do anything.

Listing 8-3. Normal timer/counter mode ISRs

```
// Toggle pin D13 which is PortB pin 5.
ISR(TIMER2_OVF_vect) {
    // Fast pin toggle.
    PINB |= (1 << PINB5);
}

// Toggle pin D12 which is PortB pin 4.
ISR(TIMER2_COMPA_vect) {
    // Fast pin toggle.
    PINB |= (1 << PINB4);
}

// Toggle pin D13 which is PortB pin 3.
ISR(TIMER2_COMPB_vect) {
    // Fast pin toggle.
    PINB |= (1 << PINB3);
}
```

If you set this up with an LED on pin D13 (or use the built-in LED), another on pin D12, and a third on pin D11, then they will all flash, so the interrupts are working. All three will flash at exactly the same rate because there is an Overflow interrupt every 256 clock ticks, and both OCR2A and OCR2B will match TCNT2 once every 256 clock ticks also.

The timer/counter is running with a frequency of

```
F_CPU / prescaler
= 16 MHz / 1024
= 15,625 Hz.
```

We are toggling every 256 counts of the clock, and it takes two toggles to make one flash of the LED, so that's

```
F_CPU / prescaler / 256 / 2
= 16 MHz / 1024 / 256 / 2
= 30.5176 Hz
```

And that means we have a flash every 32.768 milliseconds. (The period is 1/frequency.)

Attaching my Labrador oscilloscope to the LEDs one at a time shows that they all have the same frequency, and it's calculated as 31.03 Hz, so it's not far off. It's obviously my ability to accurately place the cursors to get the correct measurements that is affecting the results, but it's close enough.

Don't forget that when an interrupt fires, it disables further interrupts, plus it takes four clock cycles to process the interrupt handler jump and another four to return, and those delays are not being considered here.

So we now know that interrupts work in normal mode. What about toggling the pins by setting the various COM2An and COM2Bn bits to toggle the pins when there's a compare match? Listings 8-4 to 8-6 show an amended sketch to do just that. Note that while D13 still has the same connections, the LED on D12 has to be moved to D3 because now, we are using the timer/counter's hardware to toggle the pins and not the interrupts. The pins that the hardware toggles for us are OC2A or D11 and OC2B or D3.

Listing 8-4. Getting the timer to flash LEDs, setup()

```
//===========================================================
// This sketch uses the Timer/Counter 2 as follows:
//
// Overflow Interrupt to toggle LED_BUILTIN (D13)
// OC2A to toggle D11
// OC2B to toggle D3.
//===========================================================
```

```
void setup() {
    // Initialise Timer/counter 2 in normal mode
    // with OC2A (D11) and OC2B (D3) toggling on match.
    TCCR2A = ((1 << COM2A0) | (1 << COM2B0));        ①

    // Enable overflow interrupt (on D13 = PB5)        ②
    TIMSK2 = (1 << TOIE2);

    // Set up the compare values.                      ③
    OCR2A = 8;
    OCR2B = 172;

    // Prescale by 1024, and start the timer.          ④
    TCCR2B = ((1 << CS22) |
              (1 << CS21) |
              (1 << CS20));

    // D11, D12 and D3 are outputs.                    ⑤
    pinMode(13, OUTPUT);
    pinMode(11, OUTPUT);
    pinMode(3, OUTPUT);
}
```

① Here we put the timer/counter into normal mode again, but configure it to also toggle pins OC2A and OC2B when there is a compare match. This does not require the use of interrupts – the toggling of the pins is controlled by the timer alone. The CPU is not involved.

② We still use the Overflow interrupt to toggle D13 as before. The CPU will be involved here.

③ I'm using the same values as before.

④   The timer/counter's clock source is configured as divided by 1024, and this starts the timer/counter running.

⑤   As before, we have to set the output pins after setting up the timer/counter.

As before, the loop() function is empty and has nothing to do.

Listing 8-5. Getting the timer to flash LEDs, loop()

```
void loop() {
    // Nothing to see here, move along now!
}
```

Finally, the code in Listing 8-6 now has a single ISR. This one is required for the Overflow interrupt. The two Compare Match interrupts are no longer required as the timer/counter will toggle the LEDs without the use of the main CPU.

Listing 8-6. Getting the timer to flash LEDs, ISR

```
// Toggle pin D13 which is PortB pin 5.
ISR(TIMER2_OVF_vect) {
    // Fast pin toggle.
    PINB |= (1 << PINB5);
}
```

It looks like those settings work too. The frequency and period of the flashing LEDs are exactly as before on all the pins – 30.5176 Hz on all three LEDs. We are still getting one flash every 256 counts on the timer.

8.1.6. Clear Timer on Compare Match Mode

In Clear Timer on Compare Match (CTC) mode, the timer/counter counts upward from BOTTOM (or from the value your code wrote to TCNTn) until it reaches TOP which is the value stored in OCRnA, whereupon, *on the next timer clock pulse*, the value in TCNTn will be cleared to zero. This is mode 2 for Timer/counter 0 and Timer/counter 2 and mode 4 for Timer/counter 1. Timer/counter 1 also has mode 12 CTC, which is discussed separately in the following.

You can change the values in OCRnA and/or OCRnB at any time, but you must be careful as double buffering is not enabled on those registers in this mode. Any changes you make are written directly to the register(s) at the time that your sketch does so. In other modes, these registers do not get changed until a certain point in the count – the values are held in a working register, buffer, until the specific point is reached. This prevents what the data sheet refers to as "glitches" in those other modes. There is no such protection in CTC mode.

If you change the value to a new value close(r) to BOTTOM (zero) while the counter is running with a low, or no prescaler, then CTC mode might miss a match if the current value in TCNTn is higher than the value just written to the OCRnx register. It will count right up to the timer/counter's maximum value and then roll over to zero before it can start the normal sequence of events again – a glitch, in other words. It is better to control the changes to the OCRnx registers by utilizing the Overflow interrupt to make the changes – that way, it happens always at BOTTOM and should avoid the glitches.

At TOP, the timer/counter's value, in TCNTn, will roll over from TOP to zero – BOTTOM – on the following tick of the timer/counter's clock.

Some things happen when the timer/counter clears:

- The Timer Overflow bit, TOVn, is set in the Timer Interrupt Flag Register, TIFRn, on *the same clock tick* as the timer/counter's value became zero – after TOP + 1 counts, assuming that you didn't change TCNTn.

This flag is only ever set, and, unless your program has enabled the timer/counter's Overflow interrupt, it will remain set until manually cleared by your sketch. You manually clear this bit by writing a 1_{binary} to it.

- The Timer Overflow interrupt will be fired, if the Timer Overflow interrupt enable bit, OCFnA, is set in the Timer Interrupt Mask Register TIMSKn *and* global interrupts are enabled. In this case, the TOVn bit *will* be cleared automatically when the interrupt service routine is entered.

- Pin OCnA will perform an action. The action depends on the values in the COMnA1-0 bits, as described in Table 8-9, when TCNTn matches with OCRnA.

Table 8-9. *COMnA1:0 settings in CTC mode*

COMnA1-COMnA0	Description
00	No effect on pin OCnA
01	Pin OCnA toggles on match with OCRnA plus one clock pulse
10	Pin OCnA is cleared (LOW) on match with OCRnA plus one clock pulse
11	Pin OCnA is set (HIGH) on match with OCRnA plus one clock pulse

- Pin OCnB will perform an action. The action depends on the values in the COMB1-0 bits, as described in Table 8-10, when TCNTn matches with OCRnB.

Table 8-10. *COMnB1:0 settings in CTC mode*

COMnB1- COMnB0	Description
00	No effect on pin OCnB
01	Pin OCnB toggles on match with OCRnB plus one clock pulse
10	Pin OCnB is cleared (LOW) on match with OCRnB plus one clock pulse
11	Pin OCnB is set (HIGH) on match with OCRnB plus one clock pulse

ⓘ The value in OCRnA is *always* the TOP value. If OCRnB is higher than the value in OCRnA, then there will be no effect on the OCnB pin, as the value in TCNTn will *never* reach the value in OCRnB. You will only see the desired effect on the OCnB pin if the value in OCRnB is less than, or equal to, the value in OCRnA.

The data sheet for the ATmega328P doesn't make this clear, and many online forums have lots of confusion on the matter.

Timer/counters 0 and 2 don't have any other CTC modes, so the preceding description applies to those counters. Timer/counter 1 has two CTC modes, modes 4 and 12. In mode 4 CTC, Timer/counter 1 acts exactly as described earlier.

When Timer/counter 1 is configured in CTC mode 12, the TOP value is defined by the value in the ICR1 or Input Capture Register, and this is attached to the Input Capture Unit for this timer/counter, as described in Section 8.3, "*Input Capture Unit*." The Input Capture Unit copies the Timer/counter 1 value from TCNT1 to the ICR1 register each time an "event" occurs. This value is then used as TOP in CTC mode 12 for Timer/counter 1.

In CTC mode 12, the following will occur when TCNT1 matches ICR1:

- Bit ICF1 is set in the Timer/counter 1 Interrupt Flag
  Register TIFR1. This bit will be cleared if the Input
  Capture interrupt is enabled by setting bit ICIE1 in
  register TIMSK1, when the interrupt routine is executed.
  If interrupts are not used, then your sketch must clear
  the ICF1 flag by writing a 1_{binary} to it.

- The Input Capture interrupt will be fired, automatically
  clearing the ICF1 flag, if configured to do so.

- The effect of the COM1A1:0 and COM1B1:0 bits are exactly
  as described earlier.

While running *any* timer/counter in *any* CTC mode, you can, if you
wish, write a value to the timer/counter's counter register, TCNTn, which
can reduce the time it takes for the Overflow bit to be set or the interrupt to
be fired. The interrupt itself can write a new value to TCNTn if necessary.

8.1.6.1. Setting CTC Mode

Table 8-11 shows the settings required to put the timer/counters into CTC
mode.

Table 8-11. *CTC mode settings*

Timer	Mode	Bits	Value
0	2	WGM02–WGM00	010_{binary}
1	4	WGM13–WGM10	0100_{binary}
1	12	WGM13–WGM10	1100_{binary}
2	2	WGM22–WGM20	010_{binary}

Bits WGMn0 and WGMn1 are found in register TCCRnA, bit WGMn2 is found in TCCRnB, and, for Timer/counter 1 only, WGM13 is also found in TCCR1B.

The maximum frequency at which the OCnA and/or OCnB pins will toggle is given by

```
F = F_CPU / (2 * prescaler * (1 + OCRnA))
```

This, if OCRnA is zero, makes the maximum frequency possible equal to

```
F_CPU / (2 * prescaler))
```

The value to be loaded into OCRnA is calculated as

```
OCRnA = (F_CPU / (F * 2 * prescaler)) - 1
```

for any desired frequency "F" and provided that the answer fits onto the appropriate timer/counter's OCRnA register.

8.1.6.2. Example Sketch

Listings 8-7 and 8-8 illustrate a sketch which sets up Timer/counter 2 in CTC mode 2, turns off all interrupts from the timer/counter, and sets pins OC2A and OC2B to toggle whenever the value in TCNT2 matches either that of OCR2A or OCR2B. TCNT2 will be cleared to zero on the timer clock pulse after it equals OCR2A.

OCR2A defines the TOP value for this sketch. In Listing 8-7, it is set to 200, giving 201 counts per cycle. OCR2B is initialized to the value 86, which is less than that of OCR2A, so it will be affected by the running timer/counter and will flash. The prescaler is again 1024, giving a frequency of

```
F_CPU / (2 * prescaler * (1 + OCR2A))
```

Therefore, the expected frequency of both LEDs will be

```
16e6 / (2 * 1024 * (1 + 200))
```

```
=> 16e6 / (2048 * 201)
```

```
=> 16e6 / 411648
=   38.868159204 Hz
```

Listing 8-7 is the setup() function for the sketch.

Listing 8-7. CTC example sketch, setup() function

```
//=========================================================
// This sketch uses the Timer/Counter 2 in CTC mode 2 as
// follows:
//
// OC2A to toggle D11 when TCNT2 matches OCR2A.
// OC2B to toggle D3 when TCNT2 matches OCR2B.
//
// Frequency = F_CPU / (2 * prescaler * (OCR2A + 1)
//=========================================================

void setup() {
    // Initialise Timer/counter 2 in CTC mode. (Mode 2) ①
    TCCR2A = ((1 << WGM21) |
              (1 << COM2A0) |
              (1 << COM2B0));

    // Disable interrupts on Timer 2.                    ②
    TIMSK2 = 0;

    // Set up the compare values.                        ③
    OCR2A = 200;
    OCR2B = 86;

    // Prescale by 1024, and start the timer.            ④
    TCCR2B = ((1 << CS22) |
              (1 << CS21) |
              (1 << CS20));
```

441

```
    // D11 and D3 are outputs.                            ⑤
    pinMode(11,  OUTPUT);
    pinMode(3, OUTPUT);
}
```

① Timer/counter 2 is configured here with CTC mode
   2, and both the OC2A (D11) and OC2B (D3) pins toggle
   when there is a compare match between TCNT2 and
   either OCR2A or ORC2B.

② All interrupts are disabled for Timer/counter 2.

③ The two required match values are set up here. As
   OCR2A is higher than OCR2B, both output pins will be
   affected when the counts match.

④ This is the point where the timer/counter's prescaler
   is set to divide the system clock by 1024, which starts
   the timer/counter running.

⑤ The output pins are configured *after* the timer/
   counter, as stated in the data sheet.

Listing 8-8 shows a very empty loop() function.

Listing 8-8. CTC example sketch, loop() function

```
void loop() {
    // Nothing happening here, move along now!
}
```

Using my trusty Labrador oscilloscope, I measured a frequency of
39 Hz on both LEDs, so I was close to the expected 38.868159204 Hz.

You will notice that loop() is empty, again. The timer/counter
hardware is doing all the hard work of toggling the LEDs for us. We could
add some code to the loop to do something useful and still have the

other two LEDS flashing away unaffected. Listings 8-9 and 8-10 show the changes that need to be made to Listings 8-6 and 8-7 to get the loop() function working hard!

Add the following line to the setup() function, just after the existing pinMode() calls.

Listing 8-9. CTC example, setup() function changes

```
pinMode(LED_BUILTIN, OUTPUT);
```

Change loop() to the following:

Listing 8-10. CTC example, loop() function changes

```
void loop() {
    // Toggle D13 and use a delay().
    digitalWrite(LED_BUILTIN, LOW);
    delay(1000);
    digitalWrite(LED_BUILTIN, HIGH);
    delay(1000);
}
```

Compile and upload the sketch. The LED on D13 will toggle at the usual rate of once every second, controlled by loop(), while the other two LEDs are completely unaffected by the calls to delay() and continue "flashing" at a frequency of almost 39 Hz. I use quotes around "flashing" as the rate is quite fast on a 16 MHz Arduino, so the LEDs appear on if you stare at them directly. If you see them in your peripheral vision, you will make out a flashing.

As the frequency is roughly 39 Hz, the period is 25.64 milliseconds, or 12.82 milliseconds on and 12.82 milliseconds off. Pretty quick, but you can see it – in your peripheral vision. The human eye is truly amazing – sometimes.

ℹ️ Yes, I know I'm mixing and matching Arduino code and AVR code, but that's what happens sometimes. I've seen many sketches where the vast majority was written in Arduino code – it's far easier on the eye after all – and only the nitty gritty parts of the code were written in plain AVR language. This is usually because the facilities of the ATmega328P being used were not available in the Arduino Language.

8.1.7. PWM Modes

The timer/counters can be configured to generate pulse width modulation (PWM) on certain pins. As with the modes already discussed, the timer/counters have a given frequency – which can be changed (see PWM frequencies in the following) – however, unlike the other modes, the amount of time that the pins stay HIGH can also be changed, even on the fly as the code is running.

The frequency of a waveform is the number of times a second that it moves through a single wave – from crest to crest or trough to trough. The period is the time it takes to do so. If the frequency is 400 Hz, then the period is one over that, or 2.5 milliseconds.

In non-PWM modes, the pin connected to the waveform generator is HIGH for 50% of the time and LOW for the other 50%. With PWM waveforms, the time that the pin is HIGH in each period is adjustable and not stuck at 50%.

8.1.7.1. Duty Cycle

The amount of time that a pin stays high, during each period, is normally specified as a percentage and is called the duty cycle. On the Arduino, the duty cycle for the analogWrite() function calls is simply

```
(value * 100) / 256
```

Calling analogWrite(pin, 128) is setting a duty cycle of 50% – the pin will be HIGH for 50% of the period and LOW for 50%.

The image in Figure 8-1 was created on a Labrador oscilloscope which was monitoring pin D9 when the Arduino was executing the statement analogWrite(9, 128).

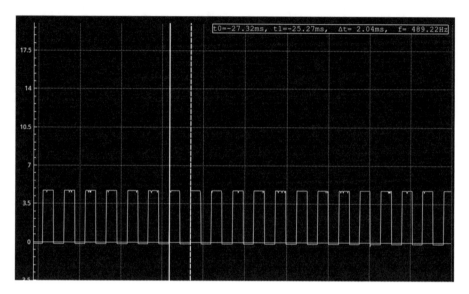

Figure 8-1. *Phase Correct PWM with 50% duty cycle*

In the top-right corner, you can see that the frequency (f) is listed as 489.22 Hz which is approximately 490 Hz as the Arduino documentation states. That will be the same on all PWM pins except D5 and D6. For those, as will be explained in the following, the image in Figure 8-2 applies.

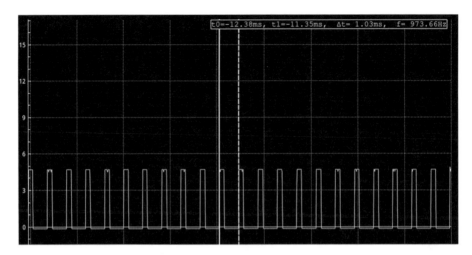

Figure 8-2. *Fast PWM with 25% duty cycle*

This time, the frequency shows as 973.66 Hz and is *roughly* the approximate 980 Hz as mentioned in the Arduino documentation. The documentation is a bit too approximate though as the actual frequency is only 976.5625 – so my measurement is a tad closer! This example trace was taken from pin D6; and the statement executing this time, to give a different graph, was analogWrite(6, 64) for a 25% duty cycle.

The general calculation to work out a duty cycle is

```
DC = (Time HIGH * 100) / (Time HIGH + Time LOW)
```

The duty cycle is useful as it causes what appears to be an analogue voltage on the output pin, rather than a digital HIGH or LOW. The voltage that appears to be present on the pin, and can be measured, is given by the formula

```
DC * HIGH Voltage
```

So if, for example, the duty cycle is 50% and VCC is 5 V, we appear to see a voltage of 2.5 V on the output pin. If the duty cycle is 25%, then we appear to see only 1.25 V on the output pin. This is why an LED can be made to fade in brightness or a motor with an appropriate driver can be made to speed up or down.

8.1.7.2. PWM Frequencies

The Arduino is set up with two fixed PWM frequencies, as explained earlier, caused by the three timer/counters being run in 8-bit mode with a divide-by-64 prescaler. Table 8-12 shows the relationship between the prescaler values and the two PWM frequencies which correspond to the prescaler value.

If necessary, you can get faster or slower PWM frequencies if your specific project requires them, by taking over the timer/counters and changing things around. If you must do this, then the following table will help you avoid having to do the arithmetic. It assumes a 16 MHz system clock and an 8-bit counter, like the Arduino.

Table 8-12. *Prescaler values and PWM frequencies*

Prescaler	Fast PWM Frequency	Fast PWM Period	Phase Correct PWM Frequency	Phase Correct PWM Period
1	62.5000 KHz	16	31.3725 KHz	31.87
8	7.8125 KHz	128	3.9216 KHz	254.99
32	1.953125 KHz	512	980.3922 Hz	1,020
64	**976.5625 Hz**	**1,024**	**490.1960 Hz**	**2,040**
128	488.28125 Hz	2,048	245.098 Hz	4,080
256	244.1406 Hz	4,096	122.5490 Hz	8,160
1024	61.0352 Hz	16,384	30.6372 Hz	32,640

> **i** All periods in Table 8-12 are measured in microseconds, or millionths of a second.

Only Timer/counter 2 can use the 32 and 128 prescaler values in the preceding table.

Be aware that changing Timer/counter 0 in this fashion will mess up things like `millis()` and `delay()` and such things that rely on a prescaler of 64 for accuracy.

> **i** The data sheet advises that when measuring PWM waveforms, the period is deemed to be measured between each TOP (highest) value of the counter.

The PWM frequency, in any PWM mode, is changed by changing the timer/counter's *prescaler.*

8.1.7.3. Fast PWM Mode

In Fast PWM mode, the value in register TCNTn will increment from zero – BOTTOM – until it reaches TOP. On the *next* clock pulse, TCNTn will be reset to zero, BOTTOM, and will then continue counting upward again. There are therefore TOP + 1 steps in each cycle. The TOP value is determined by the mode and can be

- For all timer/counters, the value 255 – this is the Arduino default.

- For all timer/counters, the value in register OCRnA.

- For Timer/counter 1 only, the value 511.

- For Timer/counter 1 only, the value 1023.

- For Timer/counter 1 only, the value in register ICR1.

 The data sheet advises that

When changing the TOP value the program must ensure that the new TOP value is higher or equal to the value of all of the Compare Registers. If the TOP value is lower than any of the Compare Registers, a compare match will never occur between the TCNTn and the OCRnx.

This PWM mode is called "single slope" as a graph of TCNTn's value would slope upward and then fall immediately back down to zero like a saw tooth. Figure 8-3 shows the slope of the count in TCNTn as it rises and resets to zero.

Each timer/counter has two pins upon which it can generate PWM waveforms. The Arduino initialization carried out in the init() function discussed in Chapter 2, for each and every sketch, sets all three timer/counters to run in 8-bit mode with a prescaler of 64 and a TOP value of 255. Timer/counter 0 is configured to run in Fast PWM mode, while the other two are configured in Phase Correct PWM mode.

Timer/counters 0 and 2 have two Fast PWM modes, modes 3 and 7. The differences are as follows:

- In mode 3, TOP is always 255 – this mode is used by the Arduino.

- In mode 7, TOP is always the value in OCRnA.

Timer/counter 0 runs Fast PWM on Arduino pins D5 and D6, which correspond to the AVR pins named PD5 and PD6.

Timer/counter 1 has five different Fast PWM modes available for use, modes 5, 6, and 7, plus modes 14 and 15. The differences are as follows:

- In mode 5, TOP is always 255 and the count in TCNT1 is always 8 bits – this mode is used by the Arduino.

- In mode 6, TOP is always 511 and the count in TCNT1 is always 9 bits.

- In mode 7, TOP is always 1023 and the count in TCNT1 is always 10 bits.

- In mode 14, TOP is always the value in register ICR1, the Input Capture Unit register.

- In mode 15, TOP is always the value in register OCR1A.

In these Fast PWM timer/counter modes

- There are TOP + 1 cycles.

- When TCNTn is zero, the appropriate PWM pin goes HIGH.

- When TCNTn equals OCRnA or OCRnB, the pin will go LOW.

The AVR microcontroller can be configured to invert the PWM output pins OCnA and OCnB, so that they go LOW instead of HIGH and HIGH instead of LOW.

ℹ️ It *should* be obvious, when running in a Fast PWM mode where TOP is defined by OCRnA, that the value in OCRnB must be less than OCRnA or the PWM will not work on that pin.

Also, in modes where OCRnA defines TOP, then you will be somewhat restricted in what you can do with pin OCnA.

The Arduino configures Timer/counter 0 to run in Fast PWM mode with a prescaler of 64. The other two times/counters are configured in Phase Correct PWM Mode.

For Fast PWM mode, the PWM frequency is calculated as

```
F_CPU / (prescaler * (TOP + 1))
```

This works out on the Arduino boards as $16e6/(64 * 256)$ or 976.5625 Hz, and this is the rate that Timer/counter 0 runs. Table 8-12 should save you the effort of working out the PWM frequencies and periods for any given prescaler.

Figure 8-3 shows the details of Fast PWM with TOP fixed at 255 which is mode 3 for Timer/counters 0 and 2 or mode 5 for Timer/counter 1.

Fast PWM

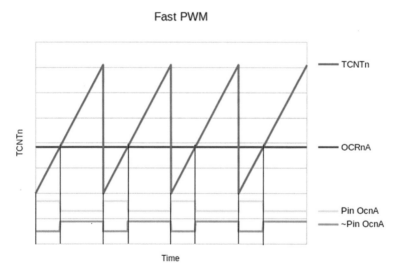

Figure 8-3. *8-bit Fast PWM with TOP at 255*

> **ℹ** In the preceding diagram, the value in OCRnA is constant as per the Arduino initialization code. It *can* be changed in code or in an interrupt handler, to vary the duty cycle of the PWM waveform, but this is not used on the Arduino.
>
> In the following description, everything that applies to OCRnA and OCnA also applies to OCRnB and OCnB, but the latter are not shown in the diagram to avoid clutter.

- The jagged line in Figure 8-3 is the value in TCNTn as it rises from zero (BOTTOM) to TOP which, in the case of an Arduino board, is set to 255 although this can be changed as per the data sheet. After 255, the value drops to zero on the next timer/counter clock pulse.

- The horizontal line is the constant value in OCRnA; in this example, it is 255 as per Arduino initialization code. The value in OCRnA can be changed, usually by the interrupt handler, if the duty cycle is required to be varied. Changes to the value in OCRnA are double buffered and applied at BOTTOM when TCNTn has just become zero.

- The two square wave lines at the bottom represent the non-inverting and the inverting waveforms generated on pin OCnA.

- If you look at the line for pin OCnA, the *non-inverting* output will be HIGH when TCNTn is zero and will then go LOW when TCNTn equals OCRnA. At the same time as the match is made, the timer/counter's Timer Compare Match interrupt flag is set.

- The bottom square wave of the two shown is the *inverting* output line, and this is simply the opposite to pin OCnA.

- The timer/counter's overflow flag will be set when TCNTn reaches BOTTOM.

The data sheet advises that *This high frequency makes the Fast PWM mode well suited for power regulation, rectification, and DAC applications. High frequency allows physically small sized external components (coils, capacitors), and therefore reduces total system cost.* It is not advised for motors as they much prefer Phase Correct PWM.

So what happens in Fast PWM? There are many things:

- When TCNTn equals TOP, the Timer n Overflow interrupt bit TOVn is set in register TIFRn, and if enabled, this interrupt can be used to update the value in the OCRnA and/or OCRnB registers to change the duty cycle of the PWM waveform. In this timer/counter mode, the OCRnA and OCRnB registers are double buffered; and the value written by your sketch, to these registers, will not be copied into the register until TCNTn resets to zero (BOTTOM). Only then do the register values change.

  This bit is not cleared unless your sketch clears it or if the interrupt handler is enabled by setting bit TOIEn in register TIMSKn in which case, assuming also that global interrupts are enabled, the bit will be automatically cleared. To clear the bit manually, in a sketch, you must write a 1_{binary} to it.

- When TCNTn reaches OCRnA, then bit OCFnA is set in register TIFRn. This bit is not cleared unless your sketch clears it or if the interrupt handler is enabled by setting bit OCIEnA in register TIMSKn in which case, assuming also that global interrupts are enabled, the bit will be automatically cleared. To clear the bit manually, in a sketch, you must write a 1_{binary} to it.

- Pin OCnA will perform an action. The action depends on the values in the COMnA1:0 bits, as described in Table 8-13, when TCNTn matches with OCRnA.

Table 8-13. *COMnA1:0 settings in Fast PWM mode*

COMnA1-COMnA0	Description
00	No effect on pin OCnA
01	<ul><li>Pin OCnA, for Timer/counters 0 and 2, in mode 3, is not affected</li><li>In mode 7, then pin OCnA will toggle when TCNTn matches OCRnA</li><li>For Timer/counter 1 in mode 14, pin OC1A will toggle when TCNT1 matches ICR1. Pin OC1B will be unaffected</li><li>In mode 15, pin OC1A will toggle when TCNT1 matches OCR1A. Pin OC1B will be unaffected</li><li>In mode 5, 6, or 7, OC1A is unaffected</li></ul>
10	Pin OCnA is LOW on match with OCRnA and HIGH at BOTTOM. This is non-inverting mode
11	Pin OCnA is HIGH on match with OCRnA and LOW at BOTTOM. This is inverting mode

- When TCNTn reaches OCRnB, then bit OCFnB is set in register TIFRn. This bit is not cleared unless your sketch clears it or the interrupt handler is enabled by setting bit OCIEnB in register TIMSKn in which case, assuming also that global interrupts are enabled, the bit will be automatically cleared. To clear the bit manually, in a sketch, you must write a 1_{binary} to it.

- Pin OCnB will perform an action. The action depends on the values in the COMnB1:0 bits, as described in Table 8-14, when TCNTn matches with OCRnB.

Table 8-14. *COMnB1:0 settings in Fast PWM mode*

COMnB1-COMnB0	Description
00	No effect on pin OCnB
01	• Reserved – do not use on Timer/counters 0 and 2 • For Timer/counter 1 in mode 14, pin OC1A will toggle when TCNT1 matches ICR1. Pin OC1B will be unaffected • In mode 15, pin OC1A will toggle when TCNT1 matches OCR1A. Pin OC1B will be unaffected • In mode 5, 6, or 7, OC1A is unaffected In other words, this setting only affects channel A on Timer/counter 1
10	Pin OCnB is LOW on match with OCRnB and HIGH at BOTTOM. This is non-inverting mode
11	Pin OCnB is HIGH on match with OCRnB and LOW at BOTTOM. This is inverting mode

8.1.7.3.1. Setting Fast PWM Mode

Table 8-15 shows the settings required to put the timer/counters into Fast PWM mode.

Table 8-15. *Fast PWM mode settings*

Timer	Mode	Bits	Value
0	3	WGM02–WGM00	011_{binary}
0	7	WGM02–WGM00	111_{binary}
1	5	WGM13–WGM10	0101_{binary}
1	6	WGM13–WGM10	0110_{binary}
1	7	WGM13–WGM10	0111_{binary}
1	14	WGM13–WGM10	1110_{binary}
1	15	WGM13–WGM10	1111_{binary}
2	3	WGM22–WGM20	011_{binary}
2	7	WGM22–WGM20	111_{binary}

Note that bits WGMn0 and WGMn1 are found in register TCCRnA, bit WGMn2 is found in TCCRnB, and, for Timer/counter 1 only, WGM13 is also found in TCCR1B.

You should be aware that because the PWM pins always go HIGH, at least in non-inverting mode, at BOTTOM, then they are always HIGH at the start of each cycle and LOW at the end, no matter what value is used for TOP. Sometimes this isn't suitable – motors apparently don't like this – and for that, you would use Phase Correct PWM instead.

8.1.7.3.2. Example Sketch

As mentioned earlier, Fast PWM is set up by the Arduino init() function for every sketch, on Timer/counter 0. The sketch in Listings 8-11, 8-12, and 8-13 is *effectively* what the init() function does to set up Timer/counter 0, but without the Overflow interrupt handler that updates millis() and micros(),and with a slower prescaler.

You might need to adjust the delay at the end of loop() if you can't see the fade up and down of the LEDs.

Listing 8-11 is a number of #defines, used to reduce the amount of bit shifting in the main code. It simply creates a definition for the two channels on Timer/counter 0, for both the HIGH and LOW states. These are used when the PWM value is 255 or 0.

Listing 8-11. Fast PWM sketch, defines

```
//==========================================================
// This sketch uses the Timer/Counter 0 in Fast PWM mode
// to fade down an LED on pin D5 while fading up an LED
// on D6. The prescaler is 1,024.
//==========================================================

#define PWM_A_LOW (~(1 << PORTD5))
#define PWM_A_HIGH ((1 << PORTD5))
#define PWM_B_LOW (~(1 << PORTD6))
#define PWM_B_HIGH ((1 << PORTD6))
```

The preceding definitions could have been declared as const uint8_t PWM_A_LOW = (~(1 << PORTD5)) and so on, which would have had the same effect. Listing 8-12 is the setup() function for the sketch.

Listing 8-12. Fast PWM sketch, setup() function

```
void setup() {
    // Set Timer 0 into Fast PWM mode 3
    // with TOP = 255 and OCOA and OCOB
    // toggling on match
    TCCR0A = ((1 << WGM01)  |                    ①
              (1 << WGM00)  |
              (1 << COM0A1) |
              (1 << COM0B1));

    // Timer 0 prescaler = 1,024.               ②
    TCCR0B = ((1 << CS02) | (1 << CS00));

    // Need to set the pins to output.    ③
    DDRD = ((1<< DDD5) | (1 << DDD6));
}
```

① This sets Timer/counter 0 into Fast PWM mode, with TOP = 255. This is the same as the Arduino init() function usually does. In addition, pins OCOA and OCOB will toggle on a compare match. These equate to pins PD5 and PD6, or Arduino pins D5 and D6.

② Unlike the Arduino's init() function, the prescaler here is set to divide by 1024.

③ This is simply pinMode(5, OUTPUT); and pinMode(6, OUTPUT); but both pins are set in one statement, not two.

The code in Listing 8-13 is that of the loop() function, which is where the hard work of fading the two LEDs up and down takes place. In the code, checks have to be made for the limits of the timer/counter – 0 and 255 – as the data sheet advises against setting those values for a PWM waveform. The analogWrite() function also checks for these values and, if found, calls digitalWrite() to set the pin LOW or HIGH as appropriate and ignores the PWM for those values.

Listing 8-13. Fast PWM sketch, loop() function

```
void loop() {
    // Current PWM duty cycle and increments.
    static uint8_t a = 0;                          ①
    static uint8_t b = 255;
    uint8_t increment = 1;

    if ((a != 0) && (a != 255)) {                  ②
        OCR0A = a;
        OCR0B = b;
    } else {                                       ③
        if (a == 255) {        // then b == 0
            PORTD |= PWM_A_HIGH;
            PORTD |= PWM_B_LOW;
        } else {               // then b == 255
            PORTD |= PWM_A_LOW;
            PORTD |= PWM_B_HIGH;
        }
    }

    a += increment;                                ④
    b -= increment;

    // Even at 1,024 prescaling, it's too quick!
    delay(1);                                      ⑤
}
```

① Declaring variables in a function as static means that they are initialized with the given value on the first call to the function. Then on the next call to the function, they have the value from the previous call – they retain their value across function call and exit, in other words.

② If a is not on a PWM limit (0 or 255), then b is not either, so simply set the OCR0x registers with the values of a and b – we have two valid PWM values which we can use.

③ If a *is* on a limit, then b *must* be on the other limit. In this case, we simply do what analogWrite() would do and effectively digitalWrite() a LOW or HIGH to the appropriate pins, depending on which limit a and b are on.

④ The fade values in a and b are incremented and decremented by the current amount.

⑤ As even the biggest prescaler runs the timer/counter way too quickly, there is a small delay to allow the fading effect to be seen. Feel free to adjust this if necessary.

The preceding code is effectively the same as analogWrite() which checks for values of 0 or 255, which the data sheet advises avoiding, and handles those separately. All other values get written to the OCR0A and OCR0B registers to control the duty cycle of the square wave generated on pins D5 and D6. An LED (and 330 Ohm resistor!) on these two pins should fade up on D5 and fade down on D6.

As variable a and b are unsigned 8-bit variables, they will roll over when increment is added or subtracted, which is why I only need to check explicitly for 0 or 255 in the code. Even if you change the increment value, it will still work.

If you run the preceding code on a normal Arduino, it might be flashing far too quickly to see properly, but one LED should be fading up while the other fades down. On a breadboard setup with the AVR microcontroller running at 8 MHz, the flashing is more obvious. You can change the delay() statement at the end of the loop() to slow things down a little, if necessary.

The LEDs will reset to their starting values when they reach the end of their fade – a will toggle from full on to full off, while b does the opposite. This means that D5 will start off, fade up to full brightness, and then drop to off again, while D6 does the opposite.

8.1.7.4. Phase Correct PWM Mode

Phase Correct PWM is called "dual slope" because the counter, TCNTn, counts from zero, BOTTOM, up to TOP and then counts back down again to BOTTOM. It takes twice as long to repeat the cycle and, thus, runs at half the frequency of the Fast PWM. The graph of the timer/counter's value against time slopes upward and then back down again and doesn't exhibit the sudden drop from TOP to BOTTOM that Fast PWM does. Figure 8-4 shows the slope of the count in TCNTn as it rises and falls back to zero.

The TOP value is determined by the mode and can be

- For all timer/counters, the value 255 – this is the Arduino default.

- For all timer/counters, the value in register OCRnA.

- For Timer/counter 1 only, the value 511.

- For Timer/counter 1 only, the value 1023.

- For Timer/counter 1 only, the value in register ICR1.

The data sheet advises that

When changing the TOP value the program must ensure that the new TOP value is higher or equal to the value of all of the Compare Registers. If the TOP value is lower than any of the Compare Registers, a compare match will never occur between the TCNT1 and the OCR1x.

It *should* be obvious, as with Fast PWM, that when running in a mode where TOP is defined by OCRnA or ICR1, the value in OCRnB must be less than OCRnA or the PWM will not work on that pin.

Also, in modes where OCRnA defines TOP, then you will be somewhat restricted in what you can do with pin OCnA.

On an Arduino, Timer/counter 1 runs Phase Correct PWM mode 1 on Arduino pins D9 and D10, which correspond to the AVR pins named PB1 and PB2. Timer/counter 2 runs Phase Correct PWM mode 1 on Arduino pins D3 and D11, which correspond to the AVR pins named PD3 and PB3.

Figure 8-4 shows the details for Phase Correct PWM with TOP fixed at 255 – mode 1 on all three timer/counters.

Phase Correct PWM

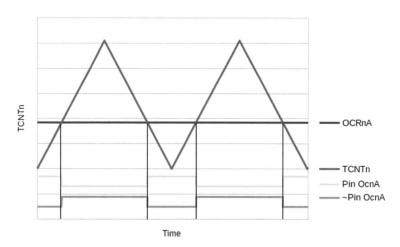

Figure 8-4. *8-bit Phase Correct PWM with TOP at 255*

ℹ In the preceding diagram, the value in OCRnA is a constant, as per the Arduino. It *can* be changed in code or in an interrupt handler and so vary the duty cycle of the PWM waveform.

In the following description, everything that applies to OCRnA and OCnA applies also to OCRnB and OCnB, but the latter are not shown in the diagram to avoid clutter.

- The triangular line is the value in TCNTn as it rises from zero (BOTTOM) to TOP which, in the case of an Arduino board, is set to 255 although this can be changed as per the data sheet. After TOP, the value counts back down to zero (BOTTOM) and then repeats as shown in the diagram. (Only two full cycles are shown here.)

- The horizontal line is the constant value in OCRnA, in this example. The value in OCRnA can be changed, usually by the interrupt handler, if the duty cycle is required to be varied. Changes to the value in OCRnA are double buffered and applied at TOP when TCNTn is at 255 on Arduino boards.

- The two square wave lines at the bottom represent the non-inverting and the inverting waveform generated on pin OCnA.

- If you look at the line for pin OCnA, the *non-inverting* output, you should see that when TCNTn reaches OCRnA while counting *upward*, the appropriate output pin will go LOW. It stays LOW until TCNTn hits OCRnA again while counting *downward* whereupon it goes HIGH. At the same time as the match is made, the timer/counter's Timer Compare Match interrupt flag is set.

- The bottom square wave of the two shown is the *inverting* output line, and this is simply the opposite to pin OCnA.

- The timer/counter's overflow flag will be set when TCNTn reaches BOTTOM.

The data sheet advises that *due to the symmetric feature of the dual-slope PWM modes, these modes are preferred for motor control applications.*

Each timer/counter has two pins upon which it can generate PWM waveforms. The Arduino initialization for each and every sketch sets the timers to all run in 8-bit mode with a prescaler of 64; however, only Timer/counters 1 and 2 are set to run in Phase Correct PWM mode.

Timer/counters 0 and 2 have two Phase Correct PWM modes, modes 1 and 5. The differences are as follows:

- In mode 1, TOP is always 255.

- In mode 5, TOP is always the value in OCRnA.

Timer/counter 1 has five different Phase Correct PWM modes available for use, modes 1, 2, and 3, plus modes 10 and 11. The differences are as follows:

- In mode 1, TOP is always 255 and the count in TCNT1 is always 8 bits.

- In mode 2, TOP is always 511 and the count in TCNT1 is always 9 bits.

- In mode 3, TOP is always 1023 and the count in TCNT1 is always 10 bits.

- In mode 10, TOP is always the value in register ICR1, the Input Capture Unit register.

- In mode 11, TOP is always the value in register OCR1A.

In these timer modes

- There are TOP $*$ 2 cycles.

- When TCNTn equals OCRnA or OCRnB while counting upward, the appropriate PWM pin goes LOW.

- When TCNTn equals OCRnA or OCRnB when counting downward, the appropriate PWM pin will go HIGH.

The AVR microcontroller can be configured to invert the output PWM pins, so that they go LOW and HIGH opposite to that specified in the preceding text.

For Phase Correct PWM mode, the PWM frequency is calculated as

```
F_CPU / (prescaler * (TOP * 2))
```

This works out on the Arduino boards as $16e6/(64 * 510)$ or 490.196078431 Hz, and this is the rate that Timer/Counters 1 and 2 run. The period of the PWM frequency is, for Phase Correct PWM configured as per the Arduino code, 2040 microseconds, or, 2.04 milliseconds.

Table 8-12 should save you the effort of working out the PWM frequencies and periods for any given prescaler.

The following lists the various changes that occur in Phase Correct PWM:

- TCNTn is only ever at TOP or BOTTOM for one clock. It will hold the value of all other counter values twice, once while counting up, once when counting down.

- When TCNTn equals BOTTOM, the Timer n Overflow interrupt bit TOVn is set in register TIFRn, and if enabled, this interrupt can be used to update the value in the OCRnA and/or OCRnB registers to change the duty cycle of the PWM waveform. In this timer mode, the OCRnA and OCRnB registers are again *double buffered*; and the value written by your sketch, to these registers, will not be copied into the register until TCNTn hits TOP. Only then do the register values change.

- This bit is not cleared unless your sketch clears it or if the interrupt handler is enabled by setting bit TOIEn in register TIMSKn in which case, assuming also that global interrupts are enabled, the bit will be automatically cleared. To clear the bit manually, in a sketch, you must write a 1_{binary} to it.

- When TCNTn reaches OCRnA, then bit OCFnA is set in register TIFRn. This bit is not cleared unless your sketch clears it or if the interrupt handler is enabled by setting bit OCIEnA in register TIMSKn in which case, assuming also that global interrupts are enabled, the bit will be automatically cleared. To clear the bit manually, in a sketch, you must write a 1_{binary} to it.

- Pin OCnA will perform an action. The action depends on the values in the COMnA1-0 bits, as described in Table 8-16, when TCNTn matches with OCRnA.

Table 8-16. *COMnA1:0 settings in Fast PWM mode*

COMnA1-COMnA0	Description
00	No effect on pin OCnA
01	• Pin OCnA, for Timer/counters 0 and 2, in mode 1, is not affected • In mode 5, pin OCnA will toggle when TCNTn matches OCRnA • For Timer/counter 1 in mode 11, pin OC1A will toggle when TCNT1 matches OCR1A, and pin OC1B will be unaffected • In modes 10, 1, 2, and 3, OC1A is unaffected
10	Pin OCnA is LOW on match with OCRnA when counting upward and HIGH on match with OCRnA when counting downward. This is non-inverting mode
11	Pin OCnA is HIGH on match with OCRnA when counting upward and LOW on match with OCRnA when counting downward. This is inverting mode

- When TCNTn reaches OCRnB, then bit OCFnB is set in register TIFRn. This bit is not cleared unless your sketch clears it or if the interrupt handler is enabled by setting bit OCIEnB in register TIMSKn in which case, assuming also that global interrupts are enabled, the bit will be automatically cleared. To clear the bit manually, in a sketch, you must write a 1_{binary} to it.

- Pin OCnB will perform an action. The action depends
  on the values in the COMnB1-0 bits, as described in
  Table 8-17, when TCNTn matches with OCRnB.

Table 8-17. *COMnB1:0 settings in Fast PWM mode*

COMnB1-COMnB0	Description
00	No effect on pin OCnB
01	• Reserved – do not use on Timer/counters 0 and 2 • For Timer/counter 1 in mode 9, pin OC1A will toggle when TCNT1 matches OCR1A, and pin OC1B will be unaffected. • In mode 1, 2, 3, or 8, OC1B is unaffected (in other words, exactly as Table 8-16)
10	Pin OCnB is LOW on match with OCR1B when counting upward and HIGH on match with OCR1B when counting downward. This is non-inverting mode
11	Pin OCnB is HIGH on match with OCR1B when counting upward and LOW on match with OCR1B when counting downward. This is inverting mode

- Only when TCNTn matches TOP are any changes made
  by the sketch to OCRnA or OCRnB applied.

8.1.7.4.1. Setting Phase Correct PWM Mode

Table 8-18 shows the settings required to put the timer/counters into
Phase Correct PWM mode.

Table 8-18. *Phase Correct PWM mode settings*

Timer	Mode	Bits	Value
0	1	WGM02–WGM00	001_{binary}
0	3	WGM02–WGM00	011_{binary}
1	1	WGM13–WGM10	0001_{binary}
1	2	WGM13–WGM10	0010_{binary}
1	3	WGM13–WGM10	0011_{binary}
1	10	WGM13–WGM10	1010_{binary}
1	11	WGM13–WGM10	1011_{binary}
2	1	WGM22–WGM20	001_{binary}
2	3	WGM22–WGM20	011_{binary}

Note that bits WGMn0 and WGMn1 are found in register TCCRnA, bit WGMn2 is found in TCCRnB, and, for Timer/counter 1 only, WGM13 is also found in TCCR1B.

8.1.7.4.2. Example Sketch

As mentioned in the preceding text, Phase Correct PWM is set up by the Arduino init() function for every sketch, on Timer/counters 1 and 2. The sketch in Listings 8-14, 8-15, and 8-16 is *effectively* what the init() function does to set up Timer/counters 1 and 2 for use with the analogWrite() function, but in the example, I'm hijacking Timer/counter 0 instead – just to be different!

> ⚠ Manipulating the PWM mode of Timer/counter 0 in this manner is harmless on the ATmega328P, but for some microcontrollers – the ATmega8 or ATmega168, for example – this will affect the accuracy of the `millis()` counter and all that which relies upon it.

You might need to adjust the delay at the end of `loop()` if you can't see the fade up and down of the LEDs.

Listing 8-14 is a number of #defines, used to reduce the amount of bit shifting in the main code. It simply creates a definition for the two channels on Timer/counter 0, for both the HIGH and LOW states. These are used when the PWM value is 255 or 0.

Listing 8-14. Phase Correct PWM sketch, defines

```
//==========================================================
// This sketch uses the Timer/Counter 0 in Phase Correct
// PWM mode to fade down an LED on pin D6 while fading up
// an LED on D5. The prescaler is 1,024.
//==========================================================

#define PWM_A_LOW (~(1 << PORTD5))
#define PWM_A_HIGH ((1 << PORTD5))
#define PWM_B_LOW (~(1 << PORTD6))
#define PWM_B_HIGH ((1 << PORTD6))
```

The preceding code could have been declared as const uint8_t PWM_A_LOW = (~(1 << PORTD5)) and so on, which would have had the same effect. Listing 8-15 is the setup() function for the demonstration sketch.

Listing 8-15. Phase Correct PWM sketch, setup() function

```
void setup() {
    // Set Timer 0 into Phase Correct PWM mode 1
    // with OC0A and OC0B toggling on match
    // and TOP = 255.
    TCCR0A = ((1 << WGM00)  |                  ①
              (1 << COM0A1) |
              (1 << COM0B1));

    // Timer 0 prescaler = 1,024.        ②
    TCCR0B = ((1 << CS02) | (1 << CS00));

    // Need to set the pins to output.
    // Using AVR speak here.
    DDRD = ((1<< DDD5) | (1 << DDD6));    ③
}
```

① This sets Timer/counter 0 into Phase Correct PWM mode, with TOP = 255. This is similar as the Arduino init() function usually does for the other two timer/counters. In addition, pins OC0A and OC0B are configured to toggle on a compare match. These equate to pins PD5 and PD6, or Arduino pins D5 and D6.

② Unlike the Arduino's init() function, the prescaler here is set to divide by 1024.

③ This is simply pinMode(5, OUTPUT); and pinMode(6, OUTPUT); but both pins are set in one statement, not two.

The code in Listing 8-16 is that of the loop() function, which is where the task of fading the two LEDs up and down lies. As we did with Fast PWM, checks have to be made for the limits of the timer/counter – 0 and

255 – as the data sheet advises against setting those values for a PWM waveform. If found, the code effectively calls digitalWrite() to set the pin LOW or HIGH as appropriate and ignores the PWM for those values.

Listing 8-16. Phase Correct PWM sketch, setup() function

```
void loop() {
    // Current PWM duty cycle and increments.
    static uint8_t a = 0;                         ①
    static uint8_t b = 255;
    uint8_t increment = 1;

    if ((a != 0) && (a != 255)) {                 ②
        OCR0A = a;
        OCR0B = b;
    } else {                                      ③
        if (a == 255) {        // then b == 0
            PORTD |= PWM_A_HIGH;
            PORTD |= PWM_B_LOW;
        } else {               // then b == 255
            PORTD |= PWM_A_LOW;
            PORTD |= PWM_B_HIGH;
        }
    }

    a += increment;                               ④
    b -= increment;

    // Even at 1,024 prescaling, it's too quick!
    delay(1);                                     ⑤
}
```

① Declaring variables in a function as static means that they are initialized with the given value on the first call to the function. Then on the next call to the function, they have the value from the previous call – they retain their value across function call and exit, in other words.

② If a is not on a PWM limit (0 or 255), then b is not either, so simply set the OCR0x registers with the values of a and b – we have two valid PWM values which we can use.

③ If a *is* on a limit, then b *must* be on the other limit. In this case, we effectively digitalWrite() a LOW or HIGH to the appropriate pins, depending on which limit a and b are on.

④ The fade values in a and b are incremented and decremented by the current amount.

⑤ As even the biggest prescaler runs the timer/counter way too quickly, there is a small delay to allow the fading effect to be seen. Feel free to adjust this if necessary.

The preceding code is effectively the same as analogWrite() which checks for values of 0 or 255, which the data sheet advises avoiding, and handles those separately. All other values get written to the OCR0A and OCR0B registers to control the duty cycle of the square wave generated on pins D5 and D6. An LED (and 330 Ohm resistor!) on these two pins should fade up on D5 and fade down on D6.

As variable a and b are unsigned 8-bit variables, they will roll over when increment is added or subtracted, which is why I only need to check explicitly for 0 or 255 in the code. Even if you change the increment value, it will still work.

If you run the preceding code on a normal Arduino, it might be flashing far too quickly to see properly, but one LED should be fading up while the other fades down. On a breadboard setup with the AVR microcontroller running at 8 MHz, the flashing is more obvious. You can change the delay() statement at the end of the loop() to slow things down a little, if necessary.

The LEDs will reset to their starting values when they reach the end of their fade – a will toggle from full on to full off, while b does the opposite. This means that D5 will start off, fade up to full brightness, and then drop to off again, while D6 does the opposite.

While the sketch is running, you should, hopefully, notice that the flickering of the LEDs is different with Phase Correct PWM from that of Fast PWM – this is noticeable when both sketches use the same delay() at the end of the loop.

8.1.7.5. Phase and Frequency Correct PWM Mode

Timer/counter 1 has an additional mode, well two modes, that the other timer/counters do not have. This is Phase and Frequency Correct PWM and is mostly identical to the previously mentioned Phase Correct PWM modes. The main difference is that the PWM generated is always symmetrical around the TOP value. This is because the OCR1A and/or ICR1 registers are updated with new values at BOTTOM, unlike Phase Correct PWM, which updates the OCRnA registers at TOP. Because of the update at BOTTOM, the count upward from BOTTOM to TOP is always the same as the count downward from TOP to BOTTOM.

The data sheet advises that

When changing the TOP value the program must ensure that the new TOP value is higher or equal to the value of all of the Compare Registers. If the TOP value is lower than any of the Compare Registers, a compare match will never occur between the TCNT1 and the OCR1x.

The data sheet also states that *there is little difference between Phase Correct and Phase and Frequency Correct PMW modes, when using a fixed* TOP *value.* However, it also states that *if you need to vary the* TOP *value, then Phase and Frequency Correct mode is best as it is _symmetrical about* TOP.

What exactly is symmetrical about this mode? As the data sheet says

The PWM period begins and ends at TOP. This means that the falling slope of the waveform, is determined by the old TOP value while the rising slope that follows, is determined by the new value in TOP. At the point where the two TOP values are different, the slopes will have a different length and thus, the period of the output waveform will be different.

i This is not a problem on the Arduino boards – none of the timer/counters are configured to run in this PWM mode.

On Timer/counter 1, the only one which has this PWM mode, the two Phase and Frequency Correct PWM modes are modes 8 and 9. The differences are as follows:

- In mode 8, TOP is always the value in register ICR1, the Input Capture Register.

- In mode 9, TOP is always the value in OCR1A.

So what happens in Phase and Frequency Correct PWM?

- TCNT1 is only ever at TOP or BOTTOM for one clock. It will hold the value of all other counter values twice, once while counting up, once when counting down. This is identical to Phase Correct PWM.

- When TCNT1 equals BOTTOM, any new value for OCR1A or OCR1B will be written into the appropriate register. Also, the Timer 1 Overflow interrupt bit TOV1 is set in register TIFR1, and if enabled, this interrupt can be used to update the value in the OCR1A and/or OCR1B registers to change the duty cycle of the PWM waveform. In this timer mode, the OCR1A and OCR1B registers are again double buffered; and the value written by your sketch, to these registers, will not be copied into the register until TCNT1 hits BOTTOM.

  This bit is not cleared unless your sketch clears it or if the interrupt handler is enabled by setting bit TOIE1 in register TIMSK1 in which case, assuming also that global interrupts are enabled, the bit will be automatically cleared. To clear the bit manually, in a sketch, you must write a 1_{binary} to it.

- When TCNT1 reaches TOP, then the OCF1A or ICF1 bit is set in register TIFR1. The bit set depends on which mode the timer/counter is executing. In mode 8, TIF1 will be set; in mode 9, it will be OCF1A.

  These two bits are not cleared unless your sketch clears them or the appropriate interrupt handler is enabled by setting bit ICIE1 in mode 8 or OCIE1A in mode 9, in register TIMSK1. In this case, assuming also that global interrupts are enabled, the bits will be automatically cleared. To clear the bits manually, in a sketch, you must write a 1_{binary} to them.

- Pin OCnA will perform an action. The action depends on the values in the COMnA1-0 bits, as described in Table 8-19, when TCNTn matches with OCRnA.

Table 8-19. *COMnA1:0 settings in Phase and Frequency Correct PWM mode*

COM1A1-COMnA0	Description
00	No effect on pin OC1A.
01	In mode 8 pin OC1A will be unaffected. In mode 9 pin OC1A will toggle when TCNT1 matches OCR1A. OC1B1 is unaffected
10	Pin OC1A is LOW on match with OCR1A when counting upward and HIGH on match with OCR1A when counting downward. This is non-inverting mode
11	Pin OC1A is HIGH on match with OCR1A when counting upward and LOW on match with OCR1A when counting downward. This is inverting mode

- When TCNT1 reaches OCR1B, then bit OCF1B is set in register TIFR1. This bit is not cleared unless your sketch clears it or if the interrupt handler is enabled by setting bit OCIE1B in register TIMSK1 in which case, assuming also that global interrupts are enabled, the bit will be automatically cleared. To clear the bit manually, in a sketch, you must write a 1_{binary} to it.

- Pin OCnB will perform an action. The action depends on the values in the COMnB1-0 bits, as described in Table 8-20, when TCNTn matches with OCRnB.

Table 8-20. *COMnB1:0 settings in Phase and Frequency Correct PWM mode*

COM1B1-COMnB0	Description
00	No effect on pin OC1B
01	This setting is exactly the same as setting bits COM1A1-0 as described earlier. Only pin OC1A is affected. In mode 8 pin OC1A will be unaffected. In mode 9 pin OC1A will toggle when TCNT1 matches OCR1A. OC1B1 is unaffected in either mode
10	Pin OC1B is LOW on match with OCR1B when counting upward and HIGH on match with OCR1B when counting downward. This is non-inverting mode
11	Pin OC1B is HIGH on match with OCR1B when counting upward and LOW on match with OCR1B when counting downward. This is inverting mode

- When TCNT1 matches BOTTOM, any changes made by the sketch to OCR1A or OCR1B are applied.

8.1.7.5.1. Setting Phase and Frequency Correct PWM Mode

Table 8-21 shows the settings required to put the timer/counters into Phase and Frequency Correct PWM mode.

Table 8-21. *Phase and Frequency Correct PWM mode settings*

Timer	Mode	Bits	Value
1	8	WGM13-WGM10	1000_{binary}
1	9	WGM13-WGM10	1001_{binary}

Note that bits WGM10 and WGM11 are found in register TCCR1A, while bits WGM12 and WGM13 are found in TCCR1B.

8.1.8. Too Much to Remember? Try AVRAssist

So many timer/counters, so many modes, so many bits to be set or cleared, etc. Does it have to be this hard?

If you point your favorite browser at https://github.com/ NormanDunbar/AVRAssist which is the AVRAssist GitHub page, you will come across my very easy to use AVR header files. These headers can be #included in your own source files, which will make life a lot easier when setting up timer/counters and the like.

In use, you end up with something like Listing 8-17.

Listing 8-17. Setting up Timer 0 with AVRAssist

```
#include <timer0.h>

using namespace AVRAssist;

ISR(TIMER0_OVF_vect) {
    ...
}

...

Timer0::initialise(MODE_FAST_PWM_255,
                Timer0::CLK_PRESCALE_64,
                Timer0::OCOA_TOGGLE | OCOB_TOGGLE,
                INT_OVERFLOW
                );

...
```

The preceding code will set Timer/counter 0 to have PWM on both pins D5 and D6 as per the Arduino `init()` function, with a prescaler of 64 and with an interrupt handler for the Timer 0 Overflow interrupt enabled, which, I think, is a little better to read and understand than a number of separate instructions listing various bit and register names, one after the other.

The preceding code *should* set up Timer/counter 0 in the mode specified and with all the settings that the Arduino sets up in the background for Timer/counter 0 when you compile a sketch. However, the preceding code *will not compile and link* when used in a sketch compiled with the Arduino IDE. This is because the IDE silently includes an interrupt handler for the Timer/counter 0 Overflow interrupt, and that means that any code in a sketch, compiled by the IDE, cannot specify an interrupt handler for that same interrupt.

If you do try this, you will get a linker error telling you that there are two separate interrupt handlers for the Overflow interrupt. Ask me how I know!

If you still wish to do something like this, you will need to compile your code outside of the Arduino IDE, and this means without using any of the Arduino Language. You will need to code in AVR C++ instead. The preceding code works perfectly in the PlatformIO environment – if, and only if, you remember to enable global interrupts – for example, and an interrupt handler for the Overflow interrupt can be defined. But then, if you do it that way, you lose the `millis()` function and all that depend on it from the Arduino environment. Decisions, decisions!

There are a few more details about AVRAssist in Appendix K.

8.2. Counting

Previously in this chapter, you learned, in some detail, all about the three timer/counters in the ATmega328P. However, all you learned about were the *timer* modes. They can also be used as *counters*; and instead of being triggered by a regular clock signal, generated from the main system clock via a prescaler, the value in TCNTn can be incremented according to an external rising or falling edge on a pair of specific pins.

ℹ️ Only Timer/counters 0 and 1 have this ability. Timer/counter 2 has other features, not available on Timer/counters 0 and 1.

8.2.1. Setting External Counting

Table 8-22 shows the configuration required to set the timer/counters into counter mode.

Table 8-22. *Setting timer/counters into counting mode*

CSn1-CSn0	Value	Description
110	6	External clock on Tn pin, counts on a falling edge
111	5	External clock on Tn pin, counts on a rising edge.

Pin T0 is physical pin 6 on the ATmega328P, Arduino pin D4, or AVR pin PD4. Pin T1 is physical pin 11 on the ATmega328P, Arduino pin D5, or AVR pin PD5. These are the only two pins that can be used in this way. If your sketch is using the pins as counter stimulus, then they obviously cannot be used as normal I/O pins.

All the Waveform Generation modes are still available when clocking from the external pins, and usually, it would be expected that some form of clock signal, perhaps generated by the ubiquitous 555 timer, would be utilized to run the counter – if a regular count was required. On the other hand, it could be used to count the number of times a door was opened in a given time – it's down to the maker to decide.

All the interrupts, matching on OCRnA or OCRnB, overflow bit setting, etc., work as expected when running in counter mode.

8.2.2. Counter Example

The circuit in Figure 8-5 and the corresponding sketch in Listings 8-18 and 8-19 show a simple model of a door counter system – the serial monitor will record "door openings" each time the switch is pressed. In real use, the switch would be debounced and mounted in such a position as to record the door opening.

---

i As I have not debounced the switch, it will also show how bouncy the particular switch I'm using happens to be.

Figure 8-5 shows the breadboard layout for this example. The circuit is very simple: the "high" side of SW1 is connected to 5 V from the Arduino. The "low" side of the switch, SW1, is connected to R1 which is a 10 K pulldown resister to GND and also to the Arduino pin D5 which is Timer/counter 1's T1 pin. The LED and R2, which is 330 Ohms, are connected between D13 and GND in the normal manner.

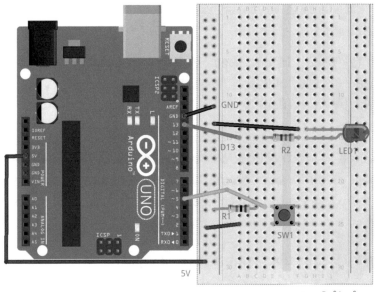

Figure 8-5. *Door counter circuit*

Listing 8-18. The door counter sketch setup()

```
void setup() {
    // Serial monitor is required.
    Serial.begin(9600);

    // Initialise Timer/counter 1 to be triggered externally
    // by a rising edge on pin D5. The timer runs in normal
    // mode as we don't need waveforms.
    TCCR1A = 0;     // Sets WGM11 and WGM10 to zero.

    // Disable interrupts on Timer 1.
    TIMSK1 = 0;

    // Clocked on a rising edge, and start the timer.
    TCCR1B = ((1 << CS12) | (1 << CS11) | (1 << CS10));
```

```
    // Make sure everything is reset.
    TCNT1 = 0;

    // T1=PD5=D5 is an input. PB5=D13 an Output.
    DDRB |= (1 << DDB5);
    DDRD |= (1 << DDD5);
}
```

Listing 8-18 sets up Timer/counter 1 to be clocked externally on a *rising* edge on pin T1 and with the timer/counter's interrupts disabled. Listing 8-19 displays the count of the number of times the door was opened.

Listing 8-19. The door counter sketch loop()

```
void loop() {
    // Save the previous value of TCNT1.
    static uint16_t lastTCNT1 = 0;
    uint16_t thisTCNT1 = TCNT1;

    if (thisTCNT1 != lastTCNT1) {
        Serial.print("TCNT1 = ");
        Serial.println(thisTCNT1);
        lastTCNT1 = thisTCNT1;
    }

    // Flash the LED and delay ...
    // ... to show that the timer still works.
    PINB |= (1 << PINB5);
    delay(2000);
}
```

Each time through the loop, the current value of TCNT1 is sent to the serial monitor if it changed since the previous count. Regardless of any changes, loop() always toggles the LED on Arduino pin D13 and then delays for 2 seconds. The delay is simply there to show that the timer/ counter will still record switch presses during a delay which is tying up the main CPU.

When the LED is on, or off, press the switch a few times quickly. When the delay is complete, the next value displayed in the serial monitor will show multiple hits have taken place and been recorded.

The following list shows the first ten results I obtained with a random switch from my spares box. These were all single presses, and the results appear quite good, not many bounces. I was of course suspicious! Surely cheap switches shouldn't be this good?

```
TCNT1 = 1
TCNT1 = 2
TCNT1 = 3
TCNT1 = 6
TCNT1 = 7
TCNT1 = 8
TCNT1 = 9
TCNT1 = 11
TCNT1 = 12
TCNT1 = 14
```

I tried a few more times with single presses, and it seems that I had picked the best switch in the world. I *mostly* only ever got a single increment. Is something wrong with the sketch? Or do I just have a really good switch?

I decided to check and remove the wire from 5 V to the high side of the switch. I then touched it to the switch side of R1, the pulldown resistor. That's better. It bounced – a lot!

> ⚠️ **Don't** touch the 5 V wire to the GND side of the resistor. You will short out the power supply and might destroy your Arduino.

```
TCNT1 = 31
TCNT1 = 32
TCNT1 = 33
TCNT1 = 35
TCNT1 = 36
TCNT1 = 104
TCNT1 = 148
TCNT1 = 243
TCNT1 = 401
TCNT1 = 417
```

The preceding first five presses used the button, and I rarely saw a bounce. The remaining five used the wire to bypass the switch. Those touches bounced massively!

> 💡 You can purchase *guaranteed non-bounce switches*, it appears. Getting hold of one and testing it against the sketch in Listings 8-18 and 8-19 might prove interesting.

In summary, as you can plainly see, setting a timer/counter to run as a counter is far, far simpler than setting one to run as timer.

8.3. Input Capture Unit

Timer/counter 1, as you know, is the only 16-bit timer on the ATmega328P. It is also the only timer/counter which has an *input capture unit*. The data sheet advertises this feature as

> *… an Input Capture unit that can capture external events and give them a time-stamp indicating time of occurrence. The external signal indicating an event, or multiple events, can be applied via the ICP1 pin or alternatively, via the analog-comparator unit. The time-stamps can then be used to calculate frequency, duty-cycle, and other features of the signal applied. Alternatively the time-stamps can be used for creating a log of the events.*

As you will see, this is not quite as useful as it sounds, but let's carry on with the data sheet, which goes on to state that:

> *When a change of the logic level (an event) occurs on the Input Capture pin (ICP1), alternatively on the Analog Comparator output (ACO), and this change confirms to the setting of the edge detector, a capture will be triggered.*

> *When a capture is triggered, the 16-bit value of the counter (TCNT1) is written to the Input Capture Register (ICR1). The Input Capture Flag (ICF1) is set at the same system clock as the TCNT1 value is copied into [the] ICR1 Register.*

> *If enabled (ICIE1 = 1), the Input Capture Flag generates an Input Capture interrupt. The ICF1 Flag is automatically cleared when the interrupt is executed. Alternatively the ICF1 Flag can be cleared by software by writing a logical one to its I/O bit location.*

Sounds useful? Maybe! Think about Timer/counter 1. It has a number of prescaler values we can use to slow down its counting frequency, the biggest of these being 1024. The Arduino's main clock runs at 16 MHz which at full speed will cause Timer/counter 1 to overflow after only 0.004096 second.

So we need to slow it down. The biggest prescaler value for Timer/counter 1 is 1024. Now it overflows every 4.194304 seconds, which is still pretty much unusable as a timestamp, as intimated in the data sheet.

We could use a uint16_t variable in our code to store the timestamp values and increment another uint16_t variable as an overflow counter every time Timer/counter 1 overflows – there's a handy interrupt that would take care of that – and use the overflow counter as the high 16 bits and the value from ICR1 in the low 16 bits. That would work, no?

Maybe. The 16-bit count of overflows would increment every 4.194304 seconds and can store up to 65,536 of those before it too overflows. That's a total of 274,877.9069 seconds which works out at 4,581.298449 minutes or 76 hours, 21 minutes, and 17.9069 seconds.

So, as long as *all* the events you wish to record, and timestamp, arrive within that time span, then having a spare 16-bit counter around to hold the overflow counts *should* work.

If 76 hours is still too short a time span for all the expected events, would using an unsigned 32-bit variable to hold the overflow count and a separate 16-bit variable to hold the TCNT1 value be any better? How long do we have to record all our events now?

We still overflow every 4.194304 seconds, but we can now accommodate 2^{32} of them. Doing the calculations, I think that works out as follows:

```
4.194304 Seconds * 2^32
=> 1.8014398e10 seconds
=> 300,239,975.2 minutes
=>     5,003,999.586 hours
=>       208,499.9827 days

=         570 years 307 days.
```

That should be long enough surely?

I have yet to see any AVR or Arduino code that uses the input capture unit. For further details of using the unit, please refer to the data sheet; however, I can't leave you in suspense, so Listings 8-20 and 8-21 show a small sketch that demonstrates using the input capture unit.

Listing 8-20. Input capture unit, setup()

```
//==========================================================
// This sketch uses the Timer/Counter 1 input capture
// unit to "timestamp" the arrival of a rising edge on
// Arduino pin D8, AVR pin ICP1/PB0, physical pin 14 on
// the ATmega328P.
//==========================================================

void setup() {
    // Initialise the LED pin (D13) as OUTPUT and
    // pin D8/PB8/ICP1 as INPUT_PULLUP.
    DDRB = (1 << DDB5);          // D13/PB5 as output.        ①
    PORTB = (1 << PORTB0);       // PB0/ICP1 as input pullup. ②

    // Initialise the ICU to no scaler, no noise cancel,
    // and rising edge detection.
    TCCR1A = 0;                      // Normal mode.          ③
    TCCR1B = ((1 << ICES1) | (1 << CS10));                    ④

    Serial.begin(9600);
}
```

① This sets all of PORTB as input, with pin PB5, aka D13, aka LED_BUILTIN as output. I'm using the built-in LED as a "flag" to show that *something* is happening while we wait for an event to happen.

② Writing to the PORT pin for an input pin enables the internal pullup resistor. This pin will be held HIGH unless pulled to ground externally.

③ Timer/counter 1 is in normal mode.

④ ICES1 enables input capture on a rising edge. CS10 enables full-speed Timer/counter clock based on the system clock.

Listing 8-21. Input capture unit, loop()

```
void loop() {
    // This is a polled wait, so it's inefficient! However
    // this loop() is not doing much else.
    //
    // Wait for ICF1 to be set in TIFR1 then send
    // ICR1 to the serial port. Toggle the built
    // in LED while we wait. (Very quickly!)
    while (!(TIFR1 & (1 << ICF1)))                        ①
        PINB |= (1 << PINB5);

        // Clear the ICF1 bit (no interrupts running you see)
        TIFR1 &= (1 << ICF1);                            ②

        // Grab the timestamp.
        Serial.println(ICR1);                            ③
}
```

① Wait here, just toggling the LED, until ICF1 goes HIGH to signal an event. That event copies the TCNT1 value into the ICR1 register while the timer carries on counting. This is a tight loop, and so the LED will appear on all the time, with the odd occasional flicker.

② Because we are not running Input Capture interrupts, we must write a 1_{binary} to the ICF1 bit to clear it for the next event.

③ Grab the event timestamp from ICR1 and write it to the serial port.

Compile and upload the sketch as shown in the preceding text and plug a jumper wire into pin D8 on your Arduino board and plug the other end into the GND location on the header.

Now open the serial monitor, which will reset the board and start the sketch running. Nothing should appear on the monitor window.

Pull the jumper wire out of the GND, the pullup resistor will start to pull the pin HIGH, and the ICU will register that as an event. The LED might flicker, briefly, and a couple of numbers will appear on the monitor output. I got these:

```
3802
4474
```

If you see only one number, well done! You managed to not cause any bounce when you removed the jumper wire.

Plug the jumper back into GND again. This will pull the pin LOW, and there *should* be no more numbers. However, given the slowness of a human being, in contrast with an AVR microcontroller running at 16 MHz, the chances are slim. You will see a few more numbers hitting the serial monitor output. Mine read

```
60412
60488
17441
19431
```

Note how the numbers count up and then appear lower, but counting up again? That's a demonstration of my point about the period available for grabbing all your events and timestamping them.

Oh, by the way, the built-in LED will appear to be always on, but it's flashing (toggling) every time `loop()` gets called from `main()`.

ℹ️ Your numbers might be bigger than mine or roll over faster. My test bed for this experiment was a breadboard *NormDuino* – see Appendix H – running on an internal 8 MHz oscillator, to free up the two pins normally used for the 16 MHz crystal.

CHAPTER 9

ATmega328P Hardware: ADC and USART

This chapter continues our look at the various hardware components of the ATmega328P. Some of them are not visible ("surfaced") in the Arduino IDE or Language, so they may at first appear new to you – the Analogue Comparator, for example.

The information in this chapter and Chapter 8 should link up with what you have already seen in Chapters 2 and 3 which covered the compilation process and the Arduino Language.

9.1. The Analogue Comparator

The ATmega328P has a built-in device, called the Analogue Comparator, which compares the input voltage on pin AIN0, the positive input, and pin AIN1, the negative input.

If the voltage on the positive input, AIN0, is higher than the voltage on the negative input, AIN1, the Analogue Comparator output bit, ACO (that's a letter OH and not a digit zero), in the Analogue Comparator Control and Status Register (ACSR), will be set to 1_{binary}.

© Norman Dunbar 2020
N. Dunbar, *Arduino Software Internals*, https://doi.org/10.1007/978-1-4842-5790-6_9

If the voltage on the positive input, AIN0, is lower than the voltage on the negative input, AIN1, then ACO is cleared to 0_{binary}.

In addition to setting the ACO bit, the comparator can also be set to trigger

- The Timer/counter 1 Input Capture function.

- A dedicated interrupt, exclusive to the Analogue Comparator. The interrupt can be configured to trigger when

  - The comparator output, ACO, is rising – from 0_{binary} to 1_{binary}.

  - The comparator output, ACO, is falling – from 1_{binary} to 0_{binary}.

  - The comparator output, ACO, is toggling – from 0_{binary} to 1_{binary} or from 1_{binary} to 0_{binary}.

Chapter 8, Section 8.3, "*Input Capture Unit*," deals with Timer/counter 1's Input Capture Unit.

Digital pins D6 and D7 are the Arduino's comparator input pins, with D6 being AIN0, the positive input, and D7 being AIN1, the negative input. D6 is therefore the reference voltage to which the voltage on D7 can be compared. However, AIN1 can optionally be configured to be any one of the ADC input pins, A0–A7 (if you have A6 and A7 of course!), as explained in the following.

ⓘ The Arduino Language does not facilitate easy access to the Analogue Comparator.

You have to do it the hard way yourself, by manipulating the individual register bits – there's no easy option here I'm afraid!

9.1.1. Reference Voltage

The reference voltage, on the positive input, AIN0, is used as the basis for the comparator. The voltage that is being sampled or compared will be checked against the voltage on the comparator's positive input. The positive input can be configured to be either

- An internally generated 1.1 V known as the bandgap reference voltage

- An external voltage supplied on the AIN0 pin also known as D6

9.1.2. Sampled Voltage

The voltage being compared against the reference voltage can be either

- The AIN1 pin, also known as D7

- Any one of the ADC input pins, which on the Arduino are A0–A5 plus A6 and A7 if your board has the surface mount version of the ATmega328P *and* the manufacturer has routed those two extra pins to a header somewhere

9.1.3. Digital Input

The pins D6 and D7 cannot be used as normal I/O pins when being used by the comparator. To this end, they should have their I/O buffers disabled – to save wasting power. This is done by setting bits AIN0D and/or AIN1D in register DIDR1, the Digital Input Disable Register 1.

Bit 0 in the DIDR1 register is AIN0D, bit 1 is AIN1D, and bits 2–7 are reserved and should not be written. They will always be zero when read.

When either AIN0D or AIN1D bit is set to 1_{binary}, the digital I/O on the AIN0 (D6) or AIN1 (D7) pin is disabled. When the pins are disabled in this manner, reading the PIND register (the input register that these two pins belong to) will always return a value of 0_{binary} for whichever of the two pins has been disabled.

The ATmega328P data sheet has this to say:

> *When an analog signal is applied to the AIN1/0 pin*
> *and the digital input from this pin is not needed,*
> *this bit should be written logic one to reduce power*
> *consumption in the digital input buffer.*

The following sections summarize the steps necessary to use the comparator.

9.1.4. Enable the Analogue Comparator

- Write a 0_{binary} to bit ACIE in the Analogue Comparator Control and Status Register – ACSR. This disables the Analogue Comparator Interrupt Enable as an interrupt can occur when the ACD bit is changed.

- Write a 0_{binary} to bit ACD in ACSR.

The preceding steps enabled the comparator and disabled interrupts from it, for now. This can be easily changed later if interrupts from the comparator are required.

9.1.5. Select Reference Voltage Source

The reference voltage applied to the positive input to the comparator can be either

- The internal bandgap reference voltage

- An external voltage on pin AIN0

Only one of these can be selected.

9.1.5.1. External Reference

To use the external reference voltage on pin AIN0, you must

- Write a 1_{binary} to bit AIN0D to disable the I/O facilities on pin D6.

- Write a 0_{binary} to bit ACBG in the ACSR register.

9.1.5.2. Internal Bandgap Reference

To use the internal reference voltage instead of AIN0, you must

- Write a 1_{binary} to bit ACBG in register ACSR.

9.1.6. Select Sampled Voltage Source Pin

The voltage to be compared with on the comparator's positive input can be either

- Pin AIN1

- One of the pins A0–A7

9.1.6.1. Sample Voltage on Pin AIN1

To compare an external reference voltage on pin AIN1 (D7), you must

- Write a 1_{binary} to bit AIN1D, in register DIDR1, to disable the I/O facilities on pin D7.

Then, either

- Write a 0_{binary} to bit ACME in register ADCSRB.

- Write a 1_{binary} to bit ACME in register ADCSRB and write a 1_{binary} to bit ADEN in register ADCSRA.

You therefore have two choices to set up the system to use AIN1.

9.1.6.2. Sample Voltage on Pins A0–A7

- Write a 0_{binary} to bit PRADC in register PRR to power the ADC.

- Write a 0_{binary} to bit ADEN in register ADCSRA to disable the ADC from using the ADC multiplexor.

- Write a 1_{binary} to bit ACME in register ADCSRB to allow the comparator to use the ADC multiplexor.

- Write the pin number, 0–7, to bits MUX2:0 in the ADMUX register to select the desired input pin from A0 through A7.

9.1.7. Sampled Voltage Summary

Table 9-1 summarizes the pin settings for all possible negative input settings.

Table 9-1. *Analogue Comparator negative input summary*

ACME	ADEN	MUX2-MUX0	Negative Input
0	?	???	AIN1
1	1	???	AIN1
1	0	000	ADC0
1	0	001	ADC1
1	0	010	ADC2
1	0	011	ADC3
1	0	100	ADC4
1	0	101	ADC5
1	0	110	ADC6
1	0	111	ADC7

9.1.8. Comparator Outputs

So far, we have looked at the numerous ways that we can set up the two inputs to the comparator. How then to we get an output from it? The Analogue Comparator Control and Status Register (ACSR) is where we need to be looking. We have already seen that bits ACD and ACBG disable/enable the comparator and select the reference voltage. The other bits areas follows:

- ACO, Analogue Comparator Output – This bit is connected to the comparator output and is synchronized with the comparator output when it changes. This synchronization takes one to two clock cycles to settle and delays changing this bit when the comparator changes.

- ACI, Analogue Comparator Interrupt Flag – This bit is set when a comparator output triggers according to the mode set in bits ACIS1:0 (see in the following). If global interrupts are enabled *and* the ACIE bit set, then the appropriate ISR will be executed and this bit cleared by hardware. Otherwise, it can be cleared by the writing of a 1_{binary} in the normal back-to-front AVR manner!

- ACIE, Analogue Comparator Interrupt Enable – This bit enables or disables the firing of an interrupt when the comparator output takes on a certain state as defined by bits ACIS1-0 which are described in the following. When the bit is 0_{binary}, no interrupts will fire.

- ACIC, Analogue Comparator Input Capture Enable – Writing this bit to 1_{binary} will enable Timer/counter 1's Input Capture function to be triggered by the Analogue Comparator. In addition to setting this bit, bit ICIE1 in register TIMSK1 must also be set to enable the Timer/counter 1 Input Capture interrupt.

- ACIS1-0, Analogue Comparator Interrupt Mode
  Select – These two bits must always be changed *after*
  disabling the comparator's ACIE bit by writing it to
  0_{binary}. These two bits select the interrupt mode for the
  comparator and determine when the interrupt will be
  fired. The possible values are

  - 00_{binary} – The interrupt fires when the comparator
    output toggles.

  - 01_{binary} – Reserved – do not use.

  - 10_{binary} – Interrupt fired on falling output edge
    (when the ACO changes from 1_{binary} to 0_{binary}).

  - 11_{binary} – Interrupt fired on rising output edge (when
    the ACO changes from 0_{binary} to 1_{binary}).

9.1.9. Comparator Example

The sketch in Listing 9-1 shows the use of the Analogue Comparator to
turn an LED on or off depending on whether the voltage at D6 is higher or
lower than the voltage at D7.

In the circuit I used for this experiment, I created a voltage divider
using two resistors. I used the same value, but it isn't necessary. The output
from this was fed into D6 and used as the reference voltage. I connected
one end to the Arduino VCC (5 V) and the other to Arduino ground.

I also wired up a potentiometer to Arduino VCC and ground and
fed the middle pin of the potentiometer to pin D7. By turning the
potentiometer, I was able to vary the voltage on pin D7, and the LED
turned off or on depending on whether the voltage was higher on D7 or
lower.

You can see the breadboarded circuit in Figure 9-1.

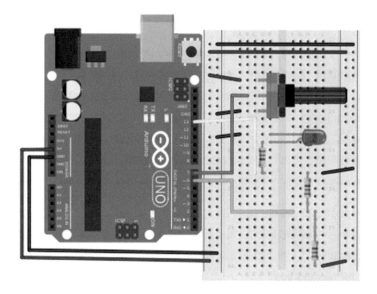

Figure 9-1. *Analogue Comparator circuit*

When the project was running, turning the potentiometer varied the voltage on D7. If the reference voltage on D6, which was 2.5 V due to my voltage divider, was higher than the variable voltage on D7, the LED turned on; otherwise, it turned off.

I've added a bigger LED to pin D13 to better show the effect, but you don't have to do this. Just remember there are two LEDs on D13 and you need to keep the current below 20 mA.

The LED I'm using has a voltage drop of 1.8 V, so subtract that from the 5 V supply from the Arduino to get 3.2 V. The resistor is 330 Ohms; and so, by division, we get 3.2/330 which gives 9.69 mA.

The Arduino has an absolute maximum of 40 mA per pin (but with other restrictions – see Appendix C for details), but 20 mA is preferred, so there should be no problems with this resistor value.

Listing 9-1. Analogue Comparator sketch

```
//=========================================================
// This sketch uses the analogue comparator with pin D6
// as the reference voltage and D7 as the voltage to be
// compared with D6. When D6 is higher than D7 then the
// LED will light. When D6 is lower than D7, the LED goes
// out. So, not a blink sketch this time!
//=========================================================

// This function sets up the comparator to fire an interrupt
// each time the ACO bit toggles. It uses D6 as the reference
// voltage and D7 as the voltage to be compared.
void setupComparator() {                              ①

    // Disable AC interrupts.
    ACSR &= ~(1 << ACIE);

    // Enable AC by disabling the AC Disable bit!
    ACSR &= ~(1 << ACD);

    // Disable digital I/O on D6 and D7.
    DIDR1 |= ((1 << AIN0D) | (1 << AIN1D));

    // D6 will be the reference voltage.
    ACSR &= ~(1 << ACBG);

    // D7 to compare with D6.
    ADCSRB &= ~(1 << ACME);

    // Fire AC interrupt on ACO toggle.
    ACSR |= ((0 << ACIS1) | (0 << ACIS0));

    // Enable AC Interrupt.
    ACSR |= (1 << ACIE);
```

```
    // Enable Global Interrupts.
    sei();
}

void setup() {
    // You can still use Arduino code as well -
    // but I'm not! D13 = output.
    DDRB |= (1 << DDB5);                              ②
    setupComparator();
}

void loop() {
    ; // Do nothing.                                 ③
}
// Analogue Comparator Interrupt Handler.Reads the ACSR
// register and sets the LED to the state of the ACO bit.

ISR(ANALOG_COMP_vect) {                              ④
    if (ACSR & (1 << ACO)) {
        PORTB |= (1 << PORTB5); // LED HIGH);
    } else {
        PORTB &= ~(1 << PORTB5); // LED LOW);
    }
}
```

① The setupComparator() function initializes the Analogue Comparator as described in the text and the code comments.

② This is just a very short pinMode(LED_BUILTIN, OUTPUT) call.

③ The loop() function does nothing. Everything happens in the ISR.

④   The ISR fires any time that the Analogue
     Comparator output toggles. It sets the LED to on, if
     the ACO bit is set; otherwise, it turns the LED off.

You should note that when the comparator output is set or reset, it
remains that way until a change is necessary. The preceding interrupt is
only called when the ACO bit toggles from set to clear, or from clear to set.
     It is effectively, like a light switch, on or off until it changes.

9.2. Analogue to Digital Converter (ADC)

The Atmega328P has a single, 10-bit Analogue to Digital Converter which
has up to nine separate inputs, depending on which ATmega328P your
Arduino is using. The Dual In-Line Package (DIP) with 28 pins has seven
inputs, while the surface mount version has all nine. On Arduino boards,
these are pins A0–A5 (or A0–A7 for the surface mount version), plus the
internal temperature sensor input. The ADC inputs can also be used by
the Analogue Comparator as described in Section 9.1, "*The Analogue
Comparator*," at the start of this chapter.
     As mentioned earlier, the ADC has 10-bit resolution which means that
it can return a value between 0 and $2^{10} - 1$, or 1023. The value is indicative
of the voltage on the AREF or AVCC pin, depending on configuration, as
compared with whichever ADC input has been selected. Only one of the
available ADC inputs can be used at a time. A result of zero represents GND,
and 1023 represents the reference voltage. The reference voltage can be
configured to one of the following three options:

- The 1.1 V internal bandgap reference voltage

- The voltage on the AVCC pin

- An external voltage on the AREF pin, which *must not*
  exceed VCC

The voltage on the ADC input pin is therefore

```
(Reference Voltage / 1024) * ADC Result
```

The ADC works by using a capacitor to sample and hold the input voltage, which is useful if the voltage changes during the time that the ADC is still calculating the result as it ensures that the sampled voltage remains stable throughout the calculation. The ADC uses successive approximation to calculate the 10 bits of the result.

In order to further improve the accuracy of the ADC, there is a special sleep mode, ADC Noise Reduction, which shuts down almost everything which is not the ADC, in order to stop all the "digital noise" that the microcontroller generates internally, so that the ADC can do its job in relative peace and quiet.

The ADC can be configured to take a single shot – as per the Arduino `analogRead()` function call – where ADC conversions are started manually on request, or to run in free running mode where each completed conversion starts another conversion automatically and only the very first conversion has to be manually started.

The ADC has an interrupt that may be configured to fire when the conversion is complete to avoid the need for your code to sit in a polling loop, waiting for the result. The interrupt is required in auto trigger mode, which can be triggered by one of many different sources – more on that later.

9.2.1. ADC Setup and Initiation

Assuming you are not using the Arduino's `analogRead()` function, then the following steps are required in order to take an ADC reading:

- Power up the ADC.

- Select a suitable prescaler to configure the ADC to run at a frequency within its required range of 50–200 KHz.

- Select a suitable reference voltage source.

- Decide on whether the result is to be left or right aligned.

- Select an input source.

- Disable digital input for the selected input pin.

- Enable interrupts, if required.

- Select single-shot or auto trigger, and if auto trigger, choose a trigger.

- Enable the ADC and initiate a conversion.

Easy?

9.2.1.1. Powering the ADC

Probably the easiest step of all, you simply have to write a 0_{binary} to the PRADC bit of the PRR register. If that bit is a 1_{binary}, then the ADC is powered off:

```
PRR &= ~(1 << PRADC);
```

9.2.1.2. Selecting the Prescaler

The ADC runs most accurately at a frequency between 50 and 200 KHz. This frequency range is mandatory if you wish to get the full 10-bit result; however, if you require less than 10-bit resolution, you can run the ADC at different frequencies. On an Arduino, the CPU is running at 16 MHz, which is a tad on the high side for the ADC. There is a prescaler for the ADC to bring the frequency down to within the desired range. To set the prescaler, you must write a suitable value to the ADPS2, ADPS1, and ADPS0 bits in the ADC Control and Status Register A, ADCSRA.

Table 9-2 shows the permitted settings for the prescaler and the resulting ADC frequencies, in KHz, for 16 MHz and 8 MHz systems.

Table 9-2. *ADC prescaler settings and frequencies*

ADPS2–ADPS0	Description	16 MHz	8 MHz
000	Divide F_CPU by 1	16,000	8,000
001	Divide F_CPU by 2	8,000	4,000
010	Divide F_CPU by 4	4,000	2,000
011	Divide F_CPU by 8	2,000	1,000
100	Divide F_CPU by 16	1,000	500
101	Divide F_CPU by 32	500	250
110	Divide F_CPU by 64	250	**125**
111	Divide F_CPU by 128	**125**	**63**

On Arduinos, only the final 111_{binary} setting, divide by 128, brings the ADC frequency down into the desired range. You *might* be successful with the 110_{binary} setting, divide by 64, which results in a frequency of 250 KHz – but it's probably not advisable especially if you need 10 bits of resolution. I *have* seen it in Arduino code – once – in the source code for an Arduino-based oscilloscope.

As I run the odd occasional NormDuino board at 8 MHz – see Appendix H – I can use either of the preceding two settings and *possibly* also the divide by 32 option, 101_{binary}.

Assuming you are running an Arduino of some kind and are bypassing analogRead(), the following code would set the desired frequency:

```
ADCSRA = ((1 << ADPS2) | (1 << ADPS1) | (1 << ADPS0));
```

ℹ️ The preceding code overwrites *all* settings in the ADCSRA register. If you are compiling in the Arduino IDE, this is a good idea as it will overwrite the Arduino's default settings.

Regardless of the IDE, doing this means that you know *exactly* where you start in the ADC setup. All further settings in ADCSRA can be ORd or ANDed in the usual manner. The examples that follow will all begin by clearing the appropriate register on its first use and adding in additional requirements on all subsequent uses.

9.2.1.3. Selecting the Reference Voltage Source

There are three separate and selectable voltage references which can be used by the ADC, although only one can be selected at any one time.

⚠️ The data sheet advises against selecting either of the two internal options if there is an external voltage already applied to the AREF pin. Doing this will most likely brick your ATmega328P. It's best to check if your particular device has anything connected *before* changing the reference voltage source.

I've looked at the schematics for the Uno and the Duemilanove, and neither of those connects the AREF pin to any voltage. NormDuino also does not have any voltages on that pin.

The same cannot be said for a number of breadboard Arduino layouts to be found on the Internet, where they connect AVCC to VCC as required, but for some reason, also connect AREF to VCC, thus creating a time bomb, just waiting to happen and for no good reason. Beware.

Even the Arduino Language delays setting the `analogReference()` until the time that `analogRead()` actually executes and the source comes with a warning against having voltage applied to AREF.

The reference voltage is set by bits REFS1 and REFS0 in the ADC Multiplexer Selection Register, also known as ADMUX. The permitted values for these two bits are shown in Table 9-3.

Table 9-3. *ADC reference voltage selection settings*

REFS1–REFS0	Description
00	Use the AREF pin as the reference voltage. The external voltage applied must not exceed VCC
01	Use the (internal) voltage on AVcc as the reference voltage. For best results, there should be a 100 nF capacitor between AREF and GND
10	Reserved
11	Use the internal 1.1 V bandgap voltage as the reference. Again, it's best to have a 100 nF capacitor between AREF and GND.

In the following example, we set the ADMUX register with an initial value for the reference voltage source, selecting the AVCC voltage, and will add to it as we progress:

```
ADMUX = ((0 << REFS1) | (1 << REFS0));
```

9.2.1.4. Left or Right Alignment?

The result of an ADC conversion is a value between 0 and 1023. This represents the voltage on the ADC input pin – see in the following – as compared with the reference voltage, both with respect to GND.

There are two registers that must be read to obtain the result, ADCH and ADCL. ADCH holds the highest bits of the result, while ADCL holds the lowest bits. Reading these registers must be done in a specific order – ADCL must be read first and then ADCH.

Once you have read ADCL, the ADC is no longer permitted to write to either ADCL or ADCH until after you have completed reading ADCH. This blocking method ensures that when you read the result of a conversion, both registers are giving you the appropriate bits of the *same* conversion result.

The ADC generates a 10-bit result, 0–1023, which is returned in the ADC data registers ADCH and ADCL. By default, the result is presented *right adjusted*, but can optionally be presented left adjusted by setting the ADLAR bit in ADMUX to a 1_{binary}:

```
ADMUX |= (1 << ADLAR);
```

The default is for the result to be right aligned, which you can ensure by

```
ADMUX &= ~(1 << ADLAR);
```

The data sheet states that *If the result is left aligned and no more than 8-bit precision is required, it is sufficient to read* ADCH.

So what is the difference? The default, right alignment, returns ADCL with bits 9–8 of the result in bits 1–0 of ADCH and bits 7–0 of the result in bits 7–0 of ADCL.

In left alignment, bits 9–2 are in bits 7–0 of ADCH, and bits 1–0 of the result are in bits 7–6 of ADCL.

In Table 9-4, "x" means we don't care about this bit of the result as it is outside the 10-bit resolution of the ADC.

Table 9-4. *ADC left/right alignment options*

ADLAR	Alignment	Result ADCH	Result ADCL
0	Right	xxxxxx98	76543210
1	Left	98765432	10xxxxxx

i In code, you can read ADCW to get the correct result and not worry about reading ADCH and ADCL in the correct order.

9.2.1.5. Selecting an Input Source

It is now time to select an input source. This is the pin that will receive the voltage that we are comparing against the reference voltage source. There are 4 bits in register ADMUX, MUX3–MUX0, which are used to select the input source. This gives up to 16 different sources, all of which are listed in Table 9-5; however, a number of the options are reserved and should not be used. ADC8, while listed in the data sheet as one of the reserved values, is actually an exception in that it *can* be safely used.

Table 9-5. *ADC input voltage source settings*

MUX3-MUX0	Description	MUX3-MUX0	Description
0000	ADC0 (Arduino A0, AVR PC0)	1000	Reserved
0001	ADC1 (Arduino A1, AVR PC1)	1001	Reserved
0010	ADC2 (Arduino A2, AVR PC2)	1010	Reserved
0011	ADC3 (Arduino A3, AVR PC3)	1011	Reserved
0100	ADC4 (Arduino A4, AVR PC4)	1100	Reserved
0101	ADC5 (Arduino A5, AVR PC5)	1101	Reserved
0110	ADC6 (Arduino A6, AVR ADC6)	1110	1.1 V internal bandgap
0111	ADC7 (Arduino A7, AVR ADC7)	1111	0 V (GND)

The data sheet has the following warnings:

- *If* ADC3, ADC2, ADC1 *or* ADC0 *are used not as ADC inputs, but as Digital Outputs, then they _must not switch while an ADC conversion is in progress._*

- *If* ADC4 *or* ADC5 *are being used for 2WI (2 Wire Interface) purposes, then using that will affect only* ADC4 *and* ADC5, *not the other ADC inputs.*

Now, the final two entries in Table 9-5 are interesting perhaps? I can only assume that they are there to enable some form of configuration perhaps. If you set MUX3:0 to 1110_{binary}, then the ADC always reads 227–229 (at least mine does) which works out at 1.11–1.12 V. Using 1111_{binary} for MUX3:0 returns zero on my devices, representing GND. Working on the assumption that this is indeed some form of configuration test, my ADC seems to be quite accurate – assuming, of course, that the 1.1 V bandgap reference voltage is itself 1.1 V of course.

---

i If your code decides to change the ADC input channel while a conversion is underway and has not yet completed, nothing will happen until the current conversion finishes.

9.2.1.6. Disable Digital Input

When using a pin as an ADC input, you are required to disable its digital input buffer by setting the appropriate bit for the pin, in the Digital Input Disable Register 0 or DIDR0.

Only the pins corresponding to ADC0 (Arduino A0) through ADC5 (Arduino A5) have the ability to have their digital input buffers disabled. Pins ADC6 and ADC7, the two new ones on surface mount versions of the ATmega328, and ADC8 do not have digital input buffers, so you cannot have them disabled.

To disable the digital input buffer for a pin, you must write a 1_{binary} to the appropriate ADCnD bit of the DIDR0 register, where the "n" represents the ADCn pin number. To disable the digital input buffer for pin ADC3, Arduino pin A3, for example, you would code

```
DIDR0 |= (1 << ADC3D);
```

Don't forget to re-enable the buffer after the pin's use as an ADC input is finished; otherwise, it will always read LOW. This is done by writing a 0_{binary} to the appropriate bit in DIDR0, as follows:

```
DIDR0 &= ~(1 << ADC3D);
```

9.2.1.7. ADC Interrupt

There is a single interrupt attached to the ADC, the ADC interrupt, or ADC Conversion Complete interrupt, accessed through ISR(ADC_vect) in your code. This interrupt is enabled by setting the ADIE, ADC Interrupt Enable, bit in register ADCSRA as follows:

```
ADCSRA |= (1 << ADIE);
```

If global interrupts are also enabled, then the interrupt will fire every time that the ADC has completed a conversion and the result is available. Any time that the ADC conversion is complete, the ADIF bit in ADCSRA will be set and will remain set until either

- The interrupt handler executes, whereupon ADIF will be automatically cleared.

- The code writes a 1_{binary} to ADIF in the usual AVR manner.

If your code is not using the ADC interrupt, it should monitor ADIF, and remember to clear it; otherwise, a further ADC conversion will not begin – unless the ADC is in free running mode, as described in the following.

⚠ The data sheet warns that we should *beware that if doing a Read-Modify-Write on* ADCSRA, *a pending interrupt can be disabled. This also applies if the* SBI *and* CBI *instructions are used.*

9.2.1.8. Single-Shot or Auto Trigger?

In single-shot mode, a single conversion is carried out, and the ADC stops working until the next request for a conversion. The conversion is started on demand by the code, and the ADC will make the reading and then stop.

In auto trigger mode, the conversion is triggered by an event or can be put in free running mode which causes the ADC to continually make a new conversion as soon as the previous one has completed. This mode usually requires the ADC interrupt to be enabled to advise the code that a conversion has finished and that the result is available. Free running mode still requires the first conversion to be manually started, as described in the following.

The various triggers available are set up in register ADCSRB by setting bits ADTS2, ADTS1, and ADTS0 as per Table 9-6.

Table 9-6. *ADC auto trigger sources*

ADTS2–ADTS0	Trigger Source
000	Free running mode
001	Analogue Comparator
010	External Interrupt Request 0
011	Timer/counter 0 Compare Match A
100	Timer/counter 0 Overflow
101	Timer/counter 1 Compare Match B
110	Timer/counter 1 Overflow
111	Timer/counter 1 Input Capture Event

These bits are only used if the ADATE bit in register ADCSRA is also set. To set the ADC into auto trigger mode with free running, the code required would be

```
ADCSRA |= (1 << ADATE);
ADCSRB = ((0 << ADTS2) | (0 << ADTS1) | (0 << ADTS0));
```

> ⚠ Register ADCSRB also contains, in bit 6, the ACME bit which is used by the Analogue Comparator – see Section 9.1, "*The Analogue Comparator.*" Setting ADCSRB in the preceding manner will clear that bit which might affect the running of the comparator if your device needs it. In that case, the preceding code should probably be changed to preserve the ACME bit before ORing the desired auto trigger bits:
>
> ```
> ADCSRA |= (1 << ADATE);
> ```
>
> ```
> ADCSRB &= (1 << ACME);
> ADCSRB |= ((0 << ADTS2) | (0 << ADTS1) | (0 << ADTS0));
> ```
>
> And yes, I know ORing with zero has no effect, but it will have an effect for other auto trigger sources.

Auto triggering is initiated when a positive edge occurs on the selected trigger signal. When this occurs, the ADC's prescaler is reset, and a new conversion is started. If the triggering signal is still positive when the current conversion finishes, a new conversion *will not* be automatically started.

Additionally, if another triggering positive edge is detected during an ADC conversion, the new triggering edge will be ignored.

The various Timer/counter 0– and Timer/counter 1–related auto triggering sources can be used to cause an ADC conversion to be initiated at regular intervals.

Even when auto triggering is enabled, your code can still manually request a single-shot conversion by initiating the conversion as described in the following.

9.2.1.9. Enabling the ADC and Initiating Conversions

Everything is now configured. All that remains is to enable the ADC and, if necessary, initiate the first conversion. The ADC is enabled by writing a 1_{binary} to the ADEN bit in register ADCSRA, as follows:

```
ADCSRA |= (1 << ADEN);
```

When ADEN is set as in the preceding text, the following events occur:

- The ADC starts consuming power.

- The ADC prescaler starts counting.

- If configured, auto triggering events will now initiate an ADC conversion.

An ADC conversion is manually requested, in single-shot or free running mode, by writing a 1_{binary} to the ADSC bit in register ADCSRA:

```
ADCSRA |= (1 << ADSC);
```

When the ADSC bit is set, the following events occur:

- The ADC prescaler is reset so that each conversion takes the same time.

- The sample and hold circuitry charges its capacitor with the voltage on the ADC input pin.

- The chosen reference voltage is enabled.

- The input channel selection is made, and the appropriate input is connected to the ADC.

- The conversion then starts at the next rising edge of the ADC clock.

9.2.1.10. ADC Conversions

The very first conversion takes 25 ADC clock cycles to complete so that the internal analogue circuitry can be initialized. Subsequent conversions take only 13 ADC clock cycles.

If the ADC's reference voltage is the internal bandgap voltage, then it will take *a certain time* for the voltage to stabilize. If it is not stabilized, the first conversion's result may be wrong. The data sheet, sadly, does not specify how long *a certain time* should be. My own code simply throws away the first reading in that mode of operation, although I have seen calls to delay(20) in some code as a suitable delay to allow the stabilization to occur.

The sample and hold of the input voltage takes place after 13.5 ADC clock cycles for the first conversion and after only 1.5 ADC clock cycles after the start of subsequent conversions.

When an ADC conversion is complete, the result is written to the data registers ADCH and ADCL, and then bit ADIF in ADCSRA is set. When running in single-shot mode, ADSC in ADCSRA is cleared simultaneously with the setting of ADIF.

If the code then sets bit ADSC to 1_{binary}, a new conversion will be initiated on the first *rising* edge of the ADC clock signal.

In any of the auto triggering modes, the ADC prescaler is reset as soon as the triggering event occurs. This ensures a fixed delay from the triggering event occurring to the start of a new ADC conversion. In this mode, the sample and hold takes place two ADC clock cycles after the rising edge on the trigger source signal. An additional three *CPU clock cycles*, not ADC clock cycles, are used for synchronization logic.

In free running mode, a new conversion will start as soon as the previous one completes, and this will occur even if the ADIF flag in the ADCSRA register is not cleared.

9.2.2. Noise Reduction

There is a sleep mode especially for the ADC. It disables many of the internal clocks leaving the ADC to make its conversion with as few noise sources internally as possible. This sleep mode is discussed in Chapter 7, Section 7.3.9.2, "*ADC Noise Reduction Sleep Mode.*"

It should be noted that this Noise Reduction mode is available only in single-shot ADC mode. The data sheet specifies the following about enabling this sleep mode:

The following procedures should be used:

Make sure that the ADC is enabled and is not busy converting.

Single Conversion mode must be selected and the ADC conversion complete interrupt must be enabled.

Enter ADC Noise Reduction mode (or Idle mode). The ADC will start a conversion once the CPU has been halted.

If no other interrupts occur before the ADC conversion completes, the ADC interrupt will wake up the CPU and execute the ADC Conversion Complete interrupt routine. If another interrupt wakes up the CPU before the ADC conversion is complete, that interrupt will be executed, and an ADC Conversion Complete interrupt request will be generated when the ADC conversion completes.

The CPU will remain in active mode until a new sleep command is executed.

It also gives the following point to note.

ℹ️ The ADC will not be automatically turned off when entering other sleep modes than Idle mode and ADC Noise Reduction mode. The user is advised to write zero to ADEN before entering such sleep modes to avoid excessive power consumption.

9.2.3. Temperature Measurement

See Appendix E for an example of using this facility of the ADC. To select this ADC input, your code needs to

- Select the internal 1.1 V bandgap as the ADC reference voltage ($\text{REFS1:0} = 11_{\text{binary}}$).

- Select ADC8 as the ADC input channel ($\text{MUX3:0} = 1000_{\text{binary}}$).

- Set the prescaler – divide by 128 on an Arduino board at 16 MHz ($\text{ADPS2:0} = 111_{\text{binary}}$).

- Execute single conversions as and when required. Auto triggering is not permitted.

The data sheet advises that readings from an *uncalibrated* sensor are

- $-40°C = 010D_{\text{hex}}$ (269_{decimal})

- $25°C = 0160_{\text{hex}}$ (352_{decimal})

- $125°C = 01E0_{\text{hex}}$ (480_{decimal})

This works out at approximately 1.2769 per degree C, and that matches with the data sheet which states that it is *approximately* 1 LSB [degrees Kelvin] or 1 degree C. The data sheet states that the temperature in degrees Centigrade is calculated as

```
Temp_C = (((((ADCH << 8) + ADCL)
       - (273 + 100 - TS_OFFSET)) * 128) / TS_GAIN)
       + 25
```

> ⚠️ Given the rules of arithmetic precedence, the preceding code would cause ADCH to be read *before* ADCL, and this would not be the correct order! Using ADCW instead of ((ADCH << 8) + ADCL) would give the correct result and cause the two registers to be read in the correct order.

- TS_OFFSET is the calibration offset for the sensor and is stored in the device itself. It is a signed two's compliment value.

- TS_GAIN is the sensor gain factor and is also stored in the device. It is an unsigned, fixed-point, 8-bit value representing 1/128th units, hence the need to multiply by 128 in the preceding text.

In the data sheet, there is a small assembly language routine to obtain both TS_OFFSET and TS_GAIN from the device. I do not use that particular method of temperature conversion, so I have not discussed that routine here.

There are, over the Internet, various methods of converting the temperature from what the ADC reads to degrees Centigrade. Some I have seen are as follows:

- ADC - an_offset – The offset is dependent on the individual AVR device.

- (ADC - 247)/1.22 – From the developer help note mentioned earlier and linked in the following.

- (((ADC - (273 - 100 - TS_OFFSET)) * 128) / TS_GAIN) + 25 – From the data sheet itself.

- ADC - 273 - From the application note on calibrating the sensor, linked in the following.

- (ADC - an_offset) a_gain_factor - From the "MySensors" code, linked in the following.

The Atmel/Microchip documents mentioned in the preceding text are as follows:

- The developer help note is at https://microchipdeveloper.com/8avr:avradc.

- The application note on calibrating the temperature sensor is at http://ww1.microchip.com/downloads/en/AppNotes/Atmel-8108-Calibration-of-the-AVRs-Internal-Temperature-Reference_ApplicationNote_AVR122.pdf, which may prove useful - if your Maths is better than mine!

- The MySensors code mentioned in the preceding text can be found at https://github.com/mysensors/MySensors/blob/bde7dadca6c50d52cc21dadd5ee6d3623be5f3c6/hal/architecture/AVR/MyHwAVR.cpp.

ℹ️ In the United Kingdom, we say *Maths*, plural, from Mathematics. I believe in the United States it is *Math*, singular (from Mathematic?), which sounds really weird to my Scottish ears. At least we agree on *Arithmetic*.

Interestingly, the calibration document mentioned in the preceding text states something a little different from the information in the data sheet, in that

> *The output from the ADC is given in LSBs or K, so the calibration values ADC_{T1} and ADC_{T2} have to be converted to degrees C. This is done by subtracting 273 from the values*

This, to my mind, implies that the temperature sensor is outputting a value representing degrees K (Kelvin) whereby 0 degrees Centigrade is 273 degrees Kelvin, hence the need to subtract 273 from the ADC reading, to get a value for Centigrade. In practice, this does not compute!

9.2.4. ADC Example

The following code initializes the ADC in free running mode and uses an interrupt to send the ADC reading to the Serial Monitor. The code was written and compiled in the Arduino IDE, but uses the plain AVR C language to set up the ADC.

This code can be run on my Uno or Duemilanove at 16MHz or on one of my 8 MHz NormDuino boards. The prescaler for the AVR is calculated based on the F_CPU chosen in the Arduino IDE, and the code correctly determines whether the board is 16 MHz or 8 MHz and sets the correct prescaler accordingly.

Figure 9-2 shows the breadboard layout where I simply connected a potentiometer to pin A0 to vary the voltage. An LED on pin D9 with a 560 Ohm resistor gave some visual feedback as it brightened and dimmed according to where I had turned the potentiometer.

The first part of the source code is shown in Listing 9-2 and is the function setupADC() which sets up the ADC directly. As mentioned earlier, it will be set up in free running auto trigger mode and will use the ADC interrupt to pass the readings to the main loop as each one becomes available.

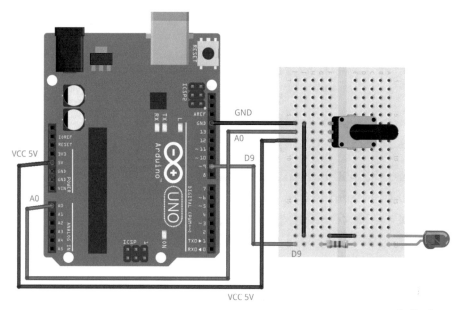

fritzing

Figure 9-2. *ADC example sketch breadboard layout*

Listing 9-2. ADC example, setupADC() function

```
void setupADC() {
   // Ensure ADC is powered.
   PRR &= ~(1 << PRADC);                                    ①

   // Slow the ADC clock down to 125 KHz
   // by dividing by 128 or 64. 128 is for a 16MHz Arduino
   // 64 for an 8MHz NormDuino. Does not cater for other
   // clock speeds here. BEWARE.
   #if F_CPU == 16000000                                   ②
   ADCSRA = (1 << ADPS2) | (1 << ADPS1) | (1 << ADPS0);
   #else
   // Non-standard 8MHz clock in use.
   ADCSRA = (1 << ADPS2) | (1 << ADPS1) | (0 << ADPS0);
```

```
  #endif

  // Initialise the ADC to use the
  // internal AVCC 5V reference voltage.
  ADMUX = (0 << REFS1) | (1 << REFS0);                    ③

  // Ensure result is right aligned.
  ADMUX &= ~(1 << ADLAR);

  // Use the ADC multiplexer input
  // ADC0 = Arduino pin A0.
  ADMUX |= (0 << MUX3) | (0 << MUX2) |                    ④
           (0 << MUX1) | (0 << MUX0);

  // Disable ADC0 Digital input buffer.
  DIDR0 |= (1 << ADC0D);

  // Use the interrupt to advise when a result is available.
  ADCSRA |= (1 << ADIE);                                 ⑤

  // Set auto-trigger on, and choose Free Running mode. As
  // we are not using the Analogue Comparator, we don't care
  // about the ACME bit in ADCSRB.
  ADCSRA |= (1 << ADATE);                                ⑥
  ADCSRB = 0;

  // Enable the ADC and wait for the voltages to settle.
  ADCSRA |= (1 << ADEN);                                 ⑦
  delay(20);
}
```

    ①   This powers the ADC by disabling the *disable the ADC* bit.

② These lines work out the prescaler for 16 MHz or 8 MHz devices. Other speeds are not catered for here. I only have two speeds on my devices.

③ This selects the internal 5 V reference voltage which is fed by pin AVCC which must be connected to VCC plus or minus 2%.

④ I know it's all zeros, but it's easy to change this line for different ADC input pins.

⑤ We are using interrupts, so they must be enabled, as must the global interrupts. This is always the case when compiling in the Arduino IDE, but not necessarily in other IDEs. Beware.

⑥ Setting ADATE enables auto trigger mode. Setting ADCSRB to zero enables free running mode. It also messes up the Analogue Comparator, but we don't care here. Other code might care, so bear it in mind.

⑦ Enable, but do not start the ADC. From here on, the ADC draws power and has initialized the reference voltage selector and the reference voltage source. It is ready to go.

After executing the code in Listing 9-2, the ADC is now fully initialized and enabled; however, it has not yet been started. In free running and single-shot modes, the ADC must be started manually. The startADC() function in Listing 9-3 does exactly that by setting bit ADSC in ADCSRA.

Listing 9-3. ADC example, startADC() function

```
void startADC() {
    ADCSRA |= (1 << ADSC);
}
```

Listing 9-4 sets up a volatile variable, ADCReading, to hold the result passed back from the interrupt handler. The variable must be defined as volatile; otherwise, the compiler might notice that it doesn't seem to be being changed in value and may simply "optimize" it away. Any global variables that you wish to change from inside an interrupt handler should be defined as volatile to prevent this happening.

Following the variable declaration, we need an interrupt handler for the ADC interrupt. All that it needs to do is to copy the ADC result from ADCW into ADCReading. The loop() function, in Listing 9-6, will do some work with this result.

Listing 9-4. ADC example, the interrupt handler

```
// Somewhere for the ADC Interrupt to store the result.
volatile uint16_t ADCReading = 0;

// The interrupt handler.
ISR(ADC_vect) {
    ADCReading = ADCW;
}
```

The setup() function, in Listing 9-5, initializes the ADC using the setupADC() function from Listing 9-4. This sets up the Serial Monitor to display the results and fires up the ADC for its first reading. Once the first reading is complete, the ADC will then be in free running mode and will constantly be initiating a new conversion as soon as the current one finishes.

Listing 9-5. ADC example, the setup() function

```
void setup() {
    setupADC();

    // Use the Serial monitor for output.
    Serial.begin(9600);
    Serial.println("Arduino Direct ADC Testing");

    // Add an LED and 560R resistor to pin 9 for feedback.
    pinMode(9, OUTPUT);

    // Now, fire up the ADC.
    startADC();
}
```

And finally, Listing 9-6 shows the loop() function, which takes the most recent ADC reading and sends it to the Serial Monitor, first as a plain value between 0 and 1023 and, second, as a voltage.

As there are 1024 different values that can be returned from the ADC and with 0 = GND and 1023 = AVCC or 5 V, anything in between must be equal to 5/1024 per division. We simply multiply ADCReading by this fraction, 0.004882812 V (4.88 milliVolts and a little bit), to get the voltage on the ADC0 or A0 pin. We must be careful to cast the result to a float, or we will lose accuracy and only see integer values.

Listing 9-6. ADC example, the loop() function

```
void loop() {
    Serial.print("ADC = ");
    Serial.print(ADCReading);

    // The voltage is ADCReading * (5V/1024)
    Serial.print(", Voltage = ");
    Serial.println((float)(ADCReading * 5.0 / 1024.0));
```

```
    // Light up the LED to a value representing the voltage
    // on pin A0 (ADC0).
    analogWrite(9, map(ADCReading, 0, 1023, 0, 255));
    delay(500);
}
```

There's a small delay at the end of the `loop()` to prevent the numbers scrolling up the screen too quickly. Don't worry about the ADC though. It will carry on taking readings and passing them back to the `loop()` as the interrupt handler works outside of `delay()` and is not affected.

9.3. USART

The USART is the Universal Synchronous/Asynchronous Receiver/ Transmitter. It's easier to type USART!

On the Arduino, it is connected from physical pins 2 and 3 to the laptop or desktop's USB port via either a separate Atmel/Microchip AVR microcontroller or an FTDI chip – depending on which Arduino you have. On an ordinary ATmega328P, it is also pins 2 and 3, but they are not connected anywhere – unless you connect them.

Pin 2 is the receive or RX pin, while pin 3 is the transmit or TX pin. You don't have to worry about this on an Arduino, but when you have your own naked ATmega328P on a breadboard or PCB and you want to communicate with it, you do. With a serial device such as an FTDI connector, at least the one I have, the pins are marked TX0 and RX0 for output. So the TX0 pin on the FTDI connects to the ATmega328P's RX pin, and the RX0 on the FTDI connects to TX on the AVR.

Confused? You should be! Some FTDI devices have the pins marked as TX and RX, and with those, you connect the TX to the TX and the RX to RX. It will not break anything if you get them crossed over, but nothing will work. If that happens to you, just swap the wires over at the AVR end.

The USART can be set up to transmit only, receive only, or do both; and it can use interrupts to facilitate this, having three dedicated interrupts available.

In synchronous modes, the USART will require a clock pin and a data pin, whereas asynchronous mode does not need a clock and can use one pin, of the two available to the USART, as the TX pin and the other for the RX pin. The Arduino uses the latter mode, asynchronous.

9.3.1. Baud Rates

The baud rate is configured by the value stored in the USART Baud Rate Register, UBRR0, where "0" is the USART number. On the ATmega328P, there is a single USART numbered 0. The Mega 2560 has four USARTs, numbered from 0 to 3.

UBRR0 is connected to a counter which counts down at the F_CPU frequency, and whenever it reaches zero, a USART clock is generated and this clock controls the USART's transmission and/or receipt of data. When the counter reaches zero, it is reloaded with the value in UBRR0. This clock is the Baud Rate Generator Clock and has the frequency given by

F_CPU / (UBRR0 + 1)

The Baud Rate Generator Clock is divided down by the USART's transmitter by 2, 8, or 16 depending on the configured mode.

The receiver circuitry, on the other hand, does no such division and uses the Baud Rate Generator Clock directly as input to its data recovery unit. Within the data recovery unit, there is a state machine which uses 2, 8, or 16 states to determine correct receipt of the transmitted data.

9.3.2. Double Speed

The transfer rate of the USART can be doubled by setting bit U2X0 in register UCSR0A. However, this bit should only be set in *asynchronous* operation; it should be zero for synchronous modes. Setting the bit causes the baud rate divider to be reduced to 8, from the usual 16, and this effectively doubles the transfer rate.

The receiver, however, will also only sample eight times, rather than 16, in the data recovery unit, thus doubling the receive speed too, but it should be noted that in this mode, a more accurate baud rate setting is required as well as a more accurate system clock. Some baud rates can cause excessive error rates – see the following for details.

For the transmission side of the USART, doubling the speed has no apparent drawbacks. (At least, that's what the data sheet says.)

9.3.3. Baud Rate Calculations

In single-speed asynchronous mode, the baud rate is calculated as

```
BAUD = F_CPU / 16 * (UBRR0 + 1)
```

Normally, however, you are more interested in setting a specific baud rate, so you would need to calculate UBRR0 for the desired rate. This is done using the formula

```
UBRR0 = (F_CPU / (16 * BAUD)) - 1
```

You will probably have figured out that you can just about define *any* baud rate you wish by setting UBRR0 to any given value.

In double-speed asynchronous mode, the formulas change to

```
BAUD = F_CPU / 8 * (UBRR0 + 1)
```

and

```
UBRR0 = (F_CPU / (8 * BAUD)) - 1
```

In synchronous (master) mode, which incidentally the Arduino cannot use, the formulas again change to

```
BAUD = F_CPU / 2 * (UBRR0 + 1)
```

and

```
UBRR0 = (F_CPU / (2 * BAUD)) - 1
```

As an example, what would the required UBRR0 setting be for an Arduino running at 16 MHz, for a baud rate of 9600 in single-speed mode?

```
UBRR0 = (F_CPU / 16 * BAUD) - 1
      = (16e6 / 16 * 9600) - 1
      = (16e6 / 153,600) - 1
      = 104.1666... - 1
      = 103.1666...
```

See the problem? We are working with registers, and registers cannot have fractions, so the preceding calculation introduces errors. Do we use the value 103 and round down or use 104 by rounding up? What are the actual baud rates obtained with those values? If we feed them back into the equation, we will see, first for UBRR0 = 103

```
BAUD = F_CPU / 16 * (UBRR0 + 1)
     = 16e6 / 16 * (103 + 1)
     = 16e6 / 16 * 104
     = 16e6 / 1664
     = 9615.384615
```

and now for UBRR0 = 104

```
BAUD = F_CPU / 16 * (UBRR0 + 1)
     = 16e6 / 16 * (104 + 1)
     = 16e6 / 16 * 105
     = 16e6 / 1680
     = 9523.809524
```

Neither of these is 9600, which we wanted, so it looks like rounding down, in this case, works out closer to our desired baud rate.

9.3.4. Baud Rate Errors

With UBRR0 set to 103 and 104, as in the preceding text, we have actual baud rates of 9615 and 9524. My rounding here is in the normal direction: less than 0.5 rounds down, more than 0.5 rounds up, and 0.5 rounds up or down to the even number.

We wanted 9600, but we got 9615 or 9524. One is running high and the other low. Which has the lowest error rate?

The data sheet calculates the error rate, as a percentage, as

```
error% = ((BAUDgot / BAUDwanted) - 1) * 100
```

The data sheet supplies numerous tables showing the desired baud rates, the UBRR0 setting, and error rates for many different values of F_CPU; and *they all appear to be wrong!*

Taking the best value calculated in the preceding text and checking the data sheet, it shows the error rate as being 0.2% for UBRR0 having the value 103. I feel the need to run a quick check myself and calculate the error rate for UBRR0 = 103:

```
error% = ((BAUDgot / BAUDwanted) - 1) * 100
       = ((9615 / 9600) - 1 ) * 100
       = (1.0015625 - 1) * 100
       = 0.15625%
```

Hmm, that's not quite the 0.2% that the data sheet mentions. So let's try again but this time, use the fractions:

```
error% = ((BAUDgot / BAUDwanted) - 1) * 100
       = ((9615.384615 / 9600) - 1 ) * 100
       = (1.001602564 - 1) * 100
       = 0.1602%
```

That's *still* not 0.2%. There are many other discrepancies in the data sheet on the matter. To be honest, I think the data sheet is rounding error rates to the nearest 0.1%.

Regardless of the data sheet's approximate error rates, the advice given is to choose a baud rate which gives an error rate of between –0.5% and +0.5%. On an Arduino board, running at 16 MHz, a 9600 baud rate is *within specifications*. Using this advice, it would seem that UBRR0 can safely be set to 103 as calculated.

9.3.5. What Is a Frame?

According to the data sheet, *A serial frame is defined to be one character of data bits with synchronization bits (start and stop bits), and optionally a parity bit for error checking.*

Start and stop bits are used to synchronize the transmitting and receiving devices, while parity bits are used to apply rudimentary error checking.

The USART is able to be configured to use any combination of the following:

- 1 start bit
- 5, 6, 7, 8, or 9 data bits
- None, even, or odd parity
- 1 or 2 stop bits

A frame always begins with the single start bit. This is followed by 5, 6, 7, 8, or 9 data bits with the least significant bit first. If parity is enabled, the parity bit is next. Finally are the 1 or 2 stop bits.

When a frame has been transmitted, it can either be followed by another frame, or the line can be set to a HIGH for idle state.

It is because of the frame structure that regarding the baud rate as the number of *characters* per second is incorrect. For an 8-bit character set, a frame can be as much as 12 bits long.

9.3.6. Parity

The USART operates, or can be configured to do so, in odd or even parity or with no parity at all. When configured to use parity, the way it is calculated is to exclusively OR, or XOR, each of the bits in the *data*, not the bits in the *frame*, and then to XOR the result with a 0_{binary} bit for even parity or a 1_{binary} bit for odd parity.

ℹ️ An exclusive OR operation takes 2 bits, and if they are both the same, the result is 0_{binary}. If they are different, the result is 1_{binary}, giving the following truth table:

```
A B | Z
----+--
0 0 | 0
0 1 | 1
1 0 | 1
1 1 | 0
```

If even parity is in use, the parity bit is used to make the number of 1_{binary} bits in the data even. Odd parity makes the number of 1 bits odd. The parity bit will be found between the final data bit and the first stop bit of a frame.

As an example, the letter "A," in ASCII, has code $65_{decimal}$, 41_{hex}, or 0100 0001_{binary}. There are 2 bits that are 1_{binary}. So for even parity, the parity bit must be a 0_{binary}; and for odd parity, it must be a 1_{binary}.

The letter "C," on the other hand, is $67_{decimal}$, 43_{hex}, and 0100 0011_{binary}. This has 3 bits that are 1_{binary}. So the parity bit in even parity will be a 1_{binary}, and for odd parity, it will be a 0_{binary}.

9.3.7. Interrupts

The USART has three separate interrupts that can be used. Two are for transmission and one for receiving data. These are

- TX Complete
- TX Data Register Empty
- RX Complete

9.3.7.1. TX Complete Interrupt

This interrupt fires when the data written to the UDR0 register has been framed in start, stop, and parity bits as appropriate and the whole of the frame has been transmitted.

9.3.7.2. TX Data Register Empty Interrupt

This interrupt fires when the data written to the UDR0 register has been written into the shift register buffer internally, to be framed. The USART *may* still be in the midst of sending the byte down the line, but the UDR0 register is empty and another byte can be written.

This is the interrupt used by the Arduino's Serial interface and allows for a slightly quicker processing of data to be written to the USART as it can be written into the UDR0 register even as the previous byte is still being wrapped and transmitted in its frame.

9.3.7.3. RX Complete

When this interrupt fires, a new data byte is waiting to be retrieved from the UDR0 register.

i It appears that the UDR0 register is used by both the transmit and receive parts of the USART. How can this be when the USART can be both transmitting and receiving? When data are read from UDR0, the byte of data recently received is returned to the calling code, while when data are written to UDR0, it is forwarded on to the transmitter side of things. The ATmega328P knows what it is doing!

9.3.8. Initializing the USART

It goes without saying that the USART will have to be initialized before *any* communication can take place. The process usually requires the USART to be powered up, choose the USART mode, set the baud rate, set the frame requirements, and then enable the transmitter and/or the receiver depending on the requirements of the code.

When running code with interrupt-driven USART operations, the global interrupts should be disabled during the setup.

If the USART needs to be reconfigured, perhaps to change the frame format or the baud rate, then the code must ensure that the existing settings have been finished with and that all current transmissions and receipts are completed. This can be carried out by checking the TXC0 and/or RXC0 bits in the UCSR0A register.

The USART has three separate control registers:

- UCSR0A is used for various error flags and transmit and receive complete flags and to set double-speed mode and multi-processor communications mode.

- UCSR0B is used to enable interrupts, to enable transmit and receive modes, and to hold bit 9 of 9-bit data frames, for transmission and receipt and one of the 3 bits used to set the data size – the other two are in UCSR0C.

- UCSR0C is used to select the USART mode, parity settings, stop bits, the remaining 2 bits of the data size settings, and the clock polarity.

In order to ensure that your USART is fully initialized, without relying on some defaults that may not be as expected, it is best to start from a known, clear configuration by clearing all three control registers:

```
UCSR0A = 0;
UCSR0B = 0;
UCSR0B = 0;
```

Any options that the code requires can now be safely ORd into the appropriate registers. The following examples will assume this mode of operation.

9.3.8.1. Powering the USART

The USART is powered up by writing a 0_{binary} to the PRUSART0 bit in the Power Reduction Register, PRR, as described in Chapter 7, Section 7.4.2, "*Power Reduction Register*":

```
PRR &= ~(1 << PRUSART0);
```

Writing a 1_{binary} to this bit shuts down the USART by stopping the clock to the module. When subsequently waking the USART again, it should be *fully* re-initialized to ensure proper operation.

9.3.8.2. Choosing the USART Mode

The USART can be operated in one of three modes:

- Asynchronous USART (the default)

- Synchronous USART

- Master SPI

The default mode is asynchronous USART, and the desired mode is defined by setting the UMSEL01 and UMSEL00 bits in the UCSR0C register, USART Control Status Register C, as defined in Table 9-7.

Table 9-7. *USART mode settings*

UMSEL01–UMSEL00	Description
00	Asynchronous USART
01	Synchronous USART
10	Reserved – do not use
11	Master SPI

ℹ️ Synchronous mode(s) requires a clock and a data line, where asynchronous mode does not. There are two pins available to the USART, so because asynchronous mode doesn't use a clock, the two pins can be configured as TX and RX.

In this mode, transmission and reception can occur at the same time – also known as *full duplex*.

Arduino boards run in asynchronous mode.

As an example, setting the USASRT to run in Master SPI mode, your code would be

```
UCSR0C |= ((1 << UMSEL01) | (1 << UMSEL00));
```

9.3.8.3. Baud Rate Setting

Setting the baud rate has been described earlier. You must calculate the appropriate value for the UBRR0 register and load it, for example:

```
// Settings for 9600 baud rate.
#define BAUD 9600
#define UBRR0_9600 ((F_CPU) / 16 * (BAUD)) - 1
...
UBRR0 = UBRR0_9600;
```

9.3.8.4. Frame Settings

The frame settings define the start bit, which is always present, the number of data bits to be transmitted/received, whether or not a parity bit is required, and the number of stop bits.

9.3.8.5. Setting Parity

Bits UPM01 and UPM00 in the UCSR0C register, USART Control Status Register C, define the USART parity mode. Table 9-8 shows the bit settings for the different parity modes.

Table 9-8. *USART parity settings*

UPM01–UPM00	Description
00	No parity (the default)
01	Reserved – do not use
10	Even parity
11	Odd parity

To configure the USART with even parity, the code would be

```
UCSR0C |= ((1 << UPM01) | (0 << UPM00));
```

9.3.8.6. Setting Stop Bits

The USBS0 bit in the UCSR0C register defines the number of stop bits as shown in Table 9-9.

Table 9-9. *USART stop bit settings*

USBS0	Description
0	1 stop bit (the default)
1	2 stop bits

The code to configure the USART with 2 stop bits would therefore be

```
UCSR0C |= ((1 << USBS0);
```

9.3.8.7. Setting Data Width

Bits UCSZ01 and UCSZ00 in register UCSR0C, along with bit UCSZ02 in register UCSR0B, define the number of data bits in a frame. The default, at power on/reset, is 8 bits. Table 9-10 shows the valid settings for the data width which the USART will use. You will note some settings are not permitted.

Table 9-10. *USART data width settings*

UCSZ02–UCSZ00	Description
000	5 bits data size
001	6 bits data size
010	7 bits data size
011	8 bits data size (the default)
100	Reserved – do not use
101	Reserved – do not use
110	Reserved – do not use
111	9 bits data size

To set, for example, 9 bits of data in the frame, your code should execute the following:

```
UCSR0B |= (1 << UCSZ02);
UCSR0C |= ((1 << UCSZ01) | (1 << UCSZ01));
```

9.3.8.8. Enabling Double-Speed Mode

To double the speed of communications, both transmission and receipt, in asynchronous mode only, set bit U2X0 in register UCSR0A as follows:

```
UCSR0A |= (1 << U2X0);
```

If the USART is to be operated in synchronous mode, this bit can be explicitly cleared, if required:

```
UCSR0A &= ~(1 << U2X0);
```

9.3.8.9. Enabling Interrupts

The USART has thee interrupts, as detailed earlier. Bits RCXCIE0, TXCIE0, and UDRIE0 control which, if any, of the interrupts will be used; and the settings are displayed in Table 9-11.

Table 9-11. *USART interrupts*

Bit	Description
RCXCIE0	RX Complete interrupt will be enabled. The code in ISR(USART_RXC_vect) will handle reading the UDR0 register to retrieve the byte just read
TXCIE0	TX Complete interrupt will be enabled. The code in ISR(USART_TXC_vect) will handle writing a new data byte to the UDR0 register ready to be transmitted
UDRIE0	USART Data Register Empty interrupt will be enabled. The code in ISR(USART_UDRE_vect) will handle writing a new data byte to the UDR0 register ready to be transmitted

The latter two interrupts *appear* do the same thing. They do, but slightly differently.

The TX Complete interrupt is fired when the data *frame* of up to 13 bits has been transmitted. At this point, any new data written to UDR0 has to be framed *before* it can be transmitted.

The USART Data Register Empty interrupt is fired whenever the date most recently written to UDR0 has been copied to the transmit shift buffer internally to the AVR microcontroller. There can be up to 9 bits of data, and so this interrupt can fire when the previous character is still in the midst of being framed and transmitted; and, in doing so, you can get a better throughput as the byte can be framed and transmitted as soon as the previous byte is on its way down the line.

The Arduino uses the USART Data Register Empty interrupt for better throughput.

Enabling these interrupts is a matter of writing a 1_{binary} to the appropriate bit in the UCSR0B register:

```
cli();
...
UCSR0B |= ((1 << RCXCIE0) | (1 << UDRIE0));
...
sei();
```

⚠️ If interrupts are to be used, it is considered best to disable global interrupts while initializing the USART. This will prevent spurious firing of the USART interrupts, possibly, when the USART is not fully configured.

9.3.8.10. Enabling Data Transmission

To enable transmission of data, the USART is configured as follows:

```
UCSR0B |= (1 << TXEN0);
```

Doing so will override the normal function of the TX pin on the AVR microcontroller. This corresponds to Arduino pin D1 or AVR pin PD1.

9.3.8.11. Enabling Data Receipt

To enable receipt of data, the USART is configured as follows:

```
UCSR0B |= (1 << RXEN0);
```

Doing so will override the normal function of the RX pin on the AVR microcontroller. This corresponds to Arduino pin D0 or AVR pin PD0.

9.3.8.12. Transmitting or Receiving 9-Bit Data

Nine-bit data? What's that about? It can happen that some data transmissions require 9 bits for each character. The ATmega328P's USART can cope with this. Given that data bytes in registers are only 8 bits long, where does the 9th bit get stored?

Bits TXB80 and RXB80 in register UCSRB0 are the places. These bits hold the 9th bit when transmitting and receiving 9-bit data. You should note that

- When transmitting data, the 9th bit must be written to TXB80 before writing the remaining 8 bits to the UDR0 register.

- When receiving data, the 9th bit must be read from RXB80 before reading the rest from UDR0.

In either case, the appropriate bit in register UCSRB0 holds the most significant bit of the 9-bit data. This will be bit number 8 – bits number from 0 upward remember. Data bits 7–0 will be in the UDR0 register when transmitting or receiving 9-bit data.

9.3.9. USART Checks

When all the initialization has been completed and the USART is now transmitting and/or receiving data quite happily, how do you check for completion or errors?

With interrupts in force, you will know when data are received and/or transmitted without problems as the appropriate interrupt will fire. However, if you are not using interrupts, you will have to poll various bits in the control registers, to see if data have been received or transmitted.

All of the bits to be checked or polled are found in register UCSR0A.

9.3.9.1. USART Receive Complete

Bit RXC0 in register UCSR0A is set when the current byte being received has been received and unframed. The data byte will be available for reading from the UDR0 register.

When the UDR0 register is subsequently read, RXC0 will be automatically cleared, as it will if the USART RX Complete interrupt is enabled and the ISR has been executed.

Code may also clear this bit by the usual manner of writing a 1_{binary} to it.

9.3.9.2. USART Transmit Complete

Bit TXC0 in register UCSR0A is set when the *frame* in the transmit buffer (a simple shift register) has been completely shifted out onto the data line, and no new data is waiting in the UDR0 register for transmission.

This bit will be automatically cleared when the USART TX Complete interrupt handler has been executed or can be cleared in code by writing a 1_{binary} to it.

9.3.9.3. USART Data Register Empty

Bit UDRE0 in register UCSR0A indicates that the register UDR0 is now empty, its previous contents having been copied into the transmit buffer ready for framing and transmission.

This bit will be automatically cleared when the USART Date Register Empty interrupt handler has been executed. Application code may also clear this bit by writing a 1_{binary} to it.

On reset or power-up, this bit is initialized to a 1_{binary} to show that the transmit data register is ready to accept new data.

9.3.9.4. USART Frame Error

Bit FE0 in register UCSR0A will be set if the received data byte had a framing error in that the *first* stop bit was detected as a 0_{binary}. The bit remains set until UDR0 is read and so should be checked prior to reading the data.

ℹ️ When writing to register UCSR0A, this bit should always be written as 0_{binary}.

9.3.9.5. USART Data Overrun

Bit DOR0 in register UCSR0A will be set whenever a Data Overrun condition is detected. A Data Overrun occurs when

- The receive buffer is full – it can hold up to two characters.

- There is a character waiting in the USART's receive shift register to be copied into the receive buffer.

- A new start bit is detected on the RX pin.

DOR0 will remain set until the receive buffer (UDR0) is read, freeing up space for new data.

ℹ️ When writing to register UCSR0A, this bit should always be written as 0_{binary}.

9.3.9.6. USART Parity Error

Bit UPE0 in register UCSR0A will be set if the next character in the receive buffer had a parity error when received but only if the USART had parity checking enabled *at the time the data was received* (Bit UPM01 in register UCSR0C was set to 1_{binary}).

UPE0 will remain set until the receive buffer (UDR0) is read.

---

i When writing to register UCSR0A, this bit should always be written as 0_{binary}.

9.3.10. USART Example

The code that follows in Listings 9-7 through 9-15 is a sketch to demonstrate the use of the USART without help from the Arduino Language and without using the Serial interface as we would normally do. The code that follows is all one sketch but is split into separate functions here for explanation.

The sketch begins with the setupUSART() function in Listing 9-7.

Listing 9-7. USART sketch, setupUSART() function

```
#define SET_UBRR0(x) ((F_CPU) / (16 * (x))) - 1          ①

void setupUSART(unsigned long baudRate) {
    // Sets up the USART to send and receive at a given baud,
    // 8 data bits, one stop bit, no parity. It doesn't use
    // interrupts or double speed.

    // Ensure we have power/clock.
    PRR &= ~(1 << PRUSART0);                              ②
```

```
    // calculate the baud rate setting.
    UBRR0 = SET_UBRR0(baudRate);                              ③

    // Initialise registers, then set TX and RX on,
    // 8 data bits. The others default appropriately.
    UCSR0A = UCSR0B = UCSR0C = 0;                             ④
    UCSR0B |= ((1 << TXEN0) | (1 << RXEN0));                  ⑤
    UCSR0C |= ((1 << UCSZ01) | (1 << UCSZ00));               ⑥
}
```

① This is a quick way to convert the desired baud rate into the required value for UBRR0.

② Always remember to power up the USART first.

③ We set the required baud rate here.

④ Clearing all the control registers is a good way to set up the system to a known configuration.

⑤ This line enables transmission and receipt of data.

⑥ These 2 bits set the data size in the frame to 8.

You will note that much of the setup was not mentioned. Where, for example, did I put the USART into asynchronous mode? My initialization of the three control registers to zero did the following for me:

- UCSR0A set double-speed and multi-processor modes off.

- UCSR0B set interrupts off.

- UCSR0C set the mode to asynchronous and defined no parity and a single stop bit.

All that the rest of setupUSART had to do was enable 8 bits of data frame size and turn on transmission and receipt of data.

The next function, shown in Listing 9-8, is the code to receive a single byte of data from the RX line. This code will block if there is nothing currently being received.

Listing 9-8. USART sketch, receiveByte() function

```
uint8_t receiveByte() {
    // Wait for bit RXC0 to be set in UCSR0A.
    loop_until_bit_is_set(UCSR0A, RXC0);        ①

    return UDR0;                                ②
}
```

   ① Wait here until the RXC0 bit gets set. Once that happens, the data in the UDR0 register is valid.

   ② Retrieve and return the character just read.

Receiving one byte at a time is okay, but sometimes you just want more! The next function, receiveText(), receives a whole string of characters. Listing 9-9 has the details.

Listing 9-9. USART sketch, receiveText() function

```
uint8_t receiveText(char *buffer, uint8_t howMany) {
    // Receive a string of text up to howMany characters
    // or until a terminating linefeed is received.
    //
    // MAKE SURE that the serial monitor is set to send a
    // NEWLINE or this code will fail to return until the
    // buffer fills.
    //
    // Assumes the caller knows what s/he is doing! The
    // buffer should be one more than howMany in length.
    uint8_t i = 0;
```

```
    while (i < howMany) {                      ①
        uint8_t c = receiveByte();
        if (c == '\n') {                       ②
            buffer[i] = '\0';
            return i;
        }
        buffer[i++] = c;                       ③
    }

    // We have received howMany characters.
    buffer[i] = '\0';                          ④
    return howMany;
}
```

① This loop will exit on one of two conditions:

- The buffer is filled up with howMany characters, and a new line has not been seen.

- The last character received was a new line.

② If the character just received as a new line, overwrite it in the buffer with a string terminator and return to the caller.

③ Otherwise, store the character just read and loop around again.

④ If we exit the loop here, we have filled the buffer with howMany characters. Add a terminating character and return.

This is a pretty simple function to be honest, but it works. As long as the buffer has howMany characters plus one, it will work perfectly if the input received is less than the buffer size, which is something that is the responsibility of the programmer.

If the received data is longer, then it is possible that the USART will suffer a Data Overrun error and lose characters. You can see this by running the sketch and holding down a key until there has been more than the buffer size typed. Then press Enter.

The first buffer full of characters will be correctly displayed, and the first two characters after that will also be displayed. Anything after those two will be lost – unless your baud rate was low enough for the characters in the array to be displayed and the following two retrieved from the internals of the USART, before the third "extra" character started to be received.

Interrupts would be better, but even the Arduino's interrupt-driven Serial interface can lose characters if there is a buffer overrun.

So far, that's all we really need for simple USART receipt of data. What about sending data out? Listing 9-10 shows how we can send a single byte down the wire via the USART.

Listing 9-10. USART sketch, sendByte() function

```
void sendByte(uint8_t c) {
    // Wait for bit UDRE0 to be set in UCSR0A then
    // buffer up the data byte.
    loop_until_bit_is_set(UCSR0A, UDRE0);      ①
    UDR0 = c;                                  ②
}
```

① Wait here until the data buffer is empty.

② Add the character to be sent to the buffer where it will be wrapped in a frame and transmitted.

Again, sending one byte is no fun, so the sendText() function in Listing 9-11 sends a whole string of characters.

Listing 9-11. USART sketch, sendText() function

```
void sendText(const uint8_t *text) {
    // Transmit a string of text. One byte
    // at a time.
    uint8_t *i = text;
    while (*i)
        sendByte(*i++);
}
```

The preceding code simply walks the passed buffer sending each character out through the USART transmitter until it finds the end of the string character, which does not get sent.

The sendNumber() function in Listing 9-12 allows you to send numeric data in almost any radix (number base) that you desire, although the default is 10. This only handles signed integer values – I leave it as an exercise for the reader to write a sendFloat() function.

Listing 9-12. USART sketch, sendNumber() function

```
void sendNumber(const long x, const uint8_t r = 10) {
    // Transmit a long integer to the USART. Only 32 bits
    // can be sent.
    char buffer[40];           ①
    ltoa(x, buffer, r);        ②
    sendText(buffer);          ③
}
```

① The length of a long is 32 bits, so 40 characters is enough of a buffer to cope without crashing. 2^{32} is 4,294,967,296 and is 10 digits in size. There's plenty room in 40 characters to hold a full unsigned number or a signed one, the smallest negative number being –2,147,483,648.

② The ltoa (long to ASCII) function does all the hard work. It also adds a terminating character to the buffer – which is another reason for having a bit extra on the end.

③ The buffered ASCII representation of the number is then transmitted.

The communicate() function in Listing 9-13 demonstrates some of the code we have seen earlier in action. It sends out the number $2^{32} - 1$ in various formats.

Listing 9-13. USART sketch, communicate() function

```
void communicate() {
    const long number = 4294967295;

    sendText("Number = 2^32 -1 in HEX: ");            ①
    sendNumber(4294967295, 16);
    sendByte('\n');

    sendText("Number = 2^32 -1 in DEC: ");            ②
    sendNumber(number, 10);
    sendByte('\n');

    sendText("Number = 2^32 -1 in OCT: ");            ③
    sendNumber(number, 8);
    sendByte('\n');

    sendText("Number = 2^32 -1 in BIN: ");            ④
    sendNumber(number, 2);
    sendByte('\n');

    sendText("\n\n");
    sendText("Type some text or numbers ... \n");
}
```

① This sends out a big number in hexadecimal. The number is $2^{32} - 1$ and is the biggest that will fit into a long data type.

② This sends out a big number in decimal. In this case, it gets printed as −1 because the parameter is signed in the call to ltoa() and $2^{32} - 1$ is indeed −1 when dealing with signed values.

③ This sends out a big number in octal.

④ This sends out a big number in binary.

The well-known and much loved setup() function is shown in Listing 9-14.

Listing 9-14. USART sketch, setup() function

```
void setup() {
    // Initialise the USART without needing Serial.
    setupUSART(9600);

    // Play with the USART.
    communicate();
}
```

This function simply initializes the USART by calling the setupUSART() function and then calls the communicate() function to "show off"! Finally, Listing 9-15 is the main loop() function.

Listing 9-15. USART sketch, loop() function

```
void loop() {
    uint8_t howManyChars;
    char buffer[101];
    // Buffer is one more than we want to receive.
    // Beware of buffer overruns, the code will lose
```

```
// characters as the USART can only store two characters.
howManyChars = receiveText(buffer, 100);
sendNumber(howManyChars);
sendByte('=');
sendByte('>');
sendText(buffer);
sendByte('\n');
}
```

The loop() function loops around – that's its job after all – and receives strings of text from the Serial Monitor. That will need to be configured to add a new line to the end of the sent text, or the code will not print any output until it has received a full buffer of 100 characters of text.

The function just receives text and prints it out, preceded by the number of characters it received. It uses two calls here to sendByte() which could, obviously, have been a single call to sendText(); but that's demonstrated in the next line.

If your input text is shorter than the buffer, the preceding discussion will work fine; if not, there's a strong possibility that characters may be lost. If, as I did, you send 102 characters to a buffer that holds 100, you get two lines of output, the first 100 characters and then the two remaining. However, if you send more than that, you get exactly the same output – the first hundred get copied to the buffer, the next two are still stored internally in the USART, and the rest, sadly, get lost due to a buffer overrun.

Welcome to the world of serial communications!

APPENDIX A

Arduino Paths

The installation paths, versions, etc. used in the book, relating to the Arduino IDE and the files to be found within that installation, are listed in the following. Be aware that these paths are valid for a download of the Arduino software as a zip file only. Downloading the installer, or, on Linux, running an install using the package manager for your distribution, may result in a different location.

My main workstation is Linux based, so most of the paths and others in the book refer to that, unless there is a specific need to refer to a Windows file or folder for any reason:

- $ARDVERS is 1.8.5.

- $ARDBASE is the location where I extracted the Arduino installation zip file. This is where you will find the file arduino.exe on Windows or arduino on Linux. These are the Arduino IDE for your operating system. My actual locations are

  - Linux – /home/norman/arduino-1.8.5

  - Windows – c:\users\norman\arduino-1.8.5

- $ARDINST is the location of the main Arduino files for AVR microcontrollers. This is $ARDBASE/hardware/arduino/avr and, on my Linux system, expands to /home/norman/arduino- 1.8.5/hardware/arduino/avr. This is where the various cores, bootloaders, variants, and so on are to be found.

© Norman Dunbar 2020
N. Dunbar, *Arduino Software Internals*, https://doi.org/10.1007/978-1-4842-5790-6

- $ARDINC is the location of many of the *.h header files and most of the *.c and *.cpp files that comprise the Arduino Language for AVR microcontrollers. This is, on my setup, $ARDINST/cores/arduino which expands to the path /home/norman/arduino- 1.8.5/hardware/arduino/avr/cores/arduino.

- Finally, $AVRINC is where the header files for the version of the AVR Library provided by the Arduino IDE are located. The Arduino Language (eventually) compiles down to calling functions within the AVR Library (henceforth referred to as AVRLib), and the header files are to be found in location $ARDBASE/hardware/tools/avr/avr/include or /home/norman/arduino-1.8.5/hardware/tools/avr/avr/include.

The following will be helpful on a Linux computer, if you wish to follow the text of the book and view the source code files referred to when I am describing the contents of such files. Listing A-1 is for Linux or MacOS users, while Listing A-2 is for Windows.

Listing A-1. shell_exports.sh for Linux and MacOS.

```
export ARDVERS=1.8.5
export ARDBASE="${HOME}"/arduino-"${ARDVERS}"
export ARDINST="${ARDBASE}"/hardware/arduino/avr
export ARDINC="${ARDINST}"/cores/arduino
export AVRINC="${ARDBASE}"/hardware/tools/avr/avr/include
```

Setting up the variable is simple:

```
source shell_exports.sh
```

The corresponding script for Windows users is shown in Listing A-2.

Listing A-2. shell_exports.bat for Windows 7

```
@echo off
set ARDVERS=1.8.5
set ARDBASE=%HOMEPATH%\arduino-%ARDVERS%
set ARDINST=%ARDBASE%\hardware\arduino\avr
set ARDINC=%ARDINST%\cores\arduino
set AVRINC=%ARDBASE%\hardware\tools\avr\avr\include
```

Alternatively, you could set the preceding environment variables up in Control Panel's System applet.

You should, obviously, change paths to suit your name and installation. You can now look at files, on Linux, by running the command

```
view ${ARDINC}/Arduino.h
```

You may, of course, replace view with your preferred editor, be it emacs, nano, or similar. If you have the xdgutils package installed, then the following command will open files in the default application:

```
xdg-open ${ARDINC}/Arduino.h
```

Similarly, on Windows, to open files in the default application, simply execute commands similar to the following, within a command-line session:

```
%ARDINC%/Arduino.h
```

This obviously assumes that files with an .h extension will have a default application set up to open them. If not, load them into your favorite text editor.

APPENDIX B

ATmega328P Pinout

Figure B-1 shows the position and names of the pins on an ATmega328P device.

ALT	Arduino	PCInt	AVR	Pin		Pin	AVR	PCInt	Arduino	ALT
RESET		PCINT14	PC6	1	U	28	PC5	PCINT13	D19/A5	SCL
RX	D0	PCINT16	PD0	2		27	PC4	PCINT12	D18/A4	SDA
TX	D1	PCINT17	PD1	3		26	PC3	PCINT11	D17/A3	
INT0	D2	PCINT18	PD2	4		25	PC2	PCINT10	D16/A2	
OC2B/INT1	D3/PWM	PCINT19	PD3	5		24	PC1	PCINT9	D15/A1	
XCK/T0	D4	PCINT20	PD4	6		23	PC0	PCINT8	D14/A0	
			VCC	7		22	GND			
			GND	8		21	AREF			
XTAL1/OSC1		PCINT6	PB6	9		20	AVCC			
XTAL2/OSC2		PCINT7	PB7	10		19	PB5	PCINT5	D13	SCK
OC0B/T1	D5/PWM	PCINT21	PD5	11		18	PB4	PCINT4	D12	MISO
OC0A/AIN0	D6/PWM	PCINT22	PD6	12		17	PB3	PCINT3	D11/PWM	OC2A/MOSI
AIN1	D7	PCINT23	PD7	13		16	PB2	PCINT2	D10/PWM	OC1B/SS
ICP1/CLKO	D8	PCINT0	PB0	14		15	PB1	PCINT1	D9/PWM	OC1A
ALT	Arduino	PCInt	AVR	Pin		Pin	AVR	PCInt	Arduino	ALT

Figure B-1. *ATmega328P pinout diagram*

In the preceding diagram, we have the following:

- The dark area in the center of the image is a representation of the ATmega328P – if you use your imagination, that is! At the top and bottom are labels identifying the contents of the appropriate columns.

© Norman Dunbar 2020
N. Dunbar, *Arduino Software Internals*, https://doi.org/10.1007/978-1-4842-5790-6

561

- Closest to the ATmega328P is the column labeled "Pin," and the numbers in those columns are the physical pin numbers on the device. The ATmega328P is a 28-pin device.

- The next column outward is labeled "AVR" and contains the names of the pins as defined by Atmel/Microchip. The Arduino uses a different naming standard. When reading the data sheet for the ATmega328P, these are the names that will be used.

- The columns labeled "PCInt" list the appropriate pin names, again defined by Atmel/Microchip, to be used when running code that handles Pin Change Interrupts. Here you see names such as PCINT0, PCINT5, etc.

- The next column outward, labeled "Arduino," indicates the Arduino pin names which can be used in your sketches. You should be familiar with names like D0, A5, etc. by now, I hope! Do remember the various Dn pins are not named like that in sketches; they just use the number. Pin D5 will be specified as just 5 in a sketch. The analogue pins, A0–A5, do use the A prefix.

- Finally, in the columns labeled "ALT," we have the list of alternate functions for a number of the pins. These alternate functions can be enabled using fuses in some cases or can be selected by setting bits in various control registers as necessary.

APPENDIX C

ATmega328P Power Restrictions

The ATmega328P is limited in the power it can source or sink:

- In total, the device can source or sink up to 200 mA maximum.

- On each port, however, only up to 100 mA maximum is allowed.

- On each individual pin, the limit is 40 mA maximum, but 20 mA is the preferred limit.

⚠️ Exceeding one or more of the power restrictions will probably damage your device and may render it useless, so take care. If you hear a click, notice a strange smell, and see blue smoke, then like me, you have overdone it!

The limits given mean that you should be thinking of using some form of a driver, a transistor, or a MOSFET, if you need to drive anything bigger than an LED on each pin. LEDs normally run around 20 mA. At least the red ones do – green and blue take more. A 2N2222 NPN transistor will safely drive up to 1000 mA and, with a 220 Ohm resistor between the Arduino and the base pin, will draw only around 15 mA from the Arduino – well within limits.

© Norman Dunbar 2020
N. Dunbar, *Arduino Software Internals*, https://doi.org/10.1007/978-1-4842-5790-6

C.1. Power in Total

The ATmega328P is restricted to a maximum of 200 mA power, sourced or sunk, in total over all the ports and pins.

C.2. Power per Port

You are advised, in the data sheet, that while each pin within a port can source or sink up to 20 mA, the total current for a single port must be limited to a maximum of 100 mA. This therefore limits each port to a maximum of five pins running at full power. However, on the ATmega328P, there are three ports, and the power restrictions on the entire chip are limited to 200 mA, so it is not possible to drive the microcontroller at capacity on all three ports.

C.3. Power per Pin

Although each pin can source or sink up to 40 mA, the data sheet warns that this should be restricted to a preferred maximum of 20 mA per pin, bearing in mind that each pin belongs to a port and ports have their own maximum power limit as does the device as a whole.

APPENDIX D

Predefined Settings

The Arduino init() function sets up a number of different features of the AVR microcontroller so that your sketch can make best use of same. These are briefly described in the following, all in one place, for reference.

D.1. Global Interrupts

Interrupts are enabled globally.

D.2. Timer/counter 0

Timer/counter 0 is configured with a divide-by-64 prescaler and in 8-bit *Fast Hardware* PWM mode to allow analogWrite() on pins D5 and D6. The PWM frequency is

```
System_clock / (Prescaler * 256)
= 16e6 / (64 * 256)
= 16e6 / 16384
= 976.5625 Hz
```

The Fast Hardware PWM mode simply counts up from 0 to 255, which is 256 different values, and then rolls over to 0 again for the next count up. The data sheet suggests that controlling motor speeds with Fast Hardware PWM isn't the best of ideas. (No, I don't know why either!) This would suggest that if you want to control motors, D5 and D6 are not the best pins to be used.

© Norman Dunbar 2020
N. Dunbar, *Arduino Software Internals*, https://doi.org/10.1007/978-1-4842-5790-6

Timer/counter 0 is also set up with an Overflow interrupt which updates the `millis()` counter via variables `timer0_millis`, `timer0_overflow_count`, and `timer0_fract`. These three variables account for the 9 bytes of Static RAM (SRAM) that every sketch uses as a minimum. There are two `unsigned longs` taking up 4 bytes each and one `unsigned char` using up the final byte.

`Timer0_millis` and `timer0_fract` are used by the `millis()` function, via the Timer/counter 0 Overflow interrupt ISR, while `timer0_overflow_count` is used by the `micros()` function and, from there, by the `delay()` function.

The Timer/counter 0 prescaler is set to divide the system clock by 64 meaning that the overflow occurs every 1 millisecond plus 24 microseconds. The `millis()` function carefully accounts for this.

Timer/counter 0 is set to use *Fast Hardware* PWM as using *Phase Correct* PWM would have interfered with the Timer/counter 0 Overflow interrupt, potentially breaking the `millis()` function by giving different values on the ATmega8 and ATmega168/ ATmega328 devices. The other two timers both use 8-bit *Phase Correct* PWM.

⚠️ If you disable timer/counter, or reconfigure it with a different prescaler value, for example, you will affect `micros()`, `millis()`, and `delay()`, as well as possibly affecting PWM on pins D5 and D6. Beware.

D.3. Timer/counters 1 and 2

Timer/counter 1 is a 16-bit timer, but is configured to provide 8-bit *Phase Correct* PWM on pins D9 and D10.

Timer/counter 2 is configured to provide 8-bit *Phase Correct* PWM on pins D3 and D11, and it is indeed an 8-bit timer.

Both timer/counters set the prescaler to divide the system clock by 64. This means that the PWM frequency is

```
System_clock / (Prescaler * 510)
= 16e6 / (64 * 510)
= 16e6 / 32649
= 490.196 Hz
```

Phase Correct PWM counts up from 0 to 255, then back down to 0, and so on. This is only 510 different values because 0 and 255 are not counted on the way up and down – the sequence would be 0, 1, 2 … 253, 254, 255, 254, 253 … 2, 1, 0, 1, 2, 3 … ad infinitum.

According to the data sheet, motors prefer Phase Correct PWM to control their speed, so if you want to control motors, D3, D9, D10, and D11 are your friends.

Disabling or reconfiguring these timer/counters will affect PWM (analogWrite()) on pins D9 and D10 (Timer/counter 1) and/or pins D3 and D11 (Timer/counter 2).

Timer/counter 2's ability to run in asynchronous mode, with an external 32 KHz crystal, *cannot* be used. This is because the Arduino boards come with a 16 MHz crystal attached to the pins that the asynchronous timer mode needs, and the ATmega328P has its fuses set to disable the calibrated internal RC oscillator so that the external one with the 16 MHz crystal can be used.

D.4. USART

The USART, which was enabled by the bootloader, is subsequently disabled by the init() function allowing pins D0 and D1 to be used as digital pins in the normal manner. This therefore requires that pins D0 and D1 be reconfigured as the USART when serial communications are required. This is automatically carried out by calling Serial.begin() in a sketch.

> **i** Some other AVR microcontrollers, notably the Mega 2560, have multiple USARTs, but the ATmega328P only has one, and it uses these two pins for communicating with the outside world.

D.5. Analogue to Digital Converter

The ADC is configured with a prescaler of 128 which divides the system clock by 128 to get an ADC clock frequency of 125 KHz, which is within the desired range of between 50 and 200 KHz. In addition, the ADC is enabled and powered on in every sketch, whether or not it is used.

You can disable the ADC and power it down to save a few microAmps, if it is not required in your sketch by adding the code in Listing D-1 to your setup() function.

Listing D-1. Disable and power down the ADC

```
#include <avr/power.h>

void setup() {
    // Disable ADC if not used.
    ADCSRA &= ~(1 << ADEN);

    // Power off ADC.
    power_adc_disable();
}
```

APPENDIX E

ADC Temperature Measuring

Some AVR microcontrollers have an internal temperature measuring device, which can be selected to be used as an input to the ADC and used to query the actual running temperature of the AVR microcontroller itself. This is not the temperature of the air around the Arduino board/AVR microcontroller; it is the temperature of the AVR microcontroller itself. Measuring the air temperature requires some kind of external temperature sensor.

This internal sensor is not accessible directly from the Arduino Language, but with a little effort, it can be done.

 The data sheet for the ATmega328P states that

If the user has a fixed voltage source connected to the AREF *pin, the user may not use the other reference voltage options in the application, as they will be shorted to the external voltage. If no external voltage is applied to the* AREF *pin, the user may switch between* AVCC *and 1.1V as reference selection.*

This means don't connect a voltage source to the AREF pin if you are going to set up the ADC to use any other reference voltage. If you do, your AVR microcontroller will possibly allow the *magic blue smoke* out and will stop working.

© Norman Dunbar 2020
N. Dunbar, *Arduino Software Internals*, https://doi.org/10.1007/978-1-4842-5790-6

Bearing the preceding warning in mind and looking at the schematics, the Arduino Duemilanove and the Uno Mark3 do not normally have AREF connected to a voltage source. There is, however, a location on one of the headers labeled "AREF" where you can supply a voltage to the AREF pin. This is limited to a maximum of 5.5 V and shouldn't be higher than the supply voltage.

As previously discussed, the ATmega328P has an on-chip temperature sensor. This can be read using channel 8 of the ADC and returns a value which represents the temperature in degrees *Kelvin*. Kelvin is similar to Centigrade, but is offset by 273 degrees, so 0 degrees Centigrade is 273 degrees Kelvin.

In order to set up the ADC to measure the AVR microcontroller's own temperature, you need to configure certain registers, as follows:

- The ADC reference voltage must be configured to use the internal 1.1 V reference by setting bits REFS1:0 to 11_{binary} in register ADMUX. You cannot use any other reference voltage for internal temperature measurements using the ADC. However, to use the internal 1.1 V reference, you **must not have the external** AREF **pin connected to any source of voltage** (see the preceding warning).

- Register ADMUX, bits MUX3-0, must be set to 1000_{binary} to enable the temperature sensor as the ADC input source.

- As with all ADC measurements, the ADC clock *must* be in the range 50–200 KHz. The Arduino runs with a 16 MHz crystal attached, so the system clock speed is far too high. In order to reduce the clock speed, the ADC prescaler must be set so that the system clock is divided down by a suitable amount to get the ADC clock into the required range. Dividing by 128 will give a value of 125 MHz, so the ADCSRA register bits ADPS2:0 should be set to 111_{binary} to achieve this.

- Register ADCSRA, bits ADEN and ADSC, should both be set to 1_{binary} to enable the ADC and to automatically start the first measurement.

---

i In the following example code, the ADC noise reduction settings are not being used. See the data sheet or Chapter 7, Section 7.3.9.2, *"ADC Noise Reduction Sleep Mode,"* for details if you wish to enable that feature. It's a special sleep mode which powers everything down apart from the ADC.

In Listing E-1, the setup() function carries out all of the preceding initialization.

Listing E-1. Initializing the ADC for temperature measurements

```
void setup() {
    // Initialise the ADC to use the
    // internal 1.1V reference voltage.
    ADMUX = (1 << REFS0) | (1 << REFS1);              ①

    // Use the ADC multiplexer input
    // number 8, the temperature sensor.
    ADMUX |= (1 << MUX3);                             ②

    // Slow the ADC clock down to 125 KHz
    // by dividing by 128. Assumes that the
    // standard Arduino 16 MHz clock is in use.
    ADCSRA = (1 << ADPS2) | (1 << ADPS1) | (1 << ADPS0);   ③
```

```
// Non-standard 8MHz clock in use.
//ADCSRA = (1 << ADPS2) | (1 << ADPS1) | (0 << ADPS0);  ④
// Enable the ADC and discard the first reading as
// it is always 351 on my device.
ADCSRA |= (1 << ADEN) | (1 << ADSC);                    ⑤
(void)readADC();

// Use the Serial monitor for output.
Serial.begin(9600);
Serial.println("Arduino Internal Temperature");
}
```

① This sets the internal 1.1 V bandgap as the ADC's reference voltage. This is mandatory when using the temperature sensor. You *must* make sure that there are no external voltages on the AREF pin of the Arduino, or else this setting makes the magic blue smoke out and causes the device to stop working. A 100 nF capacitor, between AREF and GND, is acceptable, but connecting to AREF to 5 V is not.

② This use of a reserved value for the ADMUX register is the one that selects the internal temperature sensor as the ADC input source.

③ I have an Arduino Duemilanove, an Uno, and a few homemade "NormDuinos"; and I need to uncomment one of these two lines depending on which board I'm using. My "NormDuinos" run at 8 MHz, while the Arduino boards run at 16 MHz. The main clock frequency needs to be divided down to get it into the range of 50–200 KHz.

④ This is the line for my 8 MHz devices.

⑤   I've noticed that the first reading from the ADC is
always a bit weird, at least when using the temperature
sensor. These lines start the ADC conversion and wait
for completion before throwing away the result

The readADC() function called from setup(), to throw away the first
reading, and on each pass through the loop() can be seen in Listing E-2.

Listing E-2. Reading the temperature

```
// Read the ADC result from the most recent conversion and
// start another before returning the current reading.
  uint16_t readADC() {
    // Make sure the most recent ADC read is complete.
      while ((ADCSRA & (1 << ADSC))) {                          ①
        ; // Just wait for ADC to finish.
    }

    uint16_t result = ADCW;                                     ②

    // Initiate another reading.
    ADCSRA |= (1 << ADSC);                                      ③

    return result;
}
```

①   The previous call to readADC() initiated a new read
request, so these lines simply make sure that the
request has completed and a reading is available.
The ADSC bit is used to start a conversion and
remains set to 1_{binary} until the conversion finishes,
whereupon it is cleared to 0_{binary}.

②   We grab the result from ADCW which takes care of
reading the high and low bytes of the ADC result
in the correct order. This ensures that we get the
correct value read and not some intermediate result.

③   Prior to returning the result just read from the sensor, this line initiates a new reading. The temperature sensor can only be read in single-shot mode. There's no opportunity to initiate a free running mode with the sensor.

The loop() function in Listing E-3 gathers a running average of 100 readings from the ADC and then converts the final total to degrees Centigrade which is then printed to the serial monitor.

Listing E-3. Displaying the temperature

```
void loop() {
    // Running average of the ADC Readings for
    // better accuracy.
    uint32_t ADCTotal = 0;
    float ADCAverage = 0.0;
    uint16_t ADCReading = readADC();

    for (uint8_t x = 1; x < 101; x++) {                     ①
        ADCTotal += ADCReading;
        ADCAverage = (float)ADCTotal / (float)x;

        // Uncomment if you want a running commentary!     ②
        /*
        Serial.print("ADC = ");
        Serial.print(ADCReading);
        Serial.print(" ");
        Serial.print("ADCTotal = ");
        Serial.print(ADCTotal);
        Serial.print(" ");
        Serial.print("ADCAverage = ");
        Serial.println(ADCAverage);
        */
```

```
    ADCReading = readADC();
}

// Print the ADC temperature.
float degreesC = (ADCAverage - 324.31) / 1.22;          ③
Serial.print(degreesC);
Serial.print("C, ");

// Convert to Fahrenheit. C * 1.8 + 32.                 ④
Serial.print(degreesC * 1.8 + 32);
Serial.println("F.");

// Delay a second more between readings.
delay(1000);
}
```

①   A running average of 100 readings from the sensor
    is calculated here. This avoids most of the weirdness
    that can sometimes arise, especially as the code is
    not using the ADC's Noise Reduction sleep mode
    to try and get better readings. Whatever else is
    happening on the device might be affecting the
    readings.

②   The comment says it all! If you want to see how the
    running average builds up, uncomment these lines.

③   I've decided to use this method of converting the
    ADC reading from something related to degrees
    Kelvin to degrees Centigrade. This method is closest
    to my reality and my measured temperatures in the
    office. See the following for details.

④ And for those who like their temperatures in "old money," this line converts degrees Centigrade to degrees Fahrenheit.

According to the Internet, example documents from Atmel/Microchip, and elsewhere, there are many ways to calculate the internal temperature from the reading returned by the ADC. Here are some that I've come across:

- ADC - some random offset – This is different for every device.

- (ADC - 247) / 1.22.

- ADC - 273 – This one looks promising as it corresponds to converting degrees Kelvin to Centigrade.

- (((ADC - (273 - 100 - TS_OFFSET)) ∗ 128) / TS_GAIN) + 25 – Sadly, getting the TS_OFFSET and TS_GAIN is not simple. The documents mentioned in the following warning have the details.

- (ADC - 324.31) / 1.22.

I'm using the last one, as it's the one closest to my actual temperature measurements.

Each time around the loop(), the ADC has to be coaxed into running another conversion, so bit ADSC in register ADCSRA is again set to 1_{binary} to trigger another reading.

Converting to degrees Fahrenheit, for those who still measure temperature in *old money,* is done usually by multiplying Centigrade by 1.8 and adding 32, so that's what happens next; and the resulting temperature is printed out to the Serial Monitor. Using float data types in a sketch pulls in a lot more code than normal, so it's best, if possible, to avoid them – unless you have lots of spare Flash RAM of course.

⚠ According to the data sheet, *uncalibrated* sensor data is accurate to plus or minus 10 degrees Centigrade. That's quite a range of possible temperatures then. The Application Note at `http://ww1.microchip.com/downloads/en/AppNotes/Atmel-8108-Calibration-of-the-AVRs-Internal-Temperature-Reference_ApplicationNote_AVR122.pdf` shows how the device can be calibrated, and even after that, there's only a possible best accuracy of plus or minus 2 degrees Centigrade.

APPENDIX F

Assembly Language: Briefly

I know I promised that there wouldn't be any assembly language code in the book, but I did say *probably*.

This appendix is a very brief introduction to Arduino assembly language which is supported in the IDE now, whereas it wasn't all that many versions ago that you had to make some changes to the IDE source code and recompile in order to get assembly code noticed.

One thing you must remember: assembly source files have the extension "S," in uppercase. If you have the "s" in lowercase, it won't compile as the file won't be found.

Open the Arduino IDE and create a new sketch, call it "BlinkASM," and immediately save it. Make the sketch resemble the code in Listing F-1.

Listing F-1. Arduino BlinkASM sketch

```
// Make sure the compiler can find 'blink' which is
// written elsewhere in assembly language.
extern "C" void blink();       ①

void setup() {
    pinMode(13, OUTPUT);       ②
}
```

© Norman Dunbar 2020

N. Dunbar, *Arduino Software Internals*, https://doi.org/10.1007/978-1-4842-5790-6

```
void loop() {
    blink();                        ③
    delay(1000);
}
```

① This is how we tell the IDE that we have a `void` function, called `blink`, which takes no parameters and is written in a language other than C++. We use "C" to make sure that the compiler doesn't attempt to do any C++ "name mangling" of function names and/or parameter names.

② We still need D13 as an output pin, for this example anyway.

③ This is where we call the assembly language function.

So far, so good? Nothing to be afraid of here. Next though, we have the assembly language code itself:

- Add a new tab to the opened sketch in the IDE. There's a downward arrow on the far right of the IDE's tab bar, where the tab for "BlinkASM" is currently showing. Click the arrow and choose "New Tab."

- Enter the name "BlinkASM.S" in the filename prompt area at the bottom of the screen and click OK. Make sure the file's extension is "S" in uppercase.

Now enter the assembly language code in Listing F-2 into the new tab.

Listing F-2. Arduino assembly language

```
#define __SFR_OFFSET 0                                      ①
#include <avr/io.h>                                         ②

.section .text                                              ③
.global blink                                               ④

blink:                                                      ⑤
    // digitalWrite(13, !(digitalRead(13)));                ⑥
    ldi r18, (1 << PORTB5)  ; PORTB5 = Arduino D13
    out PINB, r18           ; Toggle PORTB5 = D13
    ret
```

① Apparently, a hack! But this makes sure we get the correct offset for the PINB and PORTB names used in the following. AVRs are weird and these things – I/O addresses – have two addresses in memory (technically incorrect, but pretty much accurate!)

② This fetches the correct header file for the device we are using. This means we can refer to PORTB and PINB by name and not as a number.

③ Code, mostly, lives in the text section. We need our code to live there too.

④ As we wish to call blink() from other files, our sketch in particular, we need to make the entry point for the blink function visible.

⑤ This is the entry point to the blink() function.

⑥ This is the Arduino Language equivalent to the following two lines of assembly code.

Now compile the sketch. You can do this from either tab in the IDE. You should see the usual text scrolling up the screen – if you have verbose compilation messages enabled in the File ➤ Preferences dialogue. At the very end of the compilation, you should see the usual details on the size of the sketch and so on. Mine used 720 bytes of Flash RAM and the usual 9 bytes of Static RAM. This is another reduction in the size of the blink sketch, and we are *still* using a lot of Arduino Language code.

You should now be able to upload the sketch to your board and be amazed as the built-in LED starts blinking, yet again!

Obviously, this is a really minimal example, and unless you really need the speed and space reductions of code written in plain AVR assembly, then you should not often need to resort to assembly language, but at least it's now available in the IDE.

You do still need an `.ino` sketch file to be able to use the IDE for assembly language. That factor hasn't yet gone away – you cannot, as yet, write a complete sketch in assembly language. Well, you *can* but you would be using AVR Studio or PlatformIO to do it. The Arduino IDE or `arduino-cli` both require a sketch file.

APPENDIX G

Smallest Blink Sketch?

Okay, here's one last blink sketch, and could this one be the smallest we can get? I wonder. It requires the PlatformIO system as the Arduino IDE or command line and wraps too much extraneous code around an assembly language module. The following code in Listing G-1 compiled to 478 bytes with 9 bytes of SRAM used in the Arduino IDE and also with the arduino-cli utility. In PlatformIO, it's 162 bytes in total with no bytes of precious SRAM used.

Here's the process:

```
mkdir SmallestBlink
cd SmallestBlink
pio init --board uno
```

Listing G-1 shows what the platformio.ini file should look like for an Arduino Uno build. The framework - arduino line must be removed, or PlatformIO will compile all the usual Arduino code into the finished file. I had to add in the upload_port line as the code wouldn't upload without it and a helpful error message advised me what to do. (My Uno has an FTDI chip.)

Listing G-1. The platform.ini file

```
[env:uno]
platform = atmelavr
board = uno
upload_port = /dev/ttyUSB0
```

© Norman Dunbar 2020
N. Dunbar, *Arduino Software Internals*, https://doi.org/10.1007/978-1-4842-5790-6

We now need to determine the flash rate for a 16 MHz Arduino Uno running at a blink rate of 1 MHz with a divide-by-256 prescaler. The formula for the *frequency* of a Timer/counter 1 in CTC mode is

```
F = F_CPU / ((2 * prescaler) * (1 + OCR1A))

OCR1A = ((F_CPU / (2 * prescaler)) / Frequency) - 1
```

This gives

```
((16e6 / (2 * 256)) / 1 MHz) -1

=> (16e6 / 512) -1
=> 31,250 -1
=  31,249
```

This is the value for register OCR1A.

Type in the code shown in Listing G-2 into the file src/SmallestBlink.S.

Listing G-2. The smallest blink sketch?

```
#include <avr/io.h>

.section .text

.global main

#define FLASH_RATE 31249

main:
    ldi r18, (1 << DDB1)
    out _SFR_IO_ADDR(DDRB), r18          ; ①

    ; Set up Timer 1:
    ldi r18, (1 << COM1A0)
    sts TCCR1A, r18                      ; ②
```

```
    ldi r18, hi8(FLASH_RATE)              ; ③
    sts OCR1AH, r18

    ldi r18,lo8(FLASH_RATE)
    sts OCR1AL, r18

    ; Finish setup of Timer 1.
    ldi r18, ((1 << WGM12)|(1 << CS12))  ; ④
    sts TCCR1B, r18

loop:
    rjmp loop                            ; ⑤
```

① This sets pin 15 or PB1 or Arduino pin D9 as OUTPUT. We have to use the _SFR_IO_ADDR macro here; otherwise, the I/O register addresses used in our instructions will be 32 bytes too high!

② This puts the timer/counter into CTC mode with the pin PB1, Arduino D9, toggling every time we hit the value in OCR1A.

③ The next four lines load the value 31,249 into the OCR1A register. It must be done in two 8-bit chunks, and the high byte *must always be written first*.

④ The timer/counter is now set to run with a divide-by-256 prescaler and in CTC mode (Clear Timer on Compare). When the timer/counter's value reaches that in OCR1A, the timer/counter's value resets to zero, and the PB1 pin will toggle.

⑤ This is effectively like an empty loop() in a sketch. It does nothing except burn CPU cycles looping around itself.

⚠ As noted in the preceding text, when writing 16-bit values to *important* registers, you must note the advice in the data sheet to load the bytes in the order given. When you write the high byte, it is stored in a temporary register. When the low byte is then written, both bytes are written to the register as one operation. This prevents the possibility of a "split" value in the register.

When reading OCR1A, you read the low byte first and then the high byte to get the correct value.

Save the file, and exit the editor. Run a test compile:

```
pio run
```

There should be no errors. Now upload the code:

```
pio run -t upload
```

There should be an LED on pin D9 (PB1 or physical pin 15) on the Uno, connected to ground through an appropriate resistor – I used a 330 Ohm resistor on a 5 V setup, giving a maximum current of

```
(5V - 1.8V) / 330        ①

=> 3.2V / 330
= 9.69 milliAmps          ②
```

① This is the VCC voltage minus the forward voltage of the LED in particular. Mine is 1.8 V according to the data sheet, and this is a good default value for a red LED.

② This value is well within the *absolute* maximum value of 40 milliAmps allowed on a single pin and, also, well within the *recommended* maximum of 20 milliAmps.

The LED *should* be blinking away merrily at around 1 Hz, or 1 flash per second, but it is running faster – why? Figure G-1 shows the oscilloscope trace on the Uno's pin D9 while the code was running.

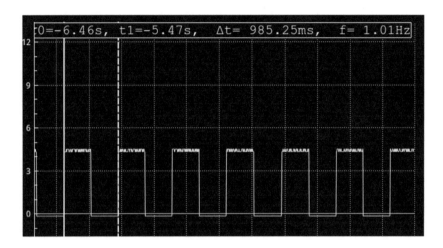

Figure G-1. *SmallestBlink Oscilloscope trace*

It clearly states in the upper-right corner that the frequency is 1 Hz. However, while that may be true, it does mean that the waveform is HIGH for 50% and LOW for the other 50% of that time; hence, the LED is actually flashing every half second. Oops! To get a 1-second *flash,* I need to calculate a 0.5 Hz frequency.

Edit the code in Listing G-2 to change one setting:

```
#define FLASH_RATE 62499
```

Recompile and upload, and finally, the LED is flashing once per second. I can check my calculations by feeding the value I recalculated back into the equation for frequency:

```
F = F_CPU / ((2 * prescaler) * (OCR1A + 1))
```

```
=> 16e6 / (( 2 * 256) * (62499 + 1))
=> 16e6 / (512 * 62500)
=> 16e6 / 32e6
=  0.5 Hz.
```

So that seems to be correct. The oscilloscope now reads 504 mHz in the upper left, so that's pretty close to 0.5 Hz. I'm happy with that.

The best thing about this blink sketch is that Timer/counter 1 is doing all the blinking by itself. The CPU is doing nothing except burning cycles in a tight loop. It would be entirely possible to put the ATmega328P to sleep to reduce power or to actually have it do "something useful" with its time.

That's it! No more blink sketches and definitely no more assembly language!

APPENDIX H

NormDuino

You can build your own "Arduino" on a breadboard and play with it there, if you feel the need. I have done this for some of the experiments in this book – just to be sure that things worked perfectly whether I was running a full-speed, 16 MHz Arduino board like my Duemilanove or my Uno or a breadboarded experimental system running at 8 MHz on the internal oscillator.

This is the sort of thing you might find interesting. After all, there's no point having a fully blown Arduino board, with all the attendant paraphernalia such as USB communications, always-on power LED, etc. – things that can waste power – when they are not needed in your finished project. It's great to use the Arduino for prototyping, but when you go into "production," you only need a handful of components.

If you look at the schematics in Figure H-1, you will notice that there's a diode between the board and the battery. This is for two reasons: it drops 0.7 V of the incoming 6 V battery supply, taking the voltage down to 5.3 V and within range of the ATmega328P's 5.5 V maximum, and it prevents damage if you connect the battery the wrong way around.

A 16 MHz crystal and a pair of 22 pF capacitors will be required if you can't get hold of an ATmega328P without the Uno bootloader already burned in. It is quite simple to burn a new bootloader so that the ATmega328P doesn't need the 16 MHz crystal and others. It is however a bit of a faff (that's a technical term) as you have to create a new entry in `boards.txt` and burn an 8 MHz bootloader and reset a couple of fuses along the way. This is the sort of thing that requires an ICSP device, although you could use an existing Arduino as the ICSP.

© Norman Dunbar 2020

N. Dunbar, *Arduino Software Internals*, https://doi.org/10.1007/978-1-4842-5790-6

So, if you have an ATmega328P with an Uno bootloader, you will
need the crystal and the capacitors plus a 6 V supply (which drops to
5.3 V, thanks to the diode); and if you get an ATmega328P without an
Uno bootloader, you will be able to run it at 3 V without the crystal and
capacitors, but 4.5 V will be better as the diode will drop that to 3.8 V which
is ample.

The following image is the schematic layout for what I'm calling
NormDuino. You can see that it is quite simple. All it needs is a power
supply, a spare ATmega328P, a couple of resistors, a switch, a diode, and a
handful of capacitors.

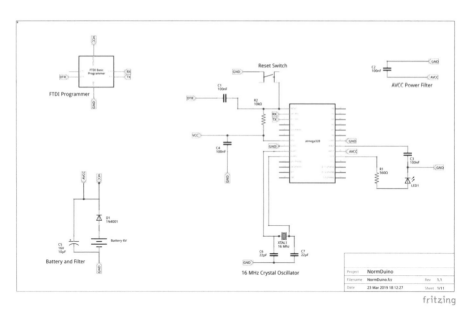

Figure H-1. *NormDuino schematic*

As you can see, there's nothing to it. You will note, I hope, that the AREF pin is not connected to anything other than a 100 nF capacitor to smooth out the power *if* you decide to connect it to VCC. For safety, and to avoid letting the magic blue smoke out, it's best to heed the warnings in the data sheet, and do not set the ADC reference voltage to the internal one if you have the AREF pin connected to an external power source.

By not connecting it in the breadboard setup, you avoid this problem and can safely use the internal 1.1 V reference for the Analogue Comparator and/or the ADC.

Figure H-2 shows how it looks when laid out on a half-sized breadboard, with power lines running down both sides.

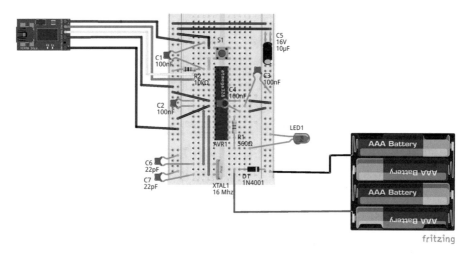

Figure H-2. *NormDuino breadboard layout*

As mentioned in the preceding text, the crystal, XTAL1; two capacitors, C6 and C7; and the two wires, at the bottom left of the breadboard, may be omitted if you have an ATmega328P without an Uno bootloader programmed in. It will, in the factory default settings, be configured to run off of the 8 MHz internal oscillator with a divide-by-8 prescaler, giving your breadboard Arduino a top speed of a whopping 1 MHz; but that can be changed.

When done and tested on the breadboard, you wouldn't want to put the breadboard into a box and use that in your finished project, so you can purchase copper-clad board that is designed to resemble a breadboard, and it's an easy task then to move each component from the breadboard to the copper board and solder it in place. You would probably need or wish to add five pins to the board as well, to allow the FTDI access to the ATmega328P, in order to reprogram it, should this ever be necessary.

Alternatively, some normal stripboard can be used, and just break each track up the middle and you have your own, handmade breadboard on a copper-clad board. I have two NormDuinos that I built in this way, one on a copper breadboard layout and the other on a simple stripboard.

ⓘ Some FTDI devices have their TX and RX pins labeled the other way around. The ATmega328P's physical pin 2 is its RX pin, and that needs to be connected to the programmer's TX pin. The ATmega328P's physical pin 3 is its TX pin, and that needs to be connected to the programmer's RX pin. On my FTDI, the pins are labeled RXO and TXO (RX and TX Output), and those need connecting to the ATmega328P's corresponding input pins, so RXO goes to TX and TXO goes to RX. Your device, of course, may well differ, so if it doesn't work, just swap the wires over and try again – you won't damage anything if the wires are crossed.

Confused? I was too. When I first started using the FTDI, I couldn't get it to see the ATmega328P, so it couldn't program it. In the end, swapping the wires over solved the problem.

Welcome to the world of old-style serial communications. Nowadays, the pins are connected like to like – so MOSI connects to MOSI and MISO connects to MISO – there's a lot less confusion that way.

Your project is now complete. The bill of materials (BOM) for the NormDuino is shown in Table H-1.

Table H-1. *BOM for a single NormDuino*

ITEM	QTY	Label	Purpose
ATmega328P	1	AVR1	The brains!
560 R resistor 1/4 W	1	R1	For the LED on D13, pin 19
10 K resistor 1/4 W	1	R2	Pullup resistor on RST pin, pin 1
Red 5 mm LED	1	LED1	The "built-in" LED, Arduino style
Momentary push button	1	S1	Reset button
100 nF ceramic capacitors	4	C1, C2, C3, C4	To decouple VCC, AVCC, and AREF and for DTR when programming
10 uF 16 V electrolytic capacitor	1	C5	Decoupling the power supply
1N4001 diode	1	D1	Reverse polarity protection, voltage dropper
16 MHz crystal	1	XTAL1	Optional: For ATmega328P with the Uno bootloader only
22 pF ceramic capacitors	2	C6, C7	Optional: For ATmega328P with the Uno bootloader only
Battery pack	1	VCC1	Power supply. 6 V for ATmega328P with the Uno bootloader, 4.5 V otherwise

If your ATmega328P came with an Uno bootloader, then you can use an FTDI device or an ICSP to program it. If the microcontroller came without a bootloader, and you don't have an ICSP of your own, you could use an existing Arduino as an ICSP, as detailed in Appendix I, which is coming next.

APPENDIX I

No ICSP? No Problem!

So you managed to buy an ATmega328P, but it came without an Uno Bootloader burned in. You don't have an ICSP to program it yourself, so what can you do? Well, you cannot burn a bootloader without an ICSP, and that could leave you a tad stuck, but Arduino to the rescue.

It's quite easy to do, and there are recent details on the Arduino Tutorials section of the Arduino web site at `www.arduino.cc/en/ Tutorial/ArduinoISP`. The steps are as follows:

- Load your Arduino with the example sketch "ArduinoISP" – go to File ➤ Examples ➤ArduinoISP ➤ ArduinoISP in the IDE.

- Compile it, and upload to your Arduino in the normal manner.

- Connect the breadboarded ATmega328P to your Arduino as detailed in the following.

- Burn the bootloader.

I.1. ArduinoISP Sketch

This is a sketch that converts an Arduino into an ICSP device. It is supplied with the IDE and can be found under File ➤ Examples ➤ ArduinoISP ➤ ArduinoISP. Simply open the sketch, compile, and upload it to your Arduino, in the normal manner.

© Norman Dunbar 2020
N. Dunbar, *Arduino Software Internals*, https://doi.org/10.1007/978-1-4842-5790-6

Your Arduino is now able to be used as an ICSP device.

ℹ️ From this point onward, the Arduino you have just programmed will be referred to as "Arduino (ICSP)," while the device you wish to program will be known as "Breadboard ATmega328P."

One thing you will also need is a 10 uF capacitor between the RESET and GND holes in the Arduino (ICSP) board header. This is required, to prevent the Arduino (ICSP) from being reset when it starts to upload the new sketch to the breadboard ATmega328P.

⚠️ The chances are that you will be using an electrolytic capacitor, so make sure that the negative lead is pushed into GND; otherwise, you might cause the capacitor to burst.

I.2. Connections

To program the breadboard ATmega328P, you need to connect four wires to it, from the Arduino ICSP, in addition to the power and ground lines of course. The connections are shown in Table I-1.

Table I-1. *ArduinoISP connections*

ICSP	ATmega328P	Description
D10	Pin 1	Used to reset the breadboard ATmega328P
D11	Pin 17	MOSI – Master Out Slave In
D12	Pin 18	MISO – Master In Slave Out
D13	Pin 19	SCK – system clock

Figure I-1 shows how the connections should look. Only the bare essential components are installed on the breadboard. This is just to burn the bootloader, nothing else. Maybe C2 and C3 are a little superfluous, but extra power supply filtering isn't a bad thing!

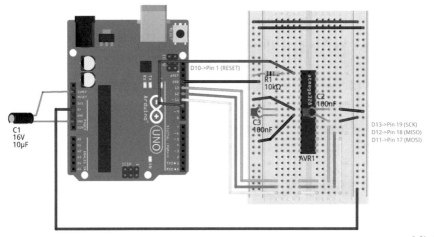

Figure I-1. *ArduinoISP*

There are three additional, but optional, connections you can make, if you are a big fan of flashing LEDs! These are optional and listed in Table I-2.

Table I-2. *ArduinoISP optional connections*

ICSP	Description
D7	Programming indicator
D8	Error indicator
D9	Heartbeat

These pins should be connected to a resistor, with a value between 330 and 560 Ohms, and from there to the positive (longest) lead of an LED. The short lead of the LED goes to GND. I use a red LED for the error indicator, green for the heartbeat, and yellow for the programming indicator. However, these are optional.

I.3. Choose Your Programmer

In the IDE, select Tools ➤ Programmer and look for the option "Arduino as ISP." Do not select "ArduinoISP" – that is not the programmer you want. Trust me. I know from bitter experience!

I.4. Burn the Bootloader

In the IDE, choose the settings you require for the breadboard ATmega328P by selecting the appropriate choices from the Tools ➤ Boards and, if required, Tools ➤Processor and so on. Normally, your selection here would be to simply pick the Uno as the board.

And finally, Tools ➤ Burn Bootloader is all you need.

After a couple of seconds, you should see a message that the bootloader has been burned. You now have burned the Uno bootloader *and* set the required fuses. The breadboard ATmega328P can now be programmed with an FTDI adaptor.

⚠️ You can only select the Uno in the preceding text, if you have the 16 MHz crystal and associated capacitors. If you don't have, and NormDuino doesn't, then Appendix J shows how you can set up a special breadboard device that runs at 8 MHz on the internal oscillator – just like NormDuino.

APPENDIX J

Breadboard 8 MHz Board Setup

The following steps should be carried out with the IDE closed.

We first need to discover if your installation has the directory named $YOUR_LOCATION/packages/arduino/hardware/avr/n.n.n/ present. N.n.n is a version number. Mine was 1.6.3 for Arduino version 1.8.5, but as I've been applying various updates, it is now at 1.8.2.

$YOUR_LOCATION is as follows:

- On Linux, look in /home/<YOUR_NAME>/.arduino15/.

- On Windows 7, look in C:\Users\<YOUR_NAME>\ AppData\Local\Arduino15a. I believe that on older versions of Windows, the file can be found in c:\ Documents and Settings\<YOUR_NAME>\Application Data\Arduino\.

- On MacOS, I believe you can look in /Users/<YOUR_ NAME>/Library/Arduino/, but I don't have access to a Mac to check, sorry.

Find the correct location and, to be sure, check to see if boards.txt, platform.txt, and programmers.txt exist. If so, you are in the correct location.

N. Dunbar, *Arduino Software Internals*, https://doi.org/10.1007/978-1-4842-5790-6

ℹ️ I know this looks like a different location from all the other files I've been discussing in the rest of this book, however, regardless of where you install or download the Arduino IDE and the software, much of the working packages and files are hidden away in the preceding locations.

Check for the existence of an 8 MHz bootloader. There should be one supplied for the ATmega boards. Look for a file named `ATmegaBOOT_168_atmega328_pro_8MHz.hex` in the directory `$YOUR_LOCATION/packages/arduino/hardware/avr/n.n.n/bootloaders/atmega/`. If you find it, all is good.

If the 8 MHz bootloader file is not found on your system, then please follow the instructions at `www.arduino.cc/en/Tutorial/ArduinoToBreadboard` instead of mine in the following. You will need a few more files to make the breadboard 8 MHz Arduino (or NormDuino) work. The section you are interested in is the one with the title *Minimal Circuit (Eliminating the External Clock)*, specifically, the numbered list of steps to follow on downloading and adding support for a breadboarded 8 MHz device.

I'm assuming that you did find the bootloader? If so, go to `$YOUR_LOCATION/packages/arduino/hardware/avr/n.n.n/` and add the code in Listing J-1, to the end of `boards.local.txt` if it exists. If it doesn't exist yet, simply create a new file with that name and add the code in Listing J-1 to it.

The code defines an "Arduino" on a breadboard, which is desired to be run on the internal oscillator, at 8 MHz, similar to NormDuino described in Appendix H. Because the bootloader already exists, all that is needed is the `boards.local.txt` file.

Listing J-1. The boards.local.txt settings

```
B8.name=Breadboard 8 MHz
B8.upload.protocol=arduino
B8.upload.maximum_size=30720
B8.upload.speed=57600
B8.bootloader.low_fuses=0xE2
B8.bootloader.high_fuses=0xDA
B8.bootloader.extended_fuses=0x05
B8.bootloader.file=atmega/ATmegaBOOT_168_atmega328_pro_8MHz.hex
B8.bootloader.unlock_bits=0x3F
B8.bootloader.lock_bits=0x0F
B8.build.mcu=atmega328p
B8.build.f_cpu=8000000L
B8.build.core=arduino:arduino
B8.build.variant=arduino:standard
B8.build.board=BB8
B8.bootloader.tool=arduino:avrdude
B8.upload.tool=arduino:avrdude
```

Once the boards.local.txt file has been saved, you may restart the IDE.

You will need an ICSP, or an Arduino as an ISP as described in Appendix I, to program the bootloader into the AVR microcontroller. The steps are as follows:

- Open the IDE and using Tools ➤ Boards, find the entry for "Breadboard 8 MHz."

- Choose the appropriate programmer. Mine is "USBtiny," but "Arduino as ISP" is another option especially if you still have the setup described in Appendix I.

- Choose Tools ➤ Burn Bootloader.

After a few seconds of activity, you should see a prompt that the bootloader has been burned. You can now remove the ICSP device and switch back to an FTDI converter to do the subsequent programming. Don't forget to select Tools ➤ Programmer in the IDE and change the programmer back to "AVRISP mk11" so that you can start using the bootloader.

You now have an Arduino-compatible device that is running on a breadboard at 8 MHz and doesn't require a 16 MHz crystal and associated capacitors and which can be easily programmed from the Arduino IDE using an FTDI adaptor.

How easy was that?

Well, I have a confession. When I was testing these on my NormDuino, I burned a bootloader successfully with the USBtiny and uploaded a sketch – yes, it was the blink sketch – using the bootloader. However, if I immediately tried to upload again with the bootloader, it failed. The situation was such that after burning a bootloader, the IDE would only ever upload a sketch *once* to the NormDuino – no matter what I did.

After much wailing and gnashing of teeth, none of which helped, I pulled the ATmega328P from my Duemilanove and swapped it for the NormDuino one. I then burned a Duemilanove bootloader, and sketches could be uploaded time after time with no errors. I then chose the 8 MHz breadboard Arduino and burned a bootloader again.

Sketches still continued to upload perfectly, while the ATmega328P sat in my Duemilanove. Time to swap it back.

On attempting to insert the microcontroller back into the breadboard, I realized that the capacitor between the RST pin, pin 1 on the ATmega328P, and the FTDI's DTR line was *not connected* to the AVR any more! Could this be the solution?

After plugging the AVR back into the breadboard and reattaching the capacitor to the RST pin, all was well.

Breadboards are fine to prototype your projects, but if you intend to keep and use the project, then it's a good idea to build it into a circuit board or at least a stripboard. Too many things fall out of breadboards.

APPENDIX K

AVRAssist

AVRAssist is a set of header files which can be #included in your AVR C++ code or #included in an Arduino sketch where you want to get down and dirty in the various hardware bits of the AVR microcontroller. The latest version of AVRAssist can always be obtained from https://github.com/NormanDunbar/AVRAssist/releases/latest on the AVRAssist GitHub repository.

K.1. Components

The following AVR internal devices can be set up with the current version of *AVRAssist*:

- Timer/counters – All three timer/counters have separate header files.

- Analogue to Digital Converter.

- The Analogue Comparator.

- The Watchdog Timer.

K.2. In Use

The *AVRAssist* header files make configuration of the various AVR registers a tad easier. As an example, the code in Listing K-1 will configure Timer/counter 0 with

N. Dunbar, *Arduino Software Internals*, https://doi.org/10.1007/978-1-4842-5790-6

- Fast PWM mode with TOP = 255

- A prescaler of 64

- OCOA and OCOB = Pins 11 and 12 = Arduino D5 and D6 = AVR PD5 and PD6 in normal GPIO mode

- Interrupt to fire on Compare Match A

- Interrupt to fire on Compare Match B

Listing K-1. AVRAssist Timer/counter 0 initialization

```
#include <timer0.h>

using namespace AVRAssist;

...

Timer0::initialise(
    Timer0::MODE_FAST_PWM_255,
    Timer0::CLK_PRESCALE_64,
    Timer0::OCOX_DISCONNECTED,
    Timer0::INT_COMP_MATCH_A | Timer0::INT_COMP_MATCH_B
);

...
```

Only the first two parameters are actually required though. The rest have *sensible* defaults (for certain values of sensible perhaps?).

Later on in the code, you can force a comparison between TCNT0 and either OCR0A or OCR0B, should you have the need. This will *not* fire any configured interrupts but will set OC0A or OC0B to the state they would take without a forced compare if they happen to match TCNT0 when forced. This is simple to do and is shown in Listing K-2.

Listing K-2. AVRAssist Timer/counter 0 force compare

```
// Force a compare between TCNT0 and OCR1A and OCR1B. Does
// not fire the interrupts but will change state appropriately
// on pins OC0A and OC0B.
```

```
Timer0::forceCompare(Timer0::FORCE_COMPARE_MATCH_A |
                     Timer0::FORCE_COMPARE_MATCH_B
             );
```

The *AVRAssist* method is, hopefully, much easier and less prone to *fat-fingered typist* syndrome (something I suffer from, frequently!) especially when attempting to type the equivalent code for Listing K-1, as displayed in Listing K-3.

Listing K-3. Equivalent code to Listing K-1

```
TCCR0A = ((0<<COM0A1) | (0<<COM0A0) | (0<<COM0B1) |
    (0<<COM0B0) | (1<<WGM00) | (1<<WGM01));

TCCR0B = ((0<<FOC0A) | (0<<FOC0B) | (0<<WGM02) |
    (0<<CS02) | (1<<CS01) | (1<<CS00));

TIMSK0 = ((1<<OCIE0A) | (1<<OCIE0B) | (0<<TOIE0));
```

Well, *I* find it easier! And, yes I did manage to type the preceding code incorrectly when writing this description. Sigh!

ℹ️ *I know*, I've set all the 0 bits in the preceding equivalent code, but that makes it easier to change the bits later, especially if I needed to change the mode, prescaler, interrupts, etc.

Index

A

Analogue Comparator Control and
    Status Register (ACSR)
  ACO bit, 494
  breadboarded circuit, 500, 501
  comparator outputs, 499, 500
  digital input, 495, 496
  enable option, 496
  pin AIN1(D7), 497
  pins A0-A7, 498
  positive input, 493
  reference voltage
    source, 495, 496
    external reference, 497
    internal reference, 497
  sampled voltage, 495
  sketch source code, 502–504
analogRead() function, 93–97
analogReference() function, 92–94
Analogue to Digital Converter
    (ADC), 568
  analogRead() function, 505
  dual in-line package (DIP), 504
  init() function, 70–72
  loop() function, 526–528
  noise reduction mode, 518
  reference voltage, 504

setupADC() function, 523, 524
setup and initiation
  disable digital input, 512
  enable conversion
    process, 516
  input source, 511, 512
  interrupts, 513
  left/right alignment, 509–511
  power selection, 506
  prescaler and frequencies,
    506–508
  reading steps, 505
  reference voltage
    source, 508, 509
  single-shot/auto trigger
    mode, 514–516
  subsequent
    conversions, 517
setup() function, 527
sketch breadboard layout,
    522, 523
startADC() function, 526
temperature conversion
  AVR microcontroller, 569
  configuration, 570
  Internet, 576
  loop() function, 574–576
  measuring device, 569

© Norman Dunbar 2020
N. Dunbar, *Arduino Software Internals*, https://doi.org/10.1007/978-1-4842-5790-6

W, X

Y, Z

Printed in the United States
By Bookmasters